HOLMAN
Old
Testament
Commentary

HOLMAN
Old Testament Commentary

Hosea, Joel, Amos, Obadia,h Jonah, Micah

GENERAL EDITOR

Max Anders

AUTHOR

Trent C. Butler

HOLMAN
REFERENCE

Nashville, Tennessee

Bible versions used in this book:

ISBN 0-8054-9477-4
Dewey Decimal Classification: 224
Subject Heading: BIBLE. O.T. HOSEA/BIBLE. O.T. JOEL/BIBLE. O.T. AMOS/
BIBLE. O.T. OBADIAH/BIBLE. O.T. JONAH/BIBLE. O.T. MICAH

Hosea-Micah / Butler, Trent

p.   cm. — (Holman Old Testament commentary)
Includes bibliographical references. (p.).
ISBN
  1. Bible. Hosea—Commentaries.   I. Title.   II. Series.

—dc21

1 2 3 4 5 6   09 08 07 06 05

*D*edicated to

Curtis and Kevin,

sons whose love has infused life with

joy and hope

⌐ Trent C. Butler ⌐

2005

Contents

Contents

Micah 6:1–7:20

Editorial Preface

Today's church hungers for Bible teaching, and Bible teachers hunger for resources to guide them in teaching God's Word. The Holman Old Testament Commentary provides the church with the food to feed the spiritually hungry in an easily digestible format. The result: new spiritual vitality that the church can readily use.

Bible teaching should result in new interest in the Scriptures, expanded Bible knowledge, discovery of specific scriptural principles, relevant applications, and exciting living. The unique format of the Holman Old Testament Commentary includes sections to achieve these results for every Old Testament book.

Opening quotations stimulate thinking and lead to an introductory illustration and discussion that draw individuals and study groups into the Word of God. Verse-by-verse commentary interprets the passage with the aim of equipping them to understand and live God's Word in a contemporary setting. A conclusion draws together the themes identified in the passage under discussion and suggests application for it. A "Life Application" section provides additional illustrative material. "Deeper Discoveries" gives the reader a closer look at some of the words, phrases, and background material that illuminate the passage. "Issues for Discussion" is a tool to enhance learning within the group. Finally, a closing prayer is suggested. Bible teachers and pastors will find the teaching outline helpful as they develop lessons and sermons.

It is the editors' prayer that this new resource for local church Bible teaching will enrich the ministry of group, as well as individual, Bible study and that it will lead God's people truly to be people of the Book, living out what God calls us to be.

Acknowledgments

This volume was written during one of those life-crisis situations as I faced retirement and then began a new professional opportunity that represented a true God-thing in my life. This placed extreme stress on those who helped and supported me.

Thus I want to say a strong word of thanks to Dr. Steve Bond, my long-time friend and faithful editor, and to George Knight, another friend and colleague who copyedited the manuscript.

Words cannot express my love and gratitude for Mary Martin and Mary Webb, who entertained themselves and offered love and support while Trent was upstairs composing.

Of course, the greatest thanks go to our God, who again and again displayed his glorious presence and affirming love during the writing process.

Holman Old Testament Commentary Contributors

Vol. 1, Genesis
ISBN 0-8054-9461-8
Kenneth O. Gangel and
Stephen J. Bramer

Vol. 2, Exodus, Leviticus, Numbers
ISBN 0-8054-9462-6
Glen Martin

Vol. 3, Deuteronomy
ISBN 0-8054-9463-4
Doug McIntosh

Vol. 4, Joshua
ISBN 0-8054-9464-2
Kenneth O. Gangel

Vol. 5, Judges, Ruth
ISBN 0-8054-9465-0
W. Gary Phillips

Vol. 6, 1 & 2 Samuel
ISBN 0-8054-9466-9
Stephen Andrews

Vol. 7, 1 & 2 Kings
ISBN 0-8054-9467-7
Gary Inrig

Vol. 8, 1 & 2 Chronicles
ISBN 0-8054-9468-5
Winfried Corduan

Vol. 9, Ezra, Nehemiah, Esther
ISBN 0-8054-9469-3
Knute Larson and Kathy Dahlen

Vol. 10, Job
ISBN 0-8054-9470-7
Steven J. Lawson

Vol. 11, Psalms 1–75
ISBN 0-8054-9471-5
Steven J. Lawson

Vol. 12, Psalms 76–150
ISBN 0-8054-9481-2
Steven J. Lawson

Vol. 13, Proverbs
ISBN 0-8054-9472-3
Max Anders

Vol. 14, Ecclesiastes, Song of Songs
ISBN 0-8054-9482-0
David George Moore and Daniel L. Akin

Vol. 15, Isaiah
ISBN 0-8054-9473-1
Trent C. Butler

Vol. 16, Jeremiah, Lamentations
ISBN 0-8054-9474-X
Fred M. Wood and Ross McLaren

Vol. 17, Ezekiel
ISBN 0-8054-9475-8
Mark F. Rooker

Vol. 18, Daniel
ISBN 0-8054-9476-6
Kenneth O. Gangel

Vol. 19, Hosea, Joel, Amos, Obadiah, Jonah, Micah
ISBN 0-8054-9477-4
Trent C. Butler

Vol. 20, Nahum, Habakkuk, Zephaniah, Haggai, Zechariah, Malachi
ISBN 0-8054-9478-2
Stephen R. Miller

Holman New Testament Commentary Contributors

Vol. 1, Matthew
ISBN 0-8054-0201-2
Stuart K. Weber

Vol. 2, Mark
ISBN 0-8054-0202-0
Rodney L. Cooper

Vol. 3, Luke
ISBN 0-8054-0203-9
Trent C. Butler

Vol. 4, John
ISBN 0-8054-0204-7
Kenneth O. Gangel

Vol. 5, Acts
ISBN 0-8054-0205-5
Kenneth O. Gangel

Vol. 6, Romans
ISBN 0-8054-0206-3
Kenneth Boa and William Kruidenier

Vol. 7, 1 & 2 Corinthians
ISBN 0-8054-0207-1
Richard L. Pratt Jr.

**Vol. 8, Galatians, Ephesians,
Philippians, Colossians**
ISBN 0-8054-0208-X
Max Anders

**Vol. 9, 1 & 2 Thessalonians,
1 & 2 Timothy, Titus, Philemon**
ISBN 0-8054-0209-8
Knute Larson

Vol. 10, Hebrews, James
ISBN 0-8054-0211-X
Thomas D. Lea

Vol. 11, 1 & 2 Peter, 1, 2, 3 John, Jude
ISBN 0-8054-0210-1
David Walls and Max Anders

Vol. 12, Revelation
ISBN 0-8054-0212-8
Kendell H. Easley

Holman Old Testament Commentary

Twenty volumes designed for Bible study and teaching to enrich the local church and God's people.

Series Editor	Max Anders
Managing Editor	Steve Bond
Project Editor	Dean Richardson
Product Development Manager	Ricky D. King
Marketing Manager	Stephanie Huffman
Executive Editor	David Shepherd
Page Composition	TF Designs, Greenbrier, TN

Introduction to

Hosea

PROPHECY PROFILE

The book is structured around lessons from the prophet's marriage experience (chs. 1–3) and his preaching (chs. 4–7). It is the second longest of the minor prophets; only Zechariah is longer. The message comes from the prophet's heart and his experience and centers on divine love for a people who prostituted themselves after other gods. Covenant requirements, as summarized in the Ten Commandments, are God's criteria for judgment. Unfaithful religious leaders bear the brunt of the burden of guilt, not having taught the people correctly. God prefers faithful love and a personal relationship of knowing him rather than religious ritual.

Hosea is referred to by several New Testament writers (Matt. 2:15; 9:13; 12:7; Luke 23:30; Rom. 9:25–28; 1 Cor. 15:55; Rev. 6:16). The author is identified in the preface mainly with the kings of Judah, though his ministry was in the Northern Kingdom (Israel).

AUTHOR PROFILE: HOSEA THE PROPHET

Hosea was the son of Beeri, who is otherwise unknown. Hosea was apparently from the Northern Kingdom, the nation to which he preached. His name means "salvation"; it is the same name in Hebrew that Joshua originally bore (Deut. 32:44) and of Israel's last king (2 Kgs. 17:1). Hosea's marriage to Gomer and the naming of his three children form the basis for the symbolic narratives of chapters 1–3. The prophet shared God's heartbreak over Israel's infidelity.

READER PROFILE: NORTHERN KINGDOM

The book can be dated by the southern kings Uzziah, Jotham, Ahaz, and Hezekiah (a possible range of 793 to 686 B.C.) and one northern king—Jeroboam II (793–753 B.C.). Hosea apparently preached in Israel from about 755 B.C. to about 715 B.C. It was the time period when Israel fell from its greatest power under Jeroboam to total destruction and exile under King Hosea (732–722 B.C.). The people of Israel knew wealth but had gained it from unjust treatment of the poor. They were proud of their religious heritage but deeply involved in syncretistic religious practices involving Baal worship. The priests and prophets used their office to please the king and to gain personal power. Hosea dealt with the unfaithfulness of the people and the faithful love of God, pointing to disaster followed by eventual hope.

Hosea 1:1–2:1

The Impossible Love Affair

I. **INTRODUCTION**
The Disaster of Unfaithful Love

II. **COMMENTARY**
A verse-by-verse explanation of these verses.

III. **CONCLUSION**
Coping with Family Losses

An overview of the principles and applications from these verses.

IV. **LIFE APPLICATION**
Loving the Ugliest

Melding these verses to life.

V. **PRAYER**
Tying these verses to life with God.

VI. **DEEPER DISCOVERIES**
Historical, geographical, and grammatical enrichment of the commentary.

VII. **TEACHING OUTLINE**
Suggested step-by-step group study of these verses.

VIII. **ISSUES FOR DISCUSSION**
Zeroing these verses in on daily life.

┌─────────────────┐
│   Q u o t e   │
└─────────────────┘

"*The* marriage [of Hosea] is an act of obedience to

Yahweh's command undertaken to dramatize the divine

indictment of Israel. Hosea is to display the predicament of

Yahweh in his covenant with Israel by wedding

a harlotrous woman!"

J a m e s L . M a y s

Hosea 1:1–2:1

IN A NUTSHELL

God charged his prophet to enact a drastic prophetic act through his own family. He married a prostitute, representing Israel's unfaithfulness, and named three children unthinkable names to symbolize the place of judgment, the reason for judgment, and the result of judgment. But God pointed to a future where faithfulness and a love relationship would be restored in Hosea's family and in God's relation to Israel.

The Impossible Love Affair

I. INTRODUCTION

The Disaster of Unfaithful Love

*T*he Vietnam era in world history produced many complex issues that continue to plague modern thinkers. The play *Miss Saigon* pictures a lonely soldier entering a bar filled with his fellow soldiers. There he meets Trim, a young woman who is just entering the world's oldest profession. Chris, the soldier, begins to live with Kim, but soon leaves Kim behind as he escapes the city before the Vietcong take it. Years later, having returned to the United States, married, and formed a family, Chris learns that Kim has given birth to his son. He returns to Vietnam to meet his child, only to have Kim commit suicide to free her child to return to the United States with his father.

Here is a picture of tragic love begun in a wrong way and leading to ultimate disaster. Some Israelites would have laughed at Hosea and taunted him for marrying a prostitute and seeing her desert him to return to her old ways. Hosea saw his situation differently. God led him into the marriage, so he committed himself to it in faithfulness and deep love. In so doing, he demonstrated God's love for a people who had forsaken him to play the field with other gods. Hosea bared his own soul to tell his story to symbolize for Israel the heartbreak God felt and to assure the people of Israel that unfaithfulness to God would lead to disaster for them.

God's people continue to have a hard time learning Hosea's lesson. We want to play the field with regard to morality and theology. Still, we expect God to take us back and bless us any time we choose. We need to listen carefully as Hosea shares with us his deepest personal experience.

II. COMMENTARY

The Impossible Love Affair

> **MAIN IDEA:** *God's love brings judgment on an unfaithful people, but then he restores a people to complete his plan for the world.*

A Revelation Received (1:1)

> **SUPPORTING IDEA:** *God sends his revelation through his prophet in specific historical circumstances.*

1:1. Prophetic books generally have an editorial preface that gives some information about the prophet and places him and his words in an exact historical situation. Hosea's preface does not introduce us to the prophet; it only says that he was the son of an otherwise unknown Beeri. What little we can infer about this northern prophet of God's love is described in the introduction to this book (see above).

The preface to the Book of Hosea focuses on the word **that came to Hosea**. The same formula introduces the books of Joel, Micah, and Zephaniah. **The word of the LORD** appears 438 times in the Hebrew Bible from Genesis 15:1 to Malachi 1:1. This is a distinctive of biblical religion: God constantly lets his people know his message. The problem lies in a people who refuse to accept and obey his message.

Hosea delivered God's message during a critical time in Israel's history (see "Deeper Discoveries"). He saw the political and economic fortunes of the Northern Kingdom and the Southern Kingdom fall from power and riches to dependency and poverty. In good times and bad times, he preached and lived out God's word before God's unfaithful people.

B The Place of Judgment: Jezreel (1:2–5)

SUPPORTING IDEA: *God finds his own ways to prepare his people for punishment when they are not faithful to him.*

1:2. A unique expression begins the actual message of the prophet: God **began to speak through Hosea**. What follows is not so much God's speech as it is a brief biography of Hosea's family life lived out in obedience to God's directions. And what a shocking family life God created for the prophet!

God's opening words appear to be words of joy: **Go, take to yourself** a wife, but then the Hebrew text describes that wife in one unexpected and unbelievable word: **adulterous**. God gives further disturbing details using the same Hebrew word: **children of unfaithfulness**. The horror of this term can be seen in the other contexts where it appears (Gen. 38:24; Nah. 3:4). Hosea's wife was in good company: Tamar, Oholah, and Nineveh! How could God possibly ask a man to marry such a woman? Scholars have sought a way out of this theological dilemma, but the biblical text offers no escape route. God chose to let his prophet endure the same hurt and shame that God experienced in his love affair with his own people.

The prophet had not only to preach God's message; he had to illustrate it in his own family. God had only one reason to offer the prophet in explaining why he must do this—because Israel was guilty of adultery **in departing from the LORD**. Hosea's ministry illustrated how Israel had abandoned God for the fertility cults of the Canaanites.

1:3. The prophet immediately demonstrated his faithfulness to God by marrying **Gomer**. We know nothing about Gomer's father or about her previous life, except that she met God's qualifications—she was a prostitute. Immediately, Hosea and Gomer fulfilled the rest of God's command as Gomer became pregnant and **bore him a son**. Here, and only here, the Hebrew text says the son was born "to him." This leaves the question open about the father of the next two children whom Gomer bore.

Commentators would love to find a way around what the text says. They do not want the Bible to let God speak in this way and cause a prophet to have such a wife. But the text shows the nature of prophetic obedience in its harshest form. God expects the prophet to carry out his message faithfully, so the prophet can in turn demand that the nation carry out God's requirements faithfully. A prophet must be willing to embody God's message, no matter how difficult it is (Isa. 20). His children must also demonstrate the Lord's message in their lives.

As Duane Garrett remarks, "The report of their births should not be passed over as a sad but merely incidental prologue to the actual prophecy; *in a real sense, they are the prophecy, and everything else is just exposition*" (NAC 19A, 55).

1:4. God not only told Hosea whom to marry and what kind of kids to have; he also named the children for Hosea. This paints a still more difficult task for the prophet. Can you imagine Hosea going into the streets, seeking his children, and having to call out their names? The first name was **Jezreel**, the name of an important geographical place in Scripture (1 Kgs. 18:45–46). The city served as the winter capital for Israel's kings. It was an important point on the highway leading from Egypt to Damascus through the Valley of Jezreel.

God had one moment in Jezreel's history in mind. King Jeroboam II represented the last strong king in the dynasty begun by **Jehu** (841–814 B.C.) and ended during the reign of Jeroboam's son, Zechariah (752 B.C.). In the Valley of Jezreel, Jehu had killed King Ahab of Israel and King Ahaziah of Judah. In the city of Jezreel, Jehu ordered Queen Jezebel's servants to throw her out the window, and so they did—to her death. Then Jehu had Ahab's seventy sons killed and their heads brought to him in Jezreel (2 Kgs. 9–10). Thus Jezreel brought horror to mind for the Israelites in the same way that "9/11" brings horror to contemporary American minds.

Jehu had done his work at God's command (2 Kgs. 9:7). Still, God told Hosea that Jehu's dynasty had not pleased him. The kings in Jehu's line had followed the same idolatrous path for which God had punished their predecessors. Thus God warned that the **Jehu** dynasty would meet the same fate at the same place where Jehu had begun his bloody reign. Not only was Israel's longest reigning dynasty coming to an end; **the kingdom of Israel** was likewise coming to **an end**. Hosea's son was therefore a sign of judgment and disaster for the political rulers of his day.

1:5. A quick verse summarizes God's plan. On the day he chooses, he will shatter the **bow** of Israel **in the Valley of Jezreel**. The bow represents the nation's military power. Such power was focused in the king of Israel. God planned to bring an end to Israel's army and its monarchy. This began when the last king of the Jehu dynasty—King Zechariah—met his death at the hand of Shallum. The Septuagint, the oldest Greek translation of the Hebrew Bible, locates this in the Valley of Jezreel (2 Kgs. 15:10). The completion also came in the Jezreel Valley when Tiglath-pileser III of Assyria defeated Israel's army and took the territory of the valley (2 Kgs. 15:29).

The Reason for Judgment: Love Lost (1:6–7)

SUPPORTING IDEA: *Human sin separates the sinner from God's love and forgiveness, but God remains free to express that love in a new way at a new time.*

1:6. Again Gomer became pregnant and bore a **daughter**. The text leaves out "to him [Hosea]" of the previous narrative. God tells the prophet to give the girl a dreadful name: "Given No Love." First Kings 3:26, Psalm 103:13, and Isaiah 49:15 demonstrate the meaning of this name, since the Hebrew word *richam* refers to the warm love and compassion a parent has for a child (Lam. 4:10). Maternal love is natural; withholding it is unthinkable. Yet Hosea's daughter had to walk down city streets dreading for anyone to call her name because she was not loved. Local residents would easily read something about her parents into the name. They could see Hosea and Gomer as having forsaken their daughter and as having proclaimed her to be illegitimate. Whether she was, the text does not say.

This girl embodies the divine word to Israel. The people must suffer as she had suffered. They must be rejected as she had been rejected. They must hear God's devastating word: **I will no longer show love to the house of Israel**. This is the final announcement of judgment. Israel had dallied with God's love too long, playing the Lord against Baal in a competition for Israel's affections. But God does not play in such competitions. He is the Lord. He had shown Israel his love in countless ways. They had rejected him, so he would remove his love from them.

The last line of verse 6 leads scholars to many different conclusions. Garrett calls the NIV translation here, **that I should at all forgive them**, "a very questionable, and one might even say impossible, translation of the Hebrew" (NAC 19A, 60). The Hebrew text reads literally, "For (or yet) lifting up, I will lift up for them." But what does *lifting* refer to in this context: lifting away or forgiving sin; lifting up people and moving them into exile; lifting up compassion and carrying it away? Some scholars even change the text slightly and have it read, "I will reject them" or "because I have been utterly betrayed by them." Obviously, the meaning of the text is not clear.

One possible explanation that retains the Hebrew text is that God is consistent and stringent in his condemnation of Israel, saving hope only for

Judah. In this case, the translation would be, "For I will surely exile them." This is the apparent meaning of the text, though it involves a rare usage of the Hebrew verb. If this is correct, then God will demonstrate the removal of his love by removing the people from the land he has given them.

However, Hosea may, here as elsewhere, reveal the paradoxical nature of God that human logic can never comprehend. If so, he says God will totally withdraw his love from Israel, only immediately to say, "Yet I will surely forgive them." God's nature contains both the holiness that destroys all sin and the love that forgives his people and renews his covenant with them. Garrett calls this the "astonishing possibility that the text means exactly what it says." He explains that "this inconsistency is the language of the vexation of a broken heart—and it also reflects the mystery of a God whose ways are above our ways." Again Garrett notes: "In Hosea absolute rejection and destruction are set alongside complete restoration and forgiveness with no transition or explanation. . . . It was nothing less than the death of a nation. . . . And yet at the same time God says, 'I will completely forgive them'" (NAC 19A, 61, 64).

1:7. The interpretation of the last line of verse 6 as carrying into exile, removing, receives support from the opening syntax of verse 7: "But **to the house of Judah** I will give compassionate **love**, and I will deliver them." Hosea's audience continued to be the Northern Kingdom (Israel). The worst political move Hosea could take was to support the Southern Kingdom (Judah) in any way. To announce judgment on the north and deliverance for the south was beyond imagination. The prophet was guilty of treason. But he proved his faithfulness to his God rather than to his nation.

In a further statement betraying the political stance of the nation, Hosea noted why the Southern Kingdom would be delivered. They would not rely on any military resources or human powers. They would let God himself win the battle as Israel of old had done under Moses and Joshua. The Northern Kingdom had taken pride in the military might of Jeroboam II and in the victories of his army. After Jeroboam, kings entered into political intrigue with Syria and other small nations in an attempt to defend themselves against the Assyrians. Hosea declared that all such political and military maneuvering would fail. The sovereign God of Israel was the only victor in battle, and he had sided with Judah, not Israel.

🆔 The Result of Judgment: Not My People (1:8–9)

SUPPORTING IDEA: *God's judgment had disastrous results because it meant the covenant was no longer valid and the people could no longer claim to be people of the God of Israel.*

1:8. Hebrew mothers usually nursed their babies until they were about three years old. This shows the prophet's patience with his wife and God's patience with Israel. Neither Gomer nor Israel proved capable of being faithful.

Both received the harsh punishment they deserved. But first Gomer produced a second **son**.

1:9. Again the Hebrew text omits the name of God and of the prophet. The terse text emphasizes only the child's name: **not my people**. This child preached a sermon to Israel with every step he took. Israel was an illegitimate child of God, just as Not My People was an illegitimate child of Hosea. Thus God nullified the covenant he had made with Israel. He would no longer say, "I will . . . be your God, and you will be my people" (Lev. 26:12). The relationship was over.

🄴 The Future: Unexpected Union (1:10–2:1)

SUPPORTING IDEA: *God has plans to recreate his people even when he has to announce judgment against them.*

1:10. As the previous statement of judgment had undone the promise to Abraham in Genesis 17:7, so without any preparation or explanation the prophet, in a sense, renews the covenant promises with Abraham in Genesis 22:17. A nation that had just been pronounced as good as dead would live again. This is similar to Ezekiel's vision of the dry bones brought to life (Ezek. 37). God in his mercy works to make salvation available to all the world.

God will reverse the judgment illustrated by Gomer's third son. The ones who were Not My People will now represent the **sons of the living God**. Only the Lord is a living God (Jer. 10:10). Israel, who has so often celebrated Baal as the god of fertility and life, will find once for all that only God can be associated with fertility, life, and hope.

1:11. It is not enough to revive a dead nation. The prophet had even more shocking news for his audience: **Judah** and **Israel will be reunited** in a great assembly, having **one leader and will come up out of the land**. Here the prophet encouraged the people and strengthened their hope. But this hope lay beyond their lifetime. They would be part of the dead generation, the punished generation, but their punishment—having God's covenant nullified—was not God's final word for the nation.

The final word pointed to future hope but not the kind of future hope the nation Israel would have described. Hosea predicted a great assembly, but he didn't explain its purpose. Such assemblies could be for providing information (Gen. 49:2), for battle (1 Sam. 28:4), for public repentance or mourning (1 Sam. 25:1), for a court of law (Isa. 43:9), for a return from exile (Neh. 1:9), for worship and sacrifice (2 Chr. 15:10–11), for crowning a king (1 Chr. 11:1–3), for rebelling against a king (2 Chr. 13:7), or even for a royal bridal search (Esth. 2:8,19).

The assembly's purpose becomes even more puzzling when we learn of its constituents: **Judah** and **Israel**. In Hosea's day such a gathering would likely be for battle—against one another. But this time they would gather to name a **leader**. Hosea doesn't call this leader a king; he is simply a "head." But the important matter is that one person will lead both Judah and Israel.

What is the occasion? **The day of Jezreel**. Here we go back to Hosea's first son. He had shown the place for God's judgment; now he shows the place for God's new salvation. This will be a great day for both Judah and Israel because they will together **come up**. This can be a military term meaning to attack, a term for returning from exile, or an agricultural term for plants springing from the soil. The name *Jezreel* means "God sows," pointing to a possible agricultural interpretation, but the earlier context identified Jezreel as a battlefield.

This new day has several possible meanings. It may be a day of renewed fertility for a deserted land. It may be a day of victory on the battlefield. It may be a new day of going up together to worship God. It may be a new day of repentance and worship. It may be a new day of political reunion in crowning a new king. Perhaps Hosea intended his audience to see many or all of these meanings in his cryptic words. Whatever the specific meaning, God wanted a people rejoicing over a new hope—a hope built on putting aside past differences and past battles and joining together in a new unity as the people who belonged to God.

2:1. Reunion of the kingdoms means a new identity for the people of God and a new interpretation of Hosea's prophetic-message-bearing children. Both Judah and Israel can call out to their sons, **my people**, and to their daughters, "ones who have received compassionate love." Covenant renewal is complete. Unity is restored. God's people are rescued from destruction and death.

> **MAIN IDEA REVIEW:** *God's love brings judgment on an unfaithful people, but then he restores a people to complete his plan for the world.*

III. CONCLUSION

Coping with Family Losses

It hurts so much to lose someone you love. On April 15, 1996, I buried my wife Mary. The hurt of that day remains a part of who I am. It took months for me to quit dwelling on my ache and get ready to face life again. Thus I can share to some extent the pain Hosea felt as he married Gomer, began a family, had to name children terrible names to signify God's dealing with his people Israel, and finally saw Gomer return to her career as a prostitute. Because God restored my life with a new wife and family, I can also rejoice with Hosea as he restored his wife to his family and saw new meaning in his children's names.

It is not only the family side of Hosea's picture that I have to identify with. I must also identify with the tragic spiritual side. Hosea's family life mirrored Israel's spiritual life. I need to get so close to God that this same deep hurt fills my soul when I disobey him. I need to be as careful in being faithful to God as I am with my family. I need to trust God to renew my relationship with him when I go astray and to depend on him for eternal hope.

PRINCIPLES

- God's love leads him to discipline and punish an unfaithful people.
- God often reveals himself in terms of our family relationships.
- God can use the most sinful people to accomplish his will.
- God's forgiveness is something he chooses to do in love, not something we can demand.
- God has a plan to restore his people in faithfulness and love.

APPLICATIONS

- Take a careful look at your life and determine in what areas you are being unfaithful to God.
- Find where God has brought his discipline and punishment into your life.
- Ask God for forgiveness for your sins.
- Practice the spiritual disciplines to develop your love affair with God.
- Expect God to reveal himself and his plans for your life.

IV. LIFE APPLICATION

Loving the Ugliest

In his book *Shields of Brass*, C. Roy Angell gives an illustration of what God's love can do in the life of a despicable human being. Miss Sadie lived at the edge of town and was despised by most of the townspeople. Then one day two ladies decided to invite Miss Sadie to the citywide revival meetings. She laughed at them, claiming that if God did save her, they would not accept her in their church. The women left, but they returned the next day to talk to Miss Sadie again. Again her scorn sent them away. Finally, during their third visit Miss Sadie promised to come to the revival if she could sit in a chair in the darkness outside the tent.

For five straight nights Miss Sadie sat in the dark as the preacher proclaimed the gospel. The two ladies joined her. The sixth night Miss Sadie moved to the back row in the tent, and then at invitation time she came down the aisle to accept Jesus as her Savior.

On Sunday morning Miss Sadie came to church and sat on the back row. A strange hush swept the congregation. Then she actually responded to the invitation. Resentment and fear winged their way through the pews. Suddenly, someone else moved—a beautiful nineteen-year-old choir member. She met Miss Sadie in the aisle, placed her arm around her, kissed her forehead, and went with her the rest of the way to the front.

Again emotion moved the members—this time they had shame and tears. Miss Sadie never missed another Sunday at church until her funeral drew one of the largest crowds the town had ever seen.

Humans don't like to work with prostitutes and ugly, despicable people. But God does. He chooses many such people to join his kingdom and become useful in his ministry. He judges their sin but changes their lives. He also challenges us to love such people as much as Hosea loved Gomer and as deeply as God loves us.

V. PRAYER

God, we are prejudiced. Certain qualities in people make us ignore them or criticize them or try to shame them. Forgive us. Teach us to love them as you love us. Amen.

VI. DEEPER DISCOVERIES

The Historical Setting of Hosea

Hosea first spoke to a prosperous people living in Israel's golden age under King Jeroboam II (793–753 B.C.), whom Walter Kaiser calls "the greatest of all the kings of northern Israel" (*A History of Israel*, p. 351). Jeroboam responded to the preaching of Jonah and restored Israel to its greatest territorial limits (2 Kgs. 14:25–28). At Jeroboam's death Israel's fortunes faded fast. His son Zechariah ruled only six months before Shallum assassinated him (2 Kgs. 15:8–12), ending the famous dynasty of Jehu. Shortly thereafter Menahem (752–742 B.C.) assassinated Shallum (2 Kgs. 15:16–22). Menahem succumbed to Assyrian domination, introducing the beginning of the end for Israel. He left the throne to his son Pekahiah (742–740 B.C.; 2 Kgs. 15:23–26), who fell to assassination by Pekah, apparently a rival from east of the Jordan River whose rule is difficult to date (perhaps 750–731 B.C.; see 2 Kgs. 15:25–29).

VII. TEACHING OUTLINE

A. INTRODUCTION

1. Lead Story: The Disaster of Unfaithful Love

2. Context: Hosea's book is set in the context of national and international history, but the opening chapter centers on the personal experiences of Hosea and his family. Hosea's tragic marriage shows God's experience with his unfaithful people.

3. Transition: Family life should be full of love and hope. But Hosea's family life turned dark in two directions. His former prostitute wife bore him children, but the identity of the father of at least one of them was uncertain. His wife Gomer returned to her career outside the home. God provided names for the children that scandalized the community while at the same time preaching a sermon of judgment to the people of Israel.

B. COMMENTARY

1. Revelation Received (1:1)

2. The Place of Judgment: Jezreel (1:2–5)

3. The Reason for Judgment: Love Lost (1:6–7)

4. The Result of Judgment: Not My People (1:8–9)

5. The Future: Unexpected Union (1:10–2:1)

C. CONCLUSION: COPING WITH FAMILY LOSSES

VIII. ISSUES FOR DISCUSSION

1. What does it say about God that he would ask Hosea to marry a prostitute and then give such hard-to-bear names to his children?

2. What does it feel like when you no longer experience God's compassion and love in your life?

3. How would you react if your pastor suddenly declared to your congregation that you were not God's people?

4. Does your church feel separated from or at odds with another church? What can your members do to bring unity and Christian love into this relationship?

Hosea 2:2–3:5

Love as the Lord Loves

I. INTRODUCTION
An Unforgettable Evening

II. COMMENTARY
A verse-by-verse explanation of these verses.

III. CONCLUSION
All's Well That Ends Well

An overview of the principles and applications from these veses.

IV. LIFE APPLICATION
God of the Unexpected

Melding these verses to life.

V. PRAYER
Tying these verses to life with God.

VI. DEEPER DISCOVERIES
Historical, geographical, and grammatical enrichment of the commentary.

VII. TEACHING OUTLINE
Suggested step-by-step group study of these verses.

VIII. ISSUES FOR DISCUSSION
Zeroing these verses in on daily life.

Q u o t e

"God does not give up. He works to turn sorrow into joy and the tragedy of unfaithfulness into the triumph of love."

J a m e s   M o n t g o m e r y   B o i c e

Hosea 2:2–3:5

I N   A   N U T S H E L L

God uses the language of Hosea's marriage to rebuke his people Israel for their unfaithfulness and to pronounce judgment that will destroy both their fertility religion and the fertility of their land. But God will again court Israel and draw her back to faithfulness and love for him. Then God will restore the land's fertility and the people's righteousness. God calls on Hosea to renew his marriage vows with his wife to illustrate God's new covenant with his people.

Love as the Lord Loves

I. INTRODUCTION

An Unforgettable Evening

I can never forget the night I met Mary Martin. You do not go to a grief support group to meet a wife just months after you have buried your sweetheart of thirty years. But somehow when this little blonde woman walked into our meeting and sat down across from me in the circle, I knew God had something special for my life. I felt a kinship with her. I was already calling the members of the grief group to check up on them between group meetings. But my conversations with Mary Martin extended longer and longer. She supplied wisdom, care, and understanding that I desperately needed, and I must have done the same for her. Two years later we were making marriage plans.

Through my experiences with Mary Martin, I have learned that God works with us through the darkest times of life—those moments when we feel most alone and separated from him. As we walk with him through the valley of the shadow, he leads us into the daylight of new hope, new promises, and new ministry.

Hosea found in his experiences with Gomer that he had to face the dark side of life before he could enjoy the dawn with her and with God. His experience, in turn, provided a living lesson for Israel.

II. COMMENTARY

Love as the Lord Loves

> **MAIN IDEA:** *God's judgment comes on an unfaithful people but is not necessarily his last word for them. He works to bring them back to him.*

A Divorcing the Adulteress (2:2–15)

> **SUPPORTING IDEA:** *God divorces an unfaithful people and strips them of their rights much as a husband does to an unfaithful wife.*

2:2–3. God speaks as the prosecuting attorney in a divorce case in which he is also the plaintiff seeking the divorce and the judge administering the sentence. He first calls the children of chapter 1 of Hosea to bring charges against their own mother. The children must give evidence that their mother is no longer behaving as their father's wife. God bases the call on his own testimony that the couple are no longer husband and wife. **She is not my wife, and I am not her husband** may well represent an Israelite divorce formula that a husband could use to end his marriage with his wife.

Unfaithfulness is just cause for divorce on both the human and divine levels. But note that this passage emphasizes the relationship of God and his people. It does not justify the breaking of a relationship on the human plane. The Hebrew text gives the purpose of the children's testimony. They are to accuse their mother so she will turn away from the **look** of fornication (or adultery, see Hos. 1:2) and from the evidence of her unfaithfulness. The "look" and "evidence" might literally have been makeup or jewelry that identified her as a prostitute or a cult prostitute of Baal, but figuratively it represents the lewd, pagan culture of Canaan and Baalism. God's lawsuit is not that of an angry husband intent on destroying the reputation and future of his wife. It is a desperate maneuver seeking to bring a wayward people back to himself after they have abandoned their relationship with him.

God is, however, serious about the relationship. He lays out the sentence if the unfaithful people refuse to return and enter into a faithful relationship with him. She likes to make love. He will take away all her adornments and **strip her naked** before her lovers. He will **bare** her body just like **the day she was born**. To say it another way, the Lord will transform Israel into a wilderness or **desert**.

Again God uses language designed to make us take notice: I will **slay her with thirst**. God has turned into an executioner of his people, making them suffer the agony of death by lack of water. He will take radical action to impress upon his chosen people the seriousness with which he takes his relationship with them. He is willing for them to be "Not My People" if that is the lifestyle they choose. He is willing to send them from the fertile valley of Jezreel into the waterless wilderness.

2:4–5. God is also willing to let his people endure the horrible experience of "Not Given Love" because they are sons of fornication. These are not his children, raised in his home to love him. They are illegitimate children fathered by false gods and raised to love false gods. Thus God will abandon his children who have already abandoned him.

Having described the sentence he will impose on his people, God gives the evidence against them, again using the figure of Hosea's wife to represent unfaithful Israel. The sentence is imposed because **their mother** has committed fornication; she has acted in a shameful manner. Indeed, she said, **I will go after my lovers, who give me my food and my water, my wool and my linen, my oil and my drink**. God has a greedy family who would rather prostitute themselves shamefully than practice faithfulness.

2:6–8. Therefore, when used by the prophets, should always catch our attention. God's pronouncement of judgment, his declaration of guilt and its consequences, generally follow "therefore." The Hebrew text next has a particle which literally means, "Look at me." God is blocking Israel's promiscuous path. He treats the nation like a dumb animal that has to be fenced in so it will not wander off. God does everything possible to put up roadblocks on the path of sin.

God knows he will not stop Israel's **chase**, but he will prevent the chase from succeeding. **Her lovers** will be nowhere to be found. Finally, the message will get through to Israel. Unable to find the false lovers, she will come to her senses and decide, "Let me go and return to my husband, the original one." The Hebrew word behind **go back** has several meanings. A person repents by *turning* from sin to God. He finds new life by *returning* home from foreign exile. So Israel needs to *turn* from sin, but the people will do this only after their exile in a foreign land. Israel's reasoning is purely selfish: **then I was better off than now**. God will use economic and selfish reasons to draw his people back to himself.

Drawn back to God, Israel did not understand the source of her blessings. She forgot the confession of faith that Israel's farmers recited as they brought offerings to God (Deut. 26:5–10). **Grain**, **new wine**, and olive **oil** represented all the agricultural blessings that God had given his people (Deut. 11:14). Israel credited **Baal** with producing the land's fertility that brought all their crops. Israel also thanked Baal for the precious metals used as mediums of exchange in commercial trade that indicated the people's wealth. So Israel took **gold** and **silver** and enhanced Baal's temples and Baal's worship rites. In so doing, Israel rejected its covenant with the true source of all blessings. Only reluctantly in exile would Israel return to the Lord when they no longer had access to Baal worship.

2:9–13. Therefore sounds its warning again. Israel wanted to be better off. That was not an acceptable motivation from God's perspective. The Lord, not Baal, controlled the agricultural seasons. He would take back Israel's agricultural produce and rob the rich farmers of their source of prosperity. He would take away the **wool** and flax used to produce the fine clothes that Israel's women loved to wear. Israel had deserted God, her true husband. Now Israel would see that the Lord would no longer fulfill the husband's duties of providing food and clothing for his wife.

The results of God's actions are clear. The Hebrew word for **expose** refers to going into exile, revealing information, uncovering, and sleeping with. The basic image is uncovering Israel's "nakedness" (or perhaps her "private parts," NIV **lewdness**) in public so she will be ashamed before her former lovers. By doing this God will reveal the true nature of Israel by sending the people into exile because they have been sleeping with the enemy. Thus the covenant curse of Deuteronomy 32:39 will be fulfilled. The curse will come on Israel with **no one** able to rescue them from God's **hands**.

Worshippers of God as well as Baal celebrated agricultural **festivals**, thanking the god for the fertile crops and seeking to ensure that the plentiful harvest would be repeated. Israel linked these celebrations to God's great saving actions in their history, particularly the deliverance from Egypt. The Canaanite Baal worshippers linked everything to mystical rituals filled with explicit sexual activities. Israel had begun celebrating the Lord's worship times in rituals borrowed from the Canaanites. He would put a stop to this (Isa. 1:13).

The Lord listed the specific times of **celebrations** when Israel expressed their joy. The *hag* (**yearly festivals**) designated the three annual Jewish festivals (Passover, Weeks or Firstfruits, and Booths or Tabernacles) for which God required Israel to undertake a pilgrimage to the central sanctuary (Deut. 16:16). Each festival was tied to a particular harvest time: Passover for the spring barley harvest, Weeks for the summer wheat harvest, and Booths for the fall grape harvest. Israel assumed they would celebrate these festivals forever. God called a halt when celebration developed into sexual homage to Baal rather than memory of the Lord's great acts in Israel's history.

New Moons was a monthly celebration featuring sacrifices to God (Num. 28:11) and the sounding of trumpets (Lev. 23:23–24). Commerce and business ceased (Amos 8:5). **Sabbath days** were weekly festivals reminding Israel of God's rest in creation and of Israel's plight as slaves in Egypt. God expected Israel to stop all work and travel on these days.

God summarized his joy-stoppage order: it will affect **all her appointed feasts**. The term referred to any agreed-upon time (Ps. 75:2), but it came to designate specifically Israel's times of festival observance and national assemblies (Lev. 23:2). God thus puts an end to Israel's chief worship occasions. He preferred no worship to false worship.

The Israelites described the good life as living under one's own vine and fig tree (Mic. 4:4). Grapes and figs were especially valued as delicacies and as signs of a land's fertility and prosperity (Hos. 9:10). Hosea painted destruction and desolation in terms of the loss of fig and vine production. Israel's festivals should have celebrated God fulfilling his promise and giving Israel an abundant crop of grapes and figs. Instead, Israel praised Baal for giving figs and grapes in exchange for faithful worship.

God had a quick solution for that problem. The fertile vineyards and orchards would become a **thicket** or "undergrowth" that humans could not harvest. Only **wild animals** would be able to enjoy the fruits of God's good land. Israel could not recognize her true lover and had turned to false lovers instead.

God describes Israel's sin succinctly: **but me she forgot!** The people of Israel adorned their bodies but ignored their God. He would not ignore them. God underlined this with the ominous formula: **declares the LORD** or "announcement from Yahweh." It underlines the source of the prophetic word. The announcement of doom came directly from the sovereign God of Israel.

2:14–15. Therefore again warns of divine action to come. We expect to hear an announcement of punishment. But we hear an intriguing invitation instead. God will **allure** Israel **into the desert.** The Hebrew text may mean "persuade" as well as "romance." This completes the message and tone of Hosea 2:7 where God's punishment forced Israel back to her first husband. Now God leads Israel to the lonely wilderness apart from the crowds and their call to worship Baal. The wilderness (NIV **desert**) represented Israel's first honeymoon period where God was with his people when he led them from Egypt into the wilderness of Sinai (Exod. 19:1). Once again alone with Israel, God will have a heart-to-heart conversation (literally, "speak on her heart"), showing Israel that the only smart decision is to return to him.

God will restore the **vineyards** he had originally turned into thickets (v. 12). The dark blot on Joshua's conquest record was the **Valley of Achor**, which separated the tribes of Judah and Benjamin (Josh. 15:7). There Joshua had to execute an Israelite family and bury them after they disobeyed God's rules for warfare (Josh. 7:24–26). Hosea joins Isaiah (Isa. 65:10) in promising a future for sinful Israel. The valley called "trouble" (Josh. 7:25–26) would now be called **hope.** God had a new day and a new plan for God's people.

B A New Day of Dedication (2:16–23)

SUPPORTING IDEA: *God's judgment and renewed courtship lead his people back to him in a day of renewed dedication and devotion.*

2:16. Hosea gives a series of brief notes marked by **in that day.** Here we see Hosea's picture of the perfect relationship between God and his people expressed again in marital metaphors and language. "In that day" is related to the Day of the Lord teaching of Scripture, but whereas the Day of the Lord is most frequently pictured in terms of judgment (Isa. 7:18–23; Ezek. 38:10–19), "in that day" often points to God's future hope for his people (Jer. 39:16–17).

Hosea renews the wedding vows between Israel and God with a play on words. Hebrew ʾish means "man" or **husband**, while *baal* means **master**, "lord," or "husband." Israel had previously acted as though the Lord and Baal were one and the same. Now Israel would correctly address God as "my man" or "my husband," not "my Baal." This would happen because the Lord had spoken.

2:17. Each local high place or worship center had its own special god, referred to as Baal followed by another divine epithet. Thus confusion reigned as to whether one god or many were worshipped under the name Baal. The one true God will turn away the very name Baal from Israel's mouths. They will **no longer** pronounce this infamous name. In fact, such names will no longer even be remembered. Israel will have a permanent Baal amnesia, so that only the Lord will be worshipped, just as the first commandment decreed (Exod. 20:3).

2:18. With Baal gone and God in control, the world will be different. God has always been a covenant-making God. He made a covenant with Noah (Gen. 9), Moses (Exod. 19–24), and David (2 Sam. 7). He promised Jeremiah a new covenant (31:27–34). Here is a part of God's new covenant. God will restore the peace of original creation. Instruments and conduct of war will disappear, along with the names of Baal. Man and beast can **lie down** securely with no one to fear. The threat and punishment of Hosea 2:12 will no longer endure. This is God's description of the life he plans for his people.

2:19. God is ready to seal the marriage contract, promising to marry Israel and pay the bridal price for his new bride. In a way this turns Hebrew law upside down. The law protected an engaged virgin from attack by another man; any man who attacked her had to pay the bridal price and marry her, giving up the possibility of ever breaking the marriage by divorce (Deut. 22:23–29). In this case, however, the bride Israel had willingly left her husband, the Lord, to dally with the Baals. The Baals, however, were not forced to wed. Rather, original husband Yahweh, the Lord, took upon himself the responsibility, paid the bridal price, entered into the engagement process, and looked to an eternal relationship, never to be broken by divorce or anything else.

How could this be? God would change the bride's lifestyle. All those characteristics of God's character would now also characterize his bride Israel. The first members of Hosea's list of characteristics require deeper investigation. They are **righteousness, justice,** and **love** (see "Deeper Discoveries").

Compassion is the warm, protective feeling mothers have for their children (1 Kgs. 3:26) or a brother has for long-separated family members (Gen. 43:30). Such emotion brings God to restore a people he has exiled in his anger (Zech. 1:16). A person aware that he does not deserve deliverance or help still calls on God, relying on his compassion (2 Sam. 24:14).

2:20. The final component of God's bridal price for Israel is **faithfulness,** a natural part of God's character (Lam. 3:23). Faithfulness is the opposite of deceit and lying (Prov. 12:22). God can be trusted. The promises he is making to Israel will come true (Ps. 33:4).

God pays the bridal price and becomes engaged to faithless Israel so Israel will "know the Lord" (not **acknowledge** as in NIV). Usually God acts so people will "know that I am God," an expression that occurs over seventy times in the Old Testament, particularly in Ezekiel. The positive statement that someone knows the Lord occurs only here and in Jeremiah 31:34—another prophetic promise for the future. Otherwise, the statement is that people do not know the sovereign God of Israel (Jer. 4:22).

God does everything he does for his people so he may have a personal, intimate relationship with them. This will involve his people having the same commitment to righteousness, justice, covenant loyalty, parental love, and faithfulness that God has. They will have these characteristics because God will give these to them in their new covenant relationship.

2:21. But Hosea does not describe this new covenant relationship in sweet-by-and-by heavenly language. He uses the concrete language of the farmer's daily life. The beasts and birds and creeping things will be involved in the new conditions (Hos. 2:18); so will the agricultural world encompassing heaven and earth. God will answer the sky's requests for rain clouds. In turn the sky will respond to the land's requests for rain. This will happen because "the Lord has spoken" (see comments on Hos. 2:9–13).

2:22. The land will respond to the plea of the **grain** seed, to the vineyard that produces **new wine**, and to the olive trees that are sources for olive **oil** by delivering the rain to the farmlands, not to the wilderness. These crops will then respond to the fertile farmland of the Valley of **Jezreel** so that it will again be the breadbasket of Israel (see comments on Hos. 1:4).

2:23. So we go back to the beginning of chapter 1 and Hosea's children with the atrocious names. Jezreel will no longer bring memories of military defeat but of agricultural fertility. **Not my loved one** will experience God's deep parental love in eternal faithfulness. **Not my people** will know they are God's beloved people as they worship him without any memories of Baal. The marriage relationship once destroyed has been rebuilt for eternity.

ⓒ Lasting Love at Last (3:1–5)

SUPPORTING IDEA: *The purpose of God's judgment is to restore his relationship with his people so they will seek him and no other god.*

3:1–3. In spite of much scholarly debate on the relationships between chapter 1 and chapter 3, the best solution is to see God calling on his prophet to restore his marriage to an unfaithful wife. Gomer must be brought back into the prophet's house even though she was loved by Hosea's neighbor or companion (NIV **another**). Hosea must accept back into his arms his adulterous wife. Only in this way could the prophet demonstrate how **the LORD loves the Israelites**. Israel must see that their sins were as rotten in God's eyes as Gomer's adultery was in Hosea's. In fact, Israel's spiritual adultery with **other gods** was worse than Gomer's physical adultery.

Raisin cakes, made of dried, compressed grapes, provided a rare delicacy in Israel's diet (Song 2:5). They apparently were part of the fertility rituals in Baal worship (Jer. 44:19). They represented part of the pay Israel thought they earned by worshipping Baal (Hos. 2:12).

The Lord was willing to go through the legal process of engagement, to pay the bridal price, and to restore Israel as his wife. So, too, the prophet had to pay for the privilege of getting his sinful wife back. Scholars debate why and to whom Hosea made such payments. Did he pay off (1) the impoverished woman's accumulated debts? (2) the new owner after she had fallen into slavery? (3) the new husband with whom she committed adultery? (4) Gomer herself to give her a dowry and parallel God's enriching of Israel through giving them rain? (5) the temple at which she plied her trade as a religious prostitute? or (6) her father to pay again a bridal price as God had again redeemed Israel after buying them out of Egypt?

The text does not answer this question. The most likely solution would involve a bridal price parallel to God's bridal payment. The amount Hosea paid for Gomer raises some problems. A **shekel** was a measure of weight equal perhaps to four-tenths of an ounce or 11.5 grams. A **homer** was about six bushels or 220 liters of grain, while a **lethek** was apparently one-half of a homer. This price was not excessive. A slave cost thirty shekels (Exod. 21:32). The bride price when Deuteronomy was written was fifty shekels (Deut. 22:29). Hosea may have had to scrape the money together. Perhaps unable to secure enough cash, he had to include payment-in-kind with grain. The important thing was the prophet's attitude in this transaction. He obeyed God without question.

The new marriage had strict limits. Gomer had to sit and wait **many days** before she would again "have" Hosea. This would be a new experience for a prostitute who was accustomed to short-term relationships. She must not return to harlotry. Her past had shown how difficult this was for Gomer. She was forbidden from having sexual relationships with another **man**. This had been her daily routine. The final phrase of the verse, "And also I to you," apparently warns Gomer that Hosea will not be her escape hatch, substituting sexual relationships with him for those to which she was accustomed. Gomer is on "probation" so to speak, as Israel is with the Lord for "many days" (Hos. 3:4).

3:4–5. As Gomer faced restrictions, so did Israel. They would lose their political freedom as Gomer had lost her sexual freedom. They would also lose religious freedom. The **sacrifice** and **ephod** were not intrinsically evil but may have been corrupted by their use in idol worship. Israel could no longer participate in the religious practices their ancestors may have enjoyed because Israel had turned those practices into forms of Baal worship. They could no longer enjoy the pleasure of worship with its **sacrifice** to Baal, **sacred stones**,

ephod for revelation, and **idol** to adore and adorn. Israel would be brought back to God.

Sacred stones were large pillars set up at Canaanite worship places. Archaeologists have discovered some in Gezer that were almost ten feet tall. They generally represented apostasy from God (Deut. 7:5; 2 Kgs. 23:14). Still, some texts show Israelites expressing worship to the Lord through setting up such stone pillars (Gen. 28:18).

The **ephod** was a part of the priest's clothing, particularly that of the high priest. The breastplate was attached to the ephod, and it contained the Urim and Thummim by which the priest gained revelation from God (Exod. 28:30). Elaborate ephods were created for foreign idols (Isa. 30:22).

Idol represents a significant Hebrew term, *teraphim,* that appears to mean "image" in a variety of contexts. Some Bible students believe a type of facial mask representing the god is meant. They were used in the worship centers devoted to other gods but were sometimes used in worship that combined legitimate and illegitimate practices (Judg. 18:17–20). They were also connected to divination practices by which a god's will was determined (Ezek. 21:21).

God's probationary period for Israel has a purpose: it will lead Israel to **return and seek the LORD**. The word *return* points in several directions. It can mean turn away from idols and to God. It can mean repent from sin and serve God. It can mean return from exile and live in the homeland again. The prophet hints at all these meanings. "Seek the LORD" can refer to seeking the Lord's direction (2 Sam. 21:1) or to praying for his favor (Zech. 8:21–22) or to trusting and obeying the Lord (Prov. 28:5). God's probation means the people of Israel will confine their seeking to one God. Returning in repentance to him, they will worship him alone.

Such return to God will be an emotional affair. Israel will **come trembling**—with trepidation, dread, and fear. They knew they did not deserve to approach his presence. They were fully aware of their repeated sins that deserved punishment. Still, they will return to God seeking grace and hope. And they will find his **blessings in the last days**.

Hosea's long speech is finished. He has acted out in his marriage the sad story of God and his rebellious people. Now he must wait for his marriage relationship to heal while the nation waits to see how God's promised future will turn out. Meanwhile, both Gomer the adulterous wife and Israel the adulterous nation must be quarantined, serving their probation until the Lord's timetable is up and the last days arrive.

MAIN IDEA REVIEW: *God's judgment comes on an unfaithful people but is not necessarily his last word for them. He works to bring them back to him.*

III. CONCLUSION

All's Well That Ends Well

A happy ending—that's what we look for as we read and as we live out our days. Hosea's family history finally found that happy ending, but only after much turmoil and shame. This mirrored Israel's history, except Hosea did not get to see Israel's happy ending. That was previewed only with Christ's coming centuries later, and we still wait for the final victorious chapter.

PRINCIPLES

- Sinners must change their ways or face God's consequences.
- Sins of parents can have horrible effects on their children.
- Seeking momentary pleasure can bring eternal destruction.
- Every good and perfect gift comes from God and not from anyone else.
- God calls his disobedient people back to himself.
- God has a plan to overcome human sin and restore his creation to fit his purposes.

APPLICATIONS

- Turn away from earthly pleasures and earthly priorities.
- Meet God's expectations of justice, righteousness, love, compassion, and faithfulness.
- Commit yourself to the Lord as the only true God and give allegiance to no other.
- Live in hope of God's promised blessings even when this seems impossible.
- Be ready to follow God's commands even when they defy human logic.

IV. LIFE APPLICATION

God of the Unexpected

God is in the business of guiding his people, even if he may do so in surprising ways. After twenty-two fulfilling years in one ministry position, I decided I wanted a new path in life, a new challenge. But who would employ a "young" man in his early sixties? Working with a job counseling specialist, I sent out résumés and attended professional seminars. Then, walking through the hundreds of book publishers' displays at a conference one afternoon, I noticed a small, handwritten notice about a position for an academic editor. When I asked about the job, I was told to "see Jane." Three months later this Baptist minister began working with Chalice Press, the publication arm of the Disciples of Christ. And I could stay in Gallatin, Tennessee, rather than moving to their headquarters in St. Louis.

Yes, God works things out for his people in the most unexpected ways. Just as he restored love and relationship in Hosea's marriage and family, so he can restore what you need in your life. But you must agree to obey and trust him, working on his timetable, not yours.

V. PRAYER

Loving God, we thank you that you work through the hard moments of life and bring results far better than what we ever expect. Show us your way for our lives. Give us faith to follow you. We commit ourselves to love, faithfulness, righteousness, justice, and compassion. Amen.

VI. DEEPER DISCOVERIES

A. Righteousness (2:19)

Righteousness is a complex concept in biblical thought. The righteousness "of the community and the individual is comportment according to God's order in every area of life, in just and proper social order (justice to the helpless, the poor, the oppressed, the widow, the orphan, the resident alien), in legal procedure, in the ritual of worship, all effected by God's [righteousness]" (J. J. Scullion, AB 5, 736). The understanding of righteousness is closely connected to our understanding of God. As Donald J. Reimer puts it, "Theological considerations automatically dominate any modern understanding of righteousness" (*NIDOTTE* 3, 746).

Righteousness is conduct that maintains the universal order of peace and wholeness that God created for and intends to maintain for his people. God's actions for his people are called *tsedeqoth* or "righteous acts of salvation" because they reestablish his intended order. The court system is set up to maintain and establish that order. Human misconduct harms this order and forces actions to restore it. In Hosea, God promises to reestablish the righteousness of his created order as he pays his bride price for Israel.

B. Justice (2:19)

Justice in biblical thought is closely related to righteousness. Justice represents the claims and the obligations a person or a society has in maintaining the world order of righteousness. The entire court process and each of its components are referred to as *mishpat* because the court has the duty and obligation to create laws and make decisions that uphold and reestablish God's created order. God thus promised through Hosea that he would take the initiative to establish the system of justice that would maintain the righteous order he desired for his people.

C. Love (2:19)

Love represents the intense Hebrew term *chesed*, which describes God's faithfulness in love to his covenant and thus to his covenant people. The term occurs 246 times in the Old Testament, the great majority referring to "the disposition and beneficent actions of God toward the faithful, Israel his people, and humanity in general" (D. A. Baer and R. P. Gordon, *NIDOTTE* 2, 211). Such faithful love is based on mutual loyalty to a relationship and mutual commitment to one another. God's steadfast commitment to his people in his *chesed* protects them in time of danger and preserves life when it is threatened.

Such *chesed* is not fleeting and ephemeral as human loyalty is (Hos. 6:4). Rather, God's faithful love is everlasting (Jer. 31:3). Israel testifies to the eternal nature of God's *chesed* (Ps. 100:5). It is God's decision, made because of his loyal character, which determines that he will restore the righteous order through justice.

VII. TEACHING OUTLINE

A. INTRODUCTION

1. Lead Story: An Unforgettable Evening
2. Context: Hosea had a wife and three oddly named children who served as symbols of God's plans for his people, Israel. Things went from bad to worse in the relationships as the wife deserted the family. How could God bring anything good out of such a tragic situation?
3. Transition: God brought discipline on the family, especially on the straying wife. Then he put her in an unbearable situation that caused her to decide to return home. This set up a problem for Hosea. Would he accept her back? Hosea went to God for help and discovered that he was to accept her back in a disciplined way.

B. COMMENTARY

1. Divorcing the Adulteress (2:2–15)
2. A New Day of Dedication (2:16–23)
3. Lasting Love at Last (3:1–5)

C. CONCLUSION: ALL'S WELL THAT ENDS WELL

VIII. ISSUES FOR DISCUSSION

1. Do the first three chapters of Hosea teach you anything about how to handle family troubles?
2. How is God calling your church to show love and compassion?
3. What issues of righteousness and justice do your church and your community face right now?
4. What changes would God have to see in your life to declare that you are faithful to him?
5. How do you know when God is calling you to return and seek him?

Hosea 4:1–5:15

Rejected Because You're Ignorant

"*M*an can live with neither other men nor with God, so long as their relationship is devoid of faithfulness. Men may cynically insist that they have no confidence in anyone, no reliance upon any relationship. But more often than not such hollow affirmations are but empty and futile efforts to drown their inner, hungry cry for the shared communion and bonds of brotherhood without which no man can achieve fullness of life."

R o y   L .   H o n e y c u t t   J r .

Hosea 4:1–5:15

 I N   A   N U T S H E L L

*G*od made a covenant with his people and listed the stipulations they must obey to be a people of the covenant. Israel refused to obey the covenant. They even refused to acknowledge that the Lord was their God. They tried to get by on worship at the traditional sacred places. God condemned their worship and called judgment down on a people who ignored him.

Rejected Because You're Ignorant

I. INTRODUCTION

The Wrong Kind of Suffering

*D*orothy Kelley Patterson testifies from an experience in her own life that poor decisions bring hardship. She and her husband moved out of state to go to seminary. Her husband expected immediate opportunities to preach and pastor in order to support the family. Such opportunities were slow in coming. So Dorothy decided to find a job even against her husband's reluctance for her to do so and fear that it would trigger her allergies. She went ahead and took three part-time jobs plus a full load of seminary work.

> As you can imagine, I quickly broke my health. "Helping" my husband by providing some initial income was soon overshadowed by the expenses that accumulated as my medical needs increased. Even to this day, despite the gracious hand of the Lord, I bear in my body the scars of abusing my health during those years. I suffered many days, propped up in bed in a darkened room, gasping for breath. But this suffering was not *for righteousness' sake;* it was because of my own stubborn pride in feeling I knew better than my husband what our family needed! Wrong choices can have far-reaching consequences (Patterson, *BeAttitudes for Women,* 226–27).

Hosea claimed Israel suffered because the people did not obey their heavenly husband and they ignored his law. As a result, they did not know God. Is it possible that the problems you face have happened because you have refused to do what God has been telling you to do for so long that you really do not know God any longer?

II. COMMENTARY

Rejected Because You're Ignorant

MAIN IDEA: *God's sinful people neither know nor seek to worship him, so they must face destruction and isolation from him until they are willing to admit their guilt and turn back to worship him.*

🅰 God's Covenant Case (4:1–3)

SUPPORTING IDEA: *God's people are guilty of not knowing him, not behaving according to his standards, and not obeying his covenant commandments.*

4:1. The court is called to order as defendant Israel is called upon to **hear the word of the LORD**. God, the prosecuting attorney and judge, will present his case. This is not an ordinary court case. The indictment is the word of the LORD (see comments on Hos. 1:1 for this technical prophetic expression). The people of Israel must listen to a litany of charges against them, knowing the case has divine authority behind it. Thus Israel has no defense as they listen to this **charge** from the Lord.

God does not use individual names. He addresses the ones **who live in the land**. Once these inhabitants of the land had been Canaanites whom God had told Israel to destroy (Josh. 9:4). Now the inhabitants were Israelites whom God had now begun to destroy.

God had good reason. He could not find the characteristics that were supposed to mark Israel off as God's people who were unlike the peoples of the land. The first of these was **faithfulness** or integrity. The term means firmness, loyalty, trustworthiness, or consistency. This certainly did not charactize Israel's relationship with God. They flirted with other gods and entered intimate relationships with them and their cultic representatives rather than being loyal to the Lord.

Israel had no faithful covenant **love** (Heb. *chesed*; see comments on Hos. 2:21). "Acknowledgment of God" was also missing from Israel's character profile. This exact phrase occurs twice in Hosea (4:1; 6:6). But in a variation on this phrase, the Bible frequently charges that people do not know God (Jer. 4:22). Such knowledge involves the intimacy of personal relationship, the recognition of God's power and authority, the confession of God's love and care, and the submission to God's will and ways. None of this characterized Israel's life with God. They stood in the same relationship to God as Pharaoh did in the exodus.

4:2. God has a list of traits that profile Israel quite accurately (for a discussion of these violations of God's Ten Commandments, see "Deeper Discoveries").

4:3. The evidence of Israel's guilt is clear. Thus the Lord pronounces the sentence. The NIV "**Because of this**" represents Hebrew *'al ken,* "therefore," the traditional form used to introduce the sentence that the guilty party must serve. The following verbs should be translated in the future, not the present: **the land** will mourn, and **all who live in it** will **waste away.** The whole creation—land, sky, and sea—are affected. Nothing in Israel's life will remain the same when God, the righteous Judge, enforces his sentence.

B God's Justice for Man's Justice System (4:4–10)

> **SUPPORTING IDEA:** *A people who delight in suing others— even priests—and priests who are negligent about teaching the law face God's justice.*

4:4. The historical situation is grave. God has to take charge. Human justice along with its court system is a complete failure. People use it only for personal advantage, not for national justice and fairness. So God calls a stop to the human court system. No person may take another person to court for any reason.

The language of verse 4b appears to warn the accused not to bring a countersuit. A society without justice is a society of contention and courtroom activity. No one is immune. Some people even bring the most holy figure in the nation to trial. God says legal justice has been turned upside down. He is the one who should be taking his people to court, and no one has any reason to contest his charges or to bring charges against anyone else. The blame cannot be shifted. Everyone in Israel is guilty as charged.

4:5. The second person singular address here, as in verse 4, points to the people Israel, not to the priests. The people will **stumble** or fall down before the enemy. Even **the prophets,** supposedly the ones who know God's will and tell it to the people, will stumble. **Day and night** gives a poetic sense of "continuously" or "completely." Placing the prophet at night may allude to false prophetic activities, or seeking God's will in a clandestine manner under the cover of night. Israel was taking their priests to court and letting prophets use pagan means to discover the divine will. No wonder the entire population would stumble in battle and suffer defeat.

I will destroy your mother represents a problem for all interpreters. The divine "I" underlines direct, divine intervention in this most unthinkable of punishments. Motherhood has always represented the most sacred, close relationship of life. Even the worst person seeks to protect his mother. Thus the most disastrous threat God can make against a people is to destroy their mothers. With such language Hosea continues the family imagery of chapters 1–3 and implies that the mothers of Israel have been no more faithful than Gomer was. Therefore, they deserve destruction.

4:6. God's emotions flood out as he continues his case against his people. They are **my people**. But they **are destroyed**. Why? **From lack of knowledge**. Does this mean God has failed to give his people his word? Of course not! Hosea's poignant ministry shows that was not the case. God has sent his word. Other prophets and priests have not faithfully delivered it, and people have refused to listen to it. God's people, hearing God's word, **have rejected knowledge**. They did not listen to or believe what God said.

God's punishment is directed first of all toward the **priests**. God rejects the priests who are supposed to teach the people his word, because the priests have forgotten (NIV **ignored**) **the law of your God**. Parents were responsible to teach God's Torah to the people (Deut. 33:10). Priests had the professional responsibility to teach Torah (Ezek.7:26). But God's people were not learning the truth from home or temple. So the God who remembers (Lev. 26:42,45) became the God who forgets. The priesthood was a family profession— **children** inherited the position from their fathers—but God would put a stop to that.

4:7. God had promised to multiply his people as part of the calling of Abraham (Gen. 15:5). The multiplying people only multiplied their sins. Even the early Hebrew scribes did not think the Hebrew text of verse 7b had been transmitted correctly. The text reads, "Their glory I will exchange for shame." The scribes read, "My glory they exchanged for shame." Modern translators often follow only one of the scribes' changes, reading as does the NIV, **they exchanged their Glory for something disgraceful**. The context features God's charges against Israel and his threat of punishment as does the present text of 7b.

The citizens of Israel thought they were riding high, rich, and powerful under Jeroboam II. God would take everything they counted as glorious and all their symbols of success and trade them in for everything that brought shame and dishonor (Prov. 3:35). Here we may find another play on words because Israel should find glory only in God, the "Glory of Israel" (1 Sam. 15:29). Instead, they would find shame as they worshipped shameful idols.

4:8. God now charges that **they feed on the sins of my people**. In context we would expect "they" to be "my people." That would mean God's people feed on their own sins, which is possible but an unlikely expression. The image of eating suggests priests partaking of sacrifices that do not please God. Apparently God changes his target here, and again, as in Hosea 4:6, he condemns the priests. They were encouraging Israel to bring sacrifices to the temple and were eating the priestly portions (Lev. 7:28–38).

The second part of the verse again raises textual questions, reading literally "they lift up his soul to their unjust action (or guilt)." Apparently "his" is used collectively here or should be changed to "their" with other Hebrew manuscripts and the early translations. The priests have sold their soul to do anything to cause Israel to bring more sinful offerings so the priests are getting richer and fatter. "Soul" here refers to the basic identity of the person and what he strives for in achieving such identity. The priests no longer gain identity from serving God. They set their aim on food and fortune.

4:9. Hosea 4:6 pointed to the destruction of the people. The "holy" and "dedicated" **priests** will fare no better. The priests sin and even cause the people to sin. God will dedicate his anointed priests to destruction. They will pay the price for their sinful **ways** and **deeds**. No profession or religious activity protects sinful people from God's punishment for sin.

4:10. God repeats the themes of food and multiplying to sum up the situation at hand, now speaking in the plural rather than the singular. The people **will eat** and always want more. The adulterous generation (Hos. 4:2) will continue their immoral ways of worship, but sexual relationships at the worship center will not lead God to fulfill his promise to multiply the population. God had promised to multiply or "spread out" his people (Gen. 28:14). He had fulfilled that promise in difficult times (Exod. 1:12), but he would cut off that promise in the time of greatest prosperity because the people and the priests had abandoned their devotion to God.

C God's Proposal for a Prostituted People (4:11–14)

SUPPORTING IDEA: *A sex-dominated society faces God's promise of ruin.*

4:11. God summarizes the people's new identity. **Prostitution** and drinking occupy their thoughts. They enjoyed Baal worship because it brought great physical pleasure. Israel sold out their history and their nation and its future for a good time in the here and now. The people have rejected knowledge. Now their indulgences dull their mental capacities so they can no longer receive knowledge.

4:12. God returns to his legal charges against the nation. The accused defendants in the case are **my people**. God's constant emotive call shows the incongruity of title and practice. They call on **wood**, not on God. They receive reports from their staff, the tool of the shepherd's trade now used to describe the wooden wand used in pagan divination practices. This **spirit of prostitution** or promiscuity that makes Israel chase after foreign gods and revel in Canaanite cults eventually **leads them astray** (Amos 2:4).

The final phrase apparently has a double meaning. It reads literally, "they prostitute themselves from under their God (gods)." They are supposed to be serving under the Lord's leadership. Instead they are seeking other gods as "lovers." They are throwing themselves under Baal in the depraved practices of Baal worship.

4:13. God had given instructions about Israel's worship at the place he would choose. Israel refused to carry out God's plans. Instead, they followed the Canaanite residue they had left in the promised land. They sacrificed on the tops of the **hills**, where the Baal altars were built, usually with a sacred grove of trees, a man-made idol, and a stone pillar. It may well be that many Israelites pronounced the name Yahweh as they worshipped at these pagan sites. They had confused pure worship of the Lord with contaminated worship. Here under the pleasant **shade** of the trees viewing nature's beauty, they engaged in explicit sexual worship practices, even devoting their own **daughters** and the wives of their sons as sacred prostitutes in the Baal worship places.

The **oak** was a big, strong tree (Amos 2:9), apparently part of the grove that provided shade for the worshippers. The **poplar** was the storax tree that produced fragrant resin. So the people enjoyed a pleasant aroma under the shade (Gen. 30:37). The **terebinth** was a large tree connected with pagan worship (translated "oak" in Ezek. 6:13). Therefore, God had good reason to take his people to court as immoral and unfaithful (see Hos. 14:1–2).

4:14. Surprisingly, the Lord promises **not** to **punish** someone in all this moral mess. He will not hold the women accountable for their **adultery**, since **the men** are even worse. They devoted themselves to sexual acts in the name of worshipping Baal. They separated themselves from their families by slipping away to a convenient spot where they could find cultic **prostitutes**. Or did they claim to be worshipping God with such immorality? This is part of their worship, giving sacrifices to the pagan god, Baal. They will come to the same end—total ruin—as the babbling fools of Proverbs 10:8–10.

D God's Preventive Measures for a Sin-Saturated Nation (4:15–19)

SUPPORTING IDEA: *God seeks to stop sin so its contagious nature will not infect Judah as it has Israel.*

4:15. Hosea prays that his own people in the nation of Judah will not follow the example of their northern kinsmen. Surely, God will have a remnant of his people who will be faithful and not fall into the Canaanite trap. **Gilgal** was Israel's first place of worship after Joshua brought the Israelites across the Jordan River and into the promised land (Josh. 5:9–10). But it was no longer a place holy to the Lord. Neither was Bethel, sarcastically spelled **Beth Aven** ("house of disaster or of injustice"), in spite of its many connections with the patriarchs (Gen. 28:19). These were not the places God had chosen for his people to worship.

Similarly, the oath formula **as surely as the LORD lives!** had long served Israel in its worship of God and its promise to keep its word (1 Kgs. 22:14).

But such an oath by people who no longer served the living God was a sin, breaking the third commandment (Jer. 5:2; see comments on Hos. 4:2).

4:16. God turns to a pastoral metaphor and a rhetorical question to get his point across. God wants to be the shepherd of his sheep (Ps. 23) and let them act like docile young **lambs**. But Israel is a **stubborn heifer**. Israel is throwing a stubborn fit of rebellion just like a young cow who does not want to obey its master. A stubborn and rebellious son deserved the death sentence (Deut. 21:18–21); did a stubborn nation deserve any less?

4:17. The word **Ephraim** was often used to signify the entire Northern Kingdom. They had **joined** or allied themselves with **idols** or false gods. They were supposed to be allies of God, members of his covenant community. Instead, they had forsaken their commitment to the Lord's covenant to make a treaty with false gods. God has one command about his stubborn people. Let them rest in peace. Don't touch them. How can he say this in face of such sin? The sentence has already been announced. Israel faces destruction.

4:18. What does Israel **dearly love**? Two passions consume them—drink (Hos. 4:11) and **prostitution** within the fertility cult (Hos. 4:12–14). Either one alone would be enough to bring the death penalty to the nation. Combined, these sinful crimes assure God's judgment.

4:19. Verse 19 introduces a new figure of speech—being wrapped in the wings of a bird (NIV **sweep them away**). The image has Hebrew *ruach* as its subject, so that it may be translated as wind, breath, spirit, or Spirit. This sounds like a positive event. Surely, God will conclude his word to Israel with a positive promise as he often does. But the spirit here is the same as that in Hosea 4:12. Israel is flying high in the spirit of adultery. Their sacrifices do not have the expected result. The land does not become fertile. The needed rains do not pour down. Abundant crops never appear. All Israel reaps is **shame**. The threat of Hosea 4:3 becomes reality. God's people must serve the sentence he has pronounced because of their sin and guilt.

🅔 God Calls an Arrogant Nation to Attention (5:1–7)

> **SUPPORTING IDEA:** *Sin has become so pervasive that the people can no longer return to their God.*

5:1. God calls the **priests** to attention. All Israel must listen up. The **royal house**, Jeroboam's family and advisors, receive a special invitation to lend an ear. God, the righteous Judge, has just pronounced the verdict on Israel. The people are guilty as charged. God's unjust people face **judgment** because they have been a **snare at Mizpah** and **a net spread out** over Mount **Tabor**. Mizpah was an ancient worship place in Gilead east of the Jordan River, and it had patriarchal connections (Gen. 31:49). Or Hosea could be referring to Mizpah in the territory of Benjamin (1 Kgs. 15:22). Mount Tabor was a high hill north of the Jezreel Valley and southwest of the Sea of Chinnereth (Ps. 89:12).

These examples stand for all the many places where Israel had traditionally worshipped God. All were corrupt. Israel's combination of worship of God with worship of Baal had turned all Israel's worship centers from a place for worshippers to a stink hole for sinners. The allure of past tradition at these places must not beckon faithful Israelites into their traps.

5:2. God issues another warning to Israel, referring to them as **rebels** who have revolted against him, removing him as their king. In all of their economic and political prosperity, they have forsaken God's justice and become murderers of the poor among their own people. They do not see any crime in what they have done, nor do they expect any punishment. God will be their instructor who brings **discipline** or punishment and puts them in shackles like prisoners.

5:3. The citizens of **Israel** thought they could live any way they pleased and not be found out. God had to remind them of the extent of his knowledge. He knew everything they did and said and thought and planned. Nothing escaped him. They could not hide. **Ephraim** has engaged in **prostitution** in the fertility cults of Baal. Thus Israel **is corrupt** or defiled, no longer pure and clean, and no longer eligible to enter the holy place where God is worshipped (2 Chr. 23:19).

5:4. Unable to enter God's holy sanctuary, the people cannot find atonement. Thus they cannot **return to their God.** "Return" (Heb. *shub*) also means repent. How can anyone be so isolated from God? The spirit of harlotry referred to in Hosea 4:12,18 dominates their life. **In their heart** is literally "in their midst." This is not so much a reference to individuals as it is to the community as a whole. All the people of Israel prefer the **prostitution** of Baal worship to the atonement of authentic worship. Thus even though God knows them (Hos. 5:3), they do not know (or **acknowledge**) the LORD (Hos. 6:3).

5:5. Continuing his use of courtroom language, Hosea places Israel on the witness stand. Surely they can give testimony to clear themselves of such drastic charges. Hosea concludes sadly that this is not the case. **Israel's** testimony is self-convicting because Israel is proud. Such arrogant pride never impresses God (Amos 6:8). Thus Israel will **stumble** (Hos. 4:5). What is even worse for Hosea is that his own people, the Southern Kingdom (**Judah**), are not exempt. They will follow Israel's example and stumble into sin and destruction. Hosea's desperate plea of 4:15 is not answered. All God's people are united in sin. God's chosen nation has become God's target for punishment and ruin.

5:6. The Israelites did not listen to the prophet. They could not stay away from their places of worship. They led their sacrificial animals to the altars at the high places and at the traditional worship centers, expecting to sacrifice them to God, receive his blessing, and find atonement for their sins. Israel claimed they were seeking the Lord. But seeking God requires repentance and humility (Zeph. 2:3), obedience, love, and justice. Even then, it is God who chooses whether to reveal himself to the seeker (Isa. 65:1), but the person who sincerely seeks the Lord can hope to **find him** (Jer. 29:13).

The Israelites who were seeking God with their sacrificial animals were in for a surprise: God had deserted the camp. He was no longer at home in their worship places. The holy God would not live in unholy surroundings, and Israel had combined worship of God and Baal worship into a sinful ritual that had no place for the God of the fathers, the Lord of the covenant, the one and only holy God.

5:7. Israel had done more than be **unfaithful to the LORD.** The Hebrew term (*bagad*) means to deal treacherously with or to depart treacherously from (Ps. 78:57). Israel had become deceptive and disruptive, even to the point of violence, severing the ties between themselves and God. They had betrayed the one they should have loved because he loved them. Their outward worship covered over their inward intentions to betray God and follow other gods. Their treacherous betrayal left concrete evidence in its wake— **illegitimate children.** They trained their legitimate children in illegitimate worship; they turned their children into worshippers of Baal. Thus they were no longer God's heirs and did not deserve to inherit his land and his blessings.

Now introduces God's word of judgment and sentencing: **their New Moon festivals will devour them** with their portions. "New Moon" refers to the religious celebration on the first day of each month (Num. 28:11). This frequent festival was misused by Israel as a fertility rite for Baal (Isa. 1:13). People and priests should join in the celebration, each eating his designated portion of the sacrificed animals. They should praise God for his saving acts for his nation in giving them their land. Instead, God's sentence said, the festival itself would eat the people with their inherited portions of the promised land.

F Battle Call to Destruction (5:8–15)

> **SUPPORTING IDEA:** *God calls faithless people to a battle they are certain to lose as he seeks to bring them back to him.*

5:8. This verse begins a new section with the watchman's call to **sound** the battle alarm on the **trumpet** or ram's **horn** (Judg. 6:34). This signal called the army to battle stations and the people to highest alert.

Gibeah was an important town in Benjamin about three miles north of Jerusalem. **Ramah** lay about five miles north of Jerusalem on the road to

Shechem. **Beth Aven** is used as in Hosea 4:15 as a defamatory substitute for Bethel, the town with patriarchal ties lying eleven miles north of Jerusalem on the northern border of Benjamin's tribal territory. This was a route by which attacking armies entered Jerusalem. God thus warned Israel to prepare for attack and invited the small tribe of **Benjamin**, shamed by Saul's failures, to **lead** the way.

No mention is made of who will attack. The normal route would be north to south taken by Assyria or Babylon. This is described south to north and may represent an attack by Ahaz, king of Judah, to regain territory from the Northern Kingdom after the Israel-Syria coalition failed to defeat Judah about 732 B.C.

5:9. The call to arms is doomed to failure. God has decreed punishment for the Northern Kingdom. The punishment will come on God's **day of reckoning** or day of punishment and rebuke. Before anyone can protest, God underlines the finality of the sentence. It will not be commuted. God has made known to the **tribes of Israel** what is trustworthy and **certain**.

5:10. God compares **Judah's leaders** to those who move the **boundary stones** of their neighbors, enlarging their territory and robbing people of their land. The Bible treats this as a heinous crime (Deut. 27:17). Thus again God has a sentence to pronounce against his people: **I will pour out my wrath on them like a flood of water**. Human sin angers God and brings forth acts of wrath against sinners. In his grace and love, he lays out a plan for sinners to be saved (Rom. 10:9–10), but his grace does not eliminate his judgment against sin.

5:11. The tone changes. God appears to take the side of the Northern Kingdom, since they are **oppressed**. But they are crushed by *mishpat*—judgment, justice, or the ordinance. The meaning here may be that God's covenant law has been enforced against Israel, bringing just punishment against them. They are receiving the oppression that they had given out to the poor, especially the poor farmers. God explained why they had to face such oppression and **judgment**: they were determined or **intent** on following vanity.

5:12. Looking back on the Syro-Ephraimitic conflict between Israel and Judah, God condemned both parties—Judah for taking northern territory and Israel for false political alliances and false worship. Thus God became the enemy of both the northern and southern nations. He was **like an** *'ash* **to Ephraim**. The term can refer to any decaying material and may intend to point to the decay in the human body represented by pus oozing from an infection. God will be **like** *raqab* **to the people of Judah**. This is another term for something rotten or decaying.

The references to sickness and sores in the following verse may point in the direction of infection or a red, rotten-looking wound in a person's body. God is no longer the faithful keeper of the covenant protecting his people. He is the agent of rot and ruin, infecting his people with sickness and horrible wounds.

5:13. Finally, God's people were observant enough to see what bad shape they were in. They should have come seeking God, but that avenue had been shut off. God had withdrawn from their places of worship. Thus they **turned to** political "allies." Help was not forthcoming because **Assyria** could offer no help for Israel's **sickness**. Assyria might give relief from immediate political and military danger, but they could not **cure** the dreadful sickness that engulfed the two nations. Assyria had no medicine to take away sin and unfaithfulness.

5:14. God had a strategy against his people. He would become a ravaging, hungry **lion** on the prowl. He would attack **Ephraim** and **Judah**, tearing their carcasses **to pieces**, satisfying his own hunger to punish these rebellious peoples. He would leave pieces of the carcass in the field for vultures and other scavengers to eat. He would then **carry** the carcasses away and hide them where no one could find them or **rescue them**. This is a veiled reference to exile for the two nations.

5:15. God would return to his own abode in the heavens since his holy dwelling places on earth had been turned into places of false worship that he could not tolerate. There he would play the waiting game until his people learned their lesson well enough to turn away from their earthly "allies" and fertility gods. When his people finally were ready to **admit their guilt** and pay the price for it, then God would pay attention to them. When they **earnestly** sought his **face**—came into his presence wanting to know and do his will—then God would hear their cries and respond. When the **misery** got bad enough, God's people would finally go searching for him. But until then, God's people faced judgment, ruin, and disaster.

> **MAIN IDEA REVIEW:** *God's sinful people neither know nor seek to worship him, so they must face destruction and isolation from him until they are willing to admit their guilt and turn back to worship him.*

III. CONCLUSION

No Guessing with God

God has clearly taught his people what he expects of us. We are not ignorant of what is right and what is wrong. Too often we act ignorant about who God is. We walk off in our own ways and ignore him, neither listening to his direction nor obeying his commands. When we live this way, what can we expect God to do?

PRINCIPLES

- God knows how we are living.
- God has made plain the basic rules for life with him.
- Serving in an office in the church does not protect you from God's judgment.
- Worshipping anyone or anything besides God brings his discipline and judgment.
- A sacred worship place may become off-limits for a disobedient people because of their sin and false worship.
- God may not be present at the place where you decide to worship him.

APPLICATIONS

- Learn God's ways and walk in them.
- Do not depend on a minister or a church ritual to establish your relationship with God.
- Turn away from anything that tempts you to disobey God or to make something a priority ahead of God.
- If you are not seeking God and acknowledging him as master of your life, expect his judgment.

IV. LIFE APPLICATION

"God Set Me Free"

Kay Arthur confesses in her book *Lord, Is It Warfare?* that she struggled for a long time with dirty thoughts and immoral dreams. She says, "I'd go to bed, pray, plead, read my Bible or a good Christian biography, but the dreams still came." Then she wrote: "Then one day, a day I'll never forget, God set me free."

Kay Arthur's former condition is shocking. Hosea described a situation just as shocking: Israel did not acknowledge or obey the God who had created them as a people, given them their land, and established them as a nation. God found that they no longer worshipped him or acknowledged him as their God.

Now it is time for your story. What is shocking about your relationship with God? What secret sins do you practice that no one else would believe? God stands ready to judge you or to free you and welcome you back. Which direction will you go?

V. PRAYER

All-powerful, all-knowing God, you know we are sinners. You know the sins we try to hide from everyone else and even from you. We know to do right, yet we do wrong. Forgive us. Deliver us. Free us. Bring us back to you once and for all. Amen.

VI. DEEPER DISCOVERIES

God's Broken Commandments (4:2)

Cursing refers to using the divine name to call down evil on an enemy or to make a covenant in the deity's name. A curse called down evil on anyone who did not keep the stipulations of the covenant or treaty agreement. When this is done without reason or with no intention of carrying out the treaty obligations, then God's name is misused, breaking the third commandment (Exod. 20:7).

Lying involves denying a fact (Josh. 7:11) or deceiving someone (Lev. 19:11). Such deception is closely related to the false testimony prohibited by the ninth commandment (Exod. 20:16).

Murder is an intentional, violent attack on an individual resulting in death; it affects the welfare of the community (Job 24:14). It goes against the precise wording of the sixth commandment (Deut. 5:17). Murder is different than unintentional manslaughter (Num. 35:12–30) and legitimate, government-sanctioned wars and executions (Gen. 9:6).

Stealing is taking another person's possessions (Exod. 22:1). This breaks the eighth commandment (Deut. 5:19).

Strictly speaking, *adultery* involves a man having sexual relationships with the wife or fiancé of another man (Jer. 29:23), though mention is also made of adulteresses (Prov. 30:20). The seventh commandment (Exod. 20:14) forbids adultery.

Bloodshed is a summary term referring to the prevailing attitude in the land where human life has no value. Such bloodshed defiles God's sacred land that he gave his people (Num. 35:33). It violates the order of creation (Gen. 9:6).

VII. TEACHING OUTLINE

A. INTRODUCTION
1. Lead Story: The Wrong Kind of Suffering

2. Context: Hosea turns from telling his story to preaching God's word. Both types of literature have the same result—a disobedient people face God's judgment.

3. Transition: What are you relying on to gain entrance into heaven when you die? Is it a one-time experience with God without following his will year after year? Is it the tradition of your church and its ministers? Is it participation in worship at a time-honored sanctuary? Watch out! None of these by themselves will get you into heaven.

B. COMMENTARY

1. God's Covenant Case (4:1–3)
2. God's Justice for Man's Justice System (4:4–10)
3. God's Proposal for a Prostituted People (4:11–14)
4. God's Preventive Measures for a Sin-Saturated Nation (4:15–19)
5. God Calls an Arrogant Nation to Attention (5:1–7)
6. Battle Call to Destruction (5:8–15)

C. CONCLUSION: NO GUESSING WITH GOD

VIII. ISSUES FOR DISCUSSION

1. What is the relationship between obeying the Ten Commandments and being saved?
2. What does it mean to know God?
3. What is the danger of going through the same worship ritual every Sunday?
4. What is the danger of having too much trust in a minister of your church?

Hosea 6:1–7:16

The Divine Desire

I. **INTRODUCTION**
Away from Self and Back to God

II. **COMMENTARY**
A verse-by-verse explanation of these verses.

III. **CONCLUSION**
"Have You Lost a Child?"

An overview of the principles and applications from these verses.

IV. **LIFE APPLICATION**
Listening to Your Lover

Melding these verses to life.

V. **PRAYER**
Tying these verses to life with God.

VI. **DEEPER DISCOVERIES**
Historical, geographical, and grammatical enrichment of the commentary.

VII. **TEACHING OUTLINE**
Suggested step-by-step group study of these verses.

VIII. **ISSUES FOR DISCUSSION**
Zeroing these verses in on daily life.

"*I* find that I need Christ just as much, and sometimes

more, in the times when everything seems to be going right

as I do in times of trouble. We make the mistake of thinking

that Christ's help is needed only for sickrooms, or in times

of overwhelming sorrow and suffering. . . . In our triumphs

we may forget that Jesus wants to rejoice with us,

as well as to weep with us."

Billy Graham

Hosea 6:1–7:16

 IN A NUTSHELL

*G*od yearns to help his sinful people but finds their claims of repentance to be false and their vows of allegiance as solid as the morning dews, so he finally has to harvest a nation that will not learn from his discipline.

The Divine Desire

I. INTRODUCTION

Away from Self and Back to God

A car wreck immediately before my college graduation, the collapse of a secure professional situation, watching my boys empty our nest, the death of a wife of thirty years—many experiences have driven me away from self and back to total dependence on God. But ever so quickly, that determination to be true and close to him slides away into more "normal" half-hearted commitment and religion by rote rather than relationship by love. Yes, I find myself all too often repeating Israel's history with God. What can I expect from God when I teach like Moses and act like the Northern Kingdom? God's call to repentance must bring a far deeper response from me that it brought from Israel. How about you?

II. COMMENTARY

The Divine Desire

> **MAIN IDEA:** *Sinful humans often expect God to return to them because they go through religious exercises and repeat words of repentance and pleas for help. But God desires much more from his people before he turns from his decision to harvest them like a person would thresh wheat.*

A Israel's Version of Repentance (6:1–3)

> **SUPPORTING IDEA:** *Repentance must focus on sorrow for sin, turning from sin, and turning to God—not on religious ritual.*

6:1. God promised his blessings to a people who returned to him with their whole heart (Deut. 30:9–10). Such repentance meant turning to God and away from all idols and false worship (1 Sam. 7:3). Repentance was a matter of the heart, not of traditional mourning rituals (Joel 2:13). But such repentance seldom happened in Israel's history (2 Kgs. 23:25). Hosea pictured a people who went through the proper community worship ritual and said the right words but had the wrong emphasis. They knew they must **return** to God in repentance. The Hebrew word *shuv* means "to turn" and "to repent." They knew God was the cause of their present desperate situation. They knew God was the only one who could **heal** their **wounds** (Hos. 5:12–13).

6:2. Israel knew they no longer lived **in** God's **presence** (Hos. 5:6). They knew that was where they belonged and that it was best for them. But Israel turned the process of repentance and healing into a magical ritual. They announced their decision to turn back to God so he had to cure them of all ills and pains. **Two days** and **third day** do not have to be taken literally, but the expression does emphasize a short period of time. Israel wanted to go through the necessary religious motions and get this thing over with and back to normal.

6:3. So Israel is ready to know God—to have an intimate relationship with him and to **acknowledge** him as God. A lack of such knowledge has been one of their problems (Hos. 5:4). The Hebrew text puts strong emphasis at this point, reading literally: "Let us know, let us pursue knowing God." Knowing God is not an automatic happening for people, even those called "my people." Knowing God is a pursuit that God's people are constantly involved in.

But again Israel makes the pursuit too easy. God's appearance to a people pursuing him is as sure as tomorrow's sunrise or like the **rains** that come in the rainy seasons of the year to water the crops. God is gracious. God is forgiving. God wants an intimate relationship in which his people truly know him, but God cannot be reduced to a law of nature that always repeats itself no matter what the people do. Repentance and knowledge of God depend on a much deeper understanding and expectation of God.

B The Divine Dilemma (6:4–11a)

SUPPORTING IDEA: *God laments his people's lack of understanding and commitment even in the face of his discipline, so he brings judgment on them.*

6:4. God enters into a one-sided conversation with his people, never giving them opportunity to respond. The deity's rhetorical questions formulate a lament, bemoaning the spiritual condition of his people. He faces a decision he does not want to make even though the answer is obvious. Israel's covenant loyalty (Heb. *chesed*) comes and goes like an early morning cloud that disappears with the heat of the sun or like the **dew** that appears on the **early** morning ground only to vanish in the sun's heat. This loyal **love** was part of God's marriage vows with his people (Hos. 2:19) and part of his earlier accusation against them (Hos. 4:1). But it was not part of Israel's life in relationship to God. The Lord had become one of Israel's many lovers to be wooed today and wronged tomorrow.

6:5. So God must boom forth the dreaded *'al ken,* **therefore,** that introduces his prediction of disaster. Here, however, God lists past discipline rather than future punishment. God has used his **prophets,** like Hosea, Amos, Isaiah, and Micah, to cut down his people like a stonecutter would **cut** to

pieces a massive rock. The prophetic **words** that came directly from God's **mouth** were the divine weapon of execution, killing his people.

6:6. If judgment and discipline are the words for the hour, what does God expect from his people? The divine voice explains with verb forms that point to past action continuing into present reality: As always, **I desire** covenant loyalty (Heb. *chesed*), **not sacrifice**, knowing **God** in a deep love relationship, not **burnt offerings**. This has been God's song to Israel ever since the original Sinai covenant (Exod. 19–20; 24; see comments on Hos. 4:1). Israel's loyalty to God has always been short-lived and suspect (Jer. 2:2). In fact, the Old Testament seldom affirms actual human loyalty toward God.

Humans love to relate to God through ritual and sacrifice rather than through covenant loyalty and obedience. But God reduces ritual and sacrifice to a second tier of priorities. Israel has acted like Canaanites. They thought in Canaanite fashion that a person showed devotion to the gods by regular sacrifices.

So Smith writes: "Their worship at their temples does not satisfy the Lord because he wants them to love him, fear him, worship only him, serve him, and obey him (Deut. 10:12). Going through the religious motions will not cut it with God" (NIV Application, 112). Israel has experienced God's deadly prophetic word and the murderous enemy armies that God has sent to discipline them. Now they have one last chance to learn their lesson and relate in love and loyalty to the God whom they can come to know. Can this really happen?

6:7. Sadly, history repeats itself. Rather than show covenant loyalty, Israel has again **broken the covenant**. This is not an illusory charge with no concrete evidence. God can point to the place where it happened. **Adam** was the town in Gilead referred to in Joshua 3:16 as Israel crossed the Jordan River. We do not know what happened at this place. God knew, and so did Israel. God uses one massive crime to characterize Israel's life with him and to show that betrayal, not loyalty, is native to the Israelite soul. To break the covenant is Israel's basic crime against God (Josh. 7:11).

6:8. **Gilead** was a large territory east of the Jordan River. It was settled by the tribes of Manasseh and Gad. The prophet poetically refers to it as a city populated by doers of injustice (Job 31:3). The streets of the city were **stained with footprints of blood**. Such behavior is treachery, unfaithfulness to God, betrayal, and thus a breaking of God's covenant. But it has a concrete illustration to prove how wicked these doers of injustice really were.

6:9. This verse is quite difficult in Hebrew. Apparently, it uses legal language to indict Israel's **priests** (cp. Hos. 4:6–10) for **murder**—among other **shameful crimes**. The particular incident occurred on the way to **Shechem** from Adam east of the Jordan River. When priests do not even stop at murder, what can we expect from the rest of the nation? Betrayal is in their nature. Covenant loyalty has vanished from their lives.

6:10. God has yet more evidence against "my people" Israel. He has seen a most **horrible thing** (Jer. 18:13). This is the same thing Hosea has focused on since chapter 1—harlotry or **prostitution**, both on the physical level and in the realm of cultic worship. Thus **Israel is defiled** and banned from God's worship.

6:11a. In terse language, God announces the sentence. This sentence falls on **Judah**. He has set a **harvest** for the people. Normally, this would sound like good news. Harvest time is what a people suffering from drought or from invading armies need most. But the harvest here is not food. The harvest is Judah herself harvested by God, acting as the Grim Reaper to bring ultimate judgment on his people.

Assassinations Without Assignments (6:11b–7:7)

> **SUPPORTING IDEA:** *God's people must not take justice and political strategy into their own hands without authorization from God.*

6:11b-7:1. In this section (6:11–7:7), God appears to be reassessing the condition of his people to determine the cause of their covenant betrayal. He uses the emotion of lament to express his findings. He begins by stating his basic desire: to **restore the fortunes** of his **people**, to **heal Israel**. He finds a major stumbling block in the way of such help for his people. It takes little effort to discover the guilt **of Ephraim** along with the evil **of Samaria**. Up to now Hosea has focused primarily on religious sin brought on by priests and worship practices. For the first time Hosea mentions Israel's capital, Samaria. Now he turns to political problems and evils within the nation.

They practice deceit. Here is the verb from Exodus 20:16. There it relates to false testimony in court. Here the people are playing politics in the worst way, making promises and joining in alliances to which they have no intention of remaining faithful.

The noun **thieves** here is related to the verb "steal" in the eighth commandment (Exod. 20:15). The raiders or **bandits** ("marauders" in Hos. 6:9) attack (or plunder) **in the streets**. Crime prevails. Government has lost control. The capital city of Israel does not deserve God's healing touch.

7:2. Israel plays politics even with God, **not** thinking God will **remember** and repay **their evil deeds**, just like politicians do not follow through on their promises. How could God forget? The evidence stares him in the face.

7:3. Their political promises and shenanigans fill the royal family with joy. The **king** and **princes** want to hear good news even if the historical moment gives no evidence for such news.

7:4. **All** of them are **adulterers** (Exod. 20:14). In the political realm, this extends beyond cultic prostitution to encompass political deceit. No one can trust a political partner. Adultery thrives on **burning** passion. So does politics. An everyday example of such burning heat comes from the baker's **oven** used for baking bread. The oven is so hot that the baker doesn't have to stoke it for a long time. The politicians are similar—so inflamed that their adultery is certain to last a long time.

7:5. The focus turns to a typical day for **our king**. Nothing in the Hebrew text makes this a **festival** day. It is simply the royal routine, a routine without work. The heat image is taken a different direction for a moment. The heat of passion turns to the heat of the drunkard. The nation's princes, the royal sons or the chief administrators, leave their duties to celebrate. The consumption of **wine** leaves them sick, their red faces flushed with heat. They are so drunk they extend their **hands** in greeting or in making a treaty with those who scoff at them.

7:6. A quick comparison of translations and commentaries here shows the wide separation of viewpoints about the text, translation, and interpretation of this verse. The hot oven image appears here, as the context would expect, but not as the syntax would demand. Still, the present text can be explained without extensive change. Israel's leaders extend their hands to scoffers for one reason: they permit them to come near with their ambush (Jer. 9:8). They do this only while **their hearts** are **an oven**. Wine has so confused their minds that they initiate irrational action.

From daily action, the text turns to nightly inaction. All **night** their baker sleeps (not **their passion smolders**, as translated by the NIV), when night is the preparation time for the next day's bread.

Quickly we turn to morning. Having slept all night, the baker awakes, burning like a blazing **fire**. He, too, has joined the daytime partygoers and suffers as they do with burning fever and hangover.

7:7. Thus Hosea draws his conclusion—**all of them are hot as an oven**. Here heat turns from the results of partying and drinking to rage at the king, since all of them—from princes to scoffers to baker—join together to **devour their rulers. All their kings fall.** This is a historical reflection on the final years of the Northern Kingdom when one royal family replaced another in quick succession through political coups and assassinations.

How could God's people get into such a condition? Hosea had one quick answer: **none of them calls on me**. Even in the period of the judges with all its intrigue, sin, and false religion, Israel returned to call on God for help in time of trouble. This generation was worse than that one. They ignored their only source of help, even when the Lord stood ready to heal.

This is God's lament. His people are so busy partying that they ignore him. How could he possibly restore their fortunes or heal their wounds? Harvest time approaches for the nations of Israel and Judah.

D Ephraim's Coming-Out Celebration (7:8–16)

SUPPORTING IDEA: *Seeking help from anyone but God is foolish, and it leads to destruction.*

7:8. God continues lamenting Israel's foolish ways. The divine lament briefly notes God's unfulfilled desires, but it centers on sorrow for the plight of God's sinful people. More figures of speech come from the baker, but these are separate from those in Hosea 7:1–7. This time the description focuses on the early preparation period as the baker **mixes** his ingredients before cooking them. Israel is all mixed up. Like the baker's ingredients, Israel has lost its identity, having fully integrated themselves among **the nations**, the neighbors living with them in the holy land or around them in bordering lands.

Ephraim is called a **cake**. This refers to a **flat** piece of bread baked in the oven and used as the main course in most Near Eastern meals. The cake is **not turned over**. Traditionally this has been explained as a cake needing to be flipped from one side to the other during cooking to keep one side from being burned while the other remains doughy. This would describe a nation so hard on one side that God cannot find entrance but so soft on the other that all the nations take advantage of it. More recently scholars have doubted whether such flat bread needed to be turned and have looked to the process of kneading and folding the bread before baking. This would continue the description of idleness and irresponsibility pictured in Hosea 7:1–7. Either way, Israel's identity is no longer determined by their relationship with God. It is now determined by their socializing and politicizing with foreign nations and foreign gods.

7:9. The nations devour Israel's **strength**. Israel has aged; its **hair is sprinkled with gray**. Israel is so mixed up and confused that its people do not know who they are. They think they are party guests honored by the host nations. They think they are still youngsters with nothing better to do than have a good time. Instead, they are old men being eaten alive, losing all their strength and vitality while partying rather than serving God as a "kingdom of priests and a holy nation" (Exod. 19:6).

7:10. Such foolish behavior deserves a one-word description—**arrogance** or pride (see comments on Hos. 5:5). God does not have to call any other witnesses to the stand. Israel's own attitude is self-convicting. Still they refuse to do the basic things God requires—**return to the LORD** (see comments on Hos. 6:1) and **search for him** (see Hos. 2:7; 3:5; 5:6,15). God laments such behavior and the destruction it brings. Israel just keeps on having a good time.

7:11. The literary image changes to birds. Israel is the silly **dove** or pigeon. **Egypt** and **Assyria** are dove hunters seeking to bag their limit. Dove Israel stands still in the roost, **calling** Egypt to come enjoy the roost, unaware of Egypt's weapons that are ready to capture and destroy. Seeing Assyria approach, dove Israel waddles out to meet the enemy army. A nation in grave danger is unaware of the peril.

7:12. Another hunter joins the fray. God has his bird **net** ready for action. He will bring them **down** like any hunter would catch birds. Israel has no understanding of who they are or what is going on in the world. But God is aware of everything and has a purpose in what he is doing. In verse 12b many commentators and translators, including the NIV, try to change the Hebrew text or find a clever interpretation of it. A straightforward reading of the text is preferable: "I will discipline them as soon as the report comes to their assembly."

The assembly would be a gathering of Israelite political leaders seeing how best to court Assyria and Egypt. The report would be either the prophetic message from God announcing his discipline on them or a report from the battlefield showing how Assyria or Egypt had attacked and conquered. By whatever means, God would use the occasion to punish his silly, easily deceived, party-happy people.

7:13. One word from God's mouth sets the tone for this entire section: **woe**. This interjection expresses dismay, often about impending disaster (Hos. 9:12). God is dismayed and hurt at what he sees as he views his people Israel. **They have strayed from me . . . they have rebelled against me**. God had done all he would do. His heart was right toward his people: **I long to redeem them**. But redemption calls for a people to turn back to God in repentance, to renew their knowledge of and relationship with God. Instead of returning to the Lord, they have **strayed** farther and farther away. The verb carries with it an undertone of fleeing or escaping, so that Israel wandered off from God intentionally, seeking to escape or flee from his presence.

God's people give no indication they want redemption. They go so far as to **speak lies against** God. Apparently, they claim one thing about the Lord as they go to worship him and an entirely different thing as they go to the high places to worship the Baals. They pledge covenant faithfulness in worship but break every commandment and every covenant expectation once they leave God's worship place. Eventually, they visit only the Baal places of worship, claiming they can worship both Baal and God there. They proclaim trust in the Lord to save them from their enemies as he had in the past, but then they go running to Egypt and Assyria, their greatest enemies, for help against the smaller neighboring enemies.

7:14. In time of need, especially in the time of the judges (Judg. 10:10), Israel cried out to God for help. Now Israel chose to **wail upon their beds**. "Wail" is a term of lamentation and mourning. We hear it as sleepless people with tearful eyes lamenting their fate and hoping for relief. A quite different meaning apparently rang in Israelite ears. Beds were part of the Canaanite worship ritual for Baal. Garrett appears to be on the right track as he writes: "This line refers to ritual wailing for the deceased Baal as part of fertility rites. Details of the rituals of the cults are lost to us, but they certainly included both prostitution at the shrines and ceremonial lamentation" (NAC, 19A, 174).

The second part of the verse raises textual questions. The more traditional interpretation is to "**gather** themselves" or "assemble themselves," while recent study has led some interpreters to suggest "debauch or fornicate themselves." The Greek Septuagint and a number of Hebrew manuscripts read "they slash themselves." Whatever the original meaning, the reference is again to types of Baal worship involved in seeking fertility for the fields and vineyards. In turning to such worship, the people were turning from God.

7:15. Hebrew syntax indicates a strong contrast here: As for me, God declares, **I trained them and strengthened them**. The Lord knew his history with his people. There were no people until he led them out of Egypt, across the Red Sea, and through the wilderness. They learned all they knew from God. But they forgot. They fled. They rebelled. They lied. It got so bad that **they plot evil against me**—again placed in a strong contrast clause. Israel's relationship with God has come to much more than simply forgetting and wandering away. It is outright rebellion and evil plotting to defeat God and win victory for Baal.

7:16. God concludes his lament over his people. The first line of the Hebrew text reads, "They returned not a height." Some commentators and translators interpret or change the text to arrive at many readings, depending on (1) whether the word "turn" means "turn to something for help" or "return to a previous source of help"; (2) whether the word for "height" means "upward," "above," or "the Most High God"; and (3) whether the word for "height" should be changed to "worthless" or "unprofitable," which would imply Baal or idols.

Verse 10 may offer a clue here. In this verse the same Hebrew term *shub,* "to turn, return, repent," describes God's expectations of an arrogant people. God here concludes the section by repeating this verb and making a play on it. The people of Israel return, but they do not repent. They turn, but not in the right direction. They return to their false worship and arrogant actions. They return upward to the high places rather than upward to **the Most High**.

Thus they are like a **bow** unprepared for the battle that their actions and attitudes have made inevitable. Instead of facing God's blessings, they face the result of their own cursing. Rather than celebrating their deliverance from Egypt in the annual Passover festival, they will find themselves again the object of ridicule and mocking in **Egypt**, having retraced the exodus journey in the opposite direction. Having failed to meet God's desires, his people will go back to stage one—slavery in Egypt.

> **MAIN IDEA REVIEW:** *Sinful humans often expect God to return to them because they go through simple religious exercises and repeat words of repentance and pleas for help. But God desires much more from his people before he turns from his decision to harvest them like a person would thresh wheat.*

III. CONCLUSION

"Have You Lost a Child?"

"Have you ever lost a child?" In his book *Cries of the Heart,* Ravi Zacharias tells how this shocking question raised by the owner of a picture frame shop stopped his wife in her tracks. He describes how his wife "was not prepared for the flood of emotion and anger that was yet to follow from this one who was still a stranger. . . . There was no masking of her bitterness and no hesitancy about where to ascribe the blame for these tragedies." A promise to pray for the woman brought forth the curt answer: "Don't bother" (pp. xi, xii).

The woman refused to turn to God and even declined to let Mrs. Zacharias call out to God on her behalf. Hosea showed God's deep feelings when his people did not turn to him sincerely. Israel tried to play at the game of religion, going through the prescribed motions at the prescribed times for every god they could find. God tried again and again through his prophet Hosea to show Israel how much he loved them and how much he wanted them to return in faithfulness to him. God's repeated discipline did not change the situation. God tried to heal his diseased nation, but they refused to recover. They returned to their sick practices and ignored God's warnings.

Israel's religious sickness brought with it political ailments, as the nation turned first to one foreign power and then another for help, while their true source of help stood ready to bring victory if only they would call on him. So the ultimate word for a people who refused to meet God's desires was military defeat, historical reversal, and slavery.

PRINCIPLES

- Religion by rote does not meet God's standards.
- Revival and restoration do not come without repentance.

- Love must be consistent, not convenient.
- Sincere faithfulness in worship and in loving actions for others meets God's desires.
- God may delay punishment, but he does not forget the actions that deserve punishment.
- False religious beliefs and practices lead to false social and political actions.
- Personal arrogance fuels faithlessness.
- God's redemption is opposed by human rebellion.

APPLICATIONS

- Check your motivation for worship: habit or homage?
- Reflect on God's discipline and your response: anger or obedience?
- Examine your ethical behavior: mercy for others or greed for self?
- Determine your reasons for your actions: political expediency or love for the divine?
- Look at your life's direction: down to human levels or up to God's desires?

IV. LIFE APPLICATION

Listening to Your Lover

"Payne, don't be so hard on yourself," Tracey Stewart encouraged her husband on the eve of the 1991 U.S. Open Golf Championship. Payne was troubled and frustrated because of his slow start in 1991 due to his neck injury, and he fretted that his point total might not be high enough to earn a spot on the 1991 Ryder Cup team representing the U.S. against an international team.

> You've already played on two Ryder Cup teams. That's two more than most guys ever get to play on. If you don't make it this year, you have nothing to be ashamed of. . . . You put so much pressure on yourself to do well. Then you get there, and you end up not performing the way you want to, and you just make yourself miserable. I love you and the kids love you, no matter what happens. You don't have anything to prove to us.

These comforting but challenging words from his beloved wife helped Payne Stewart, the late professional golf star, find a sense of freedom, letting him relax and stop being so self-critical (*Payne Stewart,* 149–50). Rather than focusing on the mechanics of golf or the pressure from his opponents, he played for the love of the game.

Israel could never learn this lesson. They continued to put more and more pressure on themselves to check every religious base, make certain they followed every religious rule, and ensure they entered into every political treaty that might guarantee their safety. They were focused on the mechanics of life. They were never comfortable in depending on God's love. They were never free to meet the desires of the one who loved them rather than the ones who frightened them. As a result, God led them into paths of defeat and destruction, always trying to bring them back to himself.

Israel lives on today in many of us. When will we learn God's standards: mercy, faithfulness, and an ongoing personal relationship in which we come to know God better and better? Will we ever see that his desires, not the world's glittering standards, are best for us?

V. PRAYER

Loving God, you have shown us what you desire in our lives. We raise your desires up as the goal of our lives. Help us know you more and more each day. Amen.

VI. DEEPER DISCOVERIES

The Meaning of "Adam" (6:7)

The Hebrew word *'adam* can mean "man," the first man "Adam," the town of "Adam," or "soil." Stuart takes the Hebrew word *'adam* in its sense of "soil," and translates, "But look—they have walked on my covenant like it was dirt" (WBC 31, 98). The NIV takes Adam as the first man. Andersen and Freedman propose that the descriptions in verses 7–9 all relate to one incident: "one act of unexampled wickedness, done by one group of people at one time and place. . . . murder, done at or near [the town of] Adam by a gang of priests; the victim (or victims) was on the way to Shechem" (AB 24, 435–436). Adam was a town in Gilead (Hos. 6:8) on the road between Succoth and Shechem (Hos. 6:9).

Garrett goes one step further and sees a pun so that Adam refers to both the first man and the city: "Like Adam (the man) they break covenants; they are faithless to me there (in the town of Adam)" (NAC, 19A, 162–63). This is appealing but is unlikely because it asks a bit too much of the reader.

VII. TEACHING OUTLINE

A. INTRODUCTION

1. Lead Story: Away from Self and Back to God

2. Context: Hosea 6 and 7 reflect a conversation between Israel and God. Israel determines to renew its religious ritual in expectation of God's automatic blessings. God seems to throw up his hands in despair, wanting to know what he can do with such a people. Thus a confrontation evolves between the people's understanding of what God desires from them and God's attempts to make the people realize his true desires for them.

3. Transition: Israel wanted to live comfortably within the lifestyle of their Canaanite neighbors and the political expectations of Egypt and Assyria, the rising military giants of the day. God wanted Israel to take his covenant with them seriously, a covenant that called for a growing relationship of love between God and people, an obedient lifestyle of ethics and mercy toward other people, and a separation from the religion and politics of Israel's neighbors.

B. COMMENTARY

1. Israel's Version of Repentance (6:1–3)
2. The Divine Dilemma (6:4–11a)
3. Assassinations Without Assignments (6:11b–7:7)
4. Ephraim's Coming-Out Celebration (7:8–16)

C. CONCLUSION: "HAVE YOU LOST A CHILD?"

VIII. ISSUES FOR DISCUSSION

1. What does it mean to return to God?
2. How do you know when God has disciplined you? What is the proper reaction?
3. What are God's greatest desires for your life?
4. What sins would God raise up as the biggest disturbance in your relationship with him?
5. Are you sure that you have experienced God's redemption? Why or why not?

Hosea 8:1–10:15

The Lord No Longer Loves

Quote

"*He* is a self-made man and worships his creator."

J o h n   B r i g h t

Hosea 8:1–10:15

IN A NUTSHELL

*G*od's love affair with Israel is finished. The sentinel's warning call sounds. The enemy approaches to punish a people who break God's covenant while claiming to be loyal to him. Their political trickery and religious idolatry disprove their claims. Their constant ignoring of God's law and their meaningless sacrifices provide more evidence against them. Their refusal to heed God's prophets stacks up the testimony against Israel. God has only one answer for his people—exile. They deserve such punishment for their continuing actions and attitudes.

The Lord No Longer Loves

I. INTRODUCTION

Blind and Embarrassed

*M*ark Lowry is a Christian singer and comedian. In his book *Out of Control,* he describes a lesson learned at church camp. He became infatuated with a young girl who provided great fun and had a great personality. She was also the first person Mark had met who was blind. On the last night of camp, the girl was invited to sing for the service, and she asked Mark to lead her on stage. In doing so, he led her right into a pole. The sound of the collision echoed through the tabernacle. Finally reaching the microphone, she said, "Well, Mark doesn't get his seeing-eye-dog license this year." The five hundred kids moaned, "Oh, Mark!" Mark was the only one not laughing. He just watched the big black-and-blue knot pop up on her forehead as she sang.

Throughout their history, Israel proved to be as blind as the girl, and they embarrassed themselves even more than Mark Lowry did. From the time they first came out of Egypt into the wilderness until they faced Hosea's prophetic warnings, Israel staggered from one sinful embarrassment to another. They walked into God's worship place and worshipped Baal. They learned God's law and lived like Canaanites with their lewd worship ceremonies honoring false gods. God announced his judgment against such a disrespectful, disobedient people. He forced Israel to ask: Do we believe God more than we believe our neighbors? Will the God of love no longer tolerate us? When will we see life with God's eyes rather than our blind eyes and stop embarrassing ourselves?

II. COMMENTARY

The Lord No Longer Loves

MAIN IDEA: *God's love for his people guarantees that they cannot act any way they want without expecting him to respond in judgment.*

A Blow the Bugle for Covenant Breakers (8:1–14)

SUPPORTING IDEA: *God has disaster in store for a people who break his covenant and worship other gods.*

8:1. Hosea caught his audience's attention as he called to a watchman to blow a **trumpet** to signal the army and the nation of an enemy's advance. The prophet saw a sign that the watchman had missed. A great bird of prey was soaring over the temple ready to eat up the remains left by an attacking army.

From this gruesome picture, the prophet turned to evidence accusing Israel of death-deserving sins mixed with threats outlining the punishment God would bring on his disobedient people. The basic accusation was simple—**the people have broken my covenant and rebelled against my law.** Those who break covenant are rebels against God. He has set out standards of behavior for his people in relationship to himself and in relationship to other people. But Israel ignored all these standards and lived by her own immoral codes. Thus the people were rebels revolting against their king.

8:2. A casual observer could serve as Israel's defense attorney. After all, they went to the regular worship times and echoed the confessions of faith. They said, "My God! We know you! Israel!" **Israel** maintained its arrogant attitude (Hos. 7:10) in claiming to "know the Lord" as "my God" because "we are Israel," the people of God. But it takes more than national tradition or racial membership to know God.

8:3. Israel **rejected** the **good** thing they had—their love relationship with God reflected in their covenant with him and in the laws he had graciously supplied. With this evidence presented, the prophet had only one conclusion—**an enemy will pursue him.** The opening call to the trumpet shows the pursuit has already begun.

8:4. God continued to list evidence against his disloyal people. They crowned **kings** one after another in Hosea's last days, but these were not kings whom God provided. Note Hosea's continued use of the word *know* to express the deep relationship God wants with his people (see Hos. 8:2,4; 11:3; 14:9). The NIV **my approval** hides this repetition of Hosea's favorite term and its indication of personal relationship rather than political approval.

Israel's resources were gifts from God. They used them, however, to **make idols for themselves** "in order that it will be cut off," that is, destroyed. "Cut" (Heb. *karath*) is also the technical term for making a covenant.

8:5. The first person speech of God gives way to the prophet's third person: "He has rejected your calf, O Samaria." The entire history of the Northern Kingdom (Israel) had been marked by worship of calves that the first king, Jeroboam I, had set up about 930 B.C. (1 Kgs. 12:28–33). God never accepted those calves as true representations of his worship. Indeed, the calves incited Israel to worship the bull that represented Baal in the Canaanite worship system.

God's first person reappears to say, **My anger burns against them.** The plural refers at least to the calves at Dan and Bethel, the two official Northern Kingdom temples, and possibly to other calves used in worship at outlying high places or even to calves in official Baal sanctuaries. God concludes the verse with a cry of exasperation, **How long?** God wanted a people who knew him so well that they would keep his laws, keep their covenant agreement, and thus enter a love relationship with him. But a look into the past showed no hope for the future.

8:6. God's exasperation continues as he exclaims that the calves are **from Israel**, made by human hands. How can people possibly worship them? Here Hosea echoes Isaiah's plaintive poetry (Isa. 40:19–20). Human artisans cannot create gods, much less the one true God. Their creations are doomed to end up as splintered ruins. They have no power.

8:7. An agricultural proverb becomes the prophet's tool to indict God's people. Israel faces judgment on the foundation of their national life, their agricultural economy. The agricultural figure is extended to focus on the certainty of judgment. Israel will not inhabit their own land or eat their own agricultural produce. They have ignored their one true God too long and will **reap the whirlwind**. The Lord can no longer ignore their sin.

8:8. Israel's land was situated between Assyria and Babylon to the northeast and Egypt to the southwest. Similarly, it stood between Asia Minor and Syria to the northwest and the trading lanes of the Arabian Desert to the southeast. All land traffic had to go through Israel, so all nations wanted to control their territory. God announced that such desire would be history. Enemies would swallow up the nation just as strangers **swallowed up** whatever grain might be produced. Arrogant Israel stood as a **worthless**, broken pot that no one wanted, and they stood on foreign soil, not their own.

8:9. God has a specific accusation against his people—**they have gone up to Assyria**. The people who were no nation became a nation because God rescued them from slavery in Egypt. But they no longer trusted the founding Father of their nation. They placed confidence in treaties with powerful Assyria rather than in their covenant with God. Such treaties cost them dearly in terms of freedom and in terms of resources when Assyria took Israel into exile in 732 B.C.

Hosea compared the people of the Northern Kingdom to a **wild** animal that roamed in the desert. So Israel isolated themselves from their history, their religious tradition, and their God. They found their treaty partner only isolated them further. Unable to live in such isolation, they hired **lovers** who proved as loyal as Hosea's Gomer. Thus Hosea paints a picture of Israel in desperation, seeking help from every source except the one that could provide aid.

8:10. The Hebrew text reads: "Even when they hire among the nations, I will now gather them. They began to be little because of the burden of the king [and] officials." "Hire" here may have a double meaning: they hired the nations to protect them or they hired themselves out among the nations, being paid for their military or commercial services but becoming more dependent on the nations all the while.

God has the solution. He will **gather them** rather than letting the foreign kings assemble them for their armies. Having gathered them, God will make them decrease in number as they serve their unfaithful kings and leaders and pay the exorbitant taxes demanded so the kings can continue to pay tribute to Assyria or other nations (2 Kgs. 15:19–20). This gathering for decrease stands in opposition to God's act of gathering the Israelites in Egypt, where he made them multiply miraculously in spite of the burdens of the Egyptian kings.

8:11. One thing multiplied in Israel—**altars**. They built altars to offer sacrifices for their sins. To all appearances such altars sought to fulfill God's demands **for sin offerings** (Lev. 16:1–34). But the unfaithful people confused offerings to the God of Israel and offerings to Baal. They confused obeying God's covenant expectations and carrying out ritual, which they thought was a guaranteed way of pleasing God. They could not learn that "I desire mercy, not sacrifice, and acknowledgment of God rather than burnt offerings" (Hos. 6:6). Thus **altars for sin offerings** became **altars for sinning** for a people who had forgotten the meaning of obedience.

8:12. God takes his accusations against Israel to an exaggerated extreme to make his point. The Hebrew text says, "I could write for him ten thousand of my laws." Hosea says God could make his expectations as specific as possible. Still Israel would ignore all ten thousand, thinking they were foreign (**alien**) intrusions into the "true religion" they were practicing as they mixed worship of God and Baal worship into an unholy conglomeration.

8:13. Using obscure technical language (see "Deeper Discoveries"), the prophet shows that Israel has turned God's sacrificial system into a feast rather than a festival of worship. Normally, at the altar the priest probably said something like, "The Lord accepts your offering. He will no longer remember your guilt and will not punish your sins. He is the God who brought you up from Egypt." Israel believed the priest's literalistic, ritualistic, automatic response was the last word. God interjected his opinion: Will you listen to the one who truly has the last word? I do not accept, am **not pleased** with your sacrifices. I do **remember** your guilt so that I will visit your **sins** upon you. **They will** certainly **return to Egypt.**

The exodus theme is turned upside down. It does not promise Israel eternal statehood, eternal safety, or eternal pardon from sin. God is free to respond to the current generation of Israel and their response or lack of it to him. He is the sovereign Lord with the right to reject sacrifices that are given in the wrong spirit, with the wrong expectations, under false theological presuppositions.

8:14. God's summary accusation explains all the others: **Israel has forgotten his Maker.** How did this play out in the real world? Israel **built** royal **palaces** or temple forts. They plotted with **Judah**, so that even the Southern

Kingdom forgot its dependence on God and turned to military bases or **forti-fied** cities. Israel and Judah thought they had unassailable protection from the enemy. They did not realize they had just made God their enemy. Nothing would protect them from him.

Ⓑ Call Off the Party for Those Deserving Punishment (9:1–9)

SUPPORTING IDEA: *Good harvests and other immediate "blessings" do not guarantee God's favor or call for God's people to celebrate when they have not changed their false religion and sinful lifestyles.*

9:1. The invasion by Tiglath-pileser III of Assyria in 732 B.C. had reduced Israel's power and resources to almost nothing. Still Israel ignored God and went on worshipping as usual, combining traditions from worship of God with those of Baal worship. Apparently one year, shortly after 732, Israel's harvest was abundant. The people gathered for the harvest festival. It was a time of joy, celebrating God's good gifts to his people.

In the middle of the celebration, Hosea appeared and commanded the people to stop the party (see "Deeper Discoveries"). Israel's harvest festival did not look like God's instructions from Deuteronomy. Their celebration followed the pattern of Baal worship with sacred prostitution and magical expectations. Israel rejoiced like the **nations**, not like the Lord wanted. No longer did they celebrate at the place God chose, his holy sanctuary. Rather, they celebrated **at every threshing floor**.

9:2. Here is God's announced punishment for a people who were celebrating in the wrong way (see "Deeper Discoveries"). The very cause of celebration will delude the people. They expected a year's worth of their basic food—grain (wheat or barley). They looked for a year's worth of their basic drink—**new wine**. But these sources of hope would fail them. God controls the earth and all its produce. When they did not worship him for providing their needs, he would withhold his blessings.

9:3. Not only would the **land** stop providing food and drink for the people; it would no longer be their home. God would take away the promised land and send them back where they came from—**to Egypt**—and into the hands of those from whom they had sought political and military help—**Assyria**. They would have **food** there, but it would be **unclean** (see comments on Hos. 5:3; 6:10).

9:4. This verse continues the figures of speech dealing with eating and worship. Mention of the **temple of the LORD** implies that the time frame of verse 4 parallels or even precedes that of verse 3. Israel was rejoicing in ways that imitated Baal's worship yet claiming they were sacrificing to God. But now no longer would they be able to **pour out wine offerings** or libations since they had no wine (v. 2). What **sacrifices** they made, God would not accept, since the food they sacrificed to him would be considered **unclean** like food touched by **mourners**, who had touched the dead (Deut. 26:13–14).

The people who celebrated and worshipped in such wrong ways would find they could no longer worship at all. What **food** they brought for worship, God would refuse to acknowledge. It would be good only to satisfy their own personal appetites. God has condemned their worship efforts. In the land they will be unclean. In exile they will be unclean—all because their worship has become unclean, polluted by the ways of the nations, contrary to the ways of the Lord.

9:5. Such judgment set up a dilemma for Israel. Three times a year they were to appear before God in annual **festival days** (Exod. 23:14–17). If God would not accept their worship, especially their offerings and sacrifices, what could they **do** on those days? The highlight of the year vanished in divine punishment. The day of greatest joy became Israel's date with judgment.

9:6. Israel did not learn God's lesson from their experiences of devastation and limitations with Tiglath-pileser III. They returned from that humiliation ready to fight again. In fact, they decided once more to trust Egypt against Assyria. In so doing they experienced the exodus in reverse. **Egypt** collected both their money and their refugees, then sent them to the city of **Memphis** twelve miles south of Cairo, where Israel was buried—filed in the list of nations that used to be significant but would never again return to historical prominence.

What a treasured possession Israel gained from the tribute they paid for Egyptian protection! The first Egyptian experience led to God's deliverance, the exodus, Sinai, and national identity. The second and last Egyptian experience led to disappearance, their homes and national identity marked only by **briers** and **thorns**. What a way to stop the party and put an end to rejoicing and celebration!

9:7. The prophet pronounced God's sentence on Israel. **Days of punishment** or visitation **are coming** or, more strongly, have come. **Days of reckoning** or "recompense" will repay Israel for their sins. The next line of the Hebrew text may read, **Let Israel know.** Hosea quoted epithets used to describe prophets whose words the people did not want to hear: **fool** and **maniac.** Hosea knew the people saw him as wild, uncontrolled, and insane in his accusations and pronouncements. He had a simple answer for such sneering remarks. The perception resulted from a people who were overloaded with injustice, guilt, and punishment.

9:8. Apparently Hosea saw himself as God's **watchman.** Often God appointed his prophets as watchmen, or guards, over his people to warn them of an enemy army's approach (Jer. 6:17). The prophets, however, sometimes warned of God's approach as an enemy to his disobedient people. This was Hosea's task. The prophet defended himself against the people's claim that he was mad. The people, not the prophet, stood under God's condemnation. In his office as watchman, he was on God's side, doing God's business.

As such the prophet was like a hunter setting traps **on all** the **paths** the people traveled, catching all the people for God to punish. The people go to the **house of** their **God**, which has become the house of their gods. They expect to find relief from the troubles the prophet is causing them. Instead they find more persecution (**snares**) and **hostility**. God's house has become more like a prisoner-of-war camp than a refuge for God's disobedient people.

9:9. Hosea concludes the section with another accusation against the people and a final announcement of God's sentence against them. He picks up the language of Genesis 6:11–12—the moral corruption of the earth in Noah's day—and intensifies it. Hosea's generation is not only corrupt; they are deeply **corrupt**. The prophet turned to another famous moment in Israel's history—the horrible rape scene perpetrated by the Benjaminites in the city of **Gibeah** (Judg. 19–20). God has a long memory when it comes to unconfessed, unforgiven sin. Hosea can pronounce the sentence with confidence. God will **punish them for their sins**.

◖C◗ Kill the Children of Those I No Longer Love (9:10–17)

> **SUPPORTING IDEA:** *A history of sin and a prophet's approval support God's decision to wipe out the people he once loved.*

9:10. A new type of literature and a new retrospective mood introduce a new direction in Hosea's thinking. Apparently the historical situation has come to a head. Israel did not learn the lesson God tried to teach through Tiglath-pileser III in 732 B.C. Now Assyria threatened again under Shalmaneser V (727–722). The end was in sight from Assyria's and Hosea's perspective but not from Israel's. The nation doggedly held on to its faith in syncretistic worship and political gamesmanship. God showed the prophet that Israel's entire history had led to this final moment of destruction and death.

God looks with fondness to the beginning of his history with Israel. He **found** them in the Egyptian wilderness and delivered them at the Red Sea. His loving action was so surprising it had to be compared to **finding grapes** in the midst of the desolate, arid wilderness (Ezek. 16:6–16). The discovery brought joy like tasting the very first sweet fig on a new **fig tree** (Isa. 28:4) after a long season without figs.

But divine joy was short-lived. Israel moved through the wilderness to **Baal Peor**. There they aligned themselves with the Canaanite gods in worship (Num. 25). Worship of such a **shameful** thing made Israel an abomination just as the idols were an abomination to God (Ezek. 5:11). Hosea ends the verse with the language of love from the first three chapters, for they **became as vile as the thing they loved**. As Gomer loved prostitution, so Israel loved false gods. This was not a one-time affair. It was a habit dating back to the wilderness. Israel did not break its habit of idolatry, so God had to break Israel.

9:11. The love image finds its natural climax in the birth process. Hosea announced judgment in words that sound as much like lamentation as like legal pronouncement. Israel was informed that their expectations of **glory** would never enter the **birth** process. Hosea described the process in reverse: No birthing, no baby in the womb (literally, "lack of stomach"), and no conceiving. Israel's dreams of glory would **fly away** like a wild **bird**.

9:12. The unexpected might happen against all odds. A child could be born to Israel. Still no glory comes to Israel since the Lord will **bereave them** of the child. What a gruesome picture of the loving Heavenly Father taking away a newborn infant from its parents. This is one more instance of how dramatic and drastic the prophetic language had to become to get a hearing from God's people. The language of lament concludes with a statement of **woe** directed toward Israel. God has just pronounced the death of a nation. God himself leads the mourning parade—a parade caused by his turning from them.

Here we recognize another play on words in the previous verse. Israel's loss of glory is not really the loss of her materialistic dreams. Israel's glory is God himself (2 Pet. 1:17), and he has turned away or, in Hosea's metaphor, flown away from Israel. Let Israel continue to depend on Baal to make the people fertile. God will show who has power over human fertility, and it is not the cult of sacred prostitution dedicated to Baal.

9:13. Tyre was a massive sea fortress city on an island off the southern coast of Phoenicia (Ezek. 27:32). This refers to Tyre as a **pleasant place**, that is, a perfect location for a city. Apparently the comparison of the two kingdoms means that both have known pleasant locations but will now face the king of Assyria, the executioner who will kill their **children**. On the spiritual plane, however, the previous verse has pictured God as the executioner, so this cannot be eliminated from the meaning. Lying behind all this may be Ephraim's (the Northern Kingdom's) tie with Tyre and its child-sacrifice religion of Baalism. Ephraim then had a pleasant home place, a pleasant religion, and a pleasant God to bring security and fertility. They traded this for the executioner represented by the Baal religion, by their own neglected God, and by the king of Assyria.

9:14. The prophet appears to take up his role as intercessor for his people to God as he begins, **Give them, O LORD**, but then he stops to ask himself a question: **what will you give them?** The answer comes to his mind, and he prays, "bereaved **wombs** and dried up **breasts**." God will rob Israel of all fertility. Ephraim will have to bring their own children to the executioner. In such a situation, the prophet cannot intercede on behalf of the people. He can only urge God on. This is a sign of the nation's desperate situation. It took such strong language to get the people's attention.

9:15. Again the prophet delved into Israel's historic tradition, going all the way back to Gilgal, Israel's first worship center after they entered the promised land under Joshua (Hos. 12:11; see comments on Hos. 4:15). Israel thought of the Gilgal days as the glory days of religion and faithfulness to God, but Hosea claimed **all their wickedness** was **in Gilgal** so that God **hated them there**. Thus God has yet another sentence that Israel must serve: **I will drive them out of my house. I will no longer love them.**

How could such a situation develop between God and his people? Hosea pointed the finger at the nation's **rebellious** or stubborn **leaders.** Israel's leaders never learned. They followed Baal and its fertility cult to the very end of their nation's existence.

9:16. Hosea turns again to the agricultural world for metaphors to describe the situation of God's people. They are beaten down like grain under hot sun without rain or under the feet of advancing enemy armies. Baal could prevent neither the famine nor the fearful enemy advance. The Lord chose not to prevent either. All the fertility efforts made in the name of Baal or in the name of God will fail because they are not the worship efforts God demands from his people. He focuses on loving the Lord, the one true God, and loving one another.

9:17. Hosea summarizes this section succinctly: **My God will reject them because they have not obeyed him.** No longer is the Lord Israel's God. He is only Hosea's God. All the rest of the nation is rejected. Just as the people wandered in the wilderness under Moses, so they will now wander among the nations they earlier sought for help. They will suffer shame and loss of power and prestige as enemies send them into exile.

What a sad picture of a people for whom God had done so much. But a disobedient people find that God no longer blesses. When grace goes away, so do the guilty people.

🅳 Bear Your Guilt Without King or Idol (10:1–8)

SUPPORTING IDEA: *Political and religious history paint God's people as sinners who must face punishment for their false worship, false politics, and false religion.*

10:1. Hosea appears to assume the role of a teacher or lecturer explaining the current historical situation to his people. In the traditional reading of this verse based on the Greek Septuagint, Hosea begins with the good old days when **Israel was a spreading vine**—a plant that grew lush and beautiful and reproduced itself plentifully. The Hebrew phrase could also be translated "a destroying vine." The participle may point to present action—Israel is a vine "being laid waste," a description of Assyria's actions. Again, the meaning of the verb is not certain in the next line: **he brought forth fruit for himself**. The prepositional phrase can mean "to be appropriate for him, be in accordance with him." Perhaps the meaning is "Israel brought forth fruit appropriate to itself." Israel's rotten actions in disobeying God and following other gods produced the fruit of destruction.

Israel's inappropriate action bringing forth the appropriate destruction is then described as false religion. As Israel's **fruit increased**, he multiplied his **altars**. Here is another double meaning. Israel saw the fruit of their harvest as a blessing from God. But the Lord saw Israel's fruits as false worship expressing itself in a vast number of illegitimate altars and **sacred** pillars. Israel thought all was well with their world, unwilling to hear God's sentence upon them or listen to a prophetic lecture setting them straight.

10:2. God's sentence was appropriate to Israel's deeds. Devious, **deceitful** hearts (more literally, "smooth, slippery hearts") must pay the price for **their guilt**. The gods the people worship cannot protect their own worship place. One greater than those gods will appear in a destructive rampage to gain vengeance for his holy name and to make Israel pay the price for their sin.

10:3. Hosea had ended his personal section by saying Israel would lose both king and worship place before God restored a Davidic king (Hos. 3:4–5). Israel appeared to place more reliance on the king of Assyria than on their own king (Hos. 5:13). Thus the nation consumes its kings, making sure each king falls and fails (Hos. 7:7). The basic reason for royal failure was ignoring Yahweh, the God of Israel. King and officials were a burden for Israel (Hos. 8:10), demanding more and more taxes to pay ever-increasing tribute.

Hosea 10 brings this cascade of royal denunciations to a climax, letting the people admit the truth the prophet had been preaching. Israel really had **no king**. This reflected the lack of personal commitment during Israel's last fifty years. It reflected religious reality during all of the Northern Kingdom's history. Israel should have thought of God as their true king. They should have anointed and served kings only when the Lord chose them. Instead, they drove themselves so deep into international dependence and debt that no king could help them.

Here is the only place where Hosea uses the language of fearing or revering the Lord—language basic to Israel's relationship to God—a relationship built on awe, respect, reverence, and fear of God (1 Sam. 12:14). Thus "fear of the LORD" is a shorthand description of the relationship God expects humans to have with him (Prov. 2:5). Without this proper religious relationship, all political relationships, commitments, and hopes were useless.

10:4. Again the prophet uses common words whose meanings can be interpreted in several ways. The literal reading is, "They speak words—swearing falsely cutting a covenant, and like a poisonous plant, justice breaks out on the field's furrows." Israel had two kinds of covenants. The first was with God. They promised to be a holy nation, a kingdom of priests for the Lord alone. The second covenant was the political agreement Israel made with their own king and then the one they made with foreign rulers such as those from Assyria and Egypt.

In both the religious and the political realm, Israel made covenants, but the documents were just words with no commitments behind them. This spread to the nation's justice system so that Israel's justice had become poison for Israel's people. Here justice can refer to the type of relationships God expected his people to have with one another. It can refer to the reality of the nation's court systems which favored the rich and powerful and left the rest to face poverty and pain. Or it can refer to any part of the legal system: the court actions Israelites brought against one another, the sentences the courts pronounced, or the unfair economic and political reality that Israel's monarchy produced. Every meaning and method of justice in Israel had become **poisonous** for the people.

10:5. Beth Aven is an insulting nickname for Bethel, Israel's central worship place. It was not the house of God (*'el*), but the house of injustice (*'aven*). This was true because a **calf-idol** lived there. It was created by King Jeroboam I at the birth of the Northern Kingdom (1 Kgs. 12:28–30). Israel may have claimed officially that the bull represented the pedestal on which the invisible sovereign Lord sat. In practice Israel confused the bull of Bethel with the bull of Baal, since Baal worship represented its god as the powerful, fertile bull. In the uncertain political conditions of Israel's final years, the people had reason to **fear** for the fate of their bull god, a god whom they "feared" with awe and reverence.

The king of Samaria controlled the temple at Bethel (Amos 7:13), and he had reason to fear for the god he served. The king's **people** were in mourning. This was a proper posture for a country whose temple and king were about to fall, but ironically this was the same posture as that taken by Baal's worshippers in the fertility rites. Baal was believed to die for a time while the soil lay fallow and then to rise again in times of sowing and harvest. During the god's dormant period, the people mourned for him and for the infertility of the fields.

Meanwhile, the false **priests** of Bethel **rejoiced**, or more exactly "celebrated in worship" around the bull pedestal. The bull calf's "glory" or **splendor** represents the gold with which the image was plated, the power and achievements the people assigned to it, and the praise that the priests and people offered to it. But because they gave glory to the calf and not to the God of their fathers, the people would see the calf dismantled, stripped of its gold, and carted **into exile**.

10:6. Even the bull calf would be **carried** away **to Assyria**. It would serve as an offering or **as tribute** to **the great king**—a title loved by the Assyrian monarchs. Yes, the god to whom they gave lavish offerings would lose all its "honor" as its only value would become the gold plate used to pay the tribute the Assyrian king demanded to "protect" Israel.

10:7. The capital city and its inhabitants face ultimate punishment. The king will be like something on **the waters**. The Hebrew word occurs only here and is variously interpreted as a piece of wood, foam, or flotsam. Failure in worship, religion, and politics will mean destruction for the god's image, the capital city, and the king of Israel.

10:8. Samaria, the center of politics for the Northern Kingdom, faced destruction. So did the center of religion, the outlying **high places**. This is the only time Hosea uses the term. In Israel's history, some high places were used to worship God (1 Kgs. 3:4–5), but most biblical references are to corrupted worship places, where both the Lord and the Canaanite gods or just the Canaanite gods were worshipped.

Hosea referred to these pagan worship centers as "high places of injustice" (Heb. *ven*). They embodied **the sin of Israel** because God had instructed his people to destroy such places and worship only where he showed them (Deut. 12:2–14). Israel's worship at the high places had no moral component and so led to injustice—the opposite of the goal of true worship of the Lord.

Such evil called for drastic divine deeds, so God would bring **thorns and thistles** to come up over **their altars**. Hosea concludes the description of punishment by noting the people's prayers not at high places but to the high **mountains** and **hills**. Such cries would not be cries for help and deliverance but cries for final destruction and escape from their misery. A people whose worship, religion, and politics were corrupt would find life was no longer worth living.

🄴 Yoke Ephraim So They Will Sow Righteousness (10:9–15)

SUPPORTING IDEA: *A history of sin represents rebellion against God's righteous purposes and calls for divine war against God's own people.*

10:9. Hosea summarizes all he has tried to teach Israel in chapters 8 through 10. Israel must accept their identity before God. They are not elect people protected from all harm because they have religious ceremonies devoted to God. Memory of the exodus does not preclude a new journey to slavery and exile. Hosea is not talking just about recent history. Israel's sins can be dated **since the days of Gibeah**. They started out in disastrous sin and have kept it up throughout their history.

The central focus of the Gibeah narrative is the destruction of the tribe of Benjamin. The first northern hero was Saul, the king from the tribe of Benjamin and the fortress city of Gibeah (1 Sam. 15:34). In Hosea's day Saul had long since lost his honor and power, and Gibeah was a minor border post called to battle alarm (Hos. 5:8). The nation of Israel had likewise lost its honor and power. **War** would **overtake** them, just as it did **the evildoers in Gibeah**.

10:10. The threatened war depended on one thing—God's desire. It would come when he pleased. It would not be a war of victory like those under Joshua. It would be a war of disgrace like that at Gibeah, since it would be a war to **punish** God's wicked people. This war would involve much more than a few tribes against another tribe. This would be a war of **nations**. It would have one cause—Israel's **double sin** or "two crimes." Israel's history of sin faced its end.

10:11. God takes a different direction to convince Israel of the seriousness of their sin. He paints an emotional picture of young Israel. Previously, Israel was described as a "stubborn heifer" or cow (Hos. 4:16). Now Israel is a young calf, the same term used in Hosea 10:5 for the calf that Israel worshipped. This calf seems to have learned her lesson because it is a **trained** (or tamed or skillful) **heifer** who **loves to** "trample." Positively, this portrays a calf learning how to trample out or thresh grain on the threshing floor. Negatively, it can indicate trampling on enemies or on powerless people as the leaders of Israel had done, creating a society without justice.

Now God reveals his plan for the trained heifer. God will make sure the young calf learns her duties. He has put the **yoke on her fair neck**. A yoke on a calf was necessary to make it work with another calf. But the yoke was also the symbol of exercising power over someone and taking them away into exile. So God continues to teach his people a history lesson. They have never been free to do as they please. In the covenant with their God, he placed his yoke of ownership on them and took the reins to lead them where they should go.

God's instructions for his people are clear. They are to be as obedient as animals harnessed to the plow to prepare God's field for harvest. The nations may be called **Judah** and **Ephraim** now, but they all go back to one ancestor, **Jacob**. As the unified nation of Jacob/Israel, God's people are to do their own plowing with God holding the reins.

10:12. Climaxing the long section reaching back to Hosea 8:1, the prophet gives Israel their job description as God's people. **Sow for yourselves** maintains the agricultural metaphor but turns from ground preparation to planting. They are to sow what produces **righteousness**. This is the only passage other than Hosea 2:19 where the prophet speaks of righteousness. There it was one of God's expectations for his eternal bride; here it is a goal that Israel sets for itself, trying to live in a way that meets God's standards and maintains the order that God has established for his creation.

Planting in a way that produces righteousness leads to the act of harvesting. This is to be done, following the Hebrew text (not the Gr. **fruit** as in NIV), according to the measure of faithful **love** (Hos. 2:19; 4:1; 6:4,6; 12:6)—making loyalty to God and his purposes the center of a person's identity and the goal of his life.

With a bit of irony, Hosea commands Israel to **break up your unplowed ground**. The farming nation that had been plowing and sowing and harvesting for centuries had allowed the ground that yielded righteousness and faithful love to go unplowed.

Turning from metaphor, Hosea expressed his expectations clearly: **it is time to seek the LORD**. This was not to be a one-time happening but a continuous lifestyle, persisted in **until he comes and showers righteousness on you**. This also placed a limit on Israel. They will have the opportunity to sow, reap, and seek only until the Lord comes. Humans cannot create righteousness in their own strength and through their own planning and actions. Human righteousness comes only as a gift from God, as Paul says in Romans (Rom. 1:16–17).

The Hebrew word for "showers" is spelled the same as a verb meaning "to teach, instruct." Hosea may have intended for both meanings to be heard here. To receive God's gift of righteousness, we must let God teach us the ways of righteousness.

10:13. Having set out his job description for Israel, God returns to reality. At present Israel certainly does not meet this job description. They have created **wickedness** and harvested injustice. They have transferred the fruit of their fields to their dinner tables and digested **the fruit of deception**. This has produced a deceitful people full of lies who make covenants they have no intention of keeping (Hos. 10:2–4).

This has happened because the people have placed their trust in themselves rather than in God. Military heroes were expected to deliver Israel, while the heroic men of God, the prophets, were ignored. Now Israel had one last chance to decide. Would they trust a human army (their own or that of a foreign covenant partner) to deliver them from the mess they were in, or would they trust the Lord of Hosts, the God of the heavenly armies, to defend their interests?

10:14. Israel refused to accept the identity God had for them. They would not meet the job description the Lord had outlined for them. God had to put on his judge's robes one more time and pronounce sentence upon his people.

Their history began with war (v. 9). God had threatened war at his pleasure (v. 10). Now he described the horrors of that nation-ending war. Tumultuous sounds fill the air. Impregnable **fortresses** fall to the ground.

10:15. The same fate awaited the people of Israel who knew God's purposes and will and refused to follow them. Here Israel is addressed as **Bethel**, the core of their evil because it was the worship place where immoral religion and pagan images dominated Israel's life. The wickedness of Israel's cult worship at Bethel spread like gangrene throughout Israel, so that worship, religion, and politics became false and wicked. At dawn the **king of Israel** will be silenced forever. When the final battle begins, the king in whom Israel has placed such strong military hopes (Hos. 10:13) will meet death. Then Israel will have no king (Hos. 10:3). The Lord will stand victorious on the battlefield, having led the charge against what was once his people but now is a defeated nation.

> **MAIN IDEA REVIEW:** *God's love for his people guarantees that they cannot act any way they want without expecting him to respond in judgment.*

III. CONCLUSION

Differing Viewpoints

Israel had a problem with their God. The way he read their history did not agree with the way they read it. They read history as God's love affair with them that would never be broken. He read history as Israel's repeated habit of sinning and turning to false gods, false religion, and false politics. Israel looked at history from the viewpoint of the exodus and Sinai. God looked at history from the viewpoint of Baal-Peor, Gilgal, and Gibeah. Israel thought their history guaranteed the life of their nation forever. God declared that their idolatry guaranteed their exile and destruction.

What caused such a difference in understanding? A major component was the definition of the Old Testament's central term—*covenant*. Israel emphasized covenant as God's promise to them. God emphasized covenant as Israel's commitment to him. A people who leaned on promise and neglected commitment found themselves in God's courtroom facing his death sentence.

PRINCIPLES

- God expects his people to keep their covenant commitments to him.
- Sin can become so habitual that the sinner is unaware that his lifestyle brings him under God's judgment.

- Verbal confessions of faith must be supported by a daily life of faith.
- Political decisions rest on religious foundations.
- True worship does not admit pagan practices into its ritual.
- Human hands cannot fashion the invisible God.
- Covenant with God cannot be mixed with agreements with those who oppose God.

APPLICATIONS

- Judge your life by God's expectations, not by the promises of traditional religious ritual.
- Realize that no other religion has a valid substitute for God's way of commitment and righteousness.
- Set your goals in line with God's call for faithful love, righteousness, and loyalty.
- Check your political commitments, actions, and policies by the standard of God's expectations.
- Depend on a personal love relationship with God, not on a historical connection with religious tradition.
- Take seriously the Bible's condemnation of sin and threat of judgment in your own life.

IV. LIFE APPLICATION

True Religion or False Alarm?

Anne Graham Lotz devotes a chapter of her book *The Glorious Dawn of God's Story* to "He Rejects Righteousness." She tells two stories that relate to Hosea's interaction with Israel. She spoke with a professor of religion in one of our nation's "most prestigious and intellectual universities." This professor said she was confused by all the other religions in the world. On a trip to India, she met with members of the Hindu religion. They impressed her with how good they were. She asked herself why her grandmother had spent so much time praying for the salvation of these people who were so good.

Lotz also relates how she and her two daughters were awakened from deep sleep in a motel. Repeatedly, she hit the alarm clock beside the bed to shut it off. Finally, sleepy eyes opened enough to see that the alarm came not from a clock but from the fire alarm on the wall. Looking out the sixth floor window, she discovered fire trucks and flames. She and her daughters had to scurry quickly down flights of steps, deluged by water from fire hoses, to escape disaster.

Israel, too, asked why another religion's practices were not a good supplement for her own. The fire alarm message Hosea brought did nothing to wake sleeping Israel from its false religion dreams. God's threat of judgment flew by their ears unheeded.

Like Israel, modern church members flirt with varied religious practices. We may label them "Far Eastern" or "New Age." They may range from mystical meditation to yoga to spiritualism to some form of devil worship. These do not replace the religious devotion we learned from our parents. They supplement it and give one more access to "god" and one more guarantee of peace and serenity here and hope for the future. If one religion is good, some people think, then two or three must be better. Israel tried this new "religious math" long ago, and the prophets met it with a call for alarm to wake the people to battle.

God has only one job description for his people. It does not include more religious practices. It includes devotion to him as the only God and devotion to righteousness and faithful love as the only way of life.

V. PRAYER

Oh Lord, we confess that we are too religious. We look into every new religious fad and practice trying to find peace of mind. Forgive us. Teach us to trust you and you alone. Tune our ears to hear your call to righteousness and love. Go with us as we follow your path. Amen.

VI. DEEPER DISCOVERIES

A. Rebellion (8:1)

"Rebel" or "rebellion" (Heb. *pasha'*) appears over 130 times in the Hebrew Bible. It can describe a nation's revolt against a ruler (2 Kgs. 1:1). More often it is used to picture Israel's attitude toward their God (Jer. 2:8,29). Such rebellion against God takes the form of refusal to obey the covenant commands contained in the law of God.

B. Textual Issues (chs. 8–10)

These chapters contain some of the Old Testament's most difficult textual questions. Most commentators find it necessary to read something besides the current Hebrew text in many of the verses in these chapters. Often they decide to follow the Septuagint, the earliest Greek translation of the Old Testament, or other ancient versions. At times they want to define a Hebrew term in a way it is not defined in any other Old Testament passage. At times they change the Hebrew text slightly to get a reading they think makes more sense.

The student of Hosea is advised to compare several translations and to pay attention to textual notes supplied in the footnotes of most translations to see what text the translator is reading and how he may be changing the Hebrew text. Our reading of the text attempts to maintain the Hebrew tradition at almost every place and so differs at several points from the NIV translation on which this commentary is based.

Here is a listing of the major differences between our reading and that of the NIV with some comments on them. Brackets in the author's translation indicate a change from the Hebrew text.

8:10: "Although they have sold themselves among the nations, I will now gather them together. They will begin to waste away under the oppression of the mighty king" (NIV).

Author: "Even when they hire among the nations, I will now gather them. They began to be small because of the burden of king [and] officials." *Note:* "Hire" and "be small" retain the ambiguity of the Hebrew text. "Mighty" is not an accurate translation for "officials."

8:13a: "They offer sacrifices given to me and they eat the meat, but the LORD is not pleased with them" (NIV).

Author: "My beloved sacrifices—they sacrifice meat and eat. Yahweh does not accept them."

9:2: "Threshing floors and winepresses will not feed the people; the new wine will fail them" (NIV).

Author: "Threshing floor and wine press do not nourish (or feed, pasture, protect, shepherd) them, while new wine will delude (let someone down, deny) in it (i. e., the land)." *Note:* Key Hebrew terms have several meanings and lend themselves to ambiguity and word play. Final pronoun is singular referring to land, not people. Final verb at least plays on the power of wine to delude or rob the people.

9:6: "Even if they escape from destruction, Egypt will gather them, and Memphis will bury them. Their treasures of silver will be taken over by briers, and thorns will overrun their tents" (NIV).

Author: "In conclusion, take notice! They have come from destruction [see 7:13; 10:14]. Egypt will gather them. Memphis will bury them. What a precious treasure (they receive) for their silver! Weeds possess them. Thornbushes are over their tents." *Note:* The Hebrew syntax probably does not represent a conditional (even if) clause (Garrett, NAC 19A, 193). The force of "take notice" should not be missed. "Escape" is the simple perfect verb, "to walk." Hebrew does not have a verb for NIV's "overrun." Weeds and thorn bushes do not overrun silver treasures. Rather, they have paid silver and received death and burial.

9:7: "The days of punishment are coming, the days of reckoning are at hand. Let Israel know this. Because your sins are so many and your hostility so great, the prophet is considered a fool, the inspired man a maniac" (NIV).

Author: "The days of visitation have come. The days of repayment have come. Israel knows: The prophet is a fool. The man of the spirit is in a crazy rage. This is because of the abundance of punishment for your guilt, indeed, the abundant persecution" (see Smith, NIV Application, 137). *Note:* The NIV seeks variety in translating the same Hebrew terms—"come," "abundance." It reads verbs as prophetic futures that may be simple past tense. It adds "this" and transforms the sentence structure, missing the connection between Israel's knowledge and its content.

9:8: "The prophet, along with my God, is the watchman over Ephraim, yet snares await him on all his paths, and hostility in the house of his God" (NIV). The Hebrew verse uses no verbs and thus makes translation difficult. Wolff says verse 8a "belongs to the most difficult texts of the book" (BKAT XIV1, 202).

Author: "The watchman of Ephraim is with my God; a prophet is a hunter's trap on all his [Ephraim's] ways; persecution is in the house of his God [or his gods]." *Note:* The NIV misses the Hebrew parallelism and turns the snares into dangers for the prophet rather than dangers for Ephraim.

9:13: The Hebrew text teases the translator with its difficulty and apparent use of double meanings. "Hosea 9:13 is a difficult, cryptic text and widely emended in almost every translation" (Smith, NIV Application, 139). The Hebrew reads literally: "Ephraim! Just like I saw (have seen) Tyre planted in a grazing place so too Ephraim bringing out to the executioner his sons."

Emended textual readings include the following:

"I have seen Ephraim, like Tyre, planted in a pleasant place. But Ephraim will bring out their children to the slayer" (NIV).

"Once I saw Ephraim as a young palm planted in a lovely meadow, but now Ephraim must lead out his children for slaughter" (NRSV).

"Ephraim, as I have seen, was like a young palm planted in a meadow; but Ephraim must lead his children out to slaughter" (ESV).

10:5: "The people who live in Samaria fear for the calf-idol of Beth Aven. Its people will mourn over it, and so will its idolatrous priests, those who had rejoiced over its splendor, because it is taken from them into exile" (NIV).

Author: "Because of the calf of Beth-aven [that is, injustice], the resident of Samaria are [sic] afraid. Indeed, his people mourned over it while his alien priests were celebrating around it. It is because of its glory that it went into exile away from them [or it]." *Note:* Again Hosea employs double meanings in his words while using syntactical connections and changes of verb patterns that lead to various translations and interpretations. The syntactical connection and meaning of "glory" raises the most difficult problem in the text. The antecedent of the pronouns is not always clear.

10:6: "It will be carried to Assyria as tribute for the great king. Ephraim will be disgraced; Israel will be ashamed of its wooden idols" (NIV).

Author: "Even it will be carried to Assyria. It is tribute for the great king. Oh, shame! Ephraim he will take away, so that Israel will be ashamed because of its counsel." *Note:* The NIV misses the note of emphasis—*Even.* For some reason the NIV changes the Hebrew text to get "idols" instead of the Hebrew "counsel." It is probable that "Oh shame" is a prophetic exclamation rather than the NIV's description of Ephraim.

10:11: "Ephraim is a trained heifer that loves to thresh; so I will put a yoke on her fair neck. I will drive Ephraim, Judah must plow, and Jacob must break up the ground" (NIV).

Author: "But Ephraim is a tamed [or skillful] calf that loves to trample, while I myself passed [a yoke] on the good thing, her neck. I will harness Ephraim. Let Judah plow. Let Jacob harrow for himself." *Note:* Most interpreters agree that a copyist has left out the word *yoke* with the same letters as "on." The NIV has ignored the Hebrew syntactic signals of "while I myself" and omitted "for himself."

10:12: "Sow for yourselves righteousness, reap the fruit of unfailing love, and break up your unplowed ground; for it is time to seek the LORD, until he comes and showers righteousness on you" (NIV).

Author: "Sow to produce righteousness for yourselves. Harvest according to the measure of faithful love. Break up for yourselves new unplowed ground while it is time to seek Yahweh before he comes and rains [or teaches] righteousness to you." *Note:* The NIV follows the Greek in reading "fruit," which is not in Hebrew and apparently misses a bit of the nuance of the prepositions used. The meaning of the syntax introducing "time to seek Yahweh" can be debated.

VII. TEACHING OUTLINE

A. INTRODUCTION

1. Lead Story: Blind and Embarrassed
2. Context: Israel had fought for independence in the Syro-Ephraimitic War of 734 to 732 B.C., but Israel lost. In the light of this defeat, the prophet seeks to explain Israel's problems and point to a solution. The people must love God and follow his ways rather than imitating their Canaanite neighbors and worshipping Baal. Indeed, they must quit mixing worship of God and worship of Baal into indistinguishable rites in the house of God that King Jeroboam built in Bethel.

Further war and disaster loom ominously because Israel has not learned to produce the righteousness and faithful love that God expects.

3. Transition: The long section of chapters 8–10 contains warnings in first-person speech from God and in third-person speech from the prophet. Both types of speech carry the same warnings. Israel must understand the times in which they live and the God they claim to worship. They are no longer the beloved darlings of God who are immune from any enemy attack. Rather, their entire history must be read as a history of sin and rebellion that deserves divine destruction. Thus the entire section must be read under the heading, "I no longer love them."

B. COMMENTARY

1. Blow the Bugle for Covenant Breakers (8:1–14)
2. Call Off the Party for Those Deserving Punishment (9:1–9)
3. Kill the Children of Those I No Longer Love (9:10–17)
4. Bear Your Guilt Without King or Idol (10:1–8)
5. Yoke Ephraim So They Will Sow Righteousness (10:9–15)

C. CONCLUSION: DIFFERING VIEWPOINTS

VIII. ISSUES FOR DISCUSSION

1. How do prophetic warnings about breaking God's law under the old covenant apply to Christians under the new covenant?
2. What causes God to tell his people, "Do not rejoice"?
3. If God is a God of love, mercy, and forgiveness, how can he tell Israel, "Even if they rear children, I will bereave them of every one" (Hos. 9:12)?
4. God identified Israel's religious rituals as sinful (Hos. 8:11). What might make God view your church's worship services as sinful?
5. What is your church doing to seek the Lord and sow seeds of righteousness?

Hosea 11:1–13:16

I Am God, Not Man

I.   **INTRODUCTION**
It's a Boy!

II. **COMMENTARY**
A verse-by-verse explanation of these verses.

III. **CONCLUSION**
Father and King

An overview of the principles and applications from these verses.

IV. **LIFE APPLICATION**
How Did You Know?

Melding these verses to life.

V.   **PRAYER**
Tying these verses to life with God.

VI. **DEEPER DISCOVERIES**
Historical, geographical, and grammatical enrichment of the commentary.

VII. **TEACHING OUTLINE**
Suggested step-by-step group study of these verses.

VIII. **ISSUES FOR DISCUSSION**
Zeroing these verses in on daily life.

Quote

"*The Old Testament thinks of God largely in terms of two different and alternative images, as king or as father. When he is thought of primarily as king, as the upholder of law, his justice receives emphasis. It is unthinkable that he should be anything but unshakably righteous, allowing no deviation from his just demands. But when he is conceived as father, it seems unthinkable that he should be anything other than compassionate. Christianity has brought the two images firmly together, with all the inevitable paradox and tension that this involves, for we habitually pray, 'Our Father ... thy kingdom come.'*"

Henry McKeating

Hosea 11:1–13:16

IN A NUTSHELL

God debates with himself over the future of his people. He recalls his history with them, looking at the deliverance from Egypt, the birth and Bethel experience of deceitful Jacob, and the leadership of Ephraim after the conquest. He also reviews his people's history of sin. Thus God questions himself about his appropriate response. Humans would naturally condemn Ephraim to destruction. But he is God, not man. What will he do?

I Am God, Not Man

I. INTRODUCTION

It's a Boy!

"*It's* a boy baby." I will never forget the doctor's words or the feeling they brought. God had blessed us with a healthy child. Mother and baby were fine. I could hold the little life in my hands. In so many ways that life lay there for me to mold. Was I up to the task? How would I respond to this child? When the child did not act exactly as I desired, how would I react?

Now, all these years later, experience has shown me that I had reason to ask those questions. Many times I have stood asking myself and my God, What should I do in this situation? Such experiences with my children have helped me understand God better because he, too, has children who cause him to ask, "How can I give you up?" Hosea pictures the inward struggles of God as he replays the story of his people and struggles with his own emotional attachments to them. Their sins anger him and lead him to feelings of anguish, but his love conquers all.

II. COMMENTARY

I Am God, Not Man

> **MAIN IDEA:** *In his love for his people, God wants to spoil his children and do everything possible for them, but in his holy justice he knows he must discipline them for their refusal to obey him.*

🅰 A Loving God and a Loathsome People (11:1–12)

> **SUPPORTING IDEA:** *In his love God debates with himself about how he should deal with his lying people.*

11:1. God takes center stage as he debates with himself about the proper course of action with his unruly children. "I offered my best," he declares. Perhaps that is all a father can hope to say in retrospect. A father hopes to trace his relationship with his child and say, "I did everything I knew how to do." Looking at his adolescent son, Israel, God the Father could certainly say that he had given them his best. He **loved** Israel. The **Egypt** experience proved that God took a nobody and created a powerful nation. He showed the strongest nation in the world that it had no power like that of God.

11:2. But the child did not turn out so well. He found young love with other gods. Exactly how Israel did that depends on how a person reads the text. The Hebrew text reads literally, "They called to them; thus they walked from before them." The Greek Septuagint reads, "Just as I called them, just so they departed from my face." The NIV follows the Septuagint. The meaning of "from before" is difficult, but it apparently means that Israel heard the call of the Baals, went to them, and then walked out of their presence to continue with their lives.

So not only did Israel center their attention on mere ritual and sacrifice (Hos. 4:13–14; 6:6; 8:13; 9:4); they even worshipped the wrong object. The carved **images** should have been burned up or chopped down (Deut. 12:3). They were the way the pagan nations worshipped—a way God refused to share (Isa. 42:8), a way that led God to punish Israel (Mic. 1:7). But Israel's history was strewn with such carved images (Isa. 10:10), whose worship Israel mixed with that of the Lord (2 Kgs. 17:41). It enraged God (Ps. 78:58). He looked to the day when Israel would throw such images away (Isa. 30:22).

11:3. Still God did not turn away. He took the toddler by his arms and **taught** the child **to walk.** He cared for the sick child, healing all the childhood diseases (Deut. 32:39). What a picture of God—the parent on hands and knees helping the baby walk and then bending over the baby's sleeping place as a pediatrician with the right medicine to stop his cough. God had done everything possible for Israel. But Israel did not **realize** (literally "know") it!

11:4. Change the image. Make God a rancher caring for farm animals. With a love beyond any feeling the animals have, God cared for his people. God used **cords of human kindness.** God did not force humans into obedience through divine sovereignty and power. Instead, he entered our world and placed human ropes on us to lead us as a farmer leads work animals to their task. These ropes were thus **ties of love.** God did not simply make work animals out of his people. God is like a farmer who knows the yoke has been too tightly attached to an animal's head or mouth, so he adjusts the yoke to make the animal more comfortable. When it says God **bent down,** it means he treated them gently. He provided everything the animals needed.

Israel fit this animal picture perfectly. They constantly welcomed foreign masters and allowed alien rulers to put yokes of tribute and slavery on their backs. Was Israel more than a dumb animal? It did not matter. God's incomparable love remained the same.

11:5. Hosea turns quickly from Israel's history to the present. The NIV translation of the verse as a question is doubtful. God does not ask; God announces. Israel sought treaties with Egypt to avoid serving Assyria or being destroyed by the Assyrian army. God's plan was different. He proclaimed that the **return to Egypt** would not happen. Rather, **Assyria** would **rule** Israel. God explained his reason for pronouncing this sentence on Israel. Israel had refused **to repent.** Here Hosea speaks explicitly of repenting, but it is the purpose behind much of the preaching of the prophets.

Just as God led Hosea to discipline his wife so she would return to him in loyal love and fidelity, so God warned his people to get them to turn away from their foreign gods and sinful ways and turn to him. Israel refused. God announced the resulting sentence. Sometimes the rebellious child had to experience the Father's discipline.

11:6. Again the Hebrew text presents the translator with problems. Much of the problem rests on the Hebrew word *bad,* which may mean, "a portion, member, solitude, carrying poles, shoots of a vine, pieces of linen, loose talk or boasting," and perhaps "oracle priest or diviner." Taking it to mean "boasting" rather than **bars of their gates**, the literal Hebrew text might best be translated, "**Swords** will whirl about in his cities; they will put an end to his boasting; they will consume **their plans**."

As in chapter 10, battle imagery is used to describe God's judgment on his people. This has been prepared for by the previous mention of the king of Assyria. Here the imagery is taken to its final stage—the battle that finishes off the nation of Israel. God's love for his people finally turns to tough love that brings judgment, even though it is a love that lets him describe himself in terms of a loving, caring Father and in terms of a human farmer tending to his animals. Israel will have no more reason to boast of its wisdom, religion, politics, or political maneuvering. All **plans** will fail. Assyria will destroy Israel's political system.

11:7. Apparently God's people have a **determined** habit of turning away from God. They call him the **Most High**, but God does nothing to lift their burdens. Calling on God with high-sounding names does no good for a people who ignore God in daily life.

11:8. God faced a crisis point. He had to decide. Would he set himself up as the final judge and execute his people, or would he execute his plan of salvation? Would justice triumph in the divine nature, or would love? Here we see the depth of divine love as God himself struggles to avoid bowing to the overwhelming evidence and sentencing his people to death. Hosea pictures God arguing with himself. How could he possibly surrender his people to another nation that worshipped another god? How could he reduce them to the fate of being mere footnotes in history like Sodom and Gomorrah's satellite cities, **Admah** and **Zeboiim** (Deut. 29:23)?

Listen to the Father agonize over his beloved children: I raised you as a child. I taught you to walk. I put everything I have into you. I delivered you out of Egypt. I gave you the land. I gave you political power. I trusted you to be instruments of my salvation for the world. Oh Israel, what will I do with you? I ought to punish you. You deserve the death sentence. You have refused to answer my call to love and repentance. Instead you have answered Assyria's call to captivity. But how can I let you go? Compassionate feelings arise within me. **My heart is changed**!

11:9. God makes up his mind. I cannot execute it, he declares. I will not execute it. Israel shall not die. I cannot give you up. My anger will not win out. Oh, Israel! I love you too much. Love is the center of my life. Does it matter what anyone else may say or ask? No! I am in control. My love will win out. Compassion burns in my breast. Why think of any other action? I will show my love to my people. That is my final word.

But how can God justify such action after the horrendous ways he has described his people? How can he announce a decision and then overrule it? Because he is divine. He acts like **God** acts. Humans have no standards by which to judge God. He sets the standards for right and wrong. God does not live by some legalistic system that says under these conditions you must do this and only this. The Lord lives by love. The **Holy One** is the totally different one. He can act as his nature tells him to act. He does not have to ask us for justification of his acts. Thus he will not destroy **Ephraim**.

11:10. So here God decides judgment cannot be his final word for his people. Love echoes a call across the nations to God's sinful, punished people. The call coming from God, the king of heaven, resembles that of a **lion**, the king of beasts. Earthly people cannot ignore the heavenly roar. The people hear and respond. They **follow the LORD** rather than walking away as in Hosea 11:2. They return, and God has a home ready for them.

The strange, unexpected word here is **west**. Egypt is a bit west of Israel, but it is viewed as being south. The west is literally "the sea" and represents the vast unknown regions. God's punishment has been so extreme that at least some of Israel has fled into the great unknown. His love is so all-encompassing that he calls Israel back to himself, even those lost hopelessly in the unknown wilds of the west.

11:11. Israel's identity came from the exodus—God's deliverance of Israel at Egypt's Red Sea. God has a second exodus in store, one from both **Assyria** and **Egypt**. Israel will flutter back home like scared **birds**, and God will again **settle them in their homes**. Once again the promised land will house the people of promise.

11:12. The God who promises new salvation is not blind. He knows the people who receive his promise. They have not changed. They are deceptive. They tell **lies**. The second half of the verse is open to several translations and interpretations. It might be translated, "But Judah still roams free with God, even with the holy ones he is faithful." The "holy ones" could be the faithful people of God. So Hosea might be saying that **Judah** still walks with God and remains among the faithful saints or holy ones, a sharp contrast to Israel and a strong invitation to Israel to imitate Judah. But the word used for "God" is *El,* which sometimes refers to a pagan god, and the "holy ones" could be angels or idols, in which case Hosea is saying that Judah, just like Israel, wanders away from God to El and is faithful to idols or angels instead of Yahweh.

B True to History but Not to God (12:1–14)

SUPPORTING IDEA: *Remaining true to a history of deceit and disobedience means not remaining true to God and his faithfulness.*

12:1. God lays out Ephraim's major crime. God accuses Ephraim of dedication to futile activities. They seek to shepherd or rule **the wind**. They pursue **the east wind**, seeking to catch it so they can control it. Such futile activities make as much sense as Israel's political and commercial dealings with foreign countries in hopes of gaining economic and military protection. The **treaty** (or covenant) **with Assyria** apparently represents a military agreement to pay tribute in order to gain protection, and such a treaty would be made in the name of the god of that country. Sending **olive oil to Egypt** might mean entering into commercial activities with Egypt or paying tribute.

Both actions represent rebellion against God, who is the only one with whom Israel is supposed to have a covenant and is the one who has promised to bless Israel with economic resources. Here is Israel the prostitute seeking first one lover and then the other to protect her from the threats to her political and economic life.

12:2. Thus God has a legal case or court indictment **against Judah**, his own people. Here Judah is identified with rather than being contrasted to Israel. The lawsuit against Judah brings punishment to **Jacob**. Here Jacob is used for Israel because the following examples will come from the life of the patriarch Jacob. Jacob's punishment will be a payment for the ways he has walked and the actions he has done. God punishes on the basis of clear evidence.

12:3. Jacob's biography is briefly reported from Genesis but without interpretation about the positive or negative qualities of the actions. "Grasp the heel" represents a Hebrew term (*'aqab*) with the same basic consonants as the name Jacob (see Gen. 25:26; 27:36). **Struggled** (*yasar*) uses the same consonants as the name Israel; the contending or struggling with God is described in Genesis 32:28 in the mysterious scene at the Jabbok River. The wrestling match with the divine representative brought Jacob a new name—Israel. The Hebrew word translated **as a man** is literally "in his strength." It refers to the virility of manhood as opposed to the weakness of a baby in the womb. The same word is also used for wickedness that works itself out in futility (Hos. 12:11), injustice (Hos. 6:8), and false worship (Hos. 10:8).

12:4. As in Genesis, the wrestling match is described both as a battle with God and with an **angel**. He **wept and begged for his favor** may be an interpretation of Jacob's prayer in Genesis 32:29 or an expansion of the story to include Jacob's fear before his brother Esau in Genesis 33:3–4. Here again we see both the strength and weakness of Jacob. He met God **at Bethel** in the ladder vision of Genesis 28:10–22. Thus Jacob's story is one of struggle, weakness, deception, and victory and intimacy with God.

12:5. The prophet stops a moment to remind his audience exactly who this God is. He is not to be confused with one of the gods of Canaan or one of the deities of victorious Assyria. This is **God Almighty**, "the God of Hosts." The title "God of Hosts" represents God as the general in charge of Israel's armies whether they be earthly (Isa. 31:4) or heavenly ("their vast array" in Gen. 2:1 is literally "all their host"). Israel forgot the power of the God who fought their battles and created their nation. Israel confused this God with the various gods of their enemies and attributed equal power and influence to those gods. Israel had to remember how their God was remembered and named among them. No other god controlled the earthly and heavenly armies.

12:6. Israel not only forgot the identity of their God; they forgot the characteristics that made them people of God. To be the people of God, they **must return** to their God or repent (see comments on Hos. 6:1; 7:10). A holy God requires a holy people, so returning to God means returning to the holy lifestyle he demands. This lifestyle includes faithful **love** (Heb. *chesed*) and **justice** (Heb. *mishpat*). (For these terms, see comments on Hos. 2:19.)

Having summarized the lifestyle in relationship to other people, Hosea summarizes the relationship to God in a unique fashion: **wait for** (or "put your hope in," HCSB) **your God always**. This excludes all gods but the God of Israel, who is "your God." It shows Israel's situation as one of need in which they must wait until someone else provides the solution to their need. They are aware of their finiteness and God's infiniteness, and they have no way to satisfy their own need. Their only hope is in God (Ps. 130:5). This hope is for God's intervention to deliver them from their problems. Ultimately, this hope is fulfilled in Jesus Christ and his promise of resurrection hope.

12:7. Suddenly the charge against Israel turns away from the historic Jacob to Israel's present economic practices. They mirror Jacob's deception. The **merchant** is signified by the Hebrew term for Canaan used in its most original sense; thus Israel is described as a Canaanite. This merchant uses **scales** that weigh too heavy when he sells and too light when he buys (Amos 8:5). He loves to oppress or exploit his customers, most of whom are already mired in poverty and debt. God hates this (Mic. 6:11) and expects different behavior from his people (Lev. 19:36).

12:8. Such practices enable **Ephraim** to boast that they are **rich** or **wealthy**. Israel knows the accusations they face, and they go to the witness stand in their own defense. They know their own **wealth**. They feel others are jealous because they feel no guilt and see no sin in their practices.

12:9. God has given Israel a history lesson about the election of her namesake ancestor Jacob/Israel. Now he reminds them of his own history. He became their God in their deliverance from **Egypt** (Exod. 1–15). In that exodus he instituted ways to remember his saving acts, including the Feast of Booths or Tabernacles when Israel relived the wilderness experience of living in **tents** (Lev. 23:34–43). Hosea declared that this living in tents would become Israel's permanent mode of existence.

12:10. Israel had no excuse. They could not plead ignorance. God made his point with emphatic repetition. God **spoke to the prophets**, with the normal prophetic **visions** as the means of reception and the **parables** or comparative sayings as the prophetic method of teaching. God had spoken, but Israel refused to acknowledge the prophets as God's inspired speakers.

12:11. God turns to a new line of evidence: Since **Gilead** is unjust, surely the people are **worthless** (or have become nothing). In **Gilgal** they sacrificed **bulls**. Even their **altars** are like **stones** heaped on furrows of the **field** (see comments on Hos. 4:15; 6:8; 9:15). Israel's frontier with Syria and ultimately Assyria was unjust, so God had no reason to defend it. He placed no value on them. The sacrifices in Gilgal violated God's prohibition (Hos. 4:15). Their piles of stones that served as altars in the midst of their agricultural fields violated God's call for sacrifice only at the places he had selected. God produced evidence not only in politics and economics but also in religion. Israel had no alibi, no excuse, no hope.

12:12. Hosea turns back again to the biography of Jacob, Israel's original ancestor, but again without comment or interpretation. Having angered his brother Esau, **Jacob fled to the country of Aram**, or Syria. There in a foreign land he worked as a shepherd to earn his **wife** (Gen. 27:43–29:30). Thus Israel cannot brag about its progenitor. He owned no land, was so poor he could not pay the bride price for his wife, was so naïve that his father-in-law deceived him, and was so unimportant socially that he worked in the lowly job of a shepherd.

12:13. Again God testifies to his history with Israel. Earlier he highlighted the prophetic office as his way of informing Israel of their sin and thus giving them no excuse for sin. Now he highlights that office further by identifying Moses as a prophet (Deut. 18:15) who brought **Israel up from Egypt** and **cared for him**. Hosea uses the same Hebrew word to speak of Jacob tending sheep in Hosea 12:12 and the prophet caring for Israel here. Hosea is the prophet like Moses, tending his generation, while Israel is the insignificant Jacob of that generation, tending sheep—not people. God provided Israel the prophet they needed, but Israel would not accept that leadership or acknowledge God's care.

12:14. God summarizes the evidence in one sentence: **Ephraim** has grieved (or **provoked him to anger**) in bitterness. The Hebrew text does not have an expressed object, so that the prophet or God himself may be seen as becoming angry. The ambiguity here may be intentional, but obviously God's anger is the central focus.

Finally, God pronounces the sentence. Ephraim's Master or **Lord**, rather than their covenant partner or God, will make his slave pay the penalty literally for bloodshed—for crimes that deserved the death sentence. The Master will pay Ephraim precisely what they have earned with their **contempt** for God—their scoffing at or scorning what he has done for them and what he has taught them through the prophets. Israel has been true to the model of their forefather, Jacob. They have disobeyed God with their politics, their economics, and their religion. They deserve the death penalty, and they will receive it.

C Death Devours as Divine Compassion Disappears (13:1–16)

SUPPORTING IDEA: *Guilt eventually brings the death sentence even from a God of compassion and salvation.*

13:1. In the days of the judges, **Ephraim** tried to assert leadership and strength before the other tribes (Judg. 8:1). Again under King Jeroboam II, Ephraim as the Northern Kingdom expanded its territory and influence (2 Kgs. 14:26–27). In those days Ephraim's voice caused other tribes or other nations to tremble in terror. Hosea depicts a different Ephraim, a dead Ephraim. What caused the death of this tribe and nation? They were **guilty** in their love affair with **Baal** and suffered its punishment (Hos. 4:15; 5:15; 10:2).

13:2. But **now** Hosea begins rousing fear and wonder about what else could happen to Ephraim. One love affair did not suffice. The people went on sinning. They made their own metal images rather than destroying them as God commanded (Num. 33:52). Thus they disobeyed God's law (Exod. 34:17), bringing down the curse of Deuteronomy 27:15 on themselves. **Craftsmen**, people whose skills and resources should be dedicated to the Lord, instead dedicate them to false gods and worship what they have created.

Some translations avoid mention of **human sacrifice**, but we must not back away from the horrendous statement of the text. Human sacrifice was a problem for Israel, especially in desperate days (Judg. 11:30–40). The practices clearly violated God's law (Lev. 20:2–5). Israel's love affair turned deadly. They took over not only reverence for Baal as shown by kissing the **calf** representations of Baal. They also followed other pagan practices—the most horrible of which Hosea condemns here.

13:3. The prophetic **therefore** introduces a prediction of disaster, a warning of judgment to come. Israel appeared on the historical scene as an ephemeral entity, vanishing as quickly as **morning mist** or **early dew**. The nation came and went like **chaff** blowing in the wind or **smoke escaping through a window.**

13:4. Israel's sin represents theological amnesia. The Lord introduces himself again to his own people as their **God** who brought them **out of Egypt**. This introduction represents a shorthand version of the introduction to the Ten Commandments (Exod. 20:2; see comments on Hos. 12:9). God's goal was an intimate personal relationship with his people, Israel (see comments on Hos. 2:20; 5:3–4; 6:3; 8:2). They had such a relationship with **no** other god. Their life as a nation depended on God since he alone was their **Savior** (Isa. 45:21). Israel had no history without God. But they had turned away from him. Having abandoned him as their God, they should expect their history to end.

13:5. Hosea continued to use the intimate term *know*, rendered by the NIV as "acknowledge" in verse 4 and as **cared for** in verse 5. In Israel's most desperate situation—forty years of wandering in the **desert** or wilderness— God became intimately acquainted with his people as he cared for them, providing manna, meat, and water. **Burning heat** is a word that occurs only here in the Hebrew Bible; it could also mean "drought."

13:6. Israel took everything they could get from God. Once these cattle raisers found grazing ground for their animals, they had everything they wanted. They could dispense with the God who provided those needs. They **became proud**. The result was predictable. Their proud hearts forgot God. They had no desire for intimacy with the Lord. They became self-sufficient.

13:7–8. Israel wanted to graze their animals. God would become an attacking animal. Take your pick—**lion, leopard,** or **bear.** Disaster lurked on every **path** Israel chose to take since they refused to follow God's path.

13:9. God had revealed himself as Israel's **helper** since patriarchal times (Ps. 37:40). Now, facing the desperation of Assyrian attacks, Israel stood **against** the only one who could help. Therefore, Israel would be **destroyed.**

13:10. God stumps Israel with a rhetorical question: **Where is your king?** The Northern Kingdom's final years saw kings come and go through the land. These were Assyrian kings and their armies, besieging cities and demanding tribute from Israel's helpless kings. The politics that Israel tried to play and the military strength that she tried to buy from Egypt and elsewhere proved fatal. Israel's earliest occupation of the land occurred under the judges (**rulers**) in the years after Joshua's conquest. That time period led to Israel doing what was right in their own eyes (Judg. 21:25) and wanting a **king.**

God listened to their demand (1 Sam. 8), but Israel could not live under the political system God instituted. The system they chose to replace it proved even worse since kings led Israel to idols and Baals, not to God. Then, in time of trouble, Israel's precious king proved to be no help at all.

13:11. In **anger** at the people for demanding a king, God **gave** them Saul (1 Sam. 9). Then in **wrath** against Saul's disobedience, God rejected him (1 Sam. 15). The same can be said about Jeroboam, who became king over the northern tribes when God was angry at Rehoboam (1 Kgs. 12). Now in wrath God would take away Israel's king for good.

13:12. Ephraim's name represented the entire Northern Kingdom. Their **guilt** was wrapped up like a package; their **sins**, hidden away for safe keeping. Ephraim did not go to God for forgiveness. Ephraim did not forsake their guilty, sinful ways. In its time of greatest need, Ephraim stood guilty before God.

13:13. Hosea returns to the family metaphors of chapters 1–3 but with a horrible twist. The **pains** of **childbirth come to him**. The male who suffers is not the father but the son being born. This son is totally devoid of **wisdom** because at the proper **time** to appear, the son refuses to stand in the **opening** of the cervix. From his birth, Ephraim has gone against the rules, never showing wisdom or obedience.

13:14. God surprises the reader. Amid the horrible pictures of suffering, judgment, and doom, the light of salvation shines forth. God makes a promise to **ransom** and **redeem** Israel. The divine voice then breaks into a taunt song: "Where are your plagues (or stinging thorns), death?" God mocks the powers represented by death and Sheol, the realm of the dead. They think they have control of a defeated, foolish Ephraim. But God has other plans— plans for redemption and ransom (see comments on Hos. 7:13 for "ransom" and Mic. 4:10 for "redeem"). When God decides to buy back his sinful people, no power can stand in his way. Our loving God proved this on the cross and through the resurrection of Jesus Christ.

But the promise for salvation and redemption was not for immediate action; it was God's ultimate plan. For the present generation ominous words rang forth. The Lord is both a God of salvation and a God of discipline. For Israel, discipline would come before **compassion** and redemption appeared.

13:15. The first line of this verse puzzles commentators. The Hebrew text reads, "For he a son of brothers causes to be fruitful." **Brothers** may be a treaty term for fellow nations. The tone is ironic and sarcastic. Israel thinks they are strong and secure because of treaties with fellow nations—Egyptians, Philistines, Edomites, Syrians. This is the same picture Isaiah and Amos paint of Israel about 740 to 735 B.C. God has another picture—a hot **east wind** blasting in **from the desert**. Israel's fruitfulness wilts in the heat. Their resources vanish. An enemy army will plunder Israel's agricultural, economic, and military storehouses.

13:16. Everything Israel relied on for protection will disappear. Samaria is guilty. The people have **rebelled against their God!** Israel would have to face barbaric military practices, including the ripping open of protruding stomachs of **pregnant women** and the abuse of infant children

(Isa 13:16,18). The rebellious nation would be victimized by an army with no moral restraints.

> **MAIN IDEA REVIEW:** *In his love for his people God wants to spoil his children and do everything possible for them, but in his holy justice he knows he must discipline them for their refusal to obey him.*

III. CONCLUSION

Father and King

God is not a simple person who is easy to understand. We cannot predict his actions and reactions. He is not a robot whom we can program to do as we expect. He refuses to fit our nice, tight theological systems. He is a person, not a doctrine. As a person, God involves himself emotionally in the life of his people as community and as individuals. He has the greatest power on earth—that of an absolute monarch over the universe. He has the deepest attachment to his people—that of a committed, loving father. Our response to God determines the side of him that we experience. Obedient children snuggle up to a loving father. Rebellious people face up to the divine king and his instruments of punishment.

PRINCIPLES

- God is a father who cares for the needs of his children.
- God does not extend his care indefinitely to a people who are bent on rebellion.
- The holy God does not want to give up on his disobedient people.
- People cannot deceive God.
- Repenting and turning to God is the only hope for a sinful nation or individual.
- Wealth cannot buy off God.
- Politicians cannot outmaneuver God.
- God has power even over death.

APPLICATIONS

- Answer God's call, not that of politicians or false gods.
- Do not depend on religion to make peace with God.
- Do not reduce God to an emergency service who stands ready to get you out of trouble.
- Talk straight with God, with no attempt to deceive him.

- Treat all people with love and justice while you wait for God's salvation.
- Serve the Lord as the only true, living God of the universe.
- Give God all the credit, taking none for yourself.

IV. LIFE APPLICATION

How Did You Know?

Jogging in his neighborhood one morning, Max Lucado knew it was the first day of school. There were television interviews, parents packing stores to get last-minute supplies, and school buses rumbling past his house. Then he noticed a pretty little girl leaving her house with new clothes and a new backpack. Max waved and encouraged her: "Have a great first day of school." The six-year-old stopped in her tracks, amazed. "How did you know?"

This brought a quick comparison to Max's mind. Just as adults sense things children cannot comprehend, so God knows so much more than we do. Max writes in his book *The Great House of God,* "Take the difference between the girl and me, amplify it a million times over, and we begin to see the contrast between us and our Father. Who among us can ponder God without asking the same question the girl did: How did you know?" (pp. 37–38).

Israel experienced the same confusion. They went through all the rituals of religion. They put on their best face in God's presence. Then they left the worship place to face the "real world." There they acted like they had to so they could make a go of it in the real world. Suddenly God confronted them. You are trying to deceive me, he told them. Don't you know I see everything you do? Why do you keep on deceiving me, knowing you will never get away with it?

Our generation is no different. We practice one lifestyle on Sunday and another one during the other six days of the week. We think God must be pleased with the time we spend in church and the offerings we put in the plate each Sunday. Surely, he'll be there to help as we need him. But God's answer comes: "I have no compassion. You must bear your guilt."

V. PRAYER

Loving father, we appear to be something special on Sunday and then sneak around behind your back the rest of the week. It does not work. You know everything about us. Forgive us. Change us. Open your fatherly arms and hold us tight. Amen.

VI. DEEPER DISCOVERIES

A. God the Father (11:1–11)

Family language dominates Hosea's prophecy because God used family experiences as the foundation of the prophet's ministry (chs. 1–3). Hosea knew what it meant to be a brokenhearted lover and a brokenhearted parent. He tried to make Israel realize that they formed God's family and in so doing had broken God's heart.

Describing God as Israel's Father goes back at least to the time of Moses (Exod. 4:22). God the Father had the authority to impose rules for his children (Deut. 14:1). But his Israelite "sons" rebelled against his authority and showed him no respect (Mal. 1:6). God's response as Father included the threat of discipline (Prov. 3:12) as well as deep love and care (Jer. 31:9).

VII. TEACHING OUTLINE

A. INTRODUCTION

1. Lead Story: It's a Boy!
2. Context: Chapters 11–13 are the emotional climax of Hosea's preaching. They point to the climactic moments in the history of Israel, the Northern Kingdom. These chapters bring to a head the constant swing between God's determination to discipline and destroy his people and his eternal love that points to salvation for a disciplined people. We learn that the seeming indecision of the prophet and the book rests on the image of a loving, holy father. His holy justice calls for punishment. His loving parental nature calls for a new start. So these chapters picture God as if he were wrestling with himself over what to do with rebellious children.
3. Transition: How will God decide? Does holiness or parental love win out when God must punish his children? We must study this lesson carefully since it describes the depths of our relationship with the Heavenly Father.

B. COMMENTARY

1. A Loving God and a Loathsome People (11:1–12)
2. True to History but Not to God (12:1–14)
3. Death Devours as Divine Compassion Disappears (13:1–16)

C. CONCLUSION: FATHER AND KING

VIII. ISSUES FOR DISCUSSION

1. How can the prophet Hosea describe God as arguing with himself?
2. What religious acts please God? Which ones do not? Why?
3. How does our ancestors' history with God affect our own relationship with him?
4. What has God done in your personal life that shows him to be your loving father?
5. What must you do to return to God right now?

Hosea 14:1–9

Return to the Righteous One

Quote

"*It's* not that God sits in His heaven and determines to abuse those who make mistakes. But He forbade certain behavior because He knew it would ultimately destroy its victims. It is not God who leads to death, but sin. And sin becomes a cancer that consumes those who embrace it."

James Dobson

Hosea 14:1–9

IN A NUTSHELL

The theme of prophetic preaching is a call to turn to God in repentance because God loves and can heal.

Return to the Righteous One

I. INTRODUCTION

Where's the Right Road?

*T*his lesson hit home in a special way today. I write this from North Carolina, where I am leading a writer's conference. I rented a car, got directions to travel straight up highway 16 from Charlotte to my destination. Everything went well. I was humming along the highway enjoying the Carolina countryside thinking all was right with the world.

Then I looked up to see I could go right or left to be on Highway 10. But no direction led to Highway 16. I had strayed from the path. I had missed the road sign that corresponded to the markings on my map. I was lost. I had to find someone who could point me in the right direction. Then I had to turn around and go back where I had come from until I found Route 16 again.

Hosea issued one last plea to Israel—come back home. He pointed Israel in the right direction. "You have missed the way. Sin is destroying you. Turn around and come back home to God."

II. COMMENTARY

Return to the Righteous One

> **MAIN IDEA:** *Sinners must quit stumbling along the path of sin, find the way back to God in repentance, accept God's loving forgiveness and healing, discard their idols, find new life under God's blessing, and act with wisdom.*

🅐 Repent and Be Healed (14:1–3)

> **SUPPORTING IDEA:** *People stumbling in sin need to return to God in repentance, ask his forgiveness, and forsake their idol worship.*

14:1. The book of Hosea pictures the prophet making one last effort to persuade the people to choose the right God and serve him in the right way. Hosea had ended his opening stories about God's directions for his own family with the promise that Israel would one day turn and seek the Lord (Hos. 3:5). But for the present their evil deeds did not permit them to turn back to God (Hos. 5:4). In 6:1 Hosea pictured Israel issuing a call to turn back to God for healing. In reality even military defeat could not make Israel turn back to

God (Hos. 7:10). Refusing to return to God, Israel would return to Egypt, needing a new exodus (Hos. 11:5). So God insisted that Israel turn in repentance, love, and justice (Hos. 12:6). Chapter 14 then repeatedly issues the call to turn to God, or repent of sin. This is the climax and core of Hosea's message.

To persuade Israel to repent, Hosea had to convince them of one reality—that they were sinners. So he exclaimed, **Your sins have been your downfall**, or more literally, "You have stumbled in your guilt" (HCSB). A person stumbling down the road of sin and guilt must turn in the opposite direction. There he will find God waiting.

14:2. A people so inexperienced in repentance needed to know how to repent. Hosea mimicked the priests as they taught the people how to offer sacrifices and remain ritually clean. Israel needed to **take words**, not sacrifices, to God. With these words they could **return to the LORD**. The words were simple—"forgive all guilt and take good." Bible students have offered many interpretations of "take good," the NIV giving the most unusual with its **receive us graciously**. Apparently "good" stands in contrast to guilt and means "accept the good we are doing, namely turning to you for forgiveness."

14:3. In 734 B.C. Israel joined Syria in trying to force Judah to join them in fighting Assyria, but King Ahaz of Judah refused. Instead, he paid Assyria to deliver him from Israel and Syria. When, then, did Hosea find the Northern Kingdom saying **Assyria** could **save** them? Apparently, this must have come in the final days of Israel's existence as a nation when certain groups in the country wanted to surrender to Assyria and depend on their mercy. In a larger context, Assyria stands for all political powers in which the people of God would place their hopes. Political sovereigns have no chance against the sovereign Lord of Israel.

In a similar vein, Israel must confess to God that they cannot rely on riding into battle on **war-horses**. Israel must confess their sin of idolatry and the inability of such idols to rescue them in time of trouble (see comments on Hos. 13:2).

The final line of the verse surprises us: **for in you the fatherless find compassion**. Israel must confess that they are helpless as orphans and need God's motherly compassion. These words emphasize the confession that other gods do not display such compassion or provide help for the helpless.

𝔹 Love and Healing Replace God's Anger (14:4–8)

SUPPORTING IDEA: *God hears his people's pleas for forgiveness, turns from his anger, and heals the wounds of his repentant people.*

14:4. Continuing to play with the Hebrew term *shub*, which can mean "turn" or "return" or "repent," Hosea says God will heal his people's "turnings" or **waywardness**. The people who turned away must return. Then God will turn to them with healing because he will **love them freely**. The last word is usually used for free will or voluntary offerings. Now God's voluntary offering to a repentant people is his love—the love graphically portrayed in Hosea's family life.

God's love operates only as his **anger** dissipates, or is **turned away**. A people seeking forgiveness and surrendering their idols to God find that he surrenders his anger against them. This does not indicate that Israel has escaped the punishment predicted throughout the book. Rather, a chastised, disciplined people will emerge from exile to confess their loyalty to God and find him healing their wounds.

14:5–7. God will be as **dew to Israel**. That is, he will appear mysteriously and regularly to provide their most basic needs just as the dew appears to water the arid land. Israel will sprout like a beautiful flower from the dry ground. The phrases **his roots** and **like a cedar of Lebanon** indicate that Israel will become as famous as Lebanon for mighty trees putting down roots. His new growth (or **shoots**) will walk (or appear) so that **his splendor** will be like the **olive tree**, while his smell will be like **Lebanon**.

Israel has stumbled and is dead in sin. God will bring healing that creates a new plant with new vigor. Roots will give him a strong foundation. New growth will indicate new life for a nation thought long dead. That new growth will not produce just an ordinary tree. It will produce a tree that captures everyone's attention with its splendor and aroma.

The people dwelling **in his shade** will return (Heb. *shub*). The continuing metaphor requires that Israel be the tree giving shade. "Return" here can refer to those who accept the call of Hosea 14:1–3; it can refer to those returning from exile, or it can refer to nations returning to pay homage and tribute to Israel. The new Israel that God heals and grows will be a refuge. Israel, a nation dependent on other nations, will suddenly find itself the source of hope for the world's needy.

Like the grain fields that die and then grow again in the new year, so Israel has died and been revived through the Lord's healing. This stands parallel to "returning ones" living under Israel's shade. Israel will provide new life for those returning to God and thus returning to Israel for help. This is reinforced with "they will sprout **like a vine**." Grain and wine were the food and drink staples of the land. A revived Israel would provide the staples the nations needed rather than having to go to the surrounding nations for life's most basic resources.

Finally, Hosea promised that his memorial would be **like the wine from Lebanon**. Apparently Lebanon produced such high-quality wine that people savored its taste and aroma long after drinking it. Up to this point, Hosea has had little good to say of the memories Israel evoked. They were faithless in religion, despicable in morality, and fickle in politics. A prostitute served as the chief image for remembering Israel. God's healing would change all that. Israel's memory would be savored by God and by the peoples of the world coming to partake of Israel's material and spiritual resources.

Up to this time, the memorial Israel had left was closely connected to Lebanon. Lebanon could represent both Syria and Phoenicia. From Syria Israel gained political alliances. From Phoenicia Israel gained Baal worship. Baal was supposed to provide all the resources Israel needed. Instead, Lebanon's Baal had provided only a stinking memory of idol worship and political disaster. God would now heal Israel from Baal worship and provide everything Israel had thought they could get from the Baal of Lebanon.

14:8. God concludes with direct address to Israel, using the familiar name of **Ephraim**, the Northern Kingdom's major tribe. Picking up the term for idols from Hosea 8:4 and 13:2, God says once and for all that he is through with the topic of **idols**. Israel must turn from them. They must respond positively to the prophet's exhortation to repent. They must seek forgiveness. They must give up idols and their dependence on foreign nations once and for all. God cares for Israel as he waits to see their **answer**.

God's description of himself surprises us. He is a **pine tree** in whom Israel's **fruitfulness** is found. The pine tree symbolized divinity, kingship, and fertility in Israel's world. God set himself up as the only true reality behind such symbolism. Now Israel had to decide. Did she believe the Lord? Did she want healing? Would she return and repent and seek forgiveness?

ℂ A Word to the Wise (14:9)

SUPPORTING IDEA: *Wise people listen to God's word, understand its meaning, follow its teaching, and show that they are righteous.*

14:9. Hosea's book closes with a saying that could be taken from a collection of proverbs. It assumes the teaching that being **wise** is life's ultimate achievement. It summarizes the prophet's teaching from a different perspective than that in the rest of chapter 14. In effect, this saying provides a self-test to see if you have caught the message of the book. If you have read correctly, you will **understand** what has been taught, will apply it to your life, and will **walk** in it because the words of the prophet teach God's **ways**.

To obey the prophetic call for repentance is to be righteous and walk in God's ways. To refuse to accept the prophet's words is to stumble off the path of God's ways in rebellion. Hosea had issued a woe oracle against rebels in Hosea 7:13 and called for the trumpet alarm in Hosea 8:1 to warn a people who had rebelled against God's law that danger lurked. In Hosea 4:5 he claimed both people and prophets stumbled in not obeying God's basic expectations. In Hosea 5:5 he denounced Israel (Ephraim) for arrogantly stumbling in their sin, leading Judah to stumble with them.

Then the last words in Hosea's book (**the rebellious stumble in them**) form an artistic *inclusio* with the same thought in Hosea 14:1 (HCSB "You have stumbled in your sin"; NIV "Your sins have been your downfall!"), giving a frame to this concluding chapter. Foolish Israel stumbles through life sinning and following any path but God's. They can display their wisdom only by hearing the prophetic call to repent, turning away from their path of sin, and turning to God for forgiveness. That for Hosea is righteousness.

> **MAIN IDEA REVIEW:** *Sinners must quit stumbling along the path of sin, find the way back to God in repentance, accept God's loving forgiveness and healing, discard their idols, find new life under God's blessing, and act with wisdom.*

III. CONCLUSION

The Humiliation of Repentance

C. S. Lewis in his book *Mere Christianity* asks:

> Now what was the sort of "hole" man had got himself into? He had tried to set up on his own, to behave as if he belonged to himself. In other words, fallen man is not simply an imperfect creature who needs improvement: he is a rebel who must lay down his arms. Laying down your arms, surrendering, saying you are sorry, realising that you have been on the wrong track and getting ready to start life over again from the ground floor—that is the only way out of a "hole." This process of surrender—this movement full speed astern—is what Christians call repentance. Now repentance is no fun at all. It is something much harder than merely eating humble pie. It means unlearning all the self-conceit and self-will that we have been training ourselves into for thousands of years. It means killing part of yourself, undergoing a kind of death.
>
> Remember, this repentance, this willing submission to humiliation and a kind of death, is not something God demands of you before He will take you back and which He could let you off if He chose: it is simply a description of what going back to Him is like.

PRINCIPLES

- Sinners have one direction to go for help and hope.
- The way back to God involves repentance, turning from sin, and turning to God.

- Repentance involves confessing sin and asking God for forgiveness.
- Repentance involves obeying God rather than trying to please God through human rituals and efforts.
- Repentance involves giving up all other allegiances and committing oneself to God alone.
- God wants to heal his people and show them his love.
- God changes a repentant people into a people with splendor and beauty that attract others to him.

APPLICATIONS

- Admit you are a sinner.
- Confess your sins to God.
- Ask God to forgive you.
- Quit trying to impress God with your goodness.
- Admit that anything but God on which you rely cannot save you.
- Depend on God's healing and love to make you what he wants you to be.
- Become wise in God's eyes.

IV. LIFE APPLICATION

Coming Home to Roost

In his book *Intrigued, How I Love to Proclaim It,* Tony Cartledge compares human sinners to birds he encountered in a Buddhist temple in Thailand. He walked past an ornate gateway and saw young women with trays of small bamboo cages containing small birds. The women invite people to set the birds free so they can earn merit toward nirvana. The more money you pay to set the birds free, the more eternal merit you receive. Tourists love to have their pictures made setting the birds free. What the tourists do not realize is that the birds are trained like homing pigeons. They soar into the air, only to return to the rear of the compound so they can offer more tourists opportunities to earn nirvana merit.

Cartledge concludes that

the practice seems strange and exotic, but it is not unrelated to the belief many Christian believers have that good deeds and a periodic confession of sin are all we need to ensure future bliss. The trouble is, smugly offered penitence without life-changing commitment offers only a misguided sense of security. Lightly confessed sin may seem to fly away, but it always comes home to roost (p. 97).

Israel had rituals aplenty to deal with their sins. They rested comfortably with their oft-confessed sins, never realizing they had not satisfied God's expectations. They needed more than public ritual. They needed personal repentance—to confess their sin, to ask God to forgive it, and to turn to God. So we, too, often rely on repeated church rituals or even rote prayers admitting sin and asking for forgiveness. God wants more.

V. PRAYER

Father, we are sinners. We can bring nothing to you to deal with our sins. We ask you to forgive our sins, and we commit ourselves right now to turn away from stumbling down sin's paths. We will turn around to walk in your ways. Amen.

VI. DEEPER DISCOVERIES

Divine Compassion (14:3)

Compassion is a perfect term for Hosea's final description of God because it is central to his opening biographical revelations. The basic meaning is seen in Hosea 9:14, where the noun means "womb."

God made Hosea name his daughter Lo-Ruhamah or "Not loved," "No Compassion" (Hos. 1:6). But God still declared that he would have compassion for Judah (Hos. 1:7). His final word declared his love for his disciplined people (Hos. 2:23). God would again marry his people and be their loving husband (Hos. 2:19). The term does not appear again in Hosea until here in this final chapter. Now it is not a husband-wife relationship but a father adopting a fatherless child. This deep love implores a sinful people to forsake their sin and return to God.

VII. TEACHING OUTLINE

A. INTRODUCTION

1. Lead Story: Where's the Right Road?
2. Context: Hosea uses the language and symbols of his biographical section (chs. 1–3) to conclude his book. The final chapter assumes the sinfulness, discipline, and punishment of the preceding thirteen chapters. God issues one last call to his people.
3. Transition: God's people face God's ultimate challenge. Will they redefine their own identity? Will they give up their traditional

religious practices? Will they change their hearts? Will they turn away from sinful, idolatrous practices? Will they turn to God?

B. COMMENTARY
1. Repent and Be Healed (14:1–3)
2. Love and Healing Replace God's Anger (14:4–8)
3. A Word to the Wise (14:9)

C. CONCLUSION: THE HUMILIATION OF REPENTANCE

VIII. ISSUES FOR DISCUSSION

1. What happens in your church that resembles Israel's ritualistic way of dealing with human sin?
2. What would change in your daily life if you truly returned to the Lord?
3. List sins for which God needs to forgive you.
4. What sources of salvation do people in your town depend upon instead of God?
5. What lets you know if you are wise or foolish?

Introduction to

Joel

Introducing the Book of Joel is simple yet impossible. It is simple because Joel 1:1 tells us all we really know—this is a collection of the words God gave to an otherwise unknown man named Joel, whose father was an otherwise unknown person named Pethuel.

DIVIDING THE BOOK INTO CHAPTERS

Scholars have followed many trails of evidence seeking more knowledge about the book and its author. The first question is how to divide the book into chapters. The Hebrew text has four chapters, while the English editions follow the lead of the Latin Vulgate, placing Joel 2:28–32 at the end of chapter 2 rather than as a separate chapter as in Hebrew.

AUTHOR, AUTHORSHIP, AND EDITING

The second problem of Joel is that of unity. Many scholars want to find several editors adding material to the original book. These Bible students cannot see any literary, historical, or theological connection between Joel 1:1 to 2:27 and 2:28 to 3:21. Stuart concludes his introduction to Joel by reporting: "At present, then, virtually no consensus can be claimed for scholarship on Joel, whether as to date, or unity, or theological perspective, or even the literalness of the imagery" (WBC 31, 235).

This commentary, however, sees a collection of images used to describe the theological teaching about the Day of the Lord in both a present and a future aspect. The collection was drawn from experience with recent locust invasions, natural disasters, and military invasion. One man, named as Joel in the text, collected the imagery, listened to God, and wrote the poetry. He impressed on his audience the horror and hope connected with facing the Day of the Lord.

The author of this commentary is thus much more comfortable with Stuart's conclusion at the beginning of his introduction: "Joel shares its simple woe-then-weal overall structure with a majority of the prophetic books. . . . Joel is also somewhat more tightly organized than many of the prophetic books, with such a degree of thematic and vocabulary linkage among the pericopes, a logical progression from one pericope to the next, that it is reasonable to conclude that Joel's message was originally composed and delivered either at one time or in a relatively short span of time (perhaps a week or a month)" (WBC 31, 227).

DATING THE PROPHET AND HIS WORK

That said, finding where that one day, week, or month lay in human history is virtually impossible. As Garrett notes:

> Probably no book of the Bible has had a wider range of dates assigned to it. Scholarly opinions for the date of Joel range from the early monarchy to the late postexilic period, although the early postexilic probably is the most popular opinion today for the date of composition (NAC 19A, 286).

Arguments for any date are subject to great debate. The book does not refer to the Northern Kingdom (Israel). Failure to mention any of the kings of Judah, on the other hand, may be accidental and unimportant, though lack of their inclusion in the introductory title of 1:1 is significant. Reference to priests and elders (Joel 1:9,13–14) without reference to a king could also be important except for the fact that the subject of the particular text is ritual matters over which the priests presided and the call is to elders as representatives of the citizens of the land. The literary context, not the historical context, excludes the king.

Reference to God's people scattered among the nations (Joel 3:2) does not necessarily refer to the major exile of 586 B.C. It could just as well speak of the Northern Kingdom's fall in 721 or the Assyrian army's victories between 713 and 701. The call for the entire population to gather for a fast in Jerusalem (Joel 1:14) is literary hyperbole. The elders of the various villages would most likely have represented the rural citizens. This does not point to a postexilic moment when Judah was so depopulated that everyone could be expected to go to Jerusalem. That Judah's population was ever that small is debatable.

Joel's familiarity with the prophetic language used by Obadiah, Jeremiah, Amos, Isaiah, or other prophets may reflect a prophetic tradition of using set phrases familiar to the audience to catch their attention and remind them that such language was the work of the prophets and should not be easily dismissed.

Appearance of Greeks (Joel 3:6) does not have to mirror the power of Alexander the Great or of slightly earlier Greek intrusions into the Middle East. Rather, Greek traders had long worked with Phoenician counterparts to control the trade routes of the Mediterranean area and beyond.

Joel's references to Edom, Egypt, Philistines, and Phoenicians is no help, since they had been Israel's opponents since the time of the wilderness wandering and conquest. Even linguistic traits such as language that is related to Aramaic do not point to nearly as late a date as earlier scholars were inclined to believe. Aramaic language exercised influence in the Middle East at least from the time of the Assyrian domination. After a meticulous study of all examples of words or phrases that might depend on the Aramaic language, G. W. Ahlström concluded: "It must be clear that many of the words and phrases having been used as arguments for a late date are not late at all" (*Joel and the Temple Cult of Jerusalem*, 22).

We conclude with Garrett: "Clear pointers to the date of Joel are few and far between. Any suggested time frame for the book should be tentative, and the interpretation of the book should not depend upon a hypothetical historical setting" (NAC 19A, 294). Garrett points to a date in the 600s B.C. This may be correct, but the description of restoring the fortunes of Jerusalem and gathering the people from the nations (Joel 3:1–3) and looting the temple seems to point to a major catastrophe in Judah's history, either that of 701 or one of the early Babylonian incursions into Judah between 609 and 587 before the total destruction of the temple. In Joel the temple appears still to be standing and functioning.

THE MEANING AND MESSAGE OF THE BOOK

Joel concentrates on one theme—the Day of the Lord. He plays several variations on that theme. The day is past, being experienced in a plague of locusts and in a natural drought and famine. The day is current or imminent, carried out by an enemy military force. The day is future: *immediately* in the salvation of Jerusalem from current problems; *long-range* in the giving of the Spirit of God on all people and the deliverance of all who call on the name of the Lord; and *ultimate* in the eternal holiness of Jerusalem, protected from its enemies, flowing with fertility, lived in obedience to the one true covenant God, and enabled by God's pardon of Israel's guilt.

Joel bases his Day of the Lord theology on a theme deeply rooted in Israel's life with God—covenant. As Deuteronomy 28 warned of curses on those who disobeyed God's covenant, so Joel's Day of the Lord fulfilled those curses, first for disobedient Israel and then for their unrighteous enemies. As the covenant introduced God with the words "I am the LORD your God" (Exod. 20:1), so Joel's ultimate hope was for Israel to know and confess that "I, the LORD your God" (Exod. 20:5) live in Jerusalem. The nature of this God revealed in the covenant renewal (Exod. 34:6–7) gave Joel hope that the Lord would not totally destroy a people who turned to him in repentance (Joel 2:13–14).

The Day of the Lord theme, rooted in covenant theology, has consequences far beyond the theological classroom. Israel must do more than learn about the nature of their covenant and the God of their covenant. Israel must learn what it means to be in covenant with God. This revolves around two simple but profound themes: (1) Israel must grieve over its sin, coming to God in true repentance, and (2) Israel must realize that God is in control.

Complacency will not satisfy God. Broken hearts will. Such repentance is not a human mechanism to control God and ensure the results that humans want when they want them. Repentance is a surrender to God's will and God's way in God's time. Repentance confesses the sin of trying to take charge of the world, and repentance recognizes that the Lord has been, is, and will always be in control. Such repentance looks to God for both pardon and blessing, but it recognizes that it cannot demand and guarantee such. Only the Lord knows when blessing and pardon will come.

When these do come, a new reality comes with them. God's Spirit is poured on all nations. Everyone has opportunity to call on the name of the Lord and be delivered. This is a new type of spiritual reality never before experienced on earth. This reality was manifest at Pentecost in the Book of Acts (2:1–4), but it still awaits ultimate consummation.

THE END

Having warned his people of all the horrors that accompany the Day of the Lord, Joel finally pointed them forward to the ultimate day. Here he joined all the prophets in pointing to God's mysterious will to make himself known to the world and to restore justice, holiness, and true worship to his creation. The end is not put on a timetable. It is not described in clear details that allow close observers of nature and history to recognize its entrance into history. It is not separated into parts or ages in which some who participate are here and others are there. Joel sets out a promise: God has a plan to protect, preserve, and bring praise to Jerusalem while bringing just punishment upon his enemies.

Even here the call is not a pure separation of Jew and Gentile. The Spirit is promised to all people, and the call for deliverance is not limited to Jews. The central emphasis, however, remains on the rescue of Judah and Jerusalem from their enemies, the presence of the holy God in his holy residence with his holy people, and the gift of pardon from guilt for a Jerusalem inhabited by his people and by the Lord forever.

Joel 1:1–20

Lamenting the Locusts

I. INTRODUCTION
Confronting Crunch Time

II. COMMENTARY
A verse-by-verse explanation of these verses.

III. CONCLUSION
God Uses Tragedy

An overview of the principles and applications from these verses.

IV. LIFE APPLICATION
Lesson from a Disaster

Melding these verses to life.

V. PRAYER
Tying these verses to life with God.

VI. DEEPER DISCOVERIES
Historical, geographical, and grammatical enrichment of the commentary.

VII. TEACHING OUTLINE
Suggested step-by-step group study of these verses.

VIII. ISSUES FOR DISCUSSION
Zeroing these verses in on daily life.

"*The* day of the Lord refers to a decisive action of Yahweh to bring his plans for Israel to completion. . . . The day of the Lord is more of a theological idea than a specific event. As a theological idea it can manifest itself in human history many times and in many forms."

Duane A. Garrett

Joel 1:1-20

IN A NUTSHELL

God's word came to Joel to deliver to Jerusalem in the midst of a devastating locust plague that had destroyed the crops, made temple sacrifices impossible, and caused the priests to put on mourning clothes. The locusts represented a nation about to invade Judah, so Joel called Jerusalem to fast and pray to God for help.

Lamenting the Locusts

I. INTRODUCTION

Confronting Crunch Time

*M*emories fifty years old are as vivid as yesterday. We would wake up one morning in west Texas to a darkened sky. The crickets had paid another visit. Walk out your door, and every step went crunch, crunch, crunch as you made your way to the morning paper or the morning milk bottles by stepping on the swarming crickets that filled the sidewalks and driveways.

How can you drive when front and back windows are crawling with crickets? Shopkeepers had an even worse nightmare. The sidewalks in front of their stores as well as their plate glass windows were covered with crickets. But the worst cricket problem belonged to the farmers and gardeners. Whatever crops the perpetual west Texas drought had left, the chirping invaders gobbled up.

What a helpless feeling! All we knew to do was wait it out and sweep up the dead bodies when the swarm moved on eastward.

Joel's people faced the same problem. Locusts, locusts everywhere and not a crop to spare. Temple offerings stopped. People either drank themselves into oblivion or prayed. In such a disastrous time, God gave Joel a message—mourn, pray for help, but know this is only a sign of worse things to come.

II. COMMENTARY

Lamenting the Locusts

> **MAIN IDEA:** *Natural disasters call God's people to cry to him for help and to see if the disaster has a deeper message from God.*

A The Mission of Mourning (1:1–14)

> **SUPPORTING IDEA:** *When disaster strikes, God calls people to devote themselves to prayer and fasting and to seek his purpose and meaning in the disaster.*

1:1. The brief introduction to the Book of Joel lacks important elements present in most of the prophetic titles or introductions. No kings are named. Nothing is said of the prophet except his father's name. Nothing is said about the content of the message. Thus we have a book with no clues for dating, no information about the prophet or his family, and no indication of where Joel prophesied. Only one thing is important for the Book of Joel—God's **word** came to God's people.

Beginning in Genesis 15:1, the phrase "the word of the LORD" or "the word of God" appears 234 times in the Old Testament, 136 of these in the Prophets. God's word directs history and directs his people as they live through the intricacies and complexities of history. The prophet did not call upon any personal qualifications or training. He simply saw himself as God's messenger sent with God's authoritative message. The people needed to hear that message, recognize its source, and obey it. This is the only verse in which the prophet's name occurs—a name meaning "Yah (or Yahweh) is God."

1:2. The word from God had several different audiences. Joel began with the **elders**. These were the experienced men of the community who served as its leaders and advisers (Exod. 3:16). In times of crisis people went to them for advice and direction. Each city had a council of elders who met in the city gateway and helped solve internal disputes and make decisions for the city (Deut. 22:15). Elders also participated in making decisions for the nation (Ezek. 8:1).

Joel addressed not only the elders but also **all who live in the land**—the citizens of Judah. For the elders and the citizens, Joel had one question—have you or anyone you know ever experienced anything like this? The rhetorical question expected the obvious answer: No. Never anything like this!

1:3. Yes, this is one for the ages, Joel declared. **Tell it to your children** and grandchildren so no one will ever forget what happened in your generation. This is to go down in the lore of the people forever so they can remember what God can do.

1:4. How do you describe what is happening? You have to come up with every kind of locust you ever heard of and describe what each has done. This is not just one small group of locusts; this is the congregation of all the locusts that have ever invaded the land. The pattern of one type of locust eating what previous locusts had left is reminiscent of the language of Exodus 10:5,15 where locusts ate what the hail had left in the Egyptian plagues.

Identifying the different types of locusts is, as Stuart notes, "speculative" (p. 241). Garrett concludes: "Beyond the fact that they all in some way refer to locusts, we simply do not know what these four words denote" (NAC, 316). The **locust swarm** may refer to an adult ready to fly on its own or to a caterpillar or to the smallest type of locust or the early grub stage of the locust. It appears in Joel 2:25 and in Amos 4:9.

The great locusts apparently refers to migratory locusts with fully developed wings. Levitical laws permitted them as food (Lev. 11:22). **Young locusts** seems to be a creeping locust that is wingless (Jer. 51:14,27). **Other locusts** represents either some stage in the life of the locust or perhaps even a cockroach (Isa. 33:4).

Whatever the exact designations of these crop destroyers, the point is intensified by using so many different names. All-consuming bugs filled the fields of Judah. Nothing escaped the voracious appetites of these invaders.

Such locust invasions were not uncommon in Palestine, and they normally disappeared in a short time, so the prophet had to do something creative to magnify the image and make the people cringe at the thought of what was happening. This was not your usual locust invasion. This was eerie, mysterious—yes, supernatural. This was God caused. It could only be God ended. That is the major reason it needed to be stored up in national lore and added to the list of things God had done for his people.

1:5. Unexpectedly, Joel approached **drunkards** as his next audience. These were people who had celebrated the harvest prematurely, imbibing of the first fruits of the vineyard just before the locusts arrived. Having drunk themselves into a stupor, they would be unaware of the mysterious, ominous events of the day. Joel announced them to this unlikely crowd. Today they had no wine to drink so they could not drink themselves into oblivion and ignore the day's events. They have good reason to cry over lost wine. They needed to cry with tears of penitence to God and seek his deliverance.

1:6. Here Joel begins to let us see behind what he is describing. The locust plague is fearful enough, but this is something more. **A nation** has gone up against **my land**. The prophet continues to use the Hebrew perfect verb forms, apparently describing the immediate past reality of the locusts coming, but the prophets often used this form to describe something that God has announced even though it has not yet happened. Such a "prophetic perfect" makes a future event a present reality for the audience.

Joel then turns from the locusts and pictures them as forerunners of something far worse to come. A nation with an army **powerful and without number** is coming against God's people. The audience thought the locusts that came, destroyed, and left were horrible. They had not seen anything yet! God had another kind of army coming against them.

Lions are another image of fierceness and fear. Locusts had neither teeth nor fangs. Neither did an enemy army, but the locusts attacking the land and the army attacking the nation gave the impression of being fierce and fearful in the Judean psyche. The prophet thus piled up poetic imagery to create an emotional aura of dread, fear, helplessness, distress, and disaster.

1:7. The drunks see more than their immediate wine supply disappearing. The future supply looks even more bleak because the vineyard has become a wasteland. The plants cannot reproduce themselves for the next harvest. Fig trees that often grow in the vineyard suffer the same fate. Their protective **bark** is destroyed, leaving no future for figs. If locusts can strip the agricultural production of the nation, what can an enemy army do? Here we see the locust invasion and the army prediction merging into one.

1:8. The call to tears in verse 5 now expands into a call to "wail" or join in official lamentation ceremonies. The audience apparently shifts from the drunkards to a more general crowd, but they are given no specific identity. They are to **mourn** with the sorrow of a Hebrew girl who loses a prospective husband who had been pledged in marriage. Just as she would have to cancel the celebrations connected with the wedding, so the nation had to cancel the feasts and celebrations connected with harvest. Mourning is the mood of the moment.

1:9. **Mourning** should be expanded to include God's **house** and his **priests**. Loss of crops affects everything supposed to be brought to the temple in worship and sacrifice to God (Num. 28:1–8). Thus Israel could not maintain their covenant promises to God. They felt cut off and isolated from God. With grain and vines gone, so are the work, worship, and wages (Lev. 2:3,10) of the priests. People and priests faced the most horrible situation they could imagine.

1:10. The prophet takes inventory of the nation's agricultural resources. **Fields are ruined**, so they cannot produce anything for people or the animals to eat. **Ground is dried up** without rain, so new planting would not help even if they had seeds to plant. **Grain is destroyed**, so there is no harvest and no food. **New wine has dried up** with the destruction of the vines, so the basic beverage has vanished. Supplies of olive **oil** have been consumed, so the basic cooking oil, medicinal oil, and cosmetic oil are no longer available. Everything has been affected by this disaster.

1:11. Another audience is the one the locusts affected most seriously— the **farmers** and **vine growers**. Farmers without crops are to sink into shameful **despair**. Vineyard keepers with vines vanished are to "howl" (NIV **wail**) in public grief. Such lamentation has a concrete cause. **The harvest of the field is destroyed**—the **wheat** and **barley** harvests (Deut. 28:33,42,51).

1:12. The reasons to howl in lamentation continue. The grape-producing **vine has dried up**, and the **fig tree** has **withered** away. The **pomegranate** (Deut. 8:8), the date **palm** (Lev. 23:40), and the **apple tree** (Prov. 25:11) represent fruit that was eaten as well as objects revered for their beauty and their connection with lovers. The sweetness of life had disappeared. Throughout the section the prophet uses a play on Hebrew words meaning to be ashamed (*bosh*) and to dry up (*yabesh*). This comes to a climax here as the prophet summarizes all he has tried to say. Add up his inventory of resources, and you discover that "the jubilation has been put to shame (or withered away) from among the sons of man" (author's translation). Causes for joy are now causes for shame. Joy has dried up and withered away from Judah and Jerusalem.

1:13. Joel turns to another audience—this one quite different from the drunkards or farmers and vineyard keepers. "Get dressed to lament, you priests" (author's translation; see Isa. 15:3; Jer. 4:8 for other uses of "get dressed" in reference to mourning attire). "Lament" indicates participation in formal mourning rituals including singing (2 Sam. 1:12; Zech. 12:10–12). The most sacred task of the **priests** was ministering at God's **altar**, insuring that sacrifices were properly presented so the nation's relationship with God was maintained. God called the people away from that task to one more important at the moment—wailing to God for help.

To **spend the night in sackcloth** was most unusual and uncomfortable (1 Kgs. 21:27). For the priests **who minister before my God,** this is out of the ordinary. They are extending their rituals into the night, spending the sleeping hours in prayer for God's help in this horrendous situation. The drastic nature of the situation is described from the priests' viewpoint. They have nothing to eat because God's house has no sacrifices. God made provision for the priests to consume many of the daily sacrifices at the temple. Even worse, without sacrifices the central activity of corporate worship was missing. The priests lost their most meaningful activity and their food to a swarm of locusts. The nation lost its method of gaining access to God. This was a time for drastic mourning, not just religious ritual as usual.

The *minchah* or **grain offerings** originally referred to meat or grains offered as a gift or as tribute. It was given to another person, especially a ruler or to God, but it came to mean grain offered to God. Grain offerings were given alone or as a part of burnt offerings and peace offerings (Amos 5:22). These were sacrificed each day (Lev. 9:17). The priest was to offer a handful of this offering on the burnt offering altar as a memorial portion (Lev. 2:2,9,16) to the Lord along with the salt of the covenant (Lev. 2:13). No grain offering was to be offered on the incense altar (Exod. 30:9).

Drink offerings were also part of the daily temple worship (Num. 28:5–8), and these accompanied peace and burnt offerings (Num. 15:1–15). The drink offering appears to have been an intoxicating drink made from grain, not grapes, which produced wine (Num. 6:3). It was part of the meals that worshippers ate at the temple as part of their sacrificial worship (Deut. 14:26).

1:14. Since the priests were unable to carry out the normal worship ritual, what were they to do? Joel had specific instructions from the Lord: "Make a time holy for a fast. Declare a holy day for the assembly of the people to worship. Gather the elders. Let all the residents of the land come to the house of the Lord your God. Cry out to the Lord for help" (author's translation).

The priests had a much more important responsibility than daily worship that sought to maintain stability in the life of the nation through obedient worship. Now the stability was shattered. They had to find a way in the desperate situation to contact God and find their way back to normality and stability. To do this they had to forego the normal processes and rituals of life.

Fasting and prayer, not work and eating, were the only orders of the day. The priests had to lead out and make sure everyone in the nation was involved in crying to God for help.

B The Prophet's Prayer (1:15–20)

SUPPORTING IDEA: *God's minister not only delivers God's message in a time of disaster but also laments in prayer before God, seeking relief for God's people.*

1:15. Joel did not just deliver instructions to the priests to fast and pray. He offered his own lament to God, seeking a way out of the disaster for the nation. **Alas** (Heb. 'ahah) is an emotional expression of panic addressed to God or his messenger when the situation seems hopeless (Ezek. 4:14). What situation could cause such a response from a prophet? It is the ominous **day of the LORD**, a favorite expression with the prophets (Amos 5:18,20; Mal. 4:5). This is often reduced simply to "that day" or "day" with a distressful adjective or noun: "distress" (Jer. 16:19); "vengeance" (Isa. 34:8) "wrath" (Prov. 11:4); "evil" (Amos 6:3); "bitter" (Amos 8:10).

The preceding Scriptures paint a dark and gloomy portrait of God's special day. Apparently, this is not the original portrait painted by the average citizen and possibly by the worship leaders of Israel before the prophetic intervention. Israel looked to the day when the Lord would defeat all enemies and establish Israel as the world's strongest nation. Israel took the past experiences of victory under Moses, the judges, Joshua, and David and pushed them forward into a new day of Israelite victory under God (Amos 5:18–20).

The prophets attacked this overly optimistic picture by coloring the Day of Yahweh in dark, somber tones, warning the people that their irresponsible, optimistic picture would not hold up in the testing field of history. God was angry with his disobedient people and would come on his day to punish them severely—perhaps even destroy them.

The Babylonian destruction of Jerusalem in 586 B.C. was seen by some as a Day of the Lord (Lam. 1:12). Still, the prophets pointed to a coming Day of the Lord (Mal. 4:3,5). All the while the prophets also pointed to God's judgment on foreign nations as the Day of the Lord (Isa. 34:8; Obad. 15). The Day of the Lord is a day of deliverance and salvation for the people whom God favors but a day of destruction and ruin for his enemies.

As Joel directed his personal lament to God, he also expected the people to hear the content of his prayer. This content joined the prophetic chorus in describing the Day of the Lord in the most miserable and painful emotional tones possible. The people should pay attention, because **the day of the LORD is near** (Ezek. 30:2–3). They could not slough it off as a distant event for a future generation. God was preparing something for them—in their generation. The day would not just be a face-off with foreign armies. The day would bring **destruction** not from humans but from the **Almighty**—God himself.

1:16. The people wanted to know, what proof do you have? Joel replied that it was **before our very eyes**. The locust plague should be sufficient evidence. God had already taken away their **food**. He had silenced the **joy and gladness from the house of our God**. If the house of praise and adoration was no longer the site of joy, where could they expect to find any joy?

1:17. More proof. Joel dug deep into his poetic vocabulary, using three words that appear nowhere else in the Old Testament: **Seeds are shriveled beneath the clods**. They had no harvest. Their seeds (or perhaps "our stored provisions") were no good for the future. And all the fields had turned to clods (or perhaps the "seeds are beneath shovels," the ground being too hard to dig, there being no water in the channels where shovels would be used to direct the water into the field rows, and the seed being useless). The people had no use for places to store grain and food, so they were all **in ruins**. What **grain** they did have was **dried up** and useless.

1:18. The prophet continues his prayer to God which is also a sermon for the people. **The cattle moan**. This strong Hebrew term (*'anah*) "usually expresses an intense, negative response to terrible circumstances, actual or anticipated, often encountered as the judgment of God (Isa. 24:7–8). Lamentation over fallen Jerusalem evokes nearly half of this word's use (Lam. 1:4,11,21–22)" (David Thompson, NICOTTE).

Here in an unusual piece of poetic artistry, Joel lets the cattle moan. They express the outrage that God would let locusts destroy all the crops and deprive them of food. If the cattle are moaning, then the people are not only deprived of grain and drink offerings; they will soon be deprived of meat offerings and of meat on their tables. Even the **sheep**, able to scour the rocky hills beyond where cattle might ordinarily go, could find nothing to eat. Locusts had taken everything. Thus Israel experienced God's introduction to his day.

1:19. Joel calls out to God in prayer. He describes the desperate situation in terms of **fire**. Without water, fire runs rampant, destroying any grass or stubble that the locusts might have left. **Trees** were not only robbed of their fruit, but the fires got them, too. Israel has no agricultural resources left. God has brought the destruction. The prophet knows, and the people must learn, that only God can bring the solution and deliverance.

1:20. In another poetic leap of language, the prophet says **the wild animals pant** for God. The verb really means to "crave, long for." The animals join the prophet and the cattle in lamenting over the situation they face. They have neither food nor drink. What can they do? They can only moan and pant after God to see if he will supply their needs. This is the pattern the people also must follow. Must God's people go to the cattle and the wild beasts of the field to learn how to pray and depend on God in time of desperation and hopelessness?

MAIN IDEA REVIEW: *Natural disasters call God's people to cry to him for help and to see if the disaster has a deeper message from God.*

III. CONCLUSION

God Uses Tragedy

Disaster tests the reaction power of God's people. In her book *BeAttitudes for Women*, Dorothy Kelley Patterson shares the story of close friends who received the news that their eldest son Luel had been stricken with a malignant brain tumor. Luel endured all that modern medicine had to offer. Family and friends united in prayer. Repeatedly they saw Luel rally, only to suffer again. As Dorothy writes,

> Finally God decided to take the boy home to heaven, giving him complete healing but leaving those who loved him with an overwhelming sense of loss. Releasing him was painful, even beyond the family circle, to those who had watched and loved the boy. . . .
>
> During Luel's memorial service I became acutely aware of the blessing of affliction and suffering as I observed firsthand the spiritual grace and powerful testimony of that family who had been with the Lord and depended on him in a way few people ever experience. I saw the battle of faith in the life of my own son Armour, who had loved Luel as a brother and who had walked with him through this dark valley with no understanding of such a tragedy. Not until months later did God use this tragedy to build up Armour's own understanding of God's faithfulness (pp. 62–63).

Dorothy saw the family react with grace during the memorial service. She saw her own son struggle for months before God's answer came. The prophet Joel also saw God at work—in a locust plague. He called the people to learn a lesson from a temporary plague so they would call on God to prevent an even worse disaster of divine discipline. Israel, however, took a long time before they learned the secret of mourning, lamentation, and depending on God.

PRINCIPLES

- Natural disasters may be a message from God to a disobedient people.

- Families should discuss how they see God at work today and pass their stories on to the coming generations.

- Disaster calls all people to mourning, lamentation, and dependence on God.

- Disaster may be God's way of preparing his people to prevent or to endure a worse disaster.

- Disaster robs us of life's joy and transforms our worship from praise to mourning and lamentation.

- God's church leaders should show the people by personal example the extreme measures God expects in response to disaster.

- Disaster calls for special ceremonies in which God's people put aside all other concerns and concentrate on seeking his direction and deliverance.

- God's days of disaster point forward to his final day of judgment.

APPLICATIONS

- Begin praying now that God will not have to send disaster to call his people back to himself.

- Work with your church to develop a plan for churchwide response to national, local, and personal disasters.

- Make sure your own life is in order with God so that you are not the reason he has to discipline his people.

- Become sensitive to the needs of people who suffer personal disaster, and learn to listen to them and minister to them.

IV. LIFE APPLICATION

Lesson from a Disaster

Natural and personal disasters cause us to feel helpless. No one in the United States can forget the feeling of helplessness that 9/11 brought. Terror, shock, disbelief, hopelessness—so many feelings poured on us all at once. How did you react during the first hour after hearing the news? What part did God play in that reaction?

Joel wanted to make sure the memory of a locust disaster did not fade from his generation. He gave them pointers on how to pray, how to store up memories for future generations, and how to accept the fact that God was punishing them through the disaster.

V. PRAYER

Sovereign God, you control our world. You use all its elements to achieve your purposes. Sometimes those purposes are discipline and punishment. Show us our sins right now. Forgive us of our sins. Show us how to help our people learn from history and not have to experience your discipline anew and afresh. Amen.

VI. DEEPER DISCOVERIES

Mourning and Lament

Israel had a specific way of creating speech to respond to death and disaster. They created poetic prayers, addressed to God as well as the congregation. Mourning had a specific dress—sackcloth combined with tearing one's clothing. Mourning generally was limited to a specific time period (note the seventy days the Egyptians mourned Jacob, Joseph's father, in Gen. 50:3 and the seven-day period Joseph himself mourned in Gen. 50:10–11).

Mourning had a specific sound—the wail, extemporaneous sounds and exclamations with no literary or poetic form (Amos 5:16). This generally included the word *hoy,* "alas" or "oh, no!" Mourning included specific actions: tearing clothes, weeping, shaving the head, sitting in ashes, putting dust and ashes on the head, removing shoes, covering the bottom part of the face, cutting the body, and fasting (Jer. 6:26; Ezek. 27:30–32).

How did all these elements of mourning fit together into a whole? Nowhere does the Bible answer this question since its purpose was not to help us reconstruct the cultural and religious practices of ancient Israel. Thus we can conclude with R. W. L. Moberly:

> In sum, the precise nature of mourning ritual clearly varied according to both time and place, but in general the OT presents a consistent impression of practices that break with the normal routines of life. . . . The OT conveys the impression that its mourning practices are all part of an important ritual whereby the mourner expresses grief with a total engagement of the whole person (*NIDOTTE* 4, 873).

In our pleasure-mad, egocentric world, people do not want to hear about mourning, disaster, and lessons to be learned. Yet the Bible reminds us that there is a "a time to weep and a time to laugh, a time to mourn and a time to dance" (Eccl. 3:4).

VII. TEACHING OUTLINE

A. INTRODUCTION

1. Lead Story: Confronting Crunch Time
2. Context: Natural disaster struck Joel's land in the form of a locust plague. Farmers had no grain in the field and no seed to replant. Vineyard owners had no grapes or leaves on the vines. The animals had no food. Even water became scarce. Daily worship activities could not continue at the temple because the people had nothing to sacrifice.
3. Transition: The people were confused, angry, and frustrated. They had no idea where to turn or what to do. God sent a prophet to let them know what had happened, why, and what they must do. Today we need to learn how to respond to God in times of disaster.

B. COMMENTARY

1. The Mission of Mourning (1:1–14)
2. The Prophet's Prayer (1:15–20)

C. CONCLUSION: GOD USES TRAGEDY

VIII. ISSUES FOR DISCUSSION

1. Are disasters from "natural causes" always a sign of God's judgment and discipline?
2. What are appropriate ways for believers to express grief to God?
3. What does God expect us to do after we have completed the time of mourning and grief?
4. How can we preserve the stories of such disasters as 9/11 so future generations can learn something from them and be drawn to God?
5. How many days can be called the Day of the Lord? Do we still experience such days today? Do you believe God will bring a final Day of the Lord and judge our world once and for all?

Joel 2:1–32

God's Dreadful Day

Quote

"*One* must be a god to be able to tell successes from failures without making a mistake."

Anton Pavlovich Chekhov

Joel 2:1–32

 IN A NUTSHELL

God calls for the trumpet sound to signal the nation to battle readiness, and he describes the invading army in terms that could refer to locusts or to a military force. Then with no warning God issues a call for repentance that might bring divine reprieve. Fasting and wailing are to symbolize the people's inward repentance and change of heart. Then God surprises with a promise to renew the land's fertility and never again make them an object of mockery. So Zion hears the call to rejoice because the enemy army will be pushed back. Finally, God promises to pour his Spirit on his people and to bring deliverance to Zion on the Day of the Lord.

God's Dreadful Day

I. INTRODUCTION

Repentance Means Change

*L*arry Crabb, in his book *Inside Out*, tells the story of his friend Tony. Tony looks back to the year he entered elementary school as a turning point in his life. From then on his parents began living life as one long shouting match. Dad would leave for a week or two at a time and then come crying back. Mother cried only when Tony tried to withdraw and free himself from the intolerable situation. Meaning came to Tony only through academics. There he excelled. His rebellion against a weak father and especially against a domineering mother expressed itself in breaking curfew and by a sullen refusal to communicate.

As Tony ended his sophomore year in college, life took on new meaning as he received Christ. He sought ways to communicate with his parents and treat them better. Although his dad died during Tony's first year in seminary, the attitude Tony developed in the seminary finally softened his mother and led her to Christ.

After seminary Tony worked fourteen years in a Christian ministry, married, had three children, and settled down to a comfortable life. He turned forty, and subtle things showed up. A teacher called for a conference to report that Tony's eleven-year-old son was unmotivated, behind in his studies, and depressed. The thought of the child seeing the school psychologist caused Tony's wife to panic. Tony didn't know what to do.

A work colleague and friend then confided in Tony his unhappiness in his job and his struggle with major family problems that no one else suspected. Over the next weeks the friend then pulled back from Tony. Larry Crabb also saw Tony in ministry and personal situations and began hoping Tony would not show up for meetings because Tony was always on an artificial high and proved boring.

Then the school counselor led Tony's wife to admit her panic was not over her son but over fear that Tony would not admit the truth and deal with the problems. Tony's friend told him that confiding in Tony was not helpful because Tony did not know how to give meaningful support. Crabb told Tony he always skirted tough issues in their meetings.

Prayer and Bible study led Tony to a new view of himself. He realized that he was escaping childhood problems by retreating into an unreal world where everyone got along as his parents had not. He ignored tension and required everyone around him to be happy.

So Tony repented of his sin of self-protection and of forcing others to be what he needed them to be—happy. He learned to enter deeply into people's lives without demanding warm feedback. He discussed his own hurts with his wife and listened more caringly to hers. He discussed with his son the pressure that he was putting on the boy. Relationships with his friends became much deeper.

Still, friends saw Tony emphasizing the positive to the point of losing a sense of genuineness in life. They still saw a tendency to avoid feelings of sadness and inability to accept himself as a man. Tony again turned to Scripture and saw in Jesus the power to let suffering bring strength and weakness lead to Christlikeness.

Tony's experience demonstrates the power of repentance—to bring changes in the way a person copes with life, relates to others, and experiences relationship with God. The person who believes in God needs to repent at crucial life stages and find new ways to follow God and dispose of the unwanted baggage from the past. This is the type of repentance that Joel invited God's people to experience as they endured God's dreadful day.

II. COMMENTARY

God's Dreadful Day

MAIN IDEA: *Facing God's dreadful judgment day, God's people need to turn to him in repentance, hoping that God will refrain from the judgment he has planned.*

A The Trumpet of Tragedy (2:1–11)

SUPPORTING IDEA: *God's dreadful judgment day brings tragedy to an unrepentant people.*

2:1. The **trumpet** was a curved ram's horn used for communicating messages to the nation. The trumpet sound brought the nation to attention (Isa. 18:3). The sounding of the trumpet (Heb. *shophar*) served as a national warning that the enemy was attacking, that danger and disaster were at hand. Joel took up the military connections of the term. **Sound the alarm** translates one Hebrew word (*hari'u*) signifying a loud communal shout. Often this was the army's war cry as they launched an attack (2 Chr. 13:12). The same term was used for the triumphal shout of victory (Zech. 9:9).

Here Joel finally locates himself **in Zion**. Zion was an ancient name for parts of Jerusalem (1 Chr. 11:5), in particular the southeast ridge south of the later temple mount (1 Kgs. 8:1). This term was eventually extended to refer to the temple mount, the whole city, and the entire land and God's people. Joel uses it as a synonym for **my holy hill** to refer especially to the temple area in Jerusalem. Here God reigned as king (Ps. 9:11), and here he lived (Isa. 8:18).

Joel's audience sensed that attack was imminent, that the prophet was summoning the army to defend the holy city. Notice that Isaiah had warned of Assyrian attacks on Zion that would bring defilement to the city (Isa. 10:32). So Jerusalem's citizens anticipated Joel's call for all its residents to **tremble**. They did not anticipate the reason for trembling. This was not an ordinary battle. This was the **day of the LORD** (see comments on Joel 1:15).

2:2. Joel painted a portrait of this **day**. The words "dark . . . deep darkness . . . clouds . . . thick darkness" (author's translation) create the somber mood. Then comes the dreaded announcement: **like dawn** stretching over the mountains . . . an **army**, immense and powerful. It has never existed before. It will **never** come again. Those who see it break out in a cold sweat. Fear of the mysterious unknown grips them. The awesomeness of God at work against them begins to seep through their heads into their hearts.

2:3. Consuming **fire** in front, blazing flame behind. In front the land looks like the **garden of Eden** (see Gen. 2). Behind them is an eerie, terrifying, deserted wilderness. Nothing or no one **escapes them**. This is God's dreadful day.

2:4. War **horses** (or even chariots, the Hebrew term signifying horses or chariots) are approaching. Their speed means there is no time to escape. What can we do on God's dreadful day?

2:5. Now we hear them. **Chariots** are coming. Our hills and mountains do not deter them as we had hoped. They simply **leap over** them. Here we see Joel pulling from the imagery of the locusts to describe the approaching army in its relentless march against them. The noise of their approach reminds the people of a flaming **fire** consuming everything left by the locusts. Such a sound comes from a powerful **army** in battle formation. Such the people face as God's dreadful day approaches.

2:6. Armies writhe and tremble before the people like a woman in labor. Faces change color. Emotions run high and wild on God's dreadful day.

2:7. The enemy army comes running like heroic **warriors**. Like trained **soldiers** they scale the wall. Each soldier marches straight ahead in the route he is assigned. No one strays from his path. Such is the enemy faced by the people on the Lord's dreadful day.

2:8. Staying in line, soldiers do not push one another. Each warrior walks in his own route. They fall on or attack the enemy, marching **straight** through the enemy's arrows. Nothing stops them as they march onward. This is God's dreadful day.

2:9. Into the city they **rush**. Along its walls they **run**. Into the houses they **climb**. Through the **windows** they come. They are like **thieves**. Nothing stops them. Everything is coming under their control. This is God's dreadful day.

2:10. As the enemy comes the earth **shakes**; the heavens **tremble**. The sun and moon grow dark. The stars stop shining. Even the creation retreats in fear as the enemy advances. The people are experiencing the Lord's dreadful day.

2:11. The Lord's voice **thunders** as he shouts in front of his **army**. But who is his army—our trembling warriors or the enemy's disciplined forces? Indeed, his base camp is large. Those who obey **his command** are powerful. This sounds like the description of the enemy army in Joel 2:2. Indeed, **great** is the **day of the LORD. Who can endure it?** (Amos 7:10). Do you think you can bear up under the stress and fear of God's dreadful day?

B Do Returning and Repenting Mean Relenting and Reprieve? (2:12–17)

> **SUPPORTING IDEA:** *God's dreadful judgment day calls his people to return to him, repent of their sins, and pray that he will relent from his decision to judge.*

2:12. The scene changes with the divine **even now**. We have here the so-called oracular formula, *neum Yahweh*, **declares the LORD**. This is the voice of the Lord that catches the ear and calls for attention. The formula appears 268 times in Scripture, 238 in the prophets, but only this once in Joel.

God's words carry a plaintive invitation. You have seen the horror of God's dreadful day. What can you do about it? You have one hope—**return to me with all your heart, with fasting and weeping and mourning** rituals. God makes the invitation personal. Turn back to *me*. This assumes that in spite of what you may think, you are walking in the wrong direction. Your life is headed away from God and toward destruction. Can God's dreadful day persuade you to turn around and come back to him? That is repentance! Hebrew *shub*, "turn" or **return**, is the Hebrew word for *repent*. What does repentance involve? It begins with a decision in the innermost self. A change of will is involved.

This decision to take a new direction reveals itself in public actions. The first of these are of a ritual variety. You go to God's house. You join God's people. You give up food as unimportant in light of the dreadful situation you face. You cry real tears, regretting that the situation has come this far and that the outlook for the future is dark. You put on sackcloth. You sit in ashes. You place ashes on your head. You do all the things the people of God are doing to show their shame and sorrow at the current state of affairs. You cry out to God for deliverance from the dreadful situation.

2:13. This mourning ritual is different from most you have participated in. Usually you slash holes in the clothes you wear. Not this time. In repentance, you slash your hearts. You devote all your emotions to grief over your sins and to commitment to change. Only such a complete change can be called repentance. Only thus can you **return to the** LORD.

But why would you return to the Lord? Simply because of who he is. First, he is **your God**. Every god you have been serving—no matter how popular with the crowds, no matter how ancient the worship practices in the land, no matter how much fun and excitement the worship practices provide—is false. Every such god makes you false because they are not your gods. Only one God is your Lord. That is the God of Israel. Come back to him!

By nature God wants to be gracious to his people (Isa. 30:18), so in prayer his people call on him to be gracious to them (Ps. 9:13). They acknowledge their sins, implying that God has no reason except his own nature to be gracious to his people (Ps. 41:4). Hope for God to be gracious is qualified by a "perhaps" or "maybe," since no human action can force God to be gracious (2 Sam. 12:22). God will not forsake his people; perhaps he will act graciously toward his disobedient people (Neh. 9:17).

God is also *rachum*, **compassionate**. He "goes beyond what ought to be given" (Mike Butterworth, *NIDOTTE*). This "designates the benevolent and solicitous God who protects and preserves maternal life which is endangered" (*HALOT*), *rachum* being related to the Hebrew word for womb. "It is primarily the 'soft place' in the human being (Gen. 43:30)" (H. J. Stoebe, *TLOT*). God's compassion is the ground for humans to pray for forgiveness (Ps. 51:1). It is the basis for Joel's calling Israel to repent and turn back to God (Deut. 4:30–31).

God is *'erek 'appim*, literally "long of noses" which comes to mean "long in becoming angry," thus "patient" or **slow to anger**. This characteristic allows the loving, merciful God to forgive the sins of his people (Num. 14:18). This is patience that does not react emotionally or impulsively (Isa. 42:14).

God is *rav-chesed*, great in faithful love, **abounding in love**. This term emphasizes loyalty and faithfulness, the favor a superior like a king grants to a subordinate. It refers to acts of goodness and kindness that reflect divine faithfulness and mercy. Still, God can take away his *chesed* from his people (Jer. 16:5). Joel used standard statements about God to encourage his people to repent and return to the Lord.

2:14. What could a people expect when they repented? Joel had only a **He may** for an answer. The God of *chesed* who relates faithfully to his people might hear their penitent prayers and relent (**have pity**) as the confession of faith said he did. The result would be that he would **leave behind a blessing**, an expression that occurs nowhere else in the Old Testament. Such blessing brings life, salvation, fertility, well-being, good fortune, and God's Spirit. God is the ultimate source of all blessing, but the giver of blessing expects obedience and faithfulness from its recipients (Deut. 7:12).

Joel's contemporaries had lost all their agricultural produce, all the resources to renew agricultural fertility, and their own city to the invading locusts. God's blessing was the only hint of a future for them. If they answered God's call to repent, maybe the blessing would come. Would people see enough hope in "maybe" to repent? But Joel surprised the people. Blessing would not be to satisfy their appetites. Blessing would provide materials for them to offer to God.

2:15. The call to **blow the trumpet** is repeated (see Joel 2:1). The reason is no longer military. Now it is religious. The trumpet does not call the country to war but to worship. This worship is not that of praise, adoration, and joy. It is worship from desperation, worship seeking deliverance from disaster. Fasting is the order of the day The **sacred assembly** is a special gathering of the people of God, often connected with the final days of the annual festivals (Num. 29:35). It could also refer to pagan gatherings (2 Kgs. 10:20). Even though they had no harvest to celebrate, Joel demanded that the people join in a special assembly to mourn and to plead with God for deliverance.

2:16. No one was exempt. The priests were to **gather the people** and lead in the proper ritual acts which assured that the people were clean and undefiled and thus eligible for worship. The priests were to **consecrate the assembly**. They offered prayer to God that set the people apart as dedicated to God. This crisis was so overwhelming that all occasions for joy had to be postponed. Everyone must take off wedding dresses and festival clothes and put on mourning dress. The sacred assembly should pray for God's help and deliverance as they repented of their sins and turned to him for new life.

2:17. The priests must lead out in prayer and penitence. They should **weep** and express the nation's prayer of lamentation. The prayer had one basic petition: **Spare your people**—deliver them from the locusts and from the invading army. What happened to them symbolized God's strength and sovereign control to the nations. Continued destruction would turn Israel into a byword or proverb. The nations would use them as a negative example.

God's own people would become **an object of scorn**, meaning that the Lord himself would be scorned and mocked by the nations as they jeered and asked, **Where is their God?** The priests' lamentation thus invited God to defend his reputation as well as the reputation of his people.

⦿ Satisfied and Safe from Shame (2:18–27)

SUPPORTING IDEA: *God in his love for his people responds to their repentance in compassion, and he promises to save them from their shame.*

2:18. Worship, lament, fasting, crying, praying were not just rituals undertaken with no expectation of change. Each activity sought to bring God back to his people.

The prophet announced that God was making sure the people's activities accomplished their purpose. God had promised the land to the patriarchs (Gen. 12:1–7) and had given it to them (Josh. 1–24). The land was an essential part of the identity of his people. Threat to the land roused God's emotions. Jealousy (Heb. *qanna'* or *qin'ah*) combines both jealousy and zeal, so that *TLOT* titles its article "fervor." The cause of jealous or zealous actions "is the (possibly imagined) infringement of someone's rights or injury to the subject's honor" (H. G. L. Peels, *NIDOTTE*).

With a human subject the term involves rage, envy, and the heat roused by excitement (Isa. 11:13). God's promises to protect his people should cause them to refrain from jealous reactions against the prosperous godless (Ps. 37:1).

God's name is Jealous, and he is a jealous God (Exod. 34:14). The jealous zeal "of God is the self-preservation of the sovereign, unapproachable, holy God" (Peel, *NIDOTTE*). Idol worship makes God jealous, so that he in turn makes his errant people jealous by giving them to another nation (Deut. 32:21). A person who is faithful to God can be jealous with his jealousy (Num. 25:11). Such jealousy of God is not directed against the rival for his affections but against his own beloved people who have been disloyal to their covenant with him.

God's jealousy or zeal "acts for or against his people with nearly equal frequency" (G. Sauer, *TLOT*). Here we see the uniqueness of God's relationship with his people. The gods of the nations envied one another, but among these other peoples you never heard "of a god's zeal in relation to his worshiper" (Sauer, *TLOT*). Israel's God guards his unique claim to be the only God. He protects his position against any who would contest it. When his people worship other gods, they incite his jealousy (Deut. 32:16) and his punishment (Ezek. 5:13).

Joel shows that the jealousy and zeal of God to protect his reputation, his name, and his land also lead him to punish nations that would harm his people (Isa. 9:6; Zech. 1:14). Jealousy is a necessary side of God's love for his people. He maintains a loyal relationship with them, brings them back to him and away from his "rivals," and destroys all opposition to his position as the one true God of the universe.

Jealousy of God for his people and against their enemies raises the divine **pity** (Heb. *chamal*). This verb emphasizes the desire to pardon or spare from "an impending fate or a decreed punishment" rather than the establishing of personal relationships (H. J. Stoebe, *TLOT*).

> The religious significance of the root is limited (it does not appear in the Psalms and is only rarely used in a positive sense as in Mal. 3:17; 2 Chr. 36:15). Nevertheless, its use with the negative contributes to the Old Testament's emphasis on the seriousness of sin in God's eyes, while in its own right (and to a lesser extent) it points to the emotional and merciful aspects of his salvation (Mike Butterworth, *NIDOTTE*).

2:19. God's response is more than an emotional promise. It has concrete content—new food. What the people had lost (Joel 1:10–12,16–18) is now restored, so much so that it will **satisfy you fully.** More importantly for the long run, **never again** would God **make you an object of scorn to the nations.** Israel's reputation among the nations, so strongly established by David and Solomon and reestablished by kings like Uzziah and Josiah, would not be tarnished. The nations would have no more reason to laugh at Israel.

2:20. Now a slight clue about the nature of the enemy army appears. Locusts usually came from the south, but unusual occasions brought them from the north. The locust threat combines here with the military threat. It is from the north, but, except for Egypt, so were most of Israel's enemies, as the prophets repeatedly pointed out (Isa. 14:31; Ezek. 26:7; Dan. 11:6–15,40). This could refer to Assyria, Syria, Babylon, or even Greece, depending on the prophet's time frame.

Using poetic power, Joel paints a gruesome picture of the demise of the locusts/army. He shows the great size of the enemy—covering the entire land east to west. So the army's vanguard goes into the eastern sea (the Dead Sea), and its rear guard into the Western Sea (the Mediterranean Sea). Here is a traditional "divide and conquer" military tactic. The main body of the army will be banished into a **parched and barren land**—a description of Israel—so that the victory march may be described as pushing the enemy clear through Israel's land to the two bordering seas, or it may describe the parched wilderness south of Judah or the Arabian Desert to the east.

The lasting memory of the defeated army comes not from its size or its devastation but from its stink. Such language could apply to the rotting locust remains, but it would be even more memorable if applied to the defeated army's decaying bodies (Amos 4:10; Isa. 34:2–3). The scare of Joel 2:1–11 succumbs to the stench of Joel 2:20.

2:21. God says, **Be not afraid.** This is the reassurance formula that introduces an oracle of salvation. Hearing this relieves the tension in a desperate situation with the assurance that God is about to deliver the people (Isa. 7:4; Zeph. 3:16). **Land** here represents Hebrew *'adamah,* referring to the ground that has suffered such abuse and has become infertile. No more calls to repent, to weep, to fast. Now the call is **be glad and rejoice**. What would cause such reaction for a people so recently devastated? Only one thing brings true gladness and joy—the Lord has done great things. Israel languished and mourned because of God's punishing acts. Now Israel will rejoice because of his saving acts (Ps. 126:2–3).

2:22. The ground should not fear; neither should the **animals** (Joel 1:10,18). Even the "wilderness pastures have become green. The tree has borne its fruit. Fig tree and vine have yielded their produce" (author's translation). Have at it, dear animals, and rejoice (Joel 1:12).

2:23. Zion with all its inhabitants can join in the joy (Joel 2:1,15) because **he has given you the autumn rains in righteousness**. This is not a one-time affair. Both **autumn and spring rains** are included **as before**. Life is back to normal in God's land. Crops are growing and will continue to grow because the land will have rain.

The rain represents God's gift of righteousness, his loyalty to the covenant, his faithfulness, and thus his goodness and kindness to Israel, his people. The rain also represents a vindication of Israel's righteousness in repenting and turning back to God with fasting and prayer. It represents a gift in response to Israel's renewed loyalty. The rain is righteous in the sense that just the right amount fell. The rain was faithful in coming and loyal in adhering to the standards by which rain is normally measured.

2:24. God's jealousy and pity bring righteousness in another way—an abundant supply of **grain** and **new wine** and **oil** (Joel 1:10).

2:25. This abundance is God's design to **repay** Israel for the **great army** of **locusts** he had **sent among you**. Here again we see locust language and military language merging. The locust plague represents the forerunner symbolizing the coming army, and the locusts in their manner of destroying the fields resemble a well-trained army marching against the enemy.

2:26. Repayment is in kind. What the people lost, they will get back—food and the opportunity to praise and worship God (Joel 1:9–16). The "He may" of 2:14 has become **who has worked wonders for you**. "Wonders" (Heb. *pele'*) most often appears in the Psalms or in material related to the Psalms. It

> indicates an event that a person, judging by the customary and the expected, finds extraordinary, impossible, even wonderful. *pele'* never hinges on the phenomenon as such but includes both the unexpected event as well as one's astonished reaction to it. . . . The wonder, the astonishment, includes the recognition of the limits of one's own

power to conceptualize and comprehend. Since the *pele'* event signifies a transcendence of customary, normal expectations, it is predominantly understood as God's activity (R. Albertz, *TLOT;* cp. Gen. 18:14).

Locusts joined with foreign invaders to bring Israel shame, embarrassment, scorn, and anguish (Joel 2:6,17). No more. The Lord would take care of that. Israel has suffered shame and ridicule for the last time.

2:27. Why did God repay his people and deliver them from such atrocity and devastation? He wanted to teach them a lesson. Israel must know that "in the midst of Israel am I. I am Yahweh, your God. No other god exists" (author's translation). Thus Israel could claim the promise that they would never again suffer shame before the other nations. No nation could harm Israel if God was able to live in their midst because that would mean they had become God's holy nation where the Lord, the Holy One, could live (see Exod. 19:3–13). Here is Israel's unique statement of faith—their God lives in their midst (Num. 11:20–21). By this living in their midst, God had a unique claim on his people.

Israel's options were limited. Other nations and peoples could choose which god they wanted to go to in each situation of life. Israel had no such choice. Israel had one God for every situation in life, and this God is jealous (Joel 2:18). Thus the chorus **I am the LORD your God** rings through the Old Testament, giving Israel assurance and calling Israel to obedience (Exod. 16:12; Ezek. 28:26). The reminder "no other God exists" also drums its beat home strongly but less frequently through the Old Testament (Isa. 45:5–6). This time God promises that Israel will learn the basic theological truths and the practical implications that go along with them.

D Deliverance Through the Spirit (2:28–32)

SUPPORTING IDEA: *God's deliverance from the dreadful day of judgment comes as he pours his Spirit into his people.*

2:28–29. This verse begins a new chapter in the Hebrew text. How could God teach his people who had been so rebellious? He would teach them by changing them. Having changed the fields back to normal with rain, he will change his people back to who they are supposed to be with **my Spirit**.

We as Christians have a hard time reading this passage because we automatically read the New Testament Holy Spirit that we have experienced back into the Old Testament. We must remember the Old Testament is a pre-Pentecost book. This verse was one of the main ones used to help the church understand Pentecost, but they could use this verse only because they had experienced Pentecost (Acts 2:17–21). Our task is to see how Joel and his audience would have understood this word before we baptize it into our Pentecost experience.

The Old Testament uses the term *ruach* to refer to wind, breath, and the empowering element in a person's life. Spirit gives God's people military, political, and prophetic leaders. The Spirit of God leads people to obey his covenant expectations and points forward to new leadership and new obedience.

Joel used traditional language for God's helping and empowering his people to picture God's brilliant new promise—a promise not confined to leaders but including **all** God's people. No longer would a person have to go to prophets or priests to determine God's message. Everyone would know God's revelation. No longer could an elder generation stake out a monopoly on wisdom. The younger generation had access to God's **visions**. No longer could men exclude women because sons and daughters alike would receive God's visions.

The economically advantaged no longer had reason to claim a spiritual advantage. Even the slaves (**servants**) would receive God's Spirit of revelation and power. God planned for all people to have access to his will, to know his plan, and to have the choice to obey or disobey. Here is a central biblical text for God's mission for the world.

2:30. This great day of revelation climaxes in God's works that no person can claim credit for or duplicate. "I will give wonderful signs in the heavens and on earth" (author's translation) shows that as God lets people prophesy and understand his will, he continues to do works resembling the wonderful signs he did in Egypt (1 Chr. 16:12). God's wonderful signs included the fulfillment of curses on a disobedient people (Deut. 28:45–46). A prophet's children could function as wonderful signs reminding people of the prophet's inspired message (Isa. 8:18). Prophetic symbolic acts served as wonderful signs to the people also (Ezek. 24:24,27), as did a king's miraculous healing (2 Chr. 32:24).

Such wonders left people wondering. Were these signs of miraculous victory to come, or did they indicate the curses of disobedience? Joel's context seems to promise victory for Israel, an Israel in which everyone knows God's word and message. But Joel leaves open the possibility of violence and suffering for those who know the word and refuse to follow it. **Fire and billows of smoke** remind the reader of God's appearance with his people during the exodus (Exod. 14:19–24), but **blood** recalls God's plague of blood on the waters of Egypt (Exod. 7:14–24).

2:31. Heavenly portents go beyond expectations. They darken the great lights that God put in the skies at creation. This is not just any judgment. This is **the coming of the great and dreadful day of the LORD**. This day cannot be dismissed as one of salvation and glory for Israel. The background of locust plagues and army invasions offer historical proof that the Day of the Lord can be black and dark, and it can bring defeat. When the prophet predicts the dreadful day, you had better be ready. God's curses on the disobedient may fall on you!

2:32. A great wind of hope blows through. Just as the prediction of the work of the Spirit appeared to make the day of the Lord one of hope and revelation, so now the promise becomes clear. No matter how dark the Day of the Lord is without light from sun or moon, a ray of hope comes through. **Everyone who calls on the name of the LORD will be saved.** This goes back to the Bible's earliest days when men began to call on the name of the Lord (Gen. 4:26). God has always wanted people from all nations to devote themselves to him in worship. This is involved in calling on the Lord's name, in identifying oneself as part of the people of God.

God has poured out his Spirit in revelation. People respond to that revelation in obedience, praise, commitment, and prayer. They experience "salvation," God's deliverance from the judgment of the dreadful Day of the Lord. But this deliverance is only for **survivors whom the LORD calls.** Being on Mount Zion near God's temple is not enough. Being part of the population of Jerusalem, God's holy city, is not enough. A person calls on the name of the Lord, knowing that God took the initiative to make this possible. God brought locusts. God brought an invading army. God left survivors. God poured out his Spirit. After all God has done, now people have the invitation to call on God's name and to be delivered from this dreadful day.

> **MAIN IDEA REVIEW:** *Facing God's dreadful judgment day, God's people need to turn to him in repentance, hoping that God will refrain from the judgment he has planned.*

III. CONCLUSION

Looking for Good News

Sweat soaked my bed each morning. Pajamas required daily washing. As heat prevented sleep at three o'clock each morning, I prayed for release. Why am I in Houston, Texas, in July and August, sleeping without air conditioning? Is there no escape from 99 degrees and 99 percent humidity? Surely my summer job at the newspaper would end soon, and I would escape. I looked forward to that day of good news more than any news article I could write for the paper.

Joel had described the miserable situation his people faced from locusts and from military invaders. Now they looked for good news, escape from agricultural, military, and economic despair. Joel had a word of hope, a new Day of the Lord with God's miracles for everyone. But the people had to respond in genuine repentance. They needed different lifestyles if they were to see the good news Day of the Lord. The New Testament church experienced that great day in a marvelous way on the day of Pentecost (Acts 2). Still, God's people look forward to a new Day of the Lord, the day of Christ's return to judge the world and deliver his people. The call to us remains the same. If we expect to participate fully in that day, we must repent and obey the Lord.

PRINCIPLES

- The Day of the Lord has many faces and appears in different ways through God's history with his people.
- The coming Day of the Lord calls God's people to repentance.
- Repentance is more than ritual mourning; it is a time of changing one's lifestyle before God.
- God's nature leads him to be gracious and loving toward his people.
- No human action can force God to act; he is always the sovereign Lord who chooses when to bring discipline and when to show grace.
- God works for his people to establish his covenant relationship with them in which he is the one and only true God.
- God works to bring all people to know and obey his word.

APPLICATIONS

- Spend time in prayer affirming who God is and what he means to you.
- Accept God's discipline as a call to repentance and obedience.
- Express your grief over your sin to God.
- Ask God to deliver you from the difficulties you face today.
- Depend on God for life's daily needs.
- Rejoice with God's people over the blessings he has given you.
- Recommit yourself to let God and only God be the Lord of your life.
- Ask God to make you aware of his Spirit revealing his will to you.

IV. LIFE APPLICATION

Waiting for the Music

In his book *When Christ Comes,* Max Lucado introduces us to his daughter Sara and to Fred, her pet hamster. One day when Lucado was in charge of things at home, he lay on the couch watching Fred run up and down the family piano. The hamster's "wind sprints" brought "new meaning to 'tickling the ivories.'"

They also brought the hamster into deep trouble because he ventured over the piano cover and tumbled into the mass of piano strings and hammers.

Strings rubbed his back as he scurried around trying to escape. When Lucado and his daughter tried to squeeze their fingers in to help, Fred ran for the corner. Friendly coaxing and sergeant-like bullying did not help. Fred stayed glued to his corner. A few gentle piano notes failed to budge him. So the decision was made to dismantle the piano. With trusty Phillips screwdriver in hand, Lucado looked for a place to begin and found none.

Thinking through Fred's fix, Lucado saw how much it is like ours. We both had a good place to live and then took a fall. We are both trapped—Fred by piano wires and we by guilt, anxiety, and pride. We, too, now live in a foreign, fearful place where we were never meant to be. Our Master's hand is near to help, but we back away from it. So we don't know a way of delivery or salvation.

Like Fred, we ignore our only source of help and hope. God calls for us, coaxing softly or screaming incessantly. Still we remain silent in our helpless corner. He provides music to lure us to himself—the music of beauty and love and sacrifice. Still we ignore him. He resorts to more stringent means—discipline and punishment, dismantling our world even with locusts or armies. Even then we refuse to respond.

And then we hear God's voice. He places the choice squarely before us—repent or perish. Give your heart and life to God, or face an eternal Day of the Lord separated from him. What choice will you make?

V. PRAYER

God, we have seen your discipline, your punishment. We feel that we, like Israel, have suffered through the dark Day of the Lord. Now we hear your voice calling us to repent and live for you. Take us, cleanse us, forgive us, use us. Give us your Spirit. Let us hear and obey your word. Amen.

VI. DEEPER DISCOVERIES

The Spirit of God in the Old Testament (2:28)

The Hebrew term *ruach* occurs 378 times in the Old Testament, with its Aramaic counterpart occurring another eleven times. Its basic meaning appears to be "air that is moving, wind" (Hos. 13:15). Thus this word may in different places in the Bible refer to human or animal breath, to wind, or to the life-empowering element within man recognized by the rise and fall of the chest during breathing (Jer. 2:24; Ezek. 3:14). This Spirit of God gives life to the world as it hovers over the darkness of creation before God speaks things into being (Gen. 1:2). The Spirit thus is the breath of life with which God has created people (Isa. 42:5).

God's Spirit performs several functions in the Old Testament. The Spirit takes charge of a person, giving special powers of leadership and action (Judg. 3:10). Israel's king received the Spirit at his anointing and was expected to follow its leadership (1 Sam. 16:13–14). The expected Messiah, the new king, will be led by God's Spirit (Isa. 42:1). The Spirit gives special prophetic powers (1 Sam. 10:10). God's people should consult his Spirit as they plan to act (Isa. 30:1). God's prophets are expected to speak under the Spirit's leadership (Mic. 3:8).

But the Old Testament does not expect the Spirit to be confined to prophets and kings. God wants all his people to be ruled by the Spirit (Ezek. 11:19). This will lead to obedience to God's teachings (Ezek. 36:27). God's breath will bring new life to a dead nation (Ezek. 37:5,14). God's people will have a new heart and a new mind for obedience (Ezek. 36:26–27).

VII. TEACHING OUTLINE

A. INTRODUCTION

1. Lead Story: Repentance Means Change
2. Context: Having explained the locust plague as God's warning of deeper tragedy in the form of military invasion, Joel prepared the people by showing just how serious the Day of the Lord was and then giving them a call to action and a picture of hope.
3. Transition: The call to action involves true repentance. The Day of the Lord centers on God's delivering the remnant of his people and pouring out his Spirit on them to guide them through the life of the repentant. Here the Old Testament prepares us for the New Testament coming of the Holy Spirit at Pentecost.

B. COMMENTARY

1. The Trumpet of Tragedy (2:1–11)
2. Do Returning and Repenting Mean Relenting and Reprieve? (2:12–17)
3. Satisfied and Safe from Shame (2:18–27)
4. Deliverance Through the Spirit (2:28–32)

C. CONCLUSION: LOOKING FOR GOOD NEWS

VIII. ISSUES FOR DISCUSSION

1. Describe true repentance before God, and testify to your own experience of repentance with God.

2. How can the Day of the Lord come more than once in history, sometimes bringing the light of salvation and at other times bringing the darkness of discipline?
3. What does it mean to call on the name of the Lord for deliverance?
4. Is it good for you that God is a jealous God?

Joel 3:1–21

Judgment in Jehoshaphat

I. INTRODUCTION
"I Can't Pray for Terrorists"

II. COMMENTARY
A verse-by-verse explanation of these verses.

III. CONCLUSION
Acting on the Absurd

An overview of the principles and applications from these verses.

IV. LIFE APPLICATION
"When Did We See You?"

Melding these verses to life.

V. PRAYER
Tying these verses to life with God.

VI. DEEPER DISCOVERIES
Historical, geographical, and grammatical enrichment of the commentary.

VII. TEACHING OUTLINE
Suggested step-by-step group study of these verses.

VIII. ISSUES FOR DISCUSSION
Zeroing these verses in on daily life.

"*If* any should take offense at this particularistic presentation of divine providence, let him ponder upon the survival of the Jewish nation to be hosts of their Messiah and first messengers of the Christian faith in which we now glory, while those other nations waned into insignificance."

Leslie C. Allen

Joel 3:1–21

I N   A   N U T S H E L L

*J*oel's final chapter looks to the restoration of Judah and the punishing repayment of the nations in the Valley of Jehoshaphat for what they did to God's people. This sets up the Day of the Lord as a day of decision and as the day when God reestablishes Jerusalem as the center of his people forever.

Judgment in Jehoshaphat

I. INTRODUCTION

"I Can't Pray for Terrorists"

In her book *Battling the Prince of Darkness,* Evelyn Christenson tells about a Christian woman who came to her in Durban, South Africa. Evelyn had been teaching about the power of prayer and illustrated her teaching by describing terrorists in prison in Northern Ireland. Many people in Ireland and around the world prayed for these terrorist prisoners. As a result of such a barrage of prayer, the prisoners found Christ as their Savior. Convicted, the South African confided to Evelyn: "I can't pray for those terrorists in our country." Then searching Evelyn's face and seeing its surprised look, the lady continued, "But—what should I pray?"

"For them," the answer came quickly, "for them to find Jesus, of course. Then they won't be terrorists any more" (p. 37).

Joel faced a world in which terrorists had won. His country was devastated. God told him not to worry. The Day of the Lord was at hand. That would be a day of decision. Just as the Northern Ireland terrorists faced decision and chose Jesus, so terrorist nations attacking Judah would face decision. But this time the decision would be at the final court of appeal, the last judgment. They would have to face the consequences of their terrorism against God because the call to decision would not ring out again.

II. COMMENTARY

Judgment in Jehoshaphat

> **MAIN IDEA:** *The final Day of the Lord will bring victory and pardon for God's people, but that day of final decision will bring lasting judgment on the enemies of God's people. God will live in Zion among his people.*

A Judging Jehoshaphat's Valley (3:1–12)

> **SUPPORTING IDEA:** *On God's day of restoration for Jerusalem, he will judge all the nations who have mistreated his people.*

3:1. Joel connected his oracle against the nations to his preceding prophecy of salvation in Joel 2:28–32. Part of God's promise of salvation is elimination of the cause of the current catastrophe. When the Spirit is poured out and when the surviving people call on the name of the Lord for deliverance is the same time as **when I restore the fortunes of Judah and Jerusalem.**

"Restore the fortunes" is a technical expression (Deut. 30:3; Jer. 35:11; Ezek. 16:53), usually referring to the return from the exile. Recent study has confirmed that the meaning is "to restore the fortunes" rather than "to return from captivity," leaving a wider range of possible meanings than just reference to the exile. The Lord is always the subject of this expression.

Joel chapter 3 is in many ways a repeated chorus to chapter 2, restoring all that 1:1–2:11 destroyed. Crops, water supplies, forests, armies, cities— everything God's people lost, they now find restored. As chapter 2 pointed to verse 27, so chapter 3 points to verse 17. God's people will see their fortunes fully restored when they have answered the call to repentance and once again live in a covenant relationship with God. This is possible because God has poured out his Spirit on them (Joel 2:28).

3:2. This oracle against the nations does not limit itself to particular enemies who have fought Israel. Some enemies may eventually be listed individually, but the focus is on **all nations**. The Day of the Lord will reach beyond Israel to encompass all inhabitants of the earth. God will bring them down to the **Valley of Jehoshaphat**. Jehoshaphat was Judah's king about 873–848 B.C. (1 Chr. 3:10), but the valley seems to be mentioned here because of the meaning of the name ("Yahweh judges") rather than for any connection to the king. Tradition identifies the valley with the Kidron Valley near Jerusalem, but Scripture gives no other mention of the valley and no location for it.

Wherever the valley and whatever its original significance, Joel describes it as the place where God will take the nations to court to try their case, using the verb *shaphat* that occurs in the name of the valley. The court case concerns "my people, indeed my inheritance Israel" (author's translation). The charge against the nations is simple: **they scattered my people among the nations**, and **they divided up my land**. God had divided up the land among his tribes under Joshua (Josh. 13–21). No one else had a right to divide it up differently. God controlled his people. No one else had a right to scatter them among the nations.

3:3. God now brings specific charges against the nations. God charges them with lining his people up as captives and letting the soldiers cast lots to see which captive would become his servant (Obad. 11). They accumulate so many slaves they are willing to trade young boy captives to get a one-night stand with **prostitutes**. They would trade young captured Israelite **girls** for a glass of **wine** that they immediately drank and forgot about. Human life— Israelite human life—meant nothing to these nations. For this they would face God in court.

3:4. Two nations head the list: **Tyre and Sidon**, the two major Phoenician cities, apparently the home of the original Canaanites (Isa. 23:11). (For Tyre, see comments on Amos 1:9–10.) Sidon lay twenty-five miles north of Tyre and had a long history of leading coastal coalitions against Egypt. The two cities dominated deep-sea commercial traffic, carrying goods from many nations on their famous ships.

The question God asks is ambiguous, literally, "What you to me?" This may mean: What are your intentions? What are your relationships? What have you got to do with me? What do you mean to me? The context seems to favor, What are your intentions in dealing with me? The question continues: "Are you requiting me with a payback?" That is, Are you seeking revenge? The implication is, "Revenge for what? I and my people have done nothing. What are you up to and why?" If you are seeking a payback, God promised, watch out. "Quickly, in a hurry, I will return your requital on your head."

3:5. We are innocent, God maintains, but not you. You stole my money, my temple **treasures** (Hos. 9:6). What's more, you placed my holy objects in your pagan **temples**. You expect me to take all this lying down?

3:6. You sold my people **to the Greeks**. You think because you Phoenicians control the high seas, it does not matter what kind of trading you do. It does matter, God declares. You must never turn my precious people into a trading commodity. They are my slaves, not yours or anyone else's. They belong in my land until I send them **far from their homeland**. You have no right to send them anywhere. The Greeks (Heb. *javan*) are traced back to Japheth, Noah's son (Gen. 10:2). They are seen as a distant, unfamiliar land (Isa. 66:19).

3:7. God's work will run in two directions. He will wake up his enslaved people to lead them home, and he will gain revenge on those who have enslaved them.

3:8. Turn-about is fair play. God will enslave the Phoenicians' sons just as they enslaved his people. As they sent his enslaved sons far to the west, he will send their enslaved sons far to the southeast, to the Sabeans. In Isaiah 45:14, the Sabeans are a tall people and may be related to Africa. In Job 1:14–15 and 6:19, the Sabeans appear to be a tribe from northern Arabia. In Joel the **Sabeans** are **a nation far away**. This likely refers to southern Arabia and the kingdom of Sheba, probably the original home from which the northern Sabeans later migrated. The nomadic Arabian traders would eventually be the economic victors. What right did Joel have to promise such a reversal of fortunes for Phoenicians and Philistines? "For the Lord has spoken!" God's word would bring to pass all it had promised.

3:9. God calls the enemy armies to assemble for battle. The divine commander controls all armies and all historical events. He summons the nations to their final battle.

3:10. Peace comes when military weapons are transformed into agricultural tools (Mic. 4:3). War reverses the process. There is no time to plow the fields or trim the vines with a special vineyard knife. No time for cowards. The weakest link in the army must stand strong and proclaim, "I am a war hero." God has called the nations to send all they have to face him in battle. All must answer the call.

3:11. This verse is hard to translate. The first word may mean "hurry up" or "come, help me." "Assemble" is not an imperative in Hebrew, but it has to be here because of the context. The last line suddenly interrupts God's speech with speech addressed to him. The Septuagint or earliest Greek translation of the Old Testament reads, "The gentle must be a fighter." In spite of the textual uncertainty, the meaning remains reasonably clear: Hurry up! No time to waste! Every nation on every side of Israel, get ready for action. You know the assembly point. Muster all your soldiers there. Lord, bring your heroic **warriors** here against this enemy force.

3:12. Now God summarizes for his people what is about to happen. They are to let the nations muster themselves for battle and march out to the battleground—the **Valley of Jehoshaphat**, or the Valley of Judgment. God has chosen that as the place where he will **sit** enthroned and **judge** the surrounding **nations**. Summoned to battle, the nations will discover that the battle determines more than just one more victory or loss for the troops. It represents God's punishment on all the nations who have mistreated his people.

Ⓑ Day of Decision (3:13–16)

SUPPORTING IDEA: *The Day of the Lord will be the day of God's final decision, bringing refuge to his people and judgment to the nations.*

3:13. God addresses his people with familiar harvest imagery. But the imagery applies not to the agricultural fields but to the battlefields. There on the battlefields God will harvest the enemy and execute his sentence of death on them. Just as harvesting crops kills the plants but serves the needs of the farmer, so harvesting the enemy army will destroy the soldiers while serving the needs of God and his people. The final line of the verse pictures the final end of the grape harvest. Full vats mean a successful harvest. Blood-red juice resembles the spilled blood on the battlefield and symbolizes the destruction of the enemy. All this comes because **so great is their wickedness**!

3:14. From the agriculturally based judgment call, Joel turns to description. A noisy, raucous multitude stirs around in the **valley of decision**. The Hebrew for **multitudes** has an extensive range of meaning from "agitation" and "turmoil" to "roar, din," to "procession, pomp," to "multitudes, crowd" (see *HALOT*), with each meaning playing a part in this mob scene. Their gathering point establishes an ominous aura—the valley of decision. The Hebrew verb *charats* carries the connotation of a guilty verdict with a sentence of destruction that stands beyond appeal (Job 14:5).

This is the setting for the final, ultimate **day of the** L<small>ORD</small>. No longer will people experience a foretaste of the final reality. That reality is here. The decision is not something people will make. It is a decision God has already made to condemn and destroy those who are opposed to him.

3:15. The heavenly powers, revered by Israel's neighbors and enemies as gods, bow in darkness and mourning on the Day of the Lord (cp. Joel 2:10; Mic. 3:6). They have no power when God comes to judge. Note that **will be darkened** (Heb. *qadar*) means both to become dark and to mourn.

3:16. What is the Day of the Lord? Joel gives one final, succinct summary. It is a day of God's actions. The actions take two forms: (1) he roars **from Zion** to frighten and destroy the enemy (Amos 1:2), and (2) he is a **refuge** for his people (Prov. 14:26). The Hebrew verb *hasah*

> emphasizes human insecurity and inability in the face of calamity, and divine security and ability to harbor and preserve those in distress (Pss. 11:1; 16:1; 37:40) . . . Unlike those who are swept away by God's wrath because they have taken refuge in the lie of idolatry (Isa. 28:15,17), those who fear the Lord have a secure fortress in the day of evil (Jer. 17:17), and this legacy of faith provides a refuge for one's children as well (Prov. 14:26). Note the Lord is always a refuge, especially for those who by act of will (Ps. 73:28) and demonstration of personal faith (Ps. 71:6–7) make him such (Andrew E. Hill, *NIDOTTE*).

This is placed in parallel to *ma'oz*, **stronghold**, which often refers to hidden mountain refuges and thus secure places or military fortresses. This language, too, is often taken over and applied to the God of Israel (2 Sam. 22:33). The Day of the Lord brings no fear to God's people because they have found their security in him.

Ⓒ The Day of the Lord's Dwelling in Zion (3:17–21)

> **SUPPORTING IDEA:** *The Day of the Lord will find the holy God in his holy city on his holy hill pardoning his people but leaving his enemies desolate.*

3:17. God's purpose from the beginning of his salvation work in the exodus was to show that he and no other was their God. Over and again he used the "recognition formula" of verse 17a as proof that what he promised would come true (Exod. 29:46; Ezek. 5:13). Joel had used a variation of this formula to convince Israel that God was going to carry out his promise of salvation (Joel 2:27). Now he extended the formula to make sure the people understood exactly who was meant as **your God.** This God is the one who lives **in Zion, my holy hill.**

Israel of Joel's day might doubt this because the locusts had come and so had the enemy army. The land lay desolate. No evidence seemed to point to God's presence among his people, much less in the city where enemy armies had scaled the walls and entered the people's homes.

But present evidence does not seal the case. More evidence is forthcoming. When that evidence is presented on the final Day of the Lord, no one will have any doubt. The Lord is the God who lives in Jerusalem, and "there is no other" (Joel 2:27). The evidence then will be just what Jerusalem was waiting to hear—**Jerusalem will be holy** forever. This means that God will never again let an enemy enter the city, desecrate the holy temple, and take away the sacred treasures stored in the temple.

3:18. When this promise of the final Day of the Lord reaches fulfillment, the entire situation will be turned on its heels. The Day of the Lord will be a day of total reversal. No more complaints about locusts and droughts and armies destroying the crops. Vineyards on the mountainsides **will drip new wine** (Joel 1:10). Animals threatened with extinction by the drought and lack of pastures (Joel 1:18) will now produce so much **milk** that it will literally **flow** down the hills. Dried-up streams (cp. Joel 1:20, where the same word is used as **ravines** in Joel 3:18) will now **run with water**.

How can this happen? It will not be by natural means. **A fountain will flow out of the LORD's house**. God will be the source of fertility for his people. Biblical thought always connected the sanctity and prosperity of the temple with that of the land. A sinful, unholy land lost its holy presence and its holy temple along with the fertility of its land. A restored, holy land received anew the divine presence, the holy temple, and the material blessings on its land (Ezek. 47:1–12; Rev. 22:1–2; along with Jesus' application of the idea to himself in John 7:38).

All this would bring new life to the **valley of acacias** that flows through the Judaean desert and opens into the Kidron Valley (*HALOT;* Rudolph, KAT, XIII, 2, 86). The Eden that had become a desert waste (Joel 2:3) now returns to its intended nature as Eden. As the waters of Eden watered the world (Gen. 2:10–14), so now the waters of Jerusalem's temple will turn the desert into a flower-filled valley.

3:19. Judah's temple-based fertility will stand in stark contrast to the land of her enemies. **Egypt**, the enemy from the exodus onward, **will be desolate**. **Edom**, the uncooperative neighbor and relative (Num. 20:14–21) who joined in Babylon's desecration of the temple (Obad. 11–14), would become **a desert waste** (see comments on these verses in Obadiah).

3:20. Jerusalem and **Judah**, God's promised land, did not face the same fate. They had suffered for their sins. Locusts, armies, and droughts had brought their punishment. They were past history. God had a new promise for his people. A new Day of the Lord would bring new hope. Never again would God's people live in a desolate, deserted land. Their land would be **inhabited forever**. When God's day had come and gone, Jerusalem would stand as the victor for all generations to view. Here they could also come to know the Lord.

3:21. The translation of this verse is debated. Allen follows many modern commentators in turning the first part of the verse into a question: "Shall I leave their bloodshed unpunished? I will not" (NICOT, 117). Garrett admits the difficulty of the Hebrew and questions whether the Hebrew *dam*, "blood," can also mean "bloodguilt" and so he goes with the earliest Greek translation of the Old Testament, the Septuagint, and reads: "I will avenge their blood and not pardon" (NAC 19A, 396).

It is preferable to stick with the Hebrew text and let Joel surprise us with his final summary. His final word is not about the nations and their punishment. It is about God's people and their victory. But victory cannot come to a guilty people—a people convicted of crimes against God.

So Joel gives one final summary of his message for God's people. His ultimate focus is on the future, not the present. He looks to the time when "the Lord will be living in Zion." That can happen because of God's pardon. In his grace and love and to fulfill all his promises, God will find all the sins he has **not pardoned** and he will pardon them. What is pardoned is the most serious sin imaginable—**bloodguilt** (1 Sam. 25:26,33). Bloodguilt is "the pollution or guilt incurred when life is taken outside of the legal prescriptions defined in the Hebrew Bible" (S. David Sperling, AB I, 764).

The guilty party in a trial was sentenced with the words, "the blood be upon his head," thus clearing the other party to the trial as innocent (Josh. 2:19). Blood represents the power of life itself (Lev. 17:11) and so could never be eaten (Deut. 15:23). Atonement demands a blood ritual because only that which contains the essence of life and whose loss brings death can atone for sin (Lev. 16:14–19). Still, such atoning power resides not in the blood but in God's gift of the blood (Lev. 17:11).

Israel's many sins against God had brought the verdict—guilty and the sentence of death. But God would not carry out the sentence. On the Day of the Lord he would pardon. He had already seen his people serve their sentence and endure his discipline and punishment. That was past. The future held something different. God would live with his people eternally. But to live with them required forgiving them. This God promised to do. He would **pardon**.

Joel ends his book on an unexpected note. No more locust plagues. No more army invasions. No more natural disasters. No more punishment. The Day of the Lord will bring salvation to God's people—a salvation marked by his eternal presence with them. One thing made that possible. God pardoned, forgave, and annulled all the punishment they deserved.

> **MAIN IDEA REVIEW:** *The final Day of the Lord will bring victory and pardon for God's people, but that day of final decision will bring lasting judgment on the enemies of God's people. God will live in Zion among his people.*

III. CONCLUSION

Acting on the Absurd

In his book *What's So Amazing About Grace?*, Philip Yancey tells of being castigated and slandered for writing a tongue-in-cheek article about the absurdity of gospel mathematics: one sheep more important than ninety and nine, a widow's mite more valuable than the rich donor's millions, a one-hour worker being paid the same as the person who labored twelve hours, a year's wages of perfume poured over a man about to die. He then went to see the drama *Amadeus* and realized it presented a similar absurdity: why would God reward with such talents an undeserving young brat like Wolfgang Amadeus Mozart (pp. 59–60)?

Joel's description of the Day of the Lord follows some of the same type logic (illogic?). Joel reminds us that the Day of the Lord has a double meaning. It can be bright and victorious. It can be dark and dangerous. God's people wait for God's day. But sometimes our waiting attitude is a bit blasé. We assume everything will be all right with us, that God will bring blessing when his day comes. We forget that in his reward system God's thoughts are not our thoughts and his logic is not our logic. We cannot assume that we will be on the winning side when his day comes. The first order of business is to make sure we are on his side today.

PRINCIPLES

- God has a plan for world history in which he rewards his faithful people and punishes those who disobey him and mistreat his people.
- Sin is eventually punished.
- God is the judge of every nation and every person.
- God will protect his people when the Day of the Lord comes.
- God's ultimate purpose is to introduce himself as the only God to his people.
- All hope rests in God's forgiveness.

APPLICATIONS

- Ask God to forgive you of your sins today.
- Trust God, not worldly resources, for protection.
- Make sure you are ready to face God at his seat of judgment.
- Tell others about the one and only God.
- Do not take judgment into your own hands, but trust God to right the world's wrongs in his own time.

IV. LIFE APPLICATION

"When Did We See You?"

Ravi Zacharias, in his book *Cries of the Heart,* calls our attention to Michelangelo's masterpiece of art in which God reaches out to Adam. God's arm is extended full-length, every muscle tense and taut. Contortion shows in his face, as God strains with great effort to reach down to sinful man. As Zacharias describes the painting: "By contrast, Adam lackadaisically lets a limpish hand dangle with apathy in an attitude that seems to say, 'If it meets, it meets'" (p. 182).

Too often this is our response when we hear of God's judgment day, the Day of the Lord. As God strains to reach us, we ignore his efforts, continue obliviously on our way, assuming that all is well with our souls. The biblical message cries to us, Watch out! The Day of the Lord can be dark as well as light. It can bring horrendous surprises if you are not ready. The question stares us in the face today: Are you ready for the judgment day? Are you sure you will not be stammering out questions with the goats of Matthew 25, "When did we see you?"

V. PRAYER

Forgiving Father, only your pardon and forgiveness can prepare us for the final Day of the Lord. We are sinners. Forgive us. Cleanse us. Renew us. Make us holy so we can live for you today and be ready for you when you come again on your day. Amen.

VI. DEEPER DISCOVERIES

A Christian Reading of Prophecy

The prophets were Old Testament personalities living under the old covenant seeking to bring Jewish people to renewal of their covenant faithfulness to God. They had not yet experienced the grace and love of Jesus expressed on the cross. We have a fuller, richer experience of God's grace than they did.

This presents us with a challenge. How do we read their words? We cannot simply read them as pre-Christian believers, for that is not who we are. Yet to import the Christian gospel into the prophets' messages is to add something to their words that they did not know. We cannot be content simply with the prophet's original intention for his audience because we have already seen more fulfillment of the message than the prophets themselves ever could have expected.

What can we do? No one has the final definitive answer, so humility must rule anything we teach on this issue. But we can offer a few guidelines illustrated by Joel's Day of the Lord presentation.

1. Learn the theological truth the prophet taught and the practical application the prophet desired from his audience. Joel taught the Day of the Lord and called for repentance from his people.

2. Determine where the prophet applied predictions or descriptions to his immediate situation, where he left them to the future, and where he pointed them to the final chapter of history. The prophet Joel pointed to a pouring out of the Spirit in a time when people would call on the Lord and be saved, but he also pointed to a future for Jerusalem that would last forever.

3. See how the New Testament has expanded or deepened our understanding of the prophet's theological truth and its practical application. Determine if the New Testament has pointed to a fulfillment of the prophecy and if it has left open opportunities for still future fulfillments. Acts 2 interprets Pentecost as the fulfillment of Joel's future Day of the Lord when thousands believed and were saved, but it also points forward to an ultimate Day of the Lord.

4. Rephrase the theological truth, incorporating both the teaching of the prophet and the expanded fulfillment seen in the New Testament. The Day of the Lord is any point in history where God intervenes to bring judgment on disbelieving, disobeying people, but it has extraordinary expression in times like Pentecost and will have an ultimate expression in the final judgment. The Day of the Lord calls people to repent, trust Jesus, be baptized in his name, and act on his teachings.

5. Commit yourself to believe the theological truth and to incorporate its practical applications into your daily life.

Joel spoke of the Day of the Lord as the central theological truth of his message. He took a term already familiar to his audience and probably already in use among earlier prophetic colleagues and enriched its meaning. Following up on Amos's teaching, Joel showed a dual nature to this teaching.

The Day of the Lord was not just the traditional day of salvation that the Jewish people expected God to give them when they met their enemies on the battlefield. The Day of the Lord could also be described in terms of locust plagues, enemy armies, or natural catastrophes striking God's people. This meant the Day of the Lord could be used to describe several distinct dates on the ongoing human calendar.

Joel pointed beyond the series of days of the Lord to a day of blessing when God would pour out his Spirit on all people (Joel 2:28). Ultimately, however, Joel described a final day when "Jerusalem will be holy; never again will foreigners invade her" (Joel 3:17).

The New Testament applied Joel's teaching to the coming of the Holy Spirit at Pentecost. This was the expected Day of the Lord. It was a day when many people called on the name of the Lord and were saved (Joel 2:32; Acts 2:14–21, 41).

But the New Testament pointed far beyond Pentecost to a day of final judgment seen in Mark 13; Matthew 25; and especially the Book of Revelation. On this day every knee will bow before Jesus, the Christ, and confess that he is Lord. On that day judgment will divide the entire human population of all times into two groups—sheep and goats. On that day God's faithful sheep will receive eternal rewards and enter into eternal life, while the unbelieving goats will face final and eternal judgment.

Joel did not spell out the final judgment in terms of Jesus of Nazareth. He did not describe eternal life in New Testament terms. He did not describe hell in the way the New Testament does.

Still, Joel gives us the starting point to talk about the Day of the Lord. He prepares us to look in our own generation to extraordinary manifestations of God at work in our world to bring people to confess him as the only true God. He lets us see Pentecost as something for which God had prepared long before the amazing day of communication and salvation came. From Joel's words, we could not explain or expect everything that came from Pentecost, but with Joel's words we can more clearly understand what happened on Pentecost.

And Joel lets us look forward, knowing that God has always planned a day of final salvation and judgment. The New Testament sharpens the contours of our understanding of this day, but Joel lets us see the sharp divide between the future of God's people and the future of those who are not God's people.

Joel called on his generation to repent and seek God's pardon. He used the language of fasting and mourning rituals to describe the proper response. He used pardon for guilt as the result of such repentance. At Pentecost, Peter made the invitation even more clear: "'Repent,' Peter said to them, 'and be baptized, each of you, in the name of Jesus the Messiah for the forgiveness of your sins, and you will receive the gift of the Holy Spirit'" (Acts 2:38 HCSB).

Matthew 25 takes the practical application and the promised result a step further:

> The King will say to those on His right, 'Come, you who are blessed by My Father, inherit the kingdom prepared for you from the foundation of the world.' . . . And the King will answer them, 'I assure you: Whatever you did for one of the least of these brothers of Mine, you did for Me.' Then He will also say to those on the left, 'Depart from Me, you who are cursed, into the eternal fire prepared for the Devil and his angels.' . . . Then He will answer them, 'I assure you: Whatever you did not do for one of the least of these, you did not do for Me either.' And they will go away into eternal punishment, but the righteous into eternal life (Matt. 25:34,40–41,45–46 HCSB).

The Christian thus takes the Day of the Lord theme from Joel, extends it to a fulfillment of promise in Acts 2, and looks beyond to the final fulfillment of Matthew 25 among other passages. In so doing, the Christian reader of Joel finds a call to repent, a call to depend on God for pardon, a call to trust Jesus for salvation, and a call to carry on the ministry of Jesus to "one of the least of these" (Matt. 25:40). The Christian reader also knows that God in Jesus Christ is the Judge, and that he cannot assume any verdict, not even one for himself. He can only trust Jesus in absolute faith and follow his teaching.

VII. TEACHING OUTLINE

A. INTRODUCTION
1. Lead Story: "I Can't Pray for Terrorists"
2. Context: Joel pictured the Day of the Lord from different perspectives with different images. He comes to the final chapter to summarize not the present-day experience of the Day of the Lord, but the final event.
3. Transition: The Day of the Lord is a central biblical teaching that differentiates Christian belief from that of most other religions. It points to a final moment in history when every person who ever lived will face the Savior of the world and hear his final destiny announced.

B. COMMENTARY
1. Judging Jehoshaphat's Valley (3:1–12)
2. Day of Decision (3:13–16)
3. The Day of the LORD's Dwelling in Zion (3:17–21)

C. CONCLUSION: ACTING ON THE ABSURD

VIII. ISSUES FOR DISCUSSION

1. How can the Day of the Lord be a day of locusts, armies, and natural events that destroy Jerusalem and Judah and also be an experience of the Spirit and an experience of restoring the fortunes of Judah and Jerusalem?

2. Do modern-day believers share in the experience of Pentecost in any way?

3. Do we have the right to label a modern experience as a Day of the Lord?

4. In what way can we use the Day of the Lord predictions of Joel to condemn modern nations who do not stand for justice and righteousness?

5. Can you be certain of the verdict God will pronounce on you at the final judgment? Why or why not?

Introduction to

Amos

The first prophet to leave his message behind in written form, Amos was a shepherd and tender of fruit trees (Amos 1:1; 7:14) in the small town of Tekoa (Amos 1:1) about ten miles south of Jerusalem in the Southern Kingdom of Judah. God surprised him one day and told him to go north, into the kingdom of Israel, and prophesy. This is about as much as we know about Amos. At first glance, we may assume Amos was an uneducated man of little means, but he may have been a respected rural landowner who raised both sheep and cattle, feeding the animals with the fruit of the sycamore fig tree. He fiercely denied any connection to professional prophets or professional ministers of any kind. He ministered only because God chose to use a rural businessman to try to straighten out the religious leaders and practices of his day.

Amos did all this during the reigns of King Uzziah of Judah (792–740 B.C.) and King Jeroboam II of Israel (793–753) (Amos 1:1). But that is the only information we have about the date of his ministry except that it was two years before the earthquake (Amos 1:1). Archaeologists have found evidence of an earthquake in the excavations at Hazor that could have happened about 750 B.C. Long years later Zechariah (Zech. 14:4–5) remembered this earthquake. The Jewish historian Josephus connects the quake with the illness of King Uzziah about 760. Amos apparently addressed the nation of Israel at the highest point of its political power, which would be shortly after Jeroboam II restored Israel's boundaries to those described by Amos in 6:14. This also was around 760 B.C. (2 Kgs. 13:23–25).

Archaelogical evidence from this time shows opulence and wealth at several places in Israel, including Megiddo, Tirzah, Hazor, Dan, and Samaria. Thus we would place Amos a couple of years before 760 B.C. It may be that his brief ministry lasted less than a year.

Power came to Israel because other powers in the Ancient Near East had weakened or were preoccupied with other matters. Assyria had defeated Syria about 805 B.C. This removed Israel's chief rival. But then weak kings forced Assyria to withdraw from the power structures in Palestine. In the south kings from Libya and Sudan wrestled over Egypt, robbing it of the power to march northward and exercise control, so King Jeroboam of Israel stood alone as the man of power. Only King Uzziah of Judah provided any counterbalance to Jeroboam's thirst for territory, fame, and control.

Most importantly, Jeroboam controlled the trade routes through the Mediterranean coast and through the King's Highway east of the Jordan River. Amos spoke to a group enjoying their economic windfall (Amos 8:5–6) and their opportunity to party and live the life of ease (Amos 4:1–2).

Religion had become a big business, as people carried on the traditions of the fathers with glamorous festivals and banquets. But, as Amos was quick to show, such religion may have been in the old traditional places, but it was far from the old traditional purposes and motivations.

Five visions (Amos 7:1–3,4–6,7–9; 8:1–3; 9:1–4) provided the content for Amos's preaching along with God's ongoing revelation of his message. The result was an onerous task. Amos had to list his own Judah and Israel, his audience, among the nations foreign to God and thus facing his judgment. He had to argue with a religious people that their religious practices, though rooted in ancient tradition, made them sinners, not saints, in God's eyes. He took on common people and religious and political leaders. He accused women as well as men. He stood the nation's high priest down in face-to-face confrontation. He even stood toe to toe with God and gained time for the people as God relented from his expressed purpose of judgment.

Amos was a courageous man with a contagious faith who embarked on an outrageous mission. Ultimately, he did not succeed in gaining a hearing for God from the people. Rather, they ultimately pushed him back home to Judah, but not before the land had been warned. The citizens of Israel had no one but themselves to blame when they were unprepared to face God.

Amos did not react with joy at the bad news for his northern neighbors. He interceded for them, and God relented from his punishment (Amos 7:3,6). He prophesied only at God's command. King and priest issued contrary commands, seeking to stop the prophet, but he was loyal to his task (Amos 7:10–17). Sadly, one day God would be silent, and the people would suffer a famine of the word of God (Amos 8:12).

According to Amos, life under God includes the life of all peoples in all nations (Amos 1:3–2:16). God has expectations of how people carry out war (Amos 1:3,13; 2:2), how they treat other people and nations (Amos 1:6,9,11), how they maintain treaty and covenant commitments (Amos 1:9), how they deal with their own emotions and frustrations (Amos 1:11), and how they handle greed and power (Amos 1:13). God also controls the destiny of every nation and gives them their land just as he did for Israel (Amos 9:7). One day God will give Edom and all the nations into the hands of a restored Southern Kingdom under a descendant of David (Amos 9:11–12).

Greed and hunger for material prosperity must not determine the actions of God's people (Amos 3:9–10,15; 4:1; 5:11; 6:3–6; 8:5–6). Such materialism blinds them so they "do not know how to do right" (Amos 3:10). It makes them "complacent" with a false sense of security (Amos 6:1). They must "let justice roll on like a river, righteousness like a never-failing stream" (Amos 5:24).

Amos has one central point: Israel must "prepare to meet your God" (Amos 4:12). The Lord's people have forsaken him and created a life opposed to everything God taught them. They must face the future with fear, because God "will punish you for all your sins" (Amos 3:2). God disciplined them and sought to bring them to repentance (Amos 4:6–11). They are beginning to see disasters around them and should know that only God is capable of causing such troubles (Amos 2:3–6).

Amos has no clear promise of hope for God's sinful people. They must not expect to escape judgment. They will go into exile (Amos 5:27; 6:7–8,14; 7:17). They must not rely on their religious practices because God hates them (Amos 5:21–23). They must not look for a Day of the Lord that brings victory and salvation because God's day will be darkness and not light (Amos 5:18–20; 8:9–14). If they seek God, seek good, and maintain justice, "perhaps the LORD God Almighty will have mercy on the remnant of Joseph" (Amos 5:15).

That *perhaps* of mercy receives a small dash of definition—a definition surprising to Israel and King Jeroboam, because God promises only to "restore David's fallen tent" (Amos 9:11). This does mean the end of Israel because only the Southern Kingdom has a future, and that after it falls. Then the Southern Kingdom will again be Israel with new prosperity "never again to be uprooted from the land I have given them" (Amos 9:15). Now for the only time in the book the Lord is "your God" in the true sense of the word (Amos 2:8; 4:12; 5:26; 8:14).

Amos 1:1–2:16

Who's on God's Most-Wanted List?

"God's children need discipline to be useful members of His family."

Billy Graham

Amos 1:1–2:16

IN A NUTSHELL

God speaks from Zion, his earthly residence in Jerusalem, through his chosen prophet Amos. He details the sins of Syria, the Philistines, Tyre, Edom, the Ammonites, Moab, Judah, and Israel with the threat not to turn back his wrath from each of them. He then shows all he has done for Israel and paints the destruction faced by the sinful nation.

Who's on God's Most-Wanted List?

I. INTRODUCTION

Capturing Public Enemy #1

$\mathcal{T}$he newspaper headlines remain frozen in our memories. The joys reverberate as we recall the happy headline: "Saddam Hussein Captured!"

Amos painted equally interesting headlines for the Northern Kingdom (Israel), to whom he proclaimed God's message. He announced God's capture and punishment of each of the nations surrounding Israel. You can hear Israel shout, "Amen!" as the prophet calls the name of each nation. Then the prophet added one more name to the list—Israel. God's people find themselves on the list of God's most-wanted enemies.

II. COMMENTARY

Who's on God's Most-Wanted List?

> **MAIN IDEA:** *God's judgment awaits any nation that forgets the basic rules of human decency, but it is even more certain when God's own people forget him, his teachings, and all he has done for them.*

Amos's Message Shakes the Earth (1:1–2)

> **SUPPORTING IDEA:** *God's message of judgment comes through the human messenger.*

1:1. Amos traveled from his rural home in **Tekoa** about ten miles south of Jerusalem to announce God's judgment on **Israel**, the Northern Kingdom. Amos had learned of God's protection and care the hard way, caring for his sheep and tending his trees (Amos 7:14–15) on the border between farmland and desert. To the east of his village lay the "Desert of Tekoa" (2 Chr. 20:20).

Amos dated his ministry in both a general and specific way. Generally speaking, he prophesied during the reign of **Uzziah** in Judah (783–742 B.C.; cp. 2 Kgs. 14:21–15:34) and **Jeroboam** II in Israel (786–746 B.C.; cp. 2 Kgs. 14:23–29). More specifically, he delivered his message **two years before the earthquake** (Zech. 14:5). Some archaeological evidence may point to an earthquake about 765 to 760 B.C. (see NAC, 19B, 38). This was a time of great prosperity for both the Northern Kingdom and the Southern Kingdom as they regained territory previously lost to Syria and other small kingdoms. Reference to an earthquake following Amos's ministry reminds the reader that Amos's words came true. God brought judgment on his people shortly after Amos proclaimed God's message. The rest of the book reverberates with earthshaking news and warnings.

1:2. Almost two hundred years had passed since Jeroboam I separated the northern tribes from the southern tribes. This meant the southern prophet had a hard job trying to convince northern leaders and citizens that he had God's message for them. Amos used what appears to us as strange strategy. He announced that his message came from the God who lived in and spoke from **Jerusalem** (note that here **Zion** is simply a synonym for Jerusalem). That was precisely what northerners did not want to hear. Their worship centered in Bethel and Dan (1 Kgs. 12:29–30). They believed God spoke from Bethel and Dan, not from Jerusalem.

The citizens of the Northern Kingdom needed to hear the message. False worship at false worship centers was a major part of their sin. They needed to return to worship at the place God had chosen, not the place they wanted. Continued sin would lead to God's judgment—judgment turning the most fertile farmland and **pastures** to arid dirt, good for nothing. Mount **Carmel** represented Israel's most lush fertility (Isa. 35:2). But Amos pointed to the day when fertile Carmel would wither.

B Doom on Damascus for Military Mayhem (1:3–5)

SUPPORTING IDEA: *Gaining power through acts of terror courts divine judgment.*

1:3. Damascus is the capital of Syria today, just as it was the capital of Aram or Syria in Amos's day. It had long been a thorn in the side of Judah and Israel (1 Kg. 15:16–22; Isa. 7:6). Among their sins was that of military cruelty as they took over **Gilead**, an Israelite territory east of the Jordan River (2 Kgs. 8:12). The image comes from the grain harvest, where grain was spread on the floor and separated from the stalk by dragging an implement with iron teeth over it (Isa. 28:27). God condemned the Syrians for invading Gilead, taking prisoners of war including women and children, and treating them like grain on the threshing floor.

1:4. Hazel (1 Kgs. 19:15–17) and **Ben-Hadad** (2 Kgs. 6:24) were royal names used by the kings of Damascus. The royal house had instigated military horror, and it would be the central focus when God came in judgment.

1:5. Military crimes would receive military judgment stretching from the **Valley of Aven** to **Beth Eden**. Both names have symbolic character, *Aven* meaning idolatry, nothingness, guilt and *Beth Eden* meaning house of paradise, making a play on the garden of Eden. The Valley of Aven probably refers to the valley in Lebanon (Josh. 11:17), while Beth Eden was a Syrian (or Aramean) city-state on the Euphrates River two hundred miles from Israel (2 Kgs. 19:12). Military judgment would end the Syrian dynasty and send the people into exile. The Syrians would go back where they came from—Kir (Amos 9:7).

C Punishing the Philistines for Commerce in Captives (1:6–8)

> **SUPPORTING IDEA:** *Human beings have innate value and must not be sold like commercial cargo.*

1:6. The Philistines were part of the Sea Peoples, a group of related peoples who came from lands and islands of the northern Mediterranean and invaded the eastern and southern Mediterranean coastal lands. Among their stopping places were Crete (Jer. 47:4); Cyprus (Num. 24:24); and Ugarit. They attacked Egypt shortly before 1200 B.C. and invaded Palestine shortly after 1200 B.C. Even when Pharaoh Ramesses III of Egypt defeated them about 1190 B.C., he still had to let them settle the coast of Palestine (Deut. 2:23). They eventually centered in five cities—Gaza, Ashkelon, Ashdod, Ekron, and Gath. They were the first major threat to Israel after they settled in the promised land (1 Sam. 4:7).

The Philistines did not torment prisoners of war as Syria did. But they rejected their worth as humans and **sold them** on the open market to the highest bidder. They treated people as produce.

1:7–8. God's verdict was absolute destruction of all the Philistine cities. People are not merchandise to be used for profit. No matter their land of origin, their race, their color, their language, their past history, all people still represent God's highest creative accomplishment—the image of God himself. They must be respected as people of value and not be reduced to the role of things (Exod. 21:16).

D Trouble for Tyre, the Treaty Breaker (1:9–10)

> **SUPPORTING IDEA:** *God expects individuals and nations to be true to their word and not to break their promises.*

1:9. Tyre was a proud Phoenician city on an island off the coast of the Mediterranean Sea about twenty-five miles south of Sidon, the other major Phoenician city. David and Solomon had depended on alliances with Tyre to get building materials, builders, and access to the sea. Tyre and Sidon controlled a virtual monopoly of commercial activities in the eastern Mediterranean. Ahab's queen Jezebel from Tyre gave Baal worship a strong foothold in Israel about 870 B.C. (Josh. 19:29).

Tyre duplicated the Philistines' terroristic atrocities and went them one better. Tyre broke an international alliance **treaty**. Their prisoners of war were supposed to be their allies. Such betrayal deserves punishment.

1:10. So Tyre faced God's **fire**. Even this island stronghold was not immune to God's judgment. **Fortresses** that other nations despaired of reaching, God took in stride.

E Edom's End Comes When Family Faithfulness Fails (1:11–12)

SUPPORTING IDEA: *Nations and individuals are expected to support and protect family, so when love fails inside the family, punishment is on the way.*

1:11. Edom traced its origin to Esau, Jacob's brother (Gen. 25:30). God had given Edom special privileges (Deut. 2:4–5). Still, Edom joined with others in attacking Israel and especially Judah. This harassment reached all the way from the wilderness wanderings to King Uzziah, Amos's contemporary (Num. 20:14–21; 1 Kgs. 11:14–25). Later, other prophets would echo Amos's judgment on Edom (Isa. 34; Obad. 11).

Stifling all compassion reads literally "he destroyed his motherly love" or "his mercy." Those feelings of closeness and commitment that should characterize all family relationships had gone sour. Edom had destroyed them and taken the **sword** after his **brother**. What destroys family relationships? Edom proves example number one—**anger** that a person refuses to give up. In parallel statements the Hebrew text describes Edom's wrath as "his anger tears forever; his rage endures for the duration."

1:12. Edom's major cities faced God's destruction. **Bozrah** was Edom's ancient capital located near the modern village of Buseirah in northern Edom (1 Chr. 1:44). **Teman** means "south" in Hebrew. This apparently was the name of a city or region in southern Edom (Jer. 49:7,20). High in Edom's mountains, these cities appeared invincible. But both Tyre and Edom would discover that no fortress could protect when God decided to punish.

F Army Atrocities Assure Ammon's Anguish (1:13–15)

SUPPORTING IDEA: *Greed and hunger for power do not justify brutality in dealing with enemy captives.*

1:13. The origin of **Ammon** was connected to Lot, Abraham's nephew (Gen. 19:36–38), so here, too, family relationships are involved. During the wilderness journeys, Israel faced opposition from the Ammonites (Num. 21:21–25). These two nations separated by the Jordan River continually clashed throughout their history (1 Sam. 11:1–11; 2 Kgs. 14:25).

One sure way to weaken an enemy's armed forces is to ensure that no babies are born in the nation. To do this, armies **ripped open the pregnant women** when they captured a city. This was apparently a common warfare strategy, used especially against those being taken into exile (2 Kgs. 8:12). Ammon used this tactic in dealing with Israel, their close neighbor, as they sought to regain the land of **Gilead** taken from them by the Israelites under Moses.

1:14. The Lord had a response to such inhumane actions. God's **fire** would fall on **Rabbah**, Ammon's capital near modern Amman, Jordan (Josh. 13:25). God would use enemy armies and supernatural storms to deliver his punishment on Ammon.

1:15. God's punishment against Ammon would bring total loss for the nation. Its **king** and government **officials** would be exiled out of their land.

G Moab's Murders Mean Mourning (2:1–3)

SUPPORTING IDEA: *Even archenemies do not deserve irreverent treatment and desecration.*

2:1. Like Ammon, Moab's beginnings are traced to Abraham's nephew Lot (Gen. 19:37). Situated between Ammon and Edom and between the Dead Sea and the Arabian Desert, **Moab** had little hope for expansion. They gained Israel's enmity by refusing to allow the wilderness wanderers to pass through their territory (Num. 22:1–24:25). Worse still, Moabites lured Israelites into false worship (Num. 25:1–5). On the other hand, God protected Moab, refusing to let Israel conquer Moabite territory (Deut. 2:9).

Amos accused Moab of capturing **Edom's king** and burning his remains, even his **bones**, apparently to prevent any hope of bodily resurrection (1 Cor. 15:35–54). Here was a family feud taken to the extreme—seeking to prevent military success and to rob others of rewards beyond the grave.

2:2. Again God would use human warfare as his agent of punishment. **Kerioth** would face God's destructive **fire**. Kerioth is a Hebrew term for "cities" but also apparently the name of a Moabite town (Jer. 48:24,41). The Moabite Stone points to Kerioth as a religious center, so God would bring punishment on Moab's central religious site because they had performed horrendous atrocities against a neighbor's religious beliefs.

2:3. The exile that Ammon's officials faced was too good for Edom. Their officials would receive God's death sentence.

🄷 Judgment on Judah for Leaving the Law (2:4–5)

SUPPORTING IDEA: *God's chosen people may become foreigners in his sight if they refuse to follow his leadership.*

2:4. God had a big surprise for his people. Judgment begins at home. Listing other nations facing judgment was only a prelude. The real discipline would begin in **Judah**. They were God's chosen people. Their national center was in Jerusalem, the city from which God himself spoke (Amos 1:2). Other nations could be judged on the basis of moral law resting in the heart of every person and acknowledged by international treaties and the laws of every nation.

God's people faced even more severe punishment because they possessed God's covenant **law** and had promised to obey it (Exod. 19–20). Their history was one of disobedience of the worst kind, substituting **false gods** for the God of Israel. This violated the first of the Ten Commandments. It went against the confession of the Shema (Deut. 6:4–9) and against the covenant ceremony of Joshua 24. Such disobedience went all the way back to **their ancestors**, the original patriarchs (Gen. 31:53), who worshipped **gods** "beyond the River and in Egypt" (Josh. 24:14).

2:5. Judah believed the God of Israel would protect them forever because they were his people. Amos indicated otherwise. God's plan for Judah was just like his plan for the other foreign nations—**fire** and destruction.

🄸 Israel's Injustice Invites the Divine Doomsday (2:6–16)

SUPPORTING IDEA: *God's own people cannot escape judgment when they practice injustice, immorality, and false religion.*

2:6–8. Seven nations should complete the perfect list. It did not. God had one more surprise. He added **Israel** to the list. The Northern Kingdom to whom Amos spoke directly was included among God's most-wanted enemies.

Only here did Amos complete the list of **four** sins. They made money by selling the **righteous** poor among God's people. Those whom they did not sell, they manipulated and denigrated for their own advantage. In so doing they bypassed the entire justice system that God had established. They were equally offensive to both genders, humiliating the women with their sexual demands in flagrant opposition to God's law (Deut. 27:20). Israel was called to be holy as God was holy (Lev. 19:2). They represented the holy God to the world. To violate God's covenant rules for life was to take God's name in vain and thus to profane God's **holy name**.

The law allowed Israelites to take **garments** from a person as **pledge** for a debt, but the garments had to be returned before the cold of night set in

(Deut. 24:17). Israel joyfully attended the three sacred festivals each year. These required them to spend several days at the place of worship. There they used such pledge garments to sleep in at night. The law also allowed Israelites to fine others as restitution of damages suffered. These Israelites found excuses to fine the poor, adding to their own riches by collecting for the minor offenses of the poor (Exod. 22:14–17). Adding insult to injury, the rich took the **wine** they collected to pagan services and got drunk in the name of worship.

2:9–11. Israel had forgotten what God had done for them. He had **destroyed the Amorite** (Josh. 11:20). Early in Israel's history Amorites fought against them (Deut. 1:44). Israel should have remembered God's victories over the Amorites, but Israel forgot. Israel should have remembered God's great victories in **Egypt**. But they forgot. God's work for his people Israel was not all ancient history. God also raised **prophets** for the present generation to hear. His word should have directed their history. They should listen to the prophet, remember God's expectations, and obey.

Some did obey. God raised up **Nazirites** as examples of obedience. Israel could see and emulate their faith. Nazirites took a special vow or oath to obey God in special ways (Num. 6:1–21). One important element of the vow led Nazirites to refrain from drinking alcoholic beverages (Judg. 13:4–5).

2:12. God's actions and God's examples for the present generation meant nothing to Israel. They **made the Nazirites drink wine and commanded the prophets not to prophesy.** Israel did not want to be holy to God, and they refused to let those who proved faithful stay faithful.

2:13. God could not forget their sin. Time had run out. God described in great detail his judgment on Israel. They would be crushed like the muddy roadway under a **cart** loaded with **grain**. Or the ruts and holes in the ground create the impression of an earthquake, referring back to Amos 1:1. Whatever the exact image the prophet intended, the feeling it leaves is clear—ominous threat, impending doom.

2:14–16. Human effort, even extraordinary human abilities will be useless. No one can run fast enough to escape. No one is brave enough and skilled enough in war to win the battle. Even if the people of Israel threw away their weapons and armor and rushed away unclothed, the enemy would overtake them. Their enemy was no ordinary army. They would face God's army.

MAIN IDEA REVIEW: *God's judgment awaits any nation that forgets the basic rules of human decency, but it is even more certain when God's own people forget him, his teachings, and all he has done for them.*

III. CONCLUSION

Celebrating Freedom

Freedom is a key word for human beings. We celebrate our freedom to make choices and our freedom to relate to God and to other people. Sometimes we forget that God has freedom, too. He has the freedom to call his people to mission and the freedom to discipline those who refuse to carry out his mission. Israel regarded themselves as the people who had been chosen and blessed by God. They exercised their freedom to gain enjoyment from life and to display their greatness.

What surprises Amos sprang on them! He talked not about their freedom but about God's freedom. God was free to exercise control and discipline over all Israel's neighbors. To that Israel cried, "Amen. Get 'em, God." God is also free to exercise control and discipline over his chosen people. That message Israel did not want to hear. Turning a deaf ear to the message brought extinction for the Northern Kingdom. It can bring the same to us unless we are faithful to God.

PRINCIPLES

- God is not silent; he roars in face of his people's sin.
- All nations face judgment because they know what is right and what is wrong.
- God brings judgment on his people for their economic injustice and their religious unfaithfulness.
- God's judgment is complete, wiping out all aspects of life, religious and material.

APPLICATIONS

- Do not ask God to defeat your enemies if you are not willing to let God discipline your life.
- Do not expect the Bible to contain precise rules that cover all of life's moral decisions. Some things are so clearly wrong that they are etched deeply into your conscience.
- War does not relieve a nation from obeying God's universal moral truths.
- Stifling compassion with personal anger is never right.
- Realize that strong family ties increase moral obligations.
- Turning away from biblical teachings adds to your guilt before God.

- Take care of the poor and needy rather than using them for your own personal and economic advantage.
- Remember all that God has done for you, and worship him in obedience.

IV. LIFE APPLICATION

What Happened to JoBob?

JoBob was such a good man. Kids gathered around wherever he appeared, knowing they would get candy, a warm smile, and a funny story. Young couples often came to his door for advice and encouragement. High schoolers named him their favorite teacher and often asked him questions about life and directions for their future. One mystery surrounded JoBob's life. No one knew what he did on Sunday. He never appeared in church or anywhere else in public. Religion was just not his thing.

Looking back to my fond memories of JoBob, I now face one serious question: What happened to JoBob when he died? Could God decree eternal punishment for a man as kind and good as JoBob? Do I really believe all the stories of judgment the Bible tells me? What can I expect from God when I die?

V. PRAYER

Almighty Father, you are free to make demands on us, discipline us, and punish us. Forgive us when we flaunt our freedom and try to quench yours. Help us to listen to your message. Help us see the sins in our lives and turn away from them. Show us the people whom you want us to help. Give us the wisdom and love to help them. Amen.

VI. DEEPER DISCOVERIES

Sins (1:3,6,9,11,13; 2:1,4,6; 3:14; 4:4; 5:12)

Amos accused the nations of crimes against God. The Hebrew term *pish'e* designated a formal, legal category, including crimes of theft (Gen. 31:36), murder (1 Sam. 24:10–14), robbery (Prov. 28:24), kidnapping (Gen. 50:17), criminal claims on another's property (Exod. 22:8), breaking legal relationships (Isa. 1:28). Such serious legal offenses did not deserve or expect forgiveness, though one might ask for it (Gen. 50:17).

Pish'e was Amos's most serious description of Israel's sin. "The term refers to an open and brazen defiance of God by humans" (Alex Luc, *NIDOTTE*, H7321). "It signifies a willful, knowledgeable violation of a norm or standard.

Beyond that, it represents a willful breach of trust. It occurs most frequently to designate the disruption of an alliance through violation of a covenant" (*ABD* 6:32).

When used in a theological sense, the Hebrew term indicated a crime against God, a breaking away from God, and was often viewed as beyond forgiveness (Josh. 24:19). But the prophet could call the people to repentance for such crimes (Ezek. 14:11), and God could promise to forgive even such crimes against himself (Isa. 44:22).

> Whoever commits *pesha'* does not merely rebel or protest against Yahweh but breaks with him, takes away what is his, robs, embezzles, misappropriates it. Although it always implies a conscious behavior, the term per se does not describe the attitude but the criminal act that consists in removal of property or breach of relationship (Knierim, TLOT, 1036).

We can conclude then that

> although in most treaty violations a vassal rebels against his suzerain, in Amos *pesha'* concerns "a violation of general standards of international morality—universal laws of God—expressed in inhumane treatment of one nation by another." Each nation indicted for *pesha'* in Amos 1 and 2 is guilty of denying Yahweh's authority by asserting their own power (Andersen and Freedman, AB, 231).

VII. TEACHING OUTLINE

A. INTRODUCTION

1. Lead Story: Capturing Public Enemy #1

2. Context: Amos began his book by calling all the nations surrounding Israel to court and pronouncing the verdict for their sins. He narrowed the vision down to Israel's most immediate neighbor and relatives, the Southern Kingdom of Judah, his own people. Finally, Amos zeroed in on Israel, the Northern Kingdom, to whom he spoke directly.

3. Transition: Israel discovered they were God's public enemy #1. In spite of their long history of relationship with God in which he performed numerous miraculous acts to create and sustain them as a nation, Israel had not learned the basic facts about God's expectations and God's reactions when those expectations were not met.

B. COMMENTARY

1. Amos's Message Shakes the Earth (1:1–2)
2. Doom on Damascus for Military Mayhem (1:3–5)
3. Punishing the Philistines for Commerce in Captives (1:6–8)
4. Trouble for Tyre, the Treaty Breaker (1:9–10)
5. Edom's End Comes When Family Faithfulness Fails (1:11–12)
6. Army Atrocities Assure Ammon's Anguish (1:13–15)
7. Moab's Murders Mean Mourning (2:1–3)
8. Judgment on Judah for Leaving the Law (2:4–5)
9. Israel's Injustice Invites the Divine Doomsday (2:6–16)

C. CONCLUSION: CELEBRATING FREEDOM

VIII. ISSUES FOR DISCUSSION

1. Can you name enemies of our nation that you think God should punish? Do you really think God can punish nations in today's world? Do you think he will?
2. Are you guilty of mistreating the poor? Do you do anything in the name of religion that God condemns?
3. Are there any sins that God can list against you as an individual and against our country as a nation? Is God still judging and punishing sin?
4. How do we treat the religious leaders and spiritual role models that God gives our church and our nation?
5. What does God say about our use of drugs, alcohol, and tobacco?

Amos 3:1–15

Catastrophe for the Chosen

I. INTRODUCTION
We Lost Everything!

II. COMMENTARY
A verse-by-verse explanation of these verses.

III. CONCLUSION
Tag! You're It!

An overview of the principles and applications from these verses.

IV. LIFE APPLICATION
Return to Normal

Melding these verses to life.

V. PRAYER
Tying these verses to life with God.

VI. DEEPER DISCOVERIES
Historical, geographical, and grammatical enrichment of the commentary.

VII. TEACHING OUTLINE
Suggested step-by-step group study of these verses.

VIII. ISSUES FOR DISCUSSION
Zeroing these verses in on daily life.

Quote

" *S* in weighs more when it occurs

in the knowledge of divine salvation."

J ö r g   J e r e m i a s

Amos 3:1–15

 I N   A   N U T S H E L L

G od predicts catastrophe for the entire family he brought up from Egypt—both the Northern Kingdom and the Southern Kingdom. Being the only people God has chosen, they must face punishment for all their sins. All evidence points to the coming judgment as an act of God just as much as the exodus was. As with all his plans for his people, God announces them through his prophet. A people who do not know how to do right face destruction. The houses of worship and the houses of luxury will experience God's judgment.

Catastrophe for
the Chosen

I. INTRODUCTION

We Lost Everything!

The words, "Everything's lost! We couldn't save a thing!" haunt my memory each time I see my neighbor. The family left home for an evening of community celebration and fun. Before they returned home, the call came: fire had gutted their beautiful lakeside home. Even today it is difficult to believe how swift and complete the destruction was. The family had to start over from scratch.

Israel's case was different. God warned them again and again that they deserved destruction and that it was not far off. Israel ignored God's warnings until one day they woke up and found that everything was lost. They couldn't save a thing.

II. COMMENTARY

Catastrophe for the Chosen

> **MAIN IDEA:** *God expects a higher degree of obedience and moral living from his chosen people than from other nations, so he punishes his people more severely for their sins.*

🅰 The Covenant's Consequences (3:1–2)

> **SUPPORTING IDEA:** *God expects more from people who know him best, so their punishment is greater.*

3:1. Israel did not want to believe Amos. He started chapters 3–5 the same way with the call to **hear this word**. He showed them why they should believe his word from God and obey it.

First, they were the **people of Israel** (literally, sons of Israel). They belonged to the family of the patriarch Jacob to whom God had appeared at their sanctuary Bethel with his promise of blessing for the nation (Gen. 28:10–22).

Second, they were an extended **family**. They were not individuals looking out for themselves. They had common interests and common responsibilities.

They had to hear God's message and obey it in the interest of the larger clan, not just for their own sakes.

Third, they had a special reason for obedience—God's saving history with them. God had **brought** them up from slavery in **Egypt** to make them into a nation. The only satisfactory response would be to show their gratitude for salvation through obedience to their Savior.

3:2. God had one final reason why Israel should obey. They were the special **chosen** people of God. Out **of all the families of the earth** he had made a covenant with them (Josh. 24). They had agreed to obey the covenant regulations and expectations because they knew God would fulfill his promises to the patriarchs. God had kept his covenant promises. Israel had not kept theirs. Thus we hear the awesome prophetic word **therefore** predicting disaster. A people who do not keep covenant promises face God's covenant lawsuit where God brings charges against his people and then announces the verdict: punishment for all their sins.

B The Consistency of God's Unnatural Causes (3:3–8)

SUPPORTING IDEA: *Just as you can predict certain results in nature, so you can explain the supernatural destruction of a city as divine action.*

3:3. Dire actions have direct causes. Amos listed a series of rhetorical questions with obvious "no" answers. Israel had to draw catastrophic consequences from them. First, **two** people do not just happen to meet and travel **together**. They schedule an appointment. So Israel's walk with God was no accident. God had planned it and scheduled it, but now Israel was failing to appear for their scheduled appointment.

3:4. The world of nature, especially that of a **lion**, has an obvious lesson for us. A lion's **roar** or **growl** means the king of beasts is on the prowl and has **caught** something to eat. So God does not roar without reason. His thunderous voice warns us that he comes in judgment.

3:5. Birds, too, can become our instructors. The bird will not swoop down into a trap if it has no tempting bait. The other side of the picture is that the **trap** does not suddenly **spring up** from the ground unless a victim has set it off. God's roaring judgment doesn't just happen. Something sets it off.

3:6. In 2:6–12 Amos had listed Israel's dreadful actions, the dire causes of the punishment he predicted. Now he zeroes in on the reality of that judgment. The **trumpet** sound was the alarm signal, announcing an approaching enemy army. Certainly the **city** would **tremble** at such a sound. But Israel needed to think one stage deeper. Why would an enemy bring disaster on the city of God's people? The answer was clear—**the LORD caused it.**

3:7. Amos is ready to drive home his point. God did not bring disaster on a city on the spur of the moment. He announced his intentions to his people, and he announced them by **revealing his plan to his servants the prophets**. Amos was claiming that his preaching was God's direct warning. The people must believe and obey. If not, they would experience God's disaster.

3:8. Having heard the lion's roar (Amos 1:2), the people should have one reaction—fear. They should not condemn the prophet. He was only making the natural response to God's lion-like voice. He shared their fear, but he must proclaim the message that God had spoken.

Ⓒ The Message for the Messenger (3:9–11)

SUPPORTING IDEA: *A society that forgets how to do right can only do wrong, and it deserves God's judgment.*

3:9. God prepares heralds for international travel. They are to take messages to the Philistines and the Egyptians. In battles with Syria and Assyria, Israel constantly looked to the southwest for help, first to the Philistines and then to the Egyptians. Neither proved to be much of an ally (Amos 1:6–8).

So God turned the tables. He sent heralds or political messengers to Israel's supposed allies, calling them to be his witnesses. They should assemble on the mountains of Samaria, not to attack Israel and not to defend Israel. No, they were called to Israel's capital city to see the problems within the nation of Israel. **Great unrest** and **oppression** dominated the city. "Unrest" refers to dismay, consternation, panic, or turmoil caused by war and caused especially by God as he wins wars for or against his people (Deut. 7:23).

Oppression "frequently describe(s) various forms of social injustice by which the rich in Israelite society oppressed the poor. . . . People most likely to be mistreated and socially oppressed were those without adequate defense of their rights, viz., the widow, orphan, sojourner, and the poor" (I. Swart, *NIDOTTE*, 6943). Even foreigners could testify to the immoral situation in Israel.

3:10. How did the people of God become oppressors who caused panic among their own people? They forgot the basic lesson God had tried to teach them throughout their history. **They do not know how to do right.** They could no longer distinguish between good and bad, right and wrong. The result was that they **hoard plunder and loot in their fortresses**. These two words most often mean "violence and destruction." The prophet makes a play on words. Israel used violence and destruction of the poor to gain their wealth and then carefully hid the money away in the strongest military fortress, thinking it was safe from all intruders. God had another thought. What they hid was not wealth but violence and destruction—two sins that God must punish (Ezek. 45:9).

3:11. God's ominous **therefore** rings out. The specifics of judgment are coming. Your **plunder** is not safe because **an enemy**, mysterious by not being identified, will come to plunder the **fortresses** where the "wealth" of violence and destruction is so carefully stored. We can't take it with us when God comes calling in judgment.

D Ironic Salvation (3:12–15)

SUPPORTING IDEA: *False religion and greed join social injustice in inviting God's judgment on his people.*

3:12. This is what the LORD says, or a bit more literally "Thus says Yahweh," is a Hebrew messenger formula. A messenger or herald receives a word from his master or ruler and then delivers the message to a third party. The messenger introduces his message with this formula to indicate that the words do not come from him but from the master or ruler. Amos used the same formula to introduce each oracle against a foreign nation in chapters 1 and 2. The formula puts the authority of heaven behind the prophetic announcement.

This announcement is unusual since it uses a simile to make the point and ironically speaks of salvation in such a way as to describe destruction. Often prophets inserted messages of salvation into the dark picture of judgment they painted. At times such salvation pictures come in terms of the salvation of a remnant. That is hardly the case here.

Exodus 22:13 describes the procedure to be followed by a shepherd or some other person who had charge of animals that did not belong to him: "If it was torn to pieces by a wild animal, he shall bring in the remains as evidence and he will not be required to pay for the torn animal." The lion has the animal; the shepherd has only a few pieces, enough to show the lion's destruction. In the same way Israel will be **saved**, or more literally, "delivered"—a word used often to describe God's victory for his people in battle.

The HCSB clarifies the meaning of the last part of Amos 3:12: "So the Israelites who live in Samaria will be rescued with only the corner of a bed or the cushion of a couch." Israel will escape the enemy attack owning only a few pieces of a bed. This hardly qualifies as deliverance or salvation. Any people who have acted as Israel has acted and who still expect deliverance are in for a big surprise.

3:13. Again the messenger is called to attention. Just as Egypt and Ashdod had served as God's witnesses, now Amos is called on to hear God's message and to testify against Israel. **The house of Jacob** is a way of tying Israel closer to their patriarchal heritage, only to give a message that cancels the promises to the patriarchs. The message comes from **the LORD God Almighty**, or closer to the Hebrew text, "the Lord Yahweh, the God of Hosts." Amos stacks up traditional terms to show his authority and to prepare for the disastrous picture he must paint of Israel's future.

3:14. The day of punishment does not have to be announced. It is now assumed. Israel looked for the Day of the Lord as a day of salvation. But God would bring a dark day of disaster instead.

Religious sins and economic sins had caused judgment (Amos 2:6–8). Now Bethel, the site of religious practices, would be destroyed, and the luxurious results of economic sins would be demolished (for Bethel, see comments on Amos 4:4). The altars (Amos 2:8) would be wiped out. The **horns of the altar** were vital to the atonement rites of Israel (Exod. 29:12). An accused person could go to the worship place and grasp the horns of the altar to avoid being punished without a trial (1 Kgs. 2:28). When the altar's horns fall to the ground, so do Israel's hopes for atonement and refuge.

3:15. Israel's upper classes had so oppressed the poor that they could afford luxurious **houses**. These fancy houses apparently had an upper floor equipped to catch cool breezes for hot times and a lower story with a heating system to protect against the cold. Or the rich may have had what only kings could generally afford—a **summer house** in the hills and a **winter house** in the valleys. These **mansions** would feel the heat as God's fire ruined them. No matter how much money and effort were put into importing **ivory** for decorative inlays, wealth and power could not protect the owners against God's certain judgment.

> **MAIN IDEA REVIEW:** *God expects a higher degree of obedience and moral living from his chosen people than from other nations, and he punishes his people more severely for their sins.*

III. CONCLUSION

Tag! You're It!

"Tag! You're it!" were some of the worst words I heard as I was growing up in Sweetwater, Texas. I just happened to belong to the generation that produced the best, biggest, fastest football team in the school's history. The team went to the state finals in Texas; eighteen went on to major college scholarships. Many of the players lived in my neighborhood. Most were a year or two older than I was. All were bigger and faster. When they tagged me "It," the fun began—at least for them. They knew I could not catch one of them to make them "It."

Amos informed Israel that they were "It." No longer would God work to defeat their enemies. Now God's focus zeroed in on Israel. Just like me, they had no resources with which to escape. They were at God's mercy. The Lord had spoken. The prophet had relayed the message. The people chosen for blessing from all the families of the earth had now been chosen for God's destruction.

PRINCIPLES

- God's people are different from the rest of the world because God has chosen them.
- God's people have a greater responsibility before him because they have been given a greater opportunity for service.
- God controls the destiny of all nations.
- God has chosen to reveal his purposes to his people through his prophets.
- God's people forget the difference between right and wrong when they let sin take charge of their lives.
- God's punishment often deprives people of the things they like best and of the things involved in their sin.

APPLICATIONS

- Thank God for making you part of his chosen people.
- Examine your worship practices to see where they focus on what you enjoy rather than on expressing praise to God.
- List ways in which the material resources you own have been gathered at the expense of the impoverished people of the world.
- Find ways you can restore respect and resources to the poor of your community.
- Study the Scriptures so you will understand God's Word and ways.

IV. LIFE APPLICATION

Return to Normal

9/11! Two numbers that communicate so much to so many! A snoozing nation woke up to its vulnerability. But it wasn't long before the nation quietly returned to normal. A few inconveniences such as increased airport security have affected our lives. But the wake-up call did not last long. Most of us have gone back to business as usual.

Israel heard Amos's explicit warning. Business as usual, life as normal would not satisfy God. He expected more. He demanded that a nation become aware of its moral deficiencies and its religious hypocrisies. Amos painted a bleak picture for Israel. Forty years later the Northern Kingdom disappeared from world history, and the ten lost tribes were scattered across the

Assyrian Empire. God's people never thought it could happen. Could it happen to us today?

V. PRAYER

Father of all history, get through to our hardened, self-satisfied hearts. Convict us of our sin. Impress upon us your disciplining power. Accept our repentance. Change our hearts. Bring change and conversion—not catastrophe—on us and our nation. Amen.

VI. DEEPER DISCOVERIES

A. Divine Punishment (3:2)

God summarizes his warning to Israel in one Hebrew word: 'epqod ("I will visit you to punish you"). The Hebrew verb is used for a careful inspection or for a special visit with a distinct purpose (Ps. 17:3). Thus the commander musters his troops (1 Sam. 14:17). The census taker enrolls a person on the citizens' list (Num. 4:2) When the visit or inspection reveals a situation that deserves punishment and judgment, the verb's meaning is shifted from a general visitation to a specific action—punish (2 Kgs. 9:34).

Thus the verb occurs twice in Jeremiah 23:2. Because the rulers "have not bestowed care," God will "bestow punishment." We cannot hide our sins from God. He visits us, inspects us, observes our sins, enrolls us among the guilty, and comes to punish us (Exod. 34:7).

B. The Prophet's Vocation (3:7–8)

Amos lived in a society full of prophetic voices. Every religion has its brand of prophets. Many pagan religions in Assyria and Canaan had prophets. Often such pagan prophets were on the government payroll (1 Kgs. 18:19). Such prophets often had special ways of finding and reporting the message from their gods (Jer. 27:9). Some of these prophets were able to fool and seduce God's people into thinking they were true prophets of God (Deut. 13:2–6).

Often groups of God's prophets lived together around a popular worship place (2 Kgs. 2:7) or with the king (1 Kgs. 22). Such prophets often got bad reputations among the people (2 Kgs. 9:11). But prophets on the king's staff also faithfully delivered God's message (2 Sam. 24:11).

The Bible features individual prophets who were not tied to the court or to the temple but who functioned separately (1 Kgs. 18:36). Amos provided his own definition of a prophet—one to whom God confided his plans and one who had to speak publicly because God had roared out his message to him. When that happened, the chosen prophet had no choice. He must prophesy.

VII. TEACHING OUTLINE

A. INTRODUCTION

1. Lead Story: We Lost Everything!

2. Context: A rich nation with a long religious tradition depended on tradition and riches. They forgot God. They forgot how to worship. They forgot the difference between right and wrong. They made too much difference between the privileged few and the impoverished majority. For them God had a message.

3. Transition: The message from God came in several forms, all making the same point. The end was in sight. God planned catastrophe for his people. Could such drastic preaching sweep away the doldrums and awaken a people to revival, renewal, and real religion before it was too late?

B. COMMENTARY

1. The Covenant's Consequences (3:1–2)

2. The Consistency of God's Unnatural Causes (3:3–8)

3. The Message for the Messenger (3:9–11)

4. Ironic Salvation (3:12–15)

C. CONCLUSION: TAG! YOU'RE IT!

VIII. ISSUES FOR DISCUSSION

1. Describe what God has done to bring salvation to you just like he delivered Israel from Egypt. Is God's past history all that is needed for you to be right with him now?

2. What right does God have to punish you for your sins? Do you really believe he will do anything to you now or in the future? Why or why not?

3. In what way does God reveal his plans to his people? Do you know what plans he has for your life? Are you willing to follow his plans?

Amos 4:1-13

Invitation to Sin

I. INTRODUCTION
Sin's Invitation

II. COMMENTARY
A verse-by-verse explanation of these verses.

III. CONCLUSION
Who Runs the Show?

An overview of the principles and applications from these verses.

IV. LIFE APPLICATION
The Worship Debate

Melding these verses to life.

V. PRAYER
Tying these verses to life with God.

VI. DEEPER DISCOVERIES
Historical, geographical, and grammatical enrichment of the commentary.

VII. TEACHING OUTLINE
Suggested step-by-step group study of these verses.

VIII. ISSUES FOR DISCUSSION
Zeroing these verses in on daily life.

"*When* the fight begins within himself,

a man's worth something."

Robert Browning

Amos 4:1–13

IN A NUTSHELL

Amos takes on the women, accusing them of living from one party to the next through their abuse of the poor. He then issues a call to worship at the national shrines so the people can increase their levels of sin. In spite of all God did, Israel would not return to him, so Israel must meet God—not in worship or salvation but in judgment.

Invitation to Sin

I. INTRODUCTION

Sin's Invitation

*I*n his book *Fresh Faith*, Jim Cymbala introduces us to Wendy Alvear. As a youngster, Wendy attended a strict Spanish-speaking church three or four nights a week with her mother. The day came when she accepted Jesus and joined the church, knowing the church had a long list of rules she had to obey. One rule said women and girls wore skirts at all times.

One day Wendy joined her schoolmates in an excursion to an amusement park. Her skirt made her feel uneasy there, so she accepted a friend's invitation to lend her some pants for the afternoon. The trip ran late. Mother was waiting when the bus pulled into school. Getting off the bus in pants, Wendy knew she was trapped. The ensuing attack when she got home convinced Wendy of one thing—no more church for her. As she made the decision, she tried to make a compromise with God. *When I get married and out of this house,* she told herself, *I'll go back to church.*

By the time she was a senior, friends had done more than lend her pants. They contributed habits to her life—smoking, drinking, dance clubs. The habits in turn alienated her from her family and friends. Finally, depression took over. Only the death of her father shortly after his conversion led her back to God and to church.

The downward path to sin can sometimes begin with something simple. Many of us could document our own invitations to sin and how we accepted them. Many of us would begin with something as simple as deciding to wear a pair of pants when we really thought that was wrong. Amos, the prophet, surprised Israel by issuing his own invitation to sin. Are you on Amos's acceptance list?

II. COMMENTARY

Invitation to Sin

MAIN IDEA: *We show we have accepted sin's invitation to disaster by abusing the poor, wasting time with partying, and even by raucous religion without repentance.*

A Casting Out the Cows (4:1–3)

SUPPORTING IDEA: *Pride, prejudice, and demands for preferential treatment pave the path to punishment.*

4:1. The prophetic call to attention (Amos 3:1; 5:1) zeroes in on Israel's females in a not-so-flattering way. They are **cows of Bashan**—well-fed, hard-to-miss women seeking the center of attention at all the socialite parties. Bashan was a pastureland north of the Yarmuk River and east of the Sea of Galilee (Num. 21:33; Isa. 2:13).

The women might look like Bashan's sleek cows, but they lived in **Samaria**, the capital city of Israel. Shortly after 900 B.C., King Omri had built the city as his capital (1 Kgs. 16:23–24). In Amos's day the capital city cows cavorted through the nights with their parties and through the days calling their **husbands** to keep the strong drinks coming.

4:2–3. God responds in a solemn and threatening way. He takes the witness stand and swears an oath that what he is saying is what he will do. God puts forth his **holiness** as the guarantee of his truthfulness. The word *holiness* indicates God's absolute moral perfection, a characteristic that makes him by nature unable to tell a lie.

The content of God's witness sets an aura of terror and doom over Israel. The celebrating women of verse 1 will suffer the same fate as the men of Israel. Their nostrils will be pierced with **hooks** and **fishhooks**, and they will be taken to Assyria.

The phrase **cast out toward Harmon** gives scholars problems. No such place is known unless one changes the Hebrew text a bit and comes up with "Hermon." That would indicate the march northward to Mount Hermon, the home of the Canaanite gods and the direction one must take to end up in Assyria. These proud women and men would thus suffer even more agonizing pain and indignity than they had poured on the poor farmers whose land they had taken away and whom they had denied justice and economic opportunity. If Israel would not stand up for the rights of the poor, weak, and helpless, God would do so in unforgettable fashion.

B Call to Sinful Worship (4:4–5)

SUPPORTING IDEA: *True worship seeks to praise God, not to satisfy man's need for enjoyment.*

4:4. The southern prophet rose to his feet in a northern congregation and issued a call to worship. In so doing he imitated the priests' regular function (Joel 1:14). With irony in his voice, the prophet invited the people to come to Israel's oldest and most sacred worship places. Israel's great founding fathers, the patriarchs, had great worship experiences in **Bethel** (Gen. 13:3). Bethel played an important role in Joshua's conquest and land distribution (Josh. 8:9,12,17) and was an important political and religious center for the judges (Judg. 4:5) and in the early monarchy (1 Sam. 13:2). Bethel became most famous as the site of one of the two temples that King Jeroboam set up for the Northern Kingdom as national places of worship instead of Jerusalem (1 Kgs. 12:29,32–33). This brought God's condemnation (2 Kgs. 10:29).

Still, Bethel remained a center for prophets (2 Kgs. 2:2–3,23). Even after the Northern Kingdom went into exile and disappeared from history, Bethel served as a center of religious instruction and worship (2 Kgs. 17:28) as well as a symbol of shame and failure (Jer. 48:13). In Amos's day Bethel was a political power center for the king and his hireling priest (Amos 7:10,13). Even after the exiles returned to Jerusalem, Bethel was a significant city (Zech. 7:2; Neh. 7:32).

Gilgal near Jericho had an equally illustrious history. There the Israelites under Joshua set up their first campsite and worship site in the promised land (Josh. 4:19–20). The nation's entire male population received circumcision there, and the people celebrated Passover for the first time in the new land. This identified them once again as the obedient people of God, distinct from the murmuring generation of the wilderness years (Josh. 5:2–12). But somewhere along the way, Gilgal became a center of false worship and met prophetic condemnation, betraying its historical beginnings (Hos. 12:11).

Amos shocked and exasperated his northern brothers as he listed their favorite worship places as shrines of sin and their favorite worship practices as perversions. **Sacrifices** (Heb. *zebachim*) were animal offerings intended to create fellowship and communion with God and among the worshippers (1 Sam. 6:15). One problem with this was that the Canaanites used the same term for the same type of offering (Exod. 32:8). Israelites could easily confuse their worship practices for Yahweh, the God of Israel, with their neighbors' practices for Baal or the other gods of the Canaanites (2 Kgs. 16:15).

The tenth or **tithes** reflected both political and religious practice. Among Israel's neighbors the king often collected a tenth as his tax from a village's crops (1 Sam. 8:15,17). Sometimes this was paid to the priest because the government controlled the temple and paid the priest (Amos 7). The Israelites practiced tithing as a religious duty (Lev. 27:30–33; Matt. 23:23).

4:5. A **thank offering** and **freewill offerings** were not required by the law (Lev. 7:12–18). So the Israelites boasted about "going beyond the expected minimum" (Stewart, WBC 31, 338). They did not **love** to sacrifice; they loved to boast. But they had nothing to boast about since even their over-and-above sacrifices ignored the law. The law required unleavened bread. **Leavened bread**, bread made with yeast, was never allowed to be burnt (Lev. 2:11). The law called on Israel to love the Lord their God and their neighbor (Deut. 6:5). Tithes could help the poor and thus demonstrate love of neighbor, but Israel's love was a selfish love, a boastful love, a love that never extended beyond their own nose. Israel too readily answered Amos's ironic call to worship because Israel loved to let others see them worship and thus pour praise on themselves rather than on God.

Call to Meet Your God (4:6–13)

SUPPORTING IDEA: *Ignoring God's disciplinary acts and his calls to repentance leads to a final sentence of disaster.*

4:6. Disaster was nothing new for Israel. God had repeatedly sent disciplinary judgment on his people, calling them back to himself. Amos gave five examples of God's judgment, none of which we can date precisely, but all of which Israel remembered. Repeatedly, Israel refused to repent. God had had enough. They could ignore his discipline. They could revel in their religion rather than in the Lord's righteousness. Finally, the time had come. They would face God and hear his final sentence of disaster.

First, God said, "I gave you whiteness of teeth in all your cities and lack of bread in all your places" (author's translation). No more tooth decay problems. God had taken away all food, so nothing entered the mouth to lodge in the gaps and cause tooth decay.

Yet you have not returned to me. Here is Amos's chorus (4:6,8–11). Deuteronomy 4:29–31 and 30:1–10 showed Israel how to respond to God's judgment. God's discipline has a strong purpose—to lead his people to repent, to turn away from their frivolous, God-ignoring lifestyle, and to turn back to a God-fearing lifestyle. Israel refused to recognize God's sovereignty. They thought they could get away with worship the way they planned it and life the way they enjoyed it. Famine just called for more and better offerings in their kind of worship. But famine should call them to feast on God's Word and seek God's will. If not, the call to worship continued to be a call to sin and thus a call to judgment.

Amos emphasized the seriousness of his call with the prophetic oracle formula, literally translated "utterance of Yahweh." It designates the speech to which it is attached as the precise revelation of God. God speaks; his people ignore; judgment is on the way.

4:7–8. Baal, the chief Canaanite god, claimed to control fertility and all the conditions that produced plentiful crops. Amos contested that claim. Israel might join in Baal worship, but they got no results. Yahweh, the God of Israel, had all power over fertility and agricultural production. He **withheld rain** from his people. Yes, God was responsible for sending **rain on one town, but withheld it from another** (Deut. 28:22–24). He tried to get his people's attention and drive them back to himself. Still, people ignored God even while "two or three cities trembled along to another city for a drink of water but were never satisfied" (author's translation). They should have been traveling back to God.

4:9. If drought did not do the job, then God sent a "scorching wind and disease" (author's translation) on the crops (Deut. 28:22). "Your vast gardens and vineyards, your fig trees and olive trees the caterpillars (or perhaps locusts) devoured" (author's translation) (see Deut. 28:39–42). Without basic foodstuffs and without products to put on the market, the rural community failed. So did the proud city folk who owned much of the land. Time was ripe for repentance, but God's people turned a deaf ear to the call.

4:10. God declared through Amos that the people repeated Pharaoh's foolishness (Exod. 5–15), not listening to his threats or learning from his actions when he **sent plagues among you as I did to Egypt.** This would be something that wipes out total communities (Deut. 28:49–57). God added to that disaster for the armies, killing the robust **young men** just entering adulthood, thus endangering the future of the nation. Destroying all their **horses** meant taking away all military power and mobility, reducing the army to foot soldiers to face cavalry and chariots. Dead soldiers and horses had a gruesome effect: "I caused the stink of your camps to rise into your nostrils" (author's translation). Raising such a **stench** still raised no response. God's people would not repent.

4:11. No greater stink rose from the earth than that caused when God destroyed **Sodom and Gomorrah** for their immorality and inhumanity (Gen. 19). God brought similar disasters on some Israelite cities. Israel had as much hope and usefulness as **a burning stick snatched from the fire.** God's people burned to ashes rather than repent.

4:12. No repentance by the people called forth God's dreaded **therefore,** introducing the announcement of judgment. Destructive discipline had not produced repentance. So they faced their turn on the ultimate Judge's final docket. **Prepare to meet your God** is not an invitation that an unrepentant people delight to hear. This invitation can mean only one thing—no more opportunity to repent. A personal encounter with God will bring his final sentence of eternal judgment (Exod. 19:17). Hope has vanished. The call to repentance is silenced. Discipline is finished. Judgment is the only option.

4:13. Who is this sovereign God who issues such threats? Again Amos used the language of Israel's hymns to remind them of the God they must prepare to meet. He **forms the mountains** they cannot climb and **creates the wind** they cannot see. Yet he is no obscure God hidden in the highest heavens or unapproachable in a mountain hideaway. He **reveals his thoughts to man,** who is thus without excuse. Such a great Creator also has an awesome, fearful side. He **turns dawn to darkness,** and he **treads the high places of the earth.**

Darkness is the element of fear and mystery that threatens to return creation to chaos (Gen. 1:4–5,18). The high places are mountain peaks that humans cannot scale and the pagan worship places that God wants destroyed (1 Sam. 9:12; Mic. 1:5). This is the God whom his people must prepare to meet.

> **MAIN IDEA REVIEW:** We show we have accepted sin's invitation to disaster by abusing the poor, wasting time with partying, and even by raucous religion without repentance.

III. CONCLUSION

Who Runs the Show?

Can you worship the worship service? I remember a church where the minister of music ran the show. Prayers, offerings, sermons—all elements besides music lurked in the background. People came to see if the music minister could top last week's show or last year's pageant. When the music minister moved to another town, many members moved to another church. They looked not for fellowship or ministry or Bible study or missions involvement or an opportunity to praise and experience God. They looked for a service of thrill, enjoyment, and entertainment. Did the people of that church worship the worship service?

Amos finally had to call a halt to Israel's worship because people enjoyed what they did rather than enjoying God. The Lord had left the worship service, and no one had noticed.

PRINCIPLES

- Worship centers on God, not on human activity or enjoyment.
- Inauthentic worship can entice you to think you are right with God when you have lost all touch with him.
- Worship becomes sin when God is no longer the center of attention.

- Worship may follow traditional rules and leave out the most important elements of true worship.
- God disciplines his people to lead them back to repentance and true worship.
- A people who forsake worship, reject God, and ignore divine discipline face eternal judgment.

APPLICATIONS

- Think back on a time when you last encountered God in worship in a way that changed your life.
- Examine each element of your worship to see if it leads you to praise God or leads others to praise you.
- List ways God has brought discipline into your life.
- Determine why God has brought discipline into your life.
- Repent of any sins you are aware of, and ask God to cleanse your life from all that displeases him.
- Commit yourself anew to obey and worship God.

IV. LIFE APPLICATION

The Worship Debate

Contemporary worship style . . .
Traditional worship style . . .
Blended worship style . . .
Bible study is enough, I don't need worship . . .

Worship is controversial and divisive in many churches today. Pastors try to copy prominent, "successful" pastors and their worship styles. Debate over worship causes church splits along age lines. The world laughs at a church that cannot define its most central act.

Such division and debate among God's people is nothing new. Amos found the problem in the oldest, most revered worship places in Israel. He warned people not to go to worship because they were actually going to sin. For Israel worship had become frivolity. The bulls and cows of Bashan loved to go to worship, show off their social standing, and play can-you-top-this at offering time. Worship was for social show-offs. A people who thought they were being loyal to tradition found themselves separated from God.

Amos shocked them. God had nothing to do with their worship. Worship that ignores the one true God is not worship. Worship that focuses on the worshipper is sin. Such worship did not prepare the people to meet God. It prepared them for confession; it called them to repent or perish.

Still, Israel continued to answer the invitation to sin rather than the call to true worship. Amos issued one more call. Now attendance was mandatory, not optional. They must come and meet their God. Such a meeting would be anything but pleasant. Sin without repentance never prepares a person for a joyous time with God. It prepares him for the eternal courtroom to hear a sentence of death.

Our generation is as fraught with worship controversy as Amos's was. Too often our call to worship is really an invitation to sin. Can you ignore the controversy, hear God's call to repent, and return to worship the true and living God? Or must you get the mandatory summons to prepare to meet your God once and for all?

V. PRAYER

God, we are sorry. We have made worship a chance to judge how well the ministers perform and how poorly the congregation gets involved. We use worship as a way to enhance our reputation. We have let worship become a habit but not an experience with you. Teach us to worship. Forgive our sins of false worship and pride. Prepare us to meet you gladly at the final judgment so we can hear your sentence of well done! Amen.

VI. DEEPER DISCOVERIES

A. Sacrifices and Tithes (4:4–5)

Israel had a hobby, a favorite occupation. They loved to worship. Their worship was alive with sights, sounds, smells, tastes, and tactile feelings. The large crowds gathering at the favorite worship places brought excitement and exuberance to the worship experience. That experience included many elements. Amos mentions a few in passing.

The first element of worship was sacrifice (Heb. *zebach*). This involved slaughtering a lamb and eating the lean meat to bring fellowship and communion between the worshippers and God. Such sacrifices were sometimes used to ratify treaties or agreements (Gen. 31:54). Some sacrifices met with God's approval (Exod. 20:24), but they could also bring his anger (2 Kgs. 16:15). Even a sacrifice to other gods could be called a *zebach* (Judg. 16:23).

Pious worshippers of God made an annual pilgrimage to sacrifice to him (1 Sam. 2:19). Such sacrifices began long before Moses and Sinai (Exod. 3:18). They continued at various places in the promised land (Josh. 8:30–31). With sacrifices so important in Israel's system of worship, why did Amos condemn their practices? Douglas Stuart gives three aspects of how worship became rebellious, criminal sin: "(1) they worshipped at an improper locale;

(2) they worshipped in an improper manner (via illegitimate priests, idols, etc.); and (3) they substituted worship for righteous behavior" (WBC 31, 338). The central rite representing and cementing the relationship between God and people became sin when people participated for their own pleasure, in their own ways, for their own purposes.

The second element of Jewish worship was timing. The temple had morning and evening sacrifices (Lev. 6:8–13). Rich Israelites apparently showed their wealth and their "piety" by bringing a morning sacrifice to God. This became more of a public display than a private ritual of relationship.

The third element of worship was the tithe. The Old Testament refers frequently to a tithe that the Israelites should give to the Levites. Amos was pleased with Israel's desire to tithe. He went so far as to describe them bringing tithes every three days (literal Hebrew) rather than every three years for the poor and the Levites. But the problem was that "their motive was to magnify their generosity toward God, not to praise God's gracious provisions for them" (Smith, NAC 19b, 88).

The next element of worship was the thank offering. Israel's worship included specific occasions and rituals to offer thanks to God for specific acts of his grace. People brought offerings called "thanksgiving offerings" using the Hebrew term *todah* or thanksgiving (Ps. 107:22). Israel became experts in this ritual. But Amos claimed that Israel was mocking God's grace by bringing thanksgiving offerings because they enjoyed doing this and wanted others to see them do so rather than because they were expressing gratitude to God.

Finally, the freewill offering was a central part of Israel's worship (Deut. 16:10). Such offerings often resulted from vows or promises made to God in time of distress. These vows had to be carried out (Lev. 22:23). Supposedly, they represented "a spontaneous act of joy and devotion to God (Deut. 12:6–7)" (Gary Smith, *Amos*, 143). Such offerings represented a person's love and gratitude to God either for specific acts of deliverance or for his love in general (Ps. 54:6).

Israel loved to bring such offerings because they could shout out in a loud voice and let everyone know what they were doing. The offerings became "a means of parading . . . generosity and good deeds before . . . friends (Matt. 6:2)" instead of "the inner expression of love by a person who loved God with all his heart" (Gary Smith, 143).

B. Return to God: Repentance (4:6,8–11)

Amos relayed God's desire that Israel return to him. "Return" (Heb. *Shub*) is God's call for repentance. It describes an action of turning away from one thing and turning to another thing. Amos graphically described Israel's sins and crimes against God. Then he declared that the people had not returned to the Lord. Everything God did was meant to lead sinful Israel back to himself, but Israel never had a clue what was happening.

They never realized they had changed directions. They never knew they were following a false god. They never understood that their worship honored Baal and the Canaanite gods, not Yahweh, the God of Israel. Not knowing they were lost and going the wrong direction, they never heeded the call to return. Even God's discipline and punishment failed to catch Israel's attention. Caught in sin's trap, Israel did not hear or respond to God's call to repentance.

VII. TEACHING OUTLINE

A. INTRODUCTION

1. Lead Story: Sin's Invitation
2. Context: Having called judgment down on the nations (chs. 1–2) and on God's chosen people (ch. 3), Amos turned to Israel's elite with a shocking claim. Their riches did not reflect reward for righteousness. Their worship did not please God.
3. Transition: Amos preached fearlessly to any audience God set before him. He took on fancy ladies and called them cows. He took on regular worshippers and accused them of heresy. He stood where priests issued a call to worship and issued his own call for repentance. Who would answer such a call? Will you?

B. COMMENTARY

1. Casting Out the Cows (4:1–3)
2. Call to Sinful Worship (4:4–5)
3. Call to Meet Your God (4:6–13)

C. CONCLUSION: WHO RUNS THE SHOW?

VIII. ISSUES FOR DISCUSSION

1. What sins plague today's women? Why?
2. Can we oppress the poor by doing nothing?
3. In what way does our worship center in human vanity and pride rather than in divine praise?
4. When and why should a Christian believer experience God's discipline and punishment?
5. Does a person who attends church regularly have any reason to fear God's call to prepare to meet God?

Amos 5:1–6:14

Seek God and Live

I. **INTRODUCTION**
Seek God, Do Justice

II. **COMMENTARY**
A verse-by-verse explanation of these verses.

III. **CONCLUSION**
Our System of Justice

An overview of the principles and applications from these verses.

IV. **LIFE APPLICATION**
God's Servant for Justice in Our Community

Melding these verses to life.

V. **PRAYER**
Tying these verses to life with God.

VI. **DEEPER DISCOVERIES**
Historical, geographical, and grammatical enrichment of the commentary.

VII. **TEACHING OUTLINE**
Suggested step-by-step group study of these verses.

VIII. **ISSUES FOR DISCUSSION**
Zeroing these verses in on daily life.

"*W*ithin the boundaries of freedom, justice is a compass

which points to the future and is a guide to a daily walk that

avoids that disastrous day of judgment."

G a r y   V .   S m i t h

Amos 5:1–6:14

IN A NUTSHELL

*T*he prophet invites the people of Israel to a sneak preview of their own funeral. Their hope for life is to seek God rather than traditional worship places. They must forsake a system of justice that no longer works and implement one that rolls down for everyone. They cannot count on the Day of the Lord coming, since it will bring darkness and death, not light and life. Those enjoying the "good life" for the moment will soon face God's eternal judgment.

Seek God and Live

I. INTRODUCTION

Seek God, Do Justice

*A*fter a wearying day during the Montgomery, Alabama, bus boycott, Martin Luther King Jr. lay in bed at the point of sleep. The phone rang. With hesitation King answered only to hear a sinister voice: "Listen, nigger, we've taken all we want from you; before next week you'll be sorry you ever came to Montgomery."

One more in a series of death threats, but this one lingered in King's mind. His soul had finally reached its saturation point. He stumbled into the kitchen, made some coffee, and figured out a way to resign from his leadership position. Fearing for his newborn daughter and his wife, he testified, "I couldn't take it any longer. I was weak." Finally, searching for power to go on, he bowed his head and poured out his fears, frustrations, and concerns. "I'm at the end of my powers," he prayed. "I have nothing left."

Suddenly King sensed a power he so desperately needed. An inner voice promised, "Martin Luther, stand up for righteousness. Stand up for justice. Stand up for truth. And lo, I will be with you. Even to the end of the world" (Michael G. Long, *Martin Luther King, Jr. on Creative Living*, pp. 9–11).

In seeking God, King found the power and the purpose for fighting on. He carried out the message Amos fought so desperately to get Israel to hear. The people must seek God and do justice.

II. COMMENTARY

Seek God and Live

> **MAIN IDEA:** *Religion impacts daily living; people demonstrate their faith in God by compassionate, consistent, godly behavior focused on a relationship with him.*

A A Sneak Preview of Your Funeral (5:1–3)

> **SUPPORTING IDEA:** *Death awaits any people who seek personal pleasure and success rather than justice and eternal life.*

5:1. God placed a dirge or **lament**, a funeral song, in the prophet's mouth. It has the same poetic structure as the laments in the Book of Lamentations. **Israel**, a nation that believed they were enjoying the prime of life, had to reflect on death. This was not death in general but their own death.

5:2. God said the nation had fallen, **never to rise again**. Party-loving, prosperous Israel saw none of this. They were God's elect people enjoying God's protection. Oh no! roared the prophet. You are a nation **deserted in her own land, with no one to lift her up**. God did not guarantee them his protection forever. A disobedient nation must face the music—the music of a funeral dirge for themselves.

5:3. Israel prided themselves in their victorious armies. God would let them march out to battle once more, but this would bring disaster. Nine of every ten soldiers would not return. This did not represent a remnant with hope. This represented defeat and destruction.

B Seek God, Not Substitutes (5:4–7)

> **SUPPORTING IDEA:** *Worship ritual does not guarantee God's blessings; such a guarantee comes only when a person supports justice for everyone because it focuses on a personal relationship with God.*

5:4. Hope had not vanished. God had one last invitation: **Seek me and live**. This echoes the promise of God's law (Lev. 18:5) and God's wisdom (Prov. 15:27). This is God's call to worship. He invites his people back to true worship because worship is the foundation on which all life with God rests. Without true devotion in praise and thanksgiving, a people die. Israel had to choose—death through life as usual or life through returning to God.

5:5. Israel did not understand. They worshipped regularly. Their ancient sanctuaries were thriving. **Gilgal** went clear back to Joshua's time (Josh. 4:20). **Bethel** went back even further (Gen. 12:8; see comments on Amos 4:4). So did **Beersheba** (Gen. 22:19). History said that true worship occurred at these three ancient places. God's message said something entirely different: judgment was approaching for places where worship had turned to sin. How could holy places face judgment? Because the practice of religion there had become more important than seeking a personal relationship with God. Doing religion had replaced seeking God.

5:6. God had a Plan B for his people. Plan A called for them to seek God and live. Plan B warned that if they did not choose Plan A, then Plan B would be implemented automatically. God would become a raging fire and sweep through the Northern Kingdom, Israel, **the house of Joseph**. Those who claimed they descended from the image of perfect obedience—Joseph himself—could die in God's fire of judgment.

5:7. People who worshipped should treat other people as God would. Instead, people who worshipped were manipulating religious law, community practice, and weaker people for their own gain. They were "turning justice into wormwood" (author's translation). What should be the sweetest and normal condition for God's people—a world where justice prevails for all—

was the bitterest experience imaginable. This experience could be pictured only by bringing up images of tasting the most bitter of trees—wormwood (Jer. 9:15).

God's style of living—**righteousness**—was cast **to the ground** like rubbish. The court system depended on righteous men—the elders in the gate and the judges—to produce equity and fairness for all parties, rich or poor. Instead, the rich controlled the justice system, and the poor got only an opportunity to become poorer. Israel might go through the motions of worship. They did not seek God in doing so. Judgment loomed.

C The LORD Is His Name! Seek Him! (5:8–9)

SUPPORTING IDEA: *The people of Israel were to seek the Creator God who controls life on earth and can bring good or evil, as he chooses what is best for his people.*

5:8. At crucial points in his book (1:2; 4:13; 5:8–9; 9:5–6), Amos picked up short pieces of hymns used in Israel's worship to remind Israel of the nature of their one true God as opposed to the gods of the neighbors. He made the star constellations called the **Pleiades** (Job 38:31) **and Orion** (Isa. 13:10). Israel's neighbors saw these star clusters as deities to be worshipped and as means of revelation, giving omens that human specialists could read to determine the divine will. Israel saw them as objects that God had created and as part of the powerful army that God commanded.

Israel turned justice to wormwood or bitterness; God turned darkness into the dawn of new light and new hope. Israel could also turn the darkness of their impending funeral into light and life if they would seek God and live. The depths of the **waters of the sea** brought fear and trembling—a symbol of chaos, danger, and death. God took these waters and poured them out on the sandy beaches. In so doing he could provide needed moisture for the earth, but he could also bring the danger and chaos of the sea depths to earth. God is free to produce what pleases man, but he is also free to bring discipline and judgment to mankind.

5:9. But Israel saw themselves as strong (literal translation) since they had built up their defenses with fortified cities. That made no difference, warned Amos. God **flashes destruction** just like he sends the flashes of lightning bolts. When God chooses, he **brings the fortified city to ruin**. Don't rest on your laurels or your defenses, Amos declared. Seek God and live even when he flashes this power.

D Keep Quiet in Evil Times (5:10–13)

SUPPORTING IDEA: *God knows the sins of his people and will bring judgment on them, so the wise will observe his actions while the oppressors will face death.*

5:10. The Creator God who controlled all nations (5:8–9) was speaking. Verses 10–13 contain three activities that Israel participated in which God despised. God had a strong word for Israel: their system of justice had fallen apart. An elder of Israel had the responsibility to sit in the passageway in the city gate and hear the legal cases of the people. He decided cases and mediated in troubled situations to maintain justice in the community. The elder in the gate is **one who reproves.** He hears both sides of a case and decides who is right and who deserves punishment and then reprimands the guilty (Hab. 1:12).

One **who tells the truth** is a witness in a case who tells exactly what he experienced. But what happens to people who try to make the system of justice work? People **hate** and **despise** them. Worship had not worked in Israel because sin and selfishness—not justice and righteousness—dominated everyday life.

5:11. Amos became even more explicit in describing Israel's problem. The people who worshipped were the same ones who trampled **on the poor** and forced payment of grain. Israel's economic system depended on land staying in the hands of small landowners and within the same tribe. That was the way God intended it when he had Joshua distribute the land among the tribes (Josh. 13–21). Powerful businessmen changed all that. They got people into debt, took over their land to pay the debt, then forced the former landowners to work the soil for them and pay the largest share of the crop to rent the land.

5:12. For such worship seekers who were not God seekers, God had a final word—judgment. They would not enjoy the fruit of their labors because the all-knowing God was aware of the **sins** they had committed. He had their number—the number of times they had disobeyed him by hurting someone else. Those who sought to maintain God's way of living—the mostly poor **righteous**—faced oppression. Economic **justice** was manhandled by **bribes.** The needs of other people were ignored, indeed, were made worse by those who worshipped God.

5:13. In such sinful times God had one word of advice for his people— keep quiet. Here prophetic irony and word play again take over. **Prudent** or wise (Heb. *maskil*) can also mean "the successful man" or the "teachable man." The phrase **keeps quiet** (Heb. *damam*) can also mean to lament and wail or to die. The wise person is the one who listens to the prophet's words. He will withdraw from society's evil, seeking God's protection in the time of judgment. But the "successful" man—the great landowner facing Amos's condemnation—will wail in lamentation, become teachable, or perhaps perish from the earth. The statement is thus both an exhortation to the faithful and a warning to the worshipping oppressors.

E Seek Good, Not Evil (5:14–15)

SUPPORTING IDEA: *In evil times when God's people know they face his judgment, they need to change their lifestyle and seek good, not evil; justice, not oppression.*

5:14–15. Here, finally, a word of advice appears. God issues his invitation. **Seek good, not evil. Hate evil, love good; maintain justice in the courts.** This is how the worshipper truly demonstrates religion. Even when the times are evil, God offers one last glimmer of hope: **you may live.** "Perhaps the LORD, the God of Hosts, will be gracious" (author's translation). But only to **the remnant of Joseph.** Escape is no longer possible. God will reduce his people to a remnant. These will have one last chance to hear his invitation and adapt their daily life to the life shaped by true worship. The only way to do that is through repentance, turning from the false worship and legal oppression that God sees as evil and turning to the true worship and justice that God desires from his people.

F God Seeks Israel's Lament (5:16–17)

SUPPORTING IDEA: *Lament and anguish are the only actions left when God comes among his people to judge and punish them for their sin.*

5:16. The ominous prophetic **therefore** sounds forth to issue an ironic announcement of God's judgment. The lamentation expressed in verses 1–3 is reintroduced. Israel must lament publicly. City folk and country folk join together, even when city people have been oppressing country people. Professional **mourners** set the pace.

5:17. Even those who work in the vineyards producing the drink that brings joy must join the lamentation. What causes such national sorrow and hurt? God declared, **I will pass through your midst.** God's appearance among his people is the reason they howl in sorrow and anguish. God's presence can bring judgment rather than blessing. God's presence among sinners is devastating, especially for sinners who refuse to admit their sin and repent.

Amos had invited Israel to prepare to meet their God. Now he described what that meeting would be like. It would bring tears and sorrow as nothing had done before. Israel had seen examples of God's discipline. Now they would experience something worse—his presence in final judgment.

Ⓖ Seek Righteousness, Not Ritual (5:18–27)

SUPPORTING IDEA: *When God's woe falls on his people, they should heed his word and turn back to righteous living in which all classes and groups of people receive fairness and justice.*

5:18. The language of the funeral procession again serves the prophet's purposes as he pronounces **woe** on Israel. This Hebrew term (*hoy*) comes from mourners grief stricken over a loved one's death. Mourning and grief will pervade the nation (5:16–17). They expected God to come on **the day of the LORD** and bring salvation. They waited for God's sunshine to replace the darkness they faced. But Amos warned them not to count on their theological tradition. What they had learned about God's day was all wrong. **That day will be darkness, not light**.

5:19. God will come in judgment. Just when the people thought they had escaped the worst of the judgment, they would turn and face a bigger and fiercer opponent. Get away from a **lion**; find a **bear**. Huff and puff their way into the house, lean against the **wall** to catch their breath—and feel a poisonous **snake** nip their hand.

5:20. So Amos announced his gruesome conclusion: **Will not the day of the LORD be darkness, not light—pitch-dark, without a ray of brightness?**

5:21–23. Why would God do this to his people? Did they not go to worship every time they were supposed to? Did they not fulfill all God's worship requirements as set forth in Exodus, Leviticus, and Numbers? What had gone wrong? God had a simple answer: **I hate, I despise your religious feasts. I cannot stand your assemblies**. Worship and ritual must be more than going through the motions, checking the inspired manual to be sure you did not miss anything. Worship can be carried out to the letter of the law and still not be worship. How can that be?

The answer is not in the value of the **offerings**. You cannot pay enough to win God's favor. The answer is not in the quality of the **music** program. You cannot sing or play well enough to soothe God's anger or to guarantee his pleasure. It is the heart of worship that counts, not the quality of the performance. The church without a choir, magnificent instruments, or millionaire givers may please God much more than the modern megachurch with everything it has to offer.

5:24. God has one requirement for those who worship him: **let justice roll on like a river, righteousness like a never-failing stream**! True worship on the Lord's day depends on true righteousness lived out during the other days of the week. Only a people who obey God can truly worship him. They cannot take advantage of their neighbor on Monday, cheat on a business deal on Tuesday, tell a bunch of lies on Wednesday, cheat on their spouse on Thursday, get in a fight with their friend on Friday, take off on a drunken tangent on Saturday, and then worship on Sunday. A person's worship comes directly from his life. Only a life of obedience can bring acceptable worship to God. He demands righteousness before ritual.

5:25. But—you can hear Israel's retort—we are doing what Moses taught us to do. And God answers with a question: In your infant days as my people, when you first began to serve me in the wilderness, what did you do? Did you run around the wilderness making sure you kept all the ritual rules? Of course not! If it was not an absolute requirement then, it is not an absolute requirement now. God's deepest desire is something else. Righteousness always comes before ritual.

5:26. Look at the other side of the coin. What have you been doing instead of righteousness? **You have lifted up the shrine of your king, the pedestal of your idols, the star of your god—which you made for yourselves.**

"Your king" and "your idols" are ways the Hebrews referred to the planet Saturn, the most distant planet they knew anything about. Israel apparently learned to worship Saturn as a god by imitating their enemies, Assyria and Babylon. Amos had to remind them that the stars and planets were not gods. They had no power. The heavenly bodies were God's creation while the images they used in earthly worship were human creations.

5:27. Amos gave a simple conclusion to his message. **I will send you into exile beyond Damascus.** Syria, with Damascus as its leading city, might appear to be Israel's enemy. That was not the case. Lurking behind current Syrian claims to control territories that Israel laid claim to were Assyria and Babylon to the east. They were the enemies to fear. They were the ones who would eventually take God's people captive. One generation later, Amos's words came true as Assyria carried the Northern Kingdom into exile.

⬛ Woe to the Wealthy (6:1–7)

> **SUPPORTING IDEA:** *Wealth cannot bring security to a people who will not worship and obey God.*

6:1. Again the prophet picks up funeral oratory to condemn Israel's affluent class. Israel's elite are **complacent** or at ease **in Zion.** They are self-confident, carefree, undisturbed by the nation's situation or the prophet's predictions. They **feel secure;** they place their trust in **Mount Samaria.** As Amos had done in the opening oracles against the nations (Amos 1–2), so here he introduces the Southern Kingdom first. Mount Zion refers to Jerusalem with its religious and political traditions. It was Amos's capital city. By announcing disaster for the south, Amos gained credence and a hearing in the north. His audience in Samaria began to anticipate the day they could move south and expand their territory and power at Jerusalem's expense.

But Amos quickly shifted to Mount Samaria, the capital city of the Northern Kingdom. In his day Samaria was flying high as one of the most powerful and influential cities in the world. God's prophetic word pointed to the end of such power and prosperity. It was time to preach Samaria's funeral, but no one wanted to listen. The people of Samaria were **notable men**, dignitaries. They exercised influence in **the foremost nation**, or Israel. The **people of Israel** came to them for advice and direction. These men were too busy being important and too enthralled with power. They had no time for a southern prophet's funeral orations.

6:2. Amos had some directions of his own: **Go to Calneh**. This was a city-state in northwestern Syria. In Amos's day it faced threats from other Syrian city-states, from Assyria, and from Israel. **Hamath** was another city-state in the center of Syria on the Orontes River. It represented the northern border of Israel's land claims, and Israel exercised some claim over it in Amos's day (Num. 13:21; Ezek. 47:20). **Gath** was a Philistine city not mentioned in the list in Amos 1:6–8. Located in the interior away from the Mediterranean coast, it was the closest Philistine city to Judah. Gath had no claim to security and power in Amos's day (2 Chr. 26:6). Having conducted a tour from northeast to southwest, Amos popped the strategic question: **Are they better off than your two kingdoms?**

All three cities—Calneh, Hamath, Gath—had rich histories, but they were struggling to maintain independence in Amos's day. They were no better off than Judah and Israel, but the reverse was also true: Israel and Judah were no better off than their three neighboring city-states. Their land was no larger than Israel's or Judah's. God had the power to take neighboring land and give it to whomever he chose. He could do the same with Israel's land.

6:3. Israel's carefree leaders "postponed" **the evil day** but "invited" or "celebrated ahead of schedule" **a reign of terror** or perhaps more likely "a cessation of violence" (author's translation). Israel ignored the prophetic warning and lived as if judgment day would never come. They escaped from reality, thinking they had established a kingdom without threat so they could celebrate the absence of violence in their day. Amos apparently used a play on words here. The people expected no violence, but the same phrase in Hebrew could be understood as a "reign of violence." Amos said Israel had established just such a reign of violence. Those at ease in Zion and trusting the mountains of Samaria—the political and economic elite—carved out their lifestyles with acts of oppression on the lower economic classes.

6:4. Amos described the elite lifestyle graphically. The people would **lounge** around on expensive furniture and dine on the best meat when the people doing what amounted to slave labor for them on the farms and in the shops had little furniture and seldom ate meat at all.

6:5. These Israelite dignitaries whiled away their time making music and convincing themselves they were as good as David, Israel's premier musician. **Like David** goes with the second half of the verse, not the first. The meaning of the final phrase is not precisely clear. The verb can mean to presume, think, imagine, plan, or invent. The direct object is literally "vessels of song." They may be singing, creating songs, fantasizing about their musical creations, or inventing new songs or new instruments.

6:6. Disaster approaches, and the Isralite nobles pour bowls of fine **wine** down their throats while pouring the **finest lotions** and cosmetics on their skin. But they do **not grieve over** (or even more literally "make themselves sick over") **the ruin of Joseph**. Their nation is coming to an end. The funeral announcement has been sent. Israel's power-brokers amuse themselves with wine and beauty treatments.

6:7. The end of such lifestyles is near. Raucous **feasting and lounging** will no longer be an option. The divine **therefore** sounds ominously. These people will lead the way into **exile**. The nation is dead and headed for ruin.

⬛ An Oath of Abhorrence (6:8–14)

SUPPORTING IDEA: *God swears to bring total destruction to a people whose lifestyle has become the exact opposite of God's expectations.*

6:8. Amos piles up divine names and emotional terms to show how severe is God's decision to judge. The opening line reads literally: "The Lord Yahweh has sworn an oath by his own soul. An oracle of Yahweh, the Lord of Hosts." The Lord reminds Israel that they are dealing with the power who controls all power in the universe. He is Lord of all. God reminds Israel that they are dealing with the Lord of the exodus (Exod. 1–15) who created them as a nation, delivered them from slavery, and established a covenant with them (Exod. 19–24). The Lord of Hosts reminds a people who are proud of their military power and accomplishments that he controls the armies of Israel and the armies of heaven. No army will dare to attack his forces.

This all-powerful, all-controlling God is angry! He is repulsed by Israel's arrogant **pride**. He detests the military **fortresses** or citadels that symbolize Israel's military might and make them think their city and country are invincible. Israel thinks they will never again surrender to an enemy. God says, "I will surrender the city and all its contents" (author's translation) for you. You do not own or control the city. You do not decide when to surrender. I control the city. I will surrender it to whomever I choose. I am angry at you and have surrendered your city to the enemy. Get in line for exile.

6:9. God's surrender for Israel will not be partial. A house has **ten men** seeking refuge from the enemy. All ten will **die**. None will escape.

6:10. Finally, Israel will learn the power and presence of God, but in what a horrible way. Two people speak. One is a "beloved one" or **relative** of one of the men in the house. Either this "loved one" has become "his cremator" and speaks to an unidentified person or a second person is to burn the corpses. This shows the gravity of the situation because Israel normally did not burn or cremate bodies (Josh. 7:15,25). Either a horrible infectious disease caused this break from normal practice, or the loss of life was so great that cremation was the only practical way to deal with the large number of dead bodies.

In any case, the relative will "lift" up his loved one's "bones from the house and speak to whomever is inside the house" (author's translation). One question: **Is anyone with you?** The quick one-word answer is **No** or literally, "the end." The immediate reply: "Hush! So no one will be caused to remember the name of Yahweh."

God has brought total judgment. He has proved his awesome power and demonstrated how fierce is his hatred of Israel's pride. In such a situation, no one dare speak the divine name, lest he return for another round of destruction.

6:11. Divine judgment plays no favorites. God has issued the **command** to destroy and exile. No one will escape. Whether one's **house** is large or small, it will soon be buried by rubble.

6:12. To get his point across, the prophet turned to rhetorical questions that expect negative answers. **Do horses run on the rocky crags? Does one plow there with oxen?** Obviously not. But Israel's actions are as logical as a farmer trying to plow through the huge stone cliffs overlooking the sea. God has consistently demanded **justice**. Israel has transformed the justice that should preserve equality and fairness in the community into a poisonous plant that brings death to the community. God expects **righteousness** to characterize the people so that the stable order of the community can continue. Those who live by righteousness will produce fruit—justice. Instead, Israel's elite have produced bitter wormwood (Amos 5:7).

6:13. These people face the threat from the general who controls the heavenly hosts, and they take time to celebrate a victory over **Lo Debar**, translated literally as "No Thing." They claim, "Did we not capture for ourselves Karnaim (that is, "the horns of power") in our own strength?" (author's translation). Lo Debar was a city-state east of the Jordan River (2 Sam. 9:4–5). Karnaim, just north of the Yarmuk River, was the most important city in the northern part of Transjordan called Bashan. Apparently, Jeroboam II had recently captured these cities as he expanded his territory eastward and northward. This gave Israel a strong sense of power. Amos declared it was "nothing." God is the only one with power and might.

6:14. God would soon display his power and strength. He would raise up an enemy **nation** to oppress Israel. All the territory Jeroboam II had conquered anew for Israel (2 Kgs. 14:25), God's enemy nation would take back. **Lebo Hamath** or the Entrance to Hamath represents the southern border of the Syrian city-state mentioned in Amos 6:2 (Ezek. 48:1). **The valley of the Arabah** or the wadi of the Arabah represents a stream bed running off the Dead Sea that carried water only in the rainy season. It represented the southern extension of the conquests of King Jeroboam II.

All Israel's winnings would be lost. Israel had partied long enough. They had not taken care of God's business or heeded God's warnings. The end was in sight. When God had no impact on daily life, those living without God would soon not be living at all.

MAIN IDEA REVIEW: *Religion impacts daily living; people demonstrate their faith in God by compassionate, consistent, godly behavior focused on a relationship with him.*

III. CONCLUSION

Our System of Justice

In his book *What's So Amazing About Grace?*, Philip Yancey tells how Jeffrey Dahmer monopolized the nation's media in the early 1990s. He abused and then killed seventeen young men, cannibalizing them and storing their spare parts in his refrigerator. His story gained further attention when it became apparent that police officers had ignored the pleas of one of his victims. In prison Dahmer met a new system of justice—"prison justice"—when a fellow prisoner beat him to death with a broom handle (p. 95).

We shudder and ask how the system of justice and fairness we pride ourselves in could break down so completely. We are simply sharing Israel's thoughts and need to hear the message God spoke to them through his servant Amos. God's message continues to speak to us today about genuine worship and genuine living. Important points shout at us if we are not too deaf to listen to God.

PRINCIPLES

- True life comes when we seek God in obedience, not when we carry out traditional worship services.
- God expects his worshippers to treat other people fairly and not take advantage of them for personal gain.
- God hates our worship when we do not promote justice and righteousness during the week.
- God has a plan for bringing justice even if that means the Day of the Lord must become darkness for his people.

- The only hope for a person or for a nation is to seek a personal relationship with God.
- A personal relationship with God changes a nation's and an individual's lifestyle, creating a thirst for goodness and justice.
- Riches do not guarantee or indicate God's pleasure.

APPLICATIONS

- List five reasons you attend worship services and ask how God reacts to each one of these reasons.
- Find ways you can promote justice in your community by helping the poor, lonely, and helpless.
- Write down what you expect to happen to you when God brings his final Day of the Lord.
- Determine in what ways pride directs your actions and stirs God's hatred.
- Ask yourself how complacency and a false sense of security can separate you from God.

IV. LIFE APPLICATION

God's Servant for Justice in Our Community

Let's call him Jim. He's a pastor's favorite friend. In his easygoing, rural ways, he taught me some lessons about what church membership is all about. He never taught a class, never served as a deacon, and was quite often conspicuous by his absence from church meetings. What I learned to admire was where you could find him on Monday, Tuesday, Wednesday, Thursday, Friday, and Saturday.

On one of those days he was apt to be at the parsonage fixing something that had gone wrong. On other days he was busy with the people in the community, being their commissioner in local government and a whole lot more. Many people owed him money. Others were indebted to him for taking time to talk with their teenagers and giving them a straight-from-the-shoulder word of advice. He was making sure the tenant farmers knew their rights—even those who worked for him on his own place. He was with people of many ethnic groups helping them find solutions to major problems. He was reprimanding wayward, drunken husbands for mistreating wives and children. He was God's servant for justice in our community. Worship meant a lot to him; helping people meant much more.

Amos would have approved of this man's actions. The prophet taught Israel that God calls for righteousness over ritual if worship is to be genuine.

V. PRAYER

Just and righteous Father, we come to you with broken hearts. We have paraded our loyalty to our church and our faithfulness to its worship services. We have also paraded our dedication to ourselves and our ease and comfort, even when this has come at the expense of others who cannot share such things. Show us how we can help justice roll down so all the people may share the fruits of righteousness. Amen.

VI. DEEPER DISCOVERIES

A. Godly Seeking (5:4–6,14)

In chapter 5, Amos echoes God's demands with one word—seek (Heb. *darash*). The Hebrew term has a broad range of meanings: to seek with care, care for (either a person, Jer. 30:14 or a stray animal, Deut. 22:2), inquire about, investigate, search for, be intent on, make supplication to God, to question, to seek a word from God. Its basic meaning involves the search for knowledge. An expansion of meaning added an emotional element to the word when its objects were ideal values such as justice (Isa. 16:5), God's works (Ps. 111:2), or peace and prosperity for another person (Ezra 9:12).

Amos took a term filled with deep religious significance and turned it sarcastically on his northern audience. "The culminating point of Amos's message is that Israel now has to deal direct with Jahweh; not the Jahweh of the sanctuaries and pilgrimages, but an unknown Jahweh who was coming to perform new deeds upon Israel" (G. von Rad, *Theology of the Old Testament*, II, 134). Imitating the priest calling the people to worship, Amos called them to forsake the worship places and seek God himself.

The practice of worship is not enough. The relationship with God must be secure before worship has meaning. When worship becomes traditional and meaningless, God calls his people away from worship and back to himself. Those who seek no more than worship face death. Those who seek God will live. Those who genuinely seek God also seek something else—the good of others. For Amos, to seek God is to seek good.

VII. TEACHING OUTLINE

A. INTRODUCTION

1. Lead Story: Seek God, Do Justice
2. Context: Amos viewed the richness of Israel's worship and the riches of the people who came to worship. He then viewed the poverty of

the people who slaved for those who came to worship. Something did not add up. Worship created a society with two widely separated classes—the rich and the poor, the proud worshippers and the humble bystanders.

3. Transition: If peace, wealth, security, and self-confidence do not represent God's blessings and right standing with the Lord, what does? How can we know we are members of God's kingdom in good standing? In chapters 5 and 6 Amos had a quick response to this question.

B. COMMENTARY

1. A Sneak Preview of Your Funeral (5:1–3)
2. Seek God, Not Substitutes (5:4–7)
3. The LORD Is His Name! Seek Him! (5:8–9)
4. Keep Quiet in Evil Times (5:10–13)
5. Seek Good, Not Evil (5:14–15)
6. God Seeks Israel's Lament (5:16–17)
7. Seek Righteousness, Not Ritual (5:18–27)
8. Woe to the Wealthy (6:1–7)
9. An Oath of Abhorrence (6:8–14)

C. CONCLUSION: OUR SYSTEM OF JUSTICE

VIII. ISSUES FOR DISCUSSION

1. What elements of your church's worship please God, and what elements are displeasing?
2. List five opportunities for community service where you live that will help bring goodness and justice to those who need it most.
3. What can we do to show that we hate evil and love good?
4. Is it possible in our present political system to expect justice and righteousness in our society?

Amos 7:1–8:3

The Prophet's Profit

Quote

"*H*istory proves that it has never been possible to destroy a faith grounded in Scripture, even with the most devastating revolutions in the state."

Immanuel Kant

Amos 7:1–8:3

IN A NUTSHELL

*G*od showed Amos three visions. Swarms of locusts would strip the harvest. Amos interceded. God turned back. A judgment by fire would destroy all creation, even the great deep. Amos interceded. God turned back. God stood by a wall with a plumb line, showing the wall was built crooked. Now God would no longer spare his people. Israel faced utter defeat. Amaziah, the priest of the royal sanctuary at Bethel, confronted Amos and told him to go back south and preach to his own people. Amos testified that he was not a professional prophet but a shepherd and keeper of fruit trees. He prophesied only because he could not refuse to do what God had told him to do. He pronounced judgment on Amaziah and Israel. A final vision of a basket of fruit showed that Israel was ripe for God's final harvest.

The Prophet's Profit

I. INTRODUCTION

"We Must Visit One More Lady"

*O*ur mission trip was over, and it was time to load the vans and go to the airport. "One minute, please," the Argentine pastor interjected. "We must visit one more lady before you go."

Our group did not take that as particularly good news. Still, we walked down the block with the pastor and politely greeted the lady seated in her living room, her Bible open on the coffee table before her. "I just had to see you," she said. "I headed the planning committee for your visit, but then doctors found cancer. They operated a couple of weeks ago. I so hate it that I could not go visiting with you, but I have prayed for you every step around this community day and night."

This dying lady practiced the courage of her conviction each day. That is why we had to make one last visit, and that is why God blessed the ten days we walked the streets of Buenos Aires.

In the same way Amos helps us see that faithfulness, or obedience, means doing what God says even when no one else does.

II. COMMENTARY

The Prophet's Profit

MAIN IDEA: *God expects his people to remain faithful to him even when they are greatly outnumbered by unbelievers.*

A Power of Prophetic Prayer (7:1–6)

SUPPORTING IDEA: *God listens to faithful intercessory prayer.*

7:1. Amos interrupted his sermons to report visions that God had given him. First he saw God preparing huge **swarms of locusts**. The timing was drastic. The king had already collected his portion of the crop. Now the people waited for the final rains to come and let the grain and grass grow so they would have food for themselves and their animals. Locusts would eat up the new sprouts before they were ready to be harvested. Food for locusts meant famine for people.

7:2. The vision ended with the crops **stripped** clean. The visions did not lead to sermons. Rather, they led to prophetic protest in prayer. One word stands at the center of the prayer—**forgive**. This term usually occurs in connection with the formal rituals of the temple and always has God as its subject (Dan. 9:19).

Amos did not follow a normal process of calling Israel to confess their sin, repent, follow the laws of restitution, and renew their commitment to God. He did not ask them to bring sacrifices and go through atonement rituals. Amos simply relied on God's grace. God is not a record keeper who demands payment for each of our sins because he is a God of forgiveness (Ps. 130:3–4). He forgives because he is good and abounds in loyal covenant love (Ps. 86:5). Knowing God's love, goodness, faithfulness, and grace, Amos asked, **How can Jacob survive? He is so small!** Would God bring such terrible disaster on his people?

7:3. The Lord had regret about this. Explaining God's reaction here is no easy task. The Hebrew term *nicham* means to feel pain about something, to regret it but without an emotional expression (Judg. 2:18; Amos 7:6). This term shows us God's freedom in its most basic meaning. God "changes his dealings with men according to his sovereign purposes" (Marvin R. Wilson, *TWOT*, II, 571). God's eternal purposes do not change. His immediate reactions may change in response to human intercession or to human change.

At this point biblical religion is different from most other religions, since "God does not represent some rigid element of fate, but rather can be influenced" (J. Jeremias, OTL, 127). Thus God can report to Amos, I gave you a vision of disaster, but your intercession has caused me to change my course of action.

7:4. The second vision uses the exact same introductory and concluding formulas as the first. But the content of the vision is different. A great **fire** replaced the locusts. This would consume not only the crops. It would "eat up the great ocean deeps and eat up the inherited portion of the land" (literal translation). The **great deep** referred to the ocean depths associated with chaos in the creation account and feared by all ancient mariners (Gen. 1:2; Prov. 3:20; Jon. 2:6). Land and sea would disappear.

7:5. I beg you, stop! was Amos's reaction to the horror of the vision. No longer did he even ask for forgiveness. He wanted the visions to stop. He wanted the reality behind the visions to stop. He repeated the reason: **Jacob . . . is so small!**

7:6. Verse 6 repeats verse 3 except for a couple of small exceptions. Here we learn a lesson about prayer. "Amos manages to change God's will, and God allows Israel to survive . . . Israel is living, despite its capital guilt, solely on the basis of God's pity; God cannot bring it upon himself to destroy 'little Jacob' and thus relents from his (justified!) plan for destruction" (OTL, 128).

Here we see the prophetic office at its best. A prophet called to pronounce judgment identifies with his people and stands between the judging God and the sinful people. Through his prayers he brings God to forgive and to stop his judgment.

B Certainty of Judgment (7:7–9)

SUPPORTING IDEA: *God's patience has limits when his people refuse to repent or obey.*

7:7. The prophet received a third vision. God himself stood beside a **wall** with a **plumb line** in his hand. He was determining whether the wall was straight or not. If not, he would have to knock it down and build it again.

7:8. God asked, **What do you see, Amos?** The prophet gave the obvious reply: **a plumb line**. God's reply was far from obvious. He was **setting a plumb line among my people Israel**. He had chosen Israel. He had created them as a nation. He had conquered their land for them. He had established the kingdom and even chosen Jeroboam to start the Northern Kingdom (1 Kgs. 11:29–40). Why would God measure his own creation? Surely he had created it plumb and true!

God had created everything perfectly. But he gave his people the gift of freedom. They can choose to live in faithful obedience to him, or they can choose to go the way of the world and ignore God. When we choose the world's way, our lives become warped and out of plumb. We no longer mirror God's perfect image. We no longer serve his purposes. We become useless just like an out-of-plumb wall that is about to fall. Eventually, we must be reshaped and remolded by the Master's hand. So Amos learned in his vision that Israel had reached the point of no return. Major disciplinary action was in order: **I will spare them no longer**.

7:9. Verse 9 describes what God planned to do. Write in your own words God's plan of destructive action. Why did he emphasize **high places** and **sanctuaries**?

Isaac was the son of promise for Abraham and Sarah (Gen. 21:1–5). He was associated with the town of Beersheba (Gen. 26:25–33). Amos thus threatened southern worship places such as Beersheba where Isaac had worshipped (Amos 5:5). **Israel** was the national name for the Northern Kingdom. It originated as a secondary name for Jacob (Gen. 32:28). Destruction of worship places connected with Isaac and Jacob meant destruction of the tradition of the sons of Abraham and the covenant promise with Abraham. Israel's religious tradition was dead. God would destroy it.

No longer could the prophet pray and expect God to "relent." The day of compassion was past. Israel was untrue and faithless before God. The day of judgment had been announced. Israel's days were numbered. God is in the business of hearing prayers and showing compassion, but he is also in the business of measuring his people and bringing judgment on those who do not stay true to him.

Now the prophet's role changed. Intercession and mediation became useless and impossible. The prophet had to switch from representing the people before God to representing the God of judgment before the people. Now Israel faced a difficult decision. They must decide who was the true spokesman for the Lord.

⟨C⟩ Conflict of Loyalties (7:10–17)

SUPPORTING IDEA: *God's ministers serve at his call and command; they do not owe allegiance to any human official or institution.*

7:10. Out of nowhere appeared **Amaziah the priest of Bethel**. His role is far from what we expect from a priest. He heard the prophet's visions and word from God and immediately tattled on the prophet to the **king**. This shows that he was probably being paid by the king.

The way Amaziah reported Amos's words to the king is significant: **Amos is raising a conspiracy against you in the very heart of Israel**. Amaziah saw Amos as a threat to national security, the leader of rebellion against the king. Amos was so dangerous he needed to leave the country because **the land cannot bear all his words**. What mattered for Amaziah was the safety and continued rule of Jeroboam, king of Israel. King and country mattered more to Amaziah than God and goodness.

7:11. The priest had his own way of quoting the prophet. The prophet had reported God's words: "With my sword I will rise against the house of Jeroboam" (Amos 7:9). The priest reported that Amos had said, **Jeroboam will die by the sword, and Israel will surely go into exile, away from their native land**. Previously, Amos had warned of exile for Israel (see, e.g., Amos 5:5,27; 6:7–8). He had never said the king would be killed. The priest heightened the message to get the king's attention.

7:12–13. Having reported to his boss, the priest had a word of advice for Amos: **Go back** home to Judah and make your living there. Leave us up here in the prosperous north alone. I represent God here, and you are not welcome in **Bethel**. The king remains in control here, and speech against the king is not allowed, even if it comes directly from God.

7:14. Amos had a different slant on things. Amaziah assumed Amos was a professional prophet who made his living by religion just as Amaziah did. No! said Amos. I do not make my living by prophesying. I am not on a professional staff at a temple or worship place. I am not a son of a prophet (literal translation), a phrase that may have two meanings. Priests often gained their position by inheritance. Kings appointed a priest's son when the older priest retired or died. Amos said his father's occupation had nothing to do with his being a prophet.

The "sons of the prophets" was a technical term for a guild or group of prophets serving under a prophetic leader (1 Kgs. 20:35) at a place of worship. Amos did not belong to such a professional group. He had his own occupation. He was a **shepherd**, caring for sheep. On the side he tended **sycamore-fig trees**, preparing the fruit for sale.

7:15. While Amos plied his trade with the sheep, **the LORD** had called. The call was clear: **Go, prophesy to my people Israel**. Amos, unlike Moses, Gideon, or Jeremiah, did not ask questions about his call. He heard the call, left the sheep, and headed north. He who was not a prophet became a prophet—not to make money but to obey God.

7:16. Having explained his position, Amos could now deliver God's message one more time to Amaziah personally. Amos pitted Amaziah's word against God's word. You say . . . God says. To whom should I listen? Whom should I obey? Amaziah said, **Do not prophesy . . . stop preaching**. That went against the calling Amos had just described. He could not refuse to prophesy or preach when God had told him to do just that.

7:17. Then Amos released the prophetic hammer. Whenever you see **Therefore this is what the LORD says** in the prophetic writings, a strong word of judgment usually follows. This word was personal and specific. Amaziah's family would suffer because Amaziah had been unfaithful. His **wife** would be forced into public prostitution. Why? Apparently because she would have no husband to support her. Amaziah's **sons and daughters**, without his protection, would become victims of the invading army. Amaziah would be among the exiles of Israel in a **pagan country**. This would happen no matter how many times he told Amos not to prophesy that Israel would **go into exile**. Amaziah would **die** in exile.

𝔻 Ripe for Reaping (8:1–3)

> **SUPPORTING IDEA:** *A people who do not obey God are ripe for his harvest of judgment.*

8:1. God gave Amos a fourth vision. This involved a play on Hebrew words. Amos saw a **basket** full of figs or other **fruit** (Heb. *qayits*) harvested in the summer. Such a picture raised visions of celebration, harvest festival, worship, and feasting.

8:2. As in the third vision (Amos 7:8), God asked a simple question: **What do you see, Amos?** The prophet gave the obvious answer. God gave a not-so-obvious explanation: "The end (Heb. *qets*) has come to my people" (literal translation). A disobedient nation whose political and religious leadership was more interested in personal power and in political position than in obeying God finds they are not as secure as they thought. God can declare "time's up" for any people, even a world power.

8:3. Israel loved to worship. They raised their **temple** hymns with gusto and fervor. God was deaf to their music. His actions would change their tune from praise and joy to **wailing** and lament. Even worse, a multitude of Israelite corpses would be **flung everywhere**. No more music. **Silence.** Even the prophet's voice would cease. Worship was at an end because the nation was at its end. All this would come **in that day**, the day Israel called the Day of the Lord, the day of victory and celebration. God would win the victory on that day, and his defeated enemy would be Israel.

> **MAIN IDEA REVIEW:** *God expects his people to remain faithful to him even when they are greatly outnumbered by unbelievers.*

III. CONCLUSION

The Day You Will Never Forget

A plane flies into the World Trade Center. Flames erupt. People cry in agony. One nation under God drops into mourning, never to be the same. A city spends months cleaning up the mess.

Who will ever forget that day? But it was nothing compared to the day Amos described to Israel and its chief priest Amaziah. A minority of one faced the nation's power structure. But he proved to be the majority opinion because he knew God's mathematical formula—one plus God is always a majority.

PRINCIPLES

- God judges his own people when they are not faithful.
- Religious leaders often stand in opposition to God because their loyalties are with worldly powers, economic rewards, or professional position rather than with God and his word.
- God is patient with his people, but his patience has limits.
- God is free to respond to the prayers of his people.
- God controls the history of his people.
- God often uses laypeople to deliver his message.

APPLICATIONS

- Listen and obey God's message, not the words of people in powerful positions.
- When God calls you to do his work, obey his call.
- Prepare now for God's judgment day.

> - Worship God in reverence and holiness while you have the opportunity to do so.

IV. LIFE APPLICATION

The Moral Machine

C. S. Lewis tells the story of an English schoolboy who, when someone asked him, "What is God like?" replied, "As far as I can tell, God is the sort of person who is always snooping around to see if anyone is enjoying himself and then trying to stop it."

Lewis explains:

> I am afraid that is the sort of idea that the word Morality raises in a good many people's minds: something that interferes, something that stops you having a good time. In reality, moral rules are directions for running the human machine. Every moral rule is there to prevent a breakdown, or a strain, or a friction, in the running of that machine. . . . When you are being taught how to use any machine, the instructor keeps on saying, 'No, don't do it like that,' because, of course, there are all sorts of things that look all right and seem to you the natural way of treating the machine, but do not really work (*Mere Christianity*, p. 59).

Take a moral inventory of your attitudes and actions—as well as those of your church. Be prepared to turn from anything God shows you is wrong.

V. PRAYER

Sovereign God of the universe, you are holy and you command us to be holy. Show us how to obey. Give us the faith to obey. Help us to live so that we may be ready to meet you. Amen.

VI. DEEPER DISCOVERIES

A. The Lord Relented (7:3,6)

God is free to respond to the prayers and needs of his people. The Old Testament expresses this freedom as "God relents" (Heb. *nicham*). The word means to regret or become remorseful.

God responded to the massive dose of human sin in Noah's age by relenting or being "grieved" that he had created man on the earth (Gen. 6:6). He answered Moses' prayer for mercy and did not destroy his people (Exod. 32:12–14). In the time of the judges, he heard his oppressed people groaning and relented, having "compassion on them" (Judg. 2:18). After punishing the people because King David took an unauthorized census, God relented, being "grieved," and did not punish Jerusalem (2 Sam. 24:16).

Jeremiah promised the people that God would relent and not bring disaster if they would repent by changing their ways (Jer. 18:8). When Jeremiah was threatened, the elders looked back to the days of Hezekiah and Micah when God relented and did not carry out his prophecy of judgment (Jer. 26:19). When God exercised his freedom to relent by not bringing his threatened evil against Nineveh, the great enemy, it made his prophet mad (Jon. 3:10–4:1).

The same God who hears the pleas of his people or his prophet and relents can refuse to do so: "Therefore the earth will mourn and the heavens above grow dark, because I have spoken and will not relent, I have decided and will not turn back" (Jer. 4:28).

How do we understand this freedom of God to relent and not to relent. We must begin by acknowledging that "an explicit emotional element is absent here" (H. J. Stoebe, *TLOT*, II, 738). This is not a God reacting according to his present emotional state. Rather, the term "is never sorrowful resignation but always has concrete consequences" (Stoebe, 738). God changes his relationship to a person or people and thus changes the course of action taken for or against that people.

Mike Butterworth puts it succinctly: "God does not capriciously change his intentions or ways of acting. It is the change in Saul's behavior that leads to this expression of regret. In many cases the Lord's 'changing' of his mind is a gracious response to human factors" (*NIDOTTE*, III, 82).

God is not a static, unchanging being who can be predicted. He is a personal God who relates in freedom to his people. He listens to their intercession, sees their weakness and limits, hears an oppressed people's cries, and moves to a course of action that is the proper response at the proper moment in his relationship with his people. But this does not mean God can be coerced or predicted. He is free to decide when he will relent and when he will not.

VII. TEACHING OUTLINE

A. INTRODUCTION

1. Lead Story: "We Must Visit One More Lady"
2. Context: Amos has preached his oracles against the foreign nations and his sermons against God's people, Israel. Now he shows us why he preached, the reception he received, and the final result of his prophetic ministry.

3. Transition: Four visions and a confrontation with the national religious leader force us to face the reality of God's judgment. Judgment often comes on people who identify themselves as people of God. It comes after God has warned his people, when he has even drawn back in grace from carrying through with threatened punishment. But God's patience has limits, and his judgment day is real.

B. COMMENTARY
1. Power of Prophetic Prayer (7:1–6)
2. Certainty of Judgment (7:7–9)
3. Conflict of Loyalties (7:10–17)
4. Ripe for Reaping (8:1–3)

C. CONCLUSION: THE DAY YOU WILL NEVER FORGET

VIII. ISSUES FOR DISCUSSION

1. Does God still reveal his will to his people through visions?
2. What do God's people do or not do to bring his judgment down on themselves?
3. What does it say about God's nature when Scripture declares, "The Lord relented"?
4. What does Amos teach us about the nature of intercessory prayer?
5. What would God find in our lives and in our church if he held a plumb line beside us?

Amos 8:4–9:15

Wandering After the Word

I. INTRODUCTION
An African Hunger

II. COMMENTARY
A verse-by-verse explanation of these verses.

III. CONCLUSION
Losing Your Freedom

An overview of the principles and applications from these verses.

IV. LIFE APPLICATION
Expectations May Not Reflect Reality

Melding these verses to life.

V. PRAYER
Tying these verses to life with God.

VI. DEEPER DISCOVERIES
Historical, geographical, and grammatical enrichment of the commentary.

VII. TEACHING OUTLINE
Suggested step-by-step group study of these verses.

VIII. ISSUES FOR DISCUSSION
Zeroing these verses in on daily life.

"*W*hen God gives you a command, He is trying to protect and preserve the best He has for you. He does not want you to lose it. When God gives you a command, He is not restricting you. He is freeing you. God's purpose is that you might prosper and live."

Henry T. Blackaby and Claude V. King

Amos 8:4–9:15

IN A NUTSHELL

A people oppressing the poor and enduring worship so they can get back to the business of making money hear God's message, "I will never forget." So God warns them of judgment that will turn joy and festivity into mourning and weeping. The strongest threat comes when God announces the coming of a famine of hearing God's word.

Wandering After the Word

I. INTRODUCTION

An African Hunger

*T*he first day of a mission trip to rural Kenya I stood at a little thatched-roof building used as a church house in their village. We prayed. Suddenly, it dawned on me that I had to follow this Kenyan layman all by myself and begin witnessing along the byways of a place rampant with disease. Who would stop to hear me? We turned the first curve in the road. Five or six people stood by the road. My interpreter asked them if they would listen to me for a few moments. I simply told the story of God's love in Jesus Christ. The entire group repeated the sinner's prayer with me.

Meanwhile, an entire new group stood waiting to hear. I found how hungry people without God's word are to hear God's message. Kenya had a famine of God's word, not because God sent it but because we refused to take the word to them. In a couple of years six churches increased to 125 churches. A new Bible school served to train pastors in God's word. The famine was over.

Amos faced a people who had known the word of God for centuries. He warned them that God was taking the word away from them. A look at modern Israel and at the places where New Testament preachers established the first churches shows that God can still bring a famine of God's word.

II. COMMENTARY

Wandering After the Word

> **MAIN IDEA:** *A people who do not show God's love to the people they work and live with find God announcing judgment and taking his word away from them, but a disciplined people find God renewing his promises to them.*

A The Faithful One Never Forgets (8:4–8)

> **SUPPORTING IDEA:** *A people more devoted to commerce and coins than to the poor and to praise invite God's judgment.*

8:4. Amos issued a call to attention, a device often used by prophets to shock the audience into hearing God's opinion of who they were (Isa. 47:8; Hos. 4:1). The formula addressed the people in ways they did not expect. Those who flocked to worship in Bethel were those **who trample the needy**

and do away with the poor of the land (Amos 2:7). God had more interest in their oppressive business practices and their abhorrent social relationships than in their religious practices.

8:5. Where could God gather evidence for such an accusation? Just listen in on whispered conversations as they came to worship. One day a month, the day of the **New Moon**, the people had to leave their shops and go worship, bringing special offerings, feasting, and blowing trumpets (2 Kgs. 4:23; Hag. 1:1).

Worse still, from a business standpoint, the **Sabbath** took away a business day every week as Israel celebrated creation (Exod. 20:8–11) and the exodus (Deut. 5:12–15). Israel knew what God expected on the Sabbath and the consequences for disobedience (Exod. 31:12–17). Thus Israel went through the motions of celebrating Sabbath and New Moon, but they complained as they did, and God heard their complaints. They wanted to shut down the temple so they could open up their trade booths.

At the trade booths, they oppressed the poor who had to come to them to buy food. The rich shopkeepers reduced the amount of grain they measured out, used **scales** they knew to be inaccurate, and charged the poor higher prices (Deut. 25:13–16; Mic. 6:9–12.)

8:6. Such oppression soon emptied the pockets of the poor, who had to sell themselves into slavery to the rich or remain so deep in debt to them that they had to do whatever the rich commanded. Sometimes the price of a **pair of sandals** forced the poor man to enslave himself. The sellers went so far as to sweep up the floor at night, gathering dust and husks and anything else on the floor and mixing it with the grain to sell. How could people who did this think of themselves as God's people and of their worship as pleasing to God?

8:7. It was enough to make God take an oath to emphasize his anger and his determination to carry out his sentence. Having nothing greater than himself by which to swear the oath, he swore by **the Pride of Jacob**, apparently "an ironic name for Yahweh. Israel did not treat God as majestic. Their action demonstrated that they were not particularly proud of him, but God swears on the basis of his glorious and majestic name … to regain his glory and defend his majesty" (Gary V. Smith, *Amos*, 254–55).

The oath is ominous: **I will never forget anything they have done.** Some things we wish God would forget, but sins without repentance he cannot forget. They remain on his list until judgment day.

8:8. Israel might ignore God's oath. But the land, or perhaps even the entire earth, cannot ignore such a menacing threat. It will shake like the mighty Nile River in flood stage. The ultimate result will be mourning by **all who live in it.**

B Feasts Become Funerals (8:9–14)

> **SUPPORTING IDEA:** *God has prepared a day of judgment in which religious festivals will become funerals and the word of God will disappear.*

8:9. Amos spent eight chapters describing God's judgment on a people who failed to treat people with justice and fairness and who worshipped regularly as they were supposed to but not because they wanted to. He ended the judgment picture by describing a mysterious famine. This would happen **in that day** (Amos 8:9,13), "the days are coming" (Amos 8:11). These were indefinite expressions that could not be placed on a calendar, but they were assured dates that God had set with his disobedient people.

Portents in the natural world would usher in the famine. Darkness would rule the day—the exact opposite of what God had accomplished when he separated light and darkness and called the light day and the darkness night (Gen. 1:3–5). God's own creation would mirror the chaos of Israel's lifestyle.

8:10. The religious sector of Israel's life would likewise become chaotic in God's great reversal. Joyous festivals such as Passover and Tabernacles would lose their elements of praise and thanksgiving. **Mourning** and **weeping** would rule the temple worship at Bethel and Dan. Sabbath go-to-meeting clothes would be traded in for **sackcloth**, the symbol of lamentation, grief, and loss. The latest hairdos would be replaced by bald, shaved **heads**. The joyous festival days would become **bitter**. The only comparison that comes close to describing such a day would be the day a person had to bury his **only son**.

8:11. What could possibly make a day so horrible? The entire land would lack a vital ingredient for living. This ingredient is even more basic than food or water. God was bringing a **famine of hearing the words of the LORD**. This would be worse than any famine people had ever experienced.

8:12. Men would become just as weak from not having a daily portion of the holy **word** as they do from not eating. Thus they will **stagger** around weakly, searching for what they most need, **but they will not find it.** God's terrible punishment is upon them. They cannot find or feed on God's word.

8:13–14. Good looks and physical strength will not suffice **in that day.** Neither will religion as usual, a religion dedicated to **the shame of Samaria** and the god of **Dan** or "of the Way to Beersheba" (literal translation, apparently a reference to the pilgrimage many northerners took to the southern worship place of their forefathers Isaac and Jacob; see comments on Amos 5:5). Israel should be worshipping the Name (Heb. *Shem*). Instead, charged Amos, they worshipped the shame (Heb. *'shmah*). This is apparently a reference to the pagan Baal-Asherah symbols at Samaria (1 Kgs. 16:32–33).

Finally, God's people will learn that we do not "live on bread alone" but must have "every word that comes from the mouth of God" (Matt. 4:4). We must learn to pray, "Give us today our daily bread" (Matt. 6:11). Israel assumed they would continue to hear God's message to direct their lives. He had always sent prophets and teachers to them. Why would he stop doing so? For four hundred years after Malachi's day, Israel heard no prophet until finally John the Baptist and Jesus broke the famine of God's message for the people of Israel.

God's Presence Makes Escape Impossible (9:1–4)

SUPPORTING IDEA: *No one can escape God when he sets his eyes on his people to judge them.*

9:1. God had one more vision for Amos. This one differed from all the others in structure, in vocabulary, and in the absence of dialogue. Most of all, it differed in content. No longer did Amos see something from the natural world and connect it to God's message of judgment. Now Amos saw God himself **standing by the altar.** What an unexpected sight! God belonged in the inner sanctum of the temple, behind the thick curtains where only the high priest could go. What was God doing out in view by the altar? He was issuing commands to a mysterious, unidentified party.

The command was horrendous: **Strike the tops of the pillars so that the thresholds shake.** The pillars were strong, decorative poles that supported the roof of the temple. The tops (or capitals) were rounded, knob-shaped decorations on top of the pillars, perhaps with floral designs. The threshold was the stone under the door frame in which the pivots of the doors revolved. God thus shook the temple supports from top (capitals) to bottom (thresholds).

God made a public visit to the temple, not to enjoy the sacrifices offered to him and to revel in the worship sent his way. He came to the temple to destroy it and all its people, especially the priests like Amaziah (Amos 7:10). God meant business. Should the toppling pillars miss anyone, God himself would **kill with the sword.** Here is the image of the final inescapable judgment. Vision is no longer warning, no longer opportunity to plead for divine patience and grace. Vision is now announcement of final disaster. God has no more patience or leniency with the guilty.

9:2. God described just how serious he was in saying no one would escape. You could try digging **down to** Sheol—the place where the dead existed, the deepest imaginable place. Note the NIV translation of **grave** does not give the full import of the Hebrew *Sheol*. God would stretch out his arm, and his **hand** would **take them.** They could get on the highest mountains and keep climbing up into the **heavens.** Still they would be an arm's length away from God.

9:3. They might **hide themselves** among the cliffs, crags, and caves of Mount **Carmel** on the Mediterranean Sea coast (Judg. 6:2). God would become a hunter and hunt them down. Perhaps they were brave enough to dive into the depths of the sea with all its fearful creatures. God would issue the **command**, and the **serpent** would bite them. Amos does not identify the serpent as Leviathan (Job 3:8), but the readers would have understood the reference as to a deadly serpentine monster. From height to depth, Israel could not escape God. He is everywhere. And even the fearsome serpent obeys his command.

9:4. Perhaps Israel would take the most drastic step of all—surrender to the enemy and go into **exile**. Leaving the promised land is no way to avoid God. He is not limited to any one geographical space. He does not share his rule with other gods. He rules all lands and all countries, no matter their distant location. God's command to **slay them** is final. God will not be denied. Wherever Israel went in futile escape efforts, they would find God already there.

Normally Israel would thank God for his presence among them. Not this time because God would **fix** his **eyes** upon them **for evil and not for good**. The person who disobeys God, who refuses to repent and turn to God for forgiveness—that person finds God's acts to be evil. Not evil in the sense of absolutely bad, but evil in the sense of bringing harm and destruction to the people who are suffering God's judgment.

🄳 Identifying the Lord of Hosts (9:5–6)

> **SUPPORTING IDEA:** The Lord of Hosts controls creation and rules over it without opposition.

9:5. God's people cannot escape God's judgment. Amos turned to his collection of hymns (see Amos 4:13; 5:8–9) for proof. The nature of God as described in the hymns proved that God could bring horrendous judgment on his own people. This is the **Lord**, the Master, the one in absolute control over everything. We are slaves who must accept and obey the Lord's words. He is the LORD **Almighty**, or translated literally, "Yahweh of Hosts." Yahweh is the personal name of God revealed to Moses and Israel just before the exodus (Exod. 3:13–18). *Hosts* refers to God's army, made up of the heavenly angels and any earthly army he chooses to use. He is the commander in chief. We are privates who must obey his commands.

9:6. God **builds** a two-story dwelling for himself. The **foundation** is laid on the **earth**. The upper story reaches into the **heavens**. Can such a builder not destroy the earth, which serves only as the foundation for his home? Can he destroy an earthly temple built with human hands? Of course; he can. He has built a much better one for himself in the heavens. After all, this is the sovereign Lord who controls every body of water on earth. He can pour them out on earth to supply the water his people so desperately need, or he can pour them out to flood the world and bring havoc and destruction. God can bring judgment on the earth because he controls it. And remember what Israel learned from Moses. **The LORD** (Heb. *Yahweh*) **is his name**. Don't be fooled into worshipping any other god. This is the only God with power.

Ⓔ Protection Is Not in Claiming Election (9:7–10)

SUPPORTING IDEA: *The theological claim of election as God's people does not protect from God's judgment on a disobedient people because God controls the destiny of all nations.*

9:7. The people of Israel had an immediate reply for Amos. But you forget our history lesson. Yes, God revealed his name to Moses, as you said. God also at that time made us his special people. He chose us. He elected us. He made a covenant with us. God is tied to us on this earth. We are the only representatives he has. He has to work through us if he is to work in this world.

Oh no! Amos responds. Remember how I started out chapter 3. Aren't you just like the people of Cush near Egypt (2 Sam. 18:21–32)? You are so proud that I delivered you **from Egypt**. Remember, I did the same for the **Philistines** and the **Arameans** (or Syrians). The Philistines came to their home on the southwestern coast of Palestine from **Caphtor**, probably modern Crete (Deut. 2:23). The Arameans or Syrians came to their home in northeast Palestine from the city of **Kir** (Isa. 22:6), whose location remains uncertain.

God led Amos to make the audacious claim that God directed the history of these people just as much as he did Israel's. The prophet rejected Israel's claim to fame as the one nation whose history the Lord planned and directed. God directs the history of every nation. No nation can claim pride of place and set demands on God because they are an elect nation—the people whose history God oversees. God can pronounce judgment on all nations (Amos 1:3–2:16), and he can claim to be Lord of the history of all nations. No nation is exempt from God's discipline or destruction.

9:8. Having established God's authority to judge, Amos can relay God's decision to judge. God's **eyes . . . are on the sinful kingdom**. Normally Israel would rejoice at such words. They would mean God was about to punish Israel's enemies. But chosen Israel has become sinful Israel. Delivered from Egypt, Israel is about to become exiled to Mesopotamia. But pay attention. All is not lost. **I will not totally destroy the house of Jacob**. God will leave a remnant. That is a good sign. But first judgment must come.

9:9. God will thresh his crop of **grain**. The good kernels will fall through the sifter to the ground, but something remains behind in the sifter. These are the pebbles or rocks that have become mixed with the grain. The pebbles are too big to fall through the sieve. They remain trapped. This is the picture of Israel. God's people are trapped in God's sieve, ready to be thrown into the waste heap and destroyed. They will never reach the grain pile that God can use for his purposes.

9:10. Put it in plain terms, no figures of speech. **All the sinners among my people will die.** That should cast fear into you and make you ask questions. When God comes to judge, am I the one who dies? Have I fooled myself into thinking I am part of God's faithful people when he knows I am on the list to die in judgment? God quickly answers such questions. The sinners are those who rashly say, **Disaster will not overtake or meet us.** Just as Jesus surprised people as he identified the sheep and the goats in Matthew 25, so God surprised Israel by bringing judgment on people who felt secure in the divine arms of love.

F Restoring the Ruins (9:11–15)

SUPPORTING IDEA: *God's last word promises renewal and hope for a punished people.*

9:11. Israel's sinners face surprise. Judgment comes. Israel's faithful face surprise. Judgment is not God's final word. God will raise up **David's fallen tent.** A tent represents a booth made of twigs for temporary residence either in the battlefield (2 Sam. 11:11), for God's ark (2 Sam. 11:11), for workers in the harvest field (Isa. 1:8), or for cattle (Gen. 33:17). Here David is promised a temporary residence, not an everlasting house. Still, the residence will be rebuilt to previous specifications as in the good old days.

The promise has another element of surprise. Amos addressed his message to Israel, the Northern Kingdom. But his claim has always been that God "roars from Zion and thunders from Jerusalem" (Amos 1:2). The final promise thus centers in the Jerusalem tradition of David, not in the northern tradition of Jeroboam.

9:12. That hope is more than just a rebuilding of the monarchy. The new David will have power over the **remnant of Edom**—those people whom the prophet Obadiah condemned as betraying Jerusalem when it fell to Babylon. Indeed, the new David will have power over "all nations that are called by my name" (literal translation of Amos 9:12). How can you be sure this will happen? The same way you can be sure judgment will happen. It is Yahweh, **the LORD, who will do these things.**

9:13. Words do not adequately paint the picture of blessing. A farm metaphor fails. Reaping will not be complete before plowing begins for a new crop. New seeds will be sown before the grape harvest is turned into wine. The crop is so abundant it cannot be harvested before it is time to start another. Everywhere, grapes will appear. Their product will **flow down the** hills like rivers so people can quench their thirst without the bother of harvesting and squeezing out the juice.

9:14. When will this be? When God fulfills his promise and brings the exiles back to their homeland. **Cities** which the enemies **ruined** at God's command, Israel **will rebuild** for their use at God's command. Once again the land will be a farmer's dream as the people **plant** and harvest their crops.

9:15. How long can this last? Forever, promises God! The people are **never again to be uprooted from the land** because it is land he has given them.

God has fulfilled many of his promises. Others await fulfillment at a time of God's choosing. Even in life's darkest moments, do you depend on God to restore you and fulfill his promises to you?

> **MAIN IDEA REVIEW:** *A people who do not show God's love to the people they work and live with find God announcing judgment and taking his word away from them, but a disciplined people find God renewing his promises to them.*

III. CONCLUSION

Losing Your Freedom

One night we went for a walk with my granddaughter. We took the stroller just in case we reached the limits of her spindly two-year-old legs. Of course, she wanted to push the stroller, so we set off with her peering through the top of the stroller and pushing it down our street. Soon she needed a bit more excitement, so she found she could push the stroller and let it race down the street by itself. A couple of "No, No, don't do that" warnings did not get the job done. Finally, my wife strapped her in the stroller. A loud cry greeted this loss of freedom.

Our granddaughter resembled Israel in many ways. The people of Amos's time heard God's warnings again and again but continued to go their own way. They soon discovered that God is in the business of judging his people as well as saving them. Sadly they had to learn the final lesson: God has a day of judgment for disobedient people—a day that leaves only a small faithful remnant behind.

PRINCIPLES

- God's judgment is so severe that human words cannot describe it yet so certain that we must not ignore it.
- Judgment is more than suffering material loss. It includes loss of relationship with God expressed in the absence of his word among his people.

- Judgment is not God's final word; his eternal purpose is to create and bless a people who depend on him.

APPLICATIONS

- Devote yourself to reading God's Word daily, and be grateful that God has not taken it from you.

- Examine your religious practices such as prayer, worship, and giving to see if they meet God's standards or if they are something you do to try to win his favor.

- Determine if economic priorities govern your life rather than spiritual priorities.

- Ask God to help you discover any false gods you may be worshipping.

- Thank God for his promises of eternal salvation.

IV. LIFE APPLICATION

Expectations May Not Reflect Reality

Friends recently returned from a mission trip to Cambodia. They went with an image of a land ruined by war and ransacked by political upheaval. They returned with a report of loving people hungry to know Jesus and willing to open their arms and their homes so missionaries could tell the story of God's love. Reality turned out to be much different from their expectations.

Israel's expectations were also quite different from the picture Amos painted of God's absolute judgment on their land. Many laughed him off as a fanatic. Others took his word seriously and despaired.

Yet Amos surprised Israel with a new word—a word of hope in the midst of doom. God would bring restoration and renewal out of judgment. He struck fear into those who didn't take God seriously and gave hope to those who did. We can take a lesson from Israel. We should take his warnings of discipline seriously—but cling also to his words of hope.

V. PRAYER

Faithful judge of all the earth, help us see reality through your eyes. Do not let us create a false picture supported by false theology. Show us our sins. We repent of those sins. We turn to you in faith and obedience. Amen.

VI. DEEPER DISCOVERIES

A. Election (9:7)

Amos strikes at the heart of Israelite belief, the doctrine of God's special election of his people Israel. Deuteronomy 7:6–8 states the belief in its clearest terms:

> For you are a people holy to the LORD your God. The LORD your God has chosen you out of all the peoples on the face of the earth to be his people, his treasured possession. The LORD did not set his affection on you and choose you because you were more numerous than other peoples, for you were the fewest of all peoples. But it was because the LORD loved you and kept the oath he swore to your forefathers that he brought you out with a mighty hand and redeemed you from the land of slavery, from the power of Pharaoh king of Egypt.

This is "a novelty in the history of Ancient Near Eastern religion. The idea of Israel's special status before Yahweh is nothing short of constitutive for its faith." Amos emphasized what Israel neglected in the doctrine of election:

> Election by Yahweh must find response in the proper behavior of the elect. Without an awareness of the responsibility inherent in election, election itself is called into question. . . . Israel's election is therefore not treated in isolation, but in order to justify Yahweh's claim on Israel. Indeed, the reference to the election in Deuteromony 10:12 establishes Yahweh's comprehensive demand for obedience: to fear God, to walk in his paths, to love him, and to serve him with the whole heart and soul. Because Israel's holiness is accordingly not inherent but rests upon Yahweh's choice, however, Israel must acknowledge its obligation to behave in conformity with this act of Yahweh's free grace. The misunderstanding that Yahweh's choice may rest upon Israel's special merit is resisted vehemently (H. Wildberger, *TLOT* I, 214; see Deut. 9:4–6; 10:1–15).

Election, then, is "an absolute act of grace, grounded only in Yahweh's love for Israel, which cannot be further explained" (Wildberger, 217).

Speaking to a northern audience where election theology seems to have been extremely strong, Amos warned that election led to punishment (Amos 3:2). Election did not protect Israel from God's anger. Rather, Israel's love of cultic worship separated from a love for and obedience to God led the Lord to strip Israel of its privileged status and put them on a level playing field with all the other nations. God directed the history of every nation, not just Israel's.

If Israel saw election only as God's act in history, unconnected to covenant obedience theology, then God would disconnect Israel from himself. Now Israel had to wait for a new act of election, a new move of grace on God's part for them (Isa. 14:1). God wanted Israel to learn that "Yahweh's election does not only mean a blessed destiny. It is a summons which calls for responsibility" (W. Zimmerli, Ezekiel, *Hermeneia*, 1, 408).

VII. TEACHING OUTLINE

A. INTRODUCTION
1. Lead Story: An African Hunger
2. Context: Amos's visions and Amaziah's attempt to expel the prophet from Israel and Israel's worship places reveal the nation's desperate condition. They prepare the way for the final vision God has for the prophet and for a word of hope beyond the coming disaster.
3. Transition: Amos's final two chapters paint two contrasting pictures, the first of absolute darkness and the other of a glimmer of light beyond the darkness. What could cause God to paint such a dark picture? Does the modern church represent what Amos saw or what he hoped for? What must we do to prevent God's word of judgment becoming his final word for us?

B. COMMENTARY
1. The Faithful One Never Forgets (8:4–8)
2. Feasts Become Funerals (8:9–14)
3. God's Presence Makes Escape Impossible (9:1–4)
4. Identifying the Lord of Hosts (9:5–6)
5. Protection Is Not in Claiming Election (9:7–10)
6. Restoring the Ruins (9:11–15)

C. CONCLUSION: LOSING YOUR FREEDOM

VIII. ISSUES FOR DISCUSSION
1. What economic sins would Amos condemn you for today?
2. What marks of false religion would Amos see in your church and in your personal practices?
3. How do people try to escape from God today? What success do they have?

4. Is there any sign of a famine of God's word among us today?
5. How do we find theological ways to protect ourselves from the reality of God's discipline and judgment on his unfaithful people?

Introduction to

Obadiah

Obadiah is short and powerful. An introduction to the book must be just as short but has a difficult time being as powerful since we know virtually nothing about the prophet. His name means "slave of Yah" (or Yahweh).

Obadiah preached to Judah about Edom, an enemy of Judah at the time (586 B.C.). Edom had been Judah's ally and treaty partner since the two nations were close geographical neighbors and shared a common ancestry (Gen. 36). Sadly the nations also shared a history of enmity and violence.

Judah didn't need other enemies. Babylon had just destroyed Jerusalem and had leveled the temple. And now Judah was supposed to learn lessons from the fate of their hated enemy. The lessons are quite simple: God will punish the sins of pride, self-reliance, betrayal, and boasting over one's friends and partners. Edom's punishment was not a time for Judah to return the favor with boasting, betrayal, pride, and self-reliance of its own. Edom's punishment was time for Judah to celebrate God's kingship and devote themselves to proper worship of the eternal King until he brings Obadiah's promises to pass.

But reading Obadiah brings great temptations to us. Do we really want to serve a God who shows such wrath, violence, and vengeance? Have we joined Judah in complaining about God's injustice because we do not have faith in his promises? Do we tend to become braggarts, laughing at the bad times others receive because we view them as well-deserved punishment from God?

Obadiah challenges us to face our own pride and self-reliance, to ask God for forgiveness, to promise to let him erase these character traits from our lives, to let God insert humility into our lives in pride's place, to trust God for deliverance from life's problems rather than trying always to do it ourselves. Obadiah has one subtle lesson that many of us need to listen to and heed. He calls us to examine family relationships with immediate family and extended family. Pride and self-reliance can block us from reconciliation and peace with our families.

As we read Obadiah, we need to remember Leslie Allen's summary:

> Their religious community on the verge of extinction had to be nationalistic or perish, particularistic or disappear. Through Obadiah, Yahweh understandingly gives a word for the times. He soothes festering mental sores which developed from national humiliation, and

yet he lifts the issues to a higher plane than mere resentment and revenge. . . . [God's] pledges which must have put new luster into the downcast eyes of contemporary believers and sustained them through life's rigors, have passed, through Christ, into the possession of the Christian church. They require translation into the language of the new covenant to be meaningful today. The Book of Obadiah offers the assurance of a God of moral justice who will restore the moral equilibrium and right the blatant wrongs of this wicked world. God is in control, at work behind the scenes, working out his own plans through the chaos of human moves and countermoves. The Church triumphant is our destiny, and toward this end we are to work with confidence, however much Christian communities here and there seem to shrink and be ineffective (NICOT, 138).

Read Obadiah with hope, assurance, and humility. Read it with love for your enemies and faith in your God.

Obadiah 1–21

The Kingdom Is the Lord's

"*H*eaven's occupants are not self-centered, they are Christ-centered. You will be in your sinless state. The sinless don't protect a reputation or project an image. You won't be shamed. You'll be happy to let God do in heaven what he did on earth—be honored in your weaknesses."

M a x   L u c a d o

Obadiah 1–21

I N   A   N U T S H E L L

*G*od condemns Edom, Judah's southeastern neighbor, for pride, overconfidence, and their refusal to help in time of need, for pillaging Jerusalem while Judah was attacked by Babylon, and for capturing Judah's fleeing refugees. God thus announced the coming Day of the Lord when Edom would fall, Judah would be delivered, and the Lord's kingdom would be established.

The Kingdom Is the Lord's

INTRODUCTION

Dancing with the Devil

*I*n her book *Lord, Is It Warfare?* Kay Arthur remembers when she was seventeen years old, recently moved to a new community, and needing to make a hit with the high school kids to be noticed and appreciated. She decided to make the church canteen the place to be for the upscale youth of Shaker Heights, Ohio.

She started off with a bang, throwing a "heaven and hades dance." One side of the church hall was decorated with soft blue lighting, with angels suspended from white fluffy clouds. But hades was more inviting, or electrifying—flashing red lights, smoke curling up from the punch bowl, and a big red devil hanging on the wall with a pitchfork in his hands. Hades looked like a place where the action is, and that night it was. Heaven's hall stood empty as the teenagers flocked to hades. Kay confesses that for the next twelve years "I'd continue to dance with the devil—and didn't even realize it" (pp. 60–61).

Obadiah accused Judah's neighbor of dancing with the devil and not knowing it, of being precisely who they should not be. As we study this small book, we will look at ourselves and see how we, like Kay and like Edom, can dance with the devil and not realize it. Perhaps this study can help us find God's kingdom instead of the devil's dance before it is too late.

II. COMMENTARY

The Kingdom Is the Lord's

> **MAIN IDEA:** *Edom exhibited pride, overconfidence, refusal to help in time of need, attacking when the other person was down, and helping the enemy qualify a person and a nation for God's judgment, while God's plan is for his people to be part of his kingdom.*

A Punishing Pride (1–4)

> **SUPPORTING IDEA:** *God's judgment comes on proud, overconfident people.*

1. Obadiah means "the servant of Yah" (or Yahweh), and the prophet's name represents his task. He was God's servant, God's messenger to deliver an oracle against a foreign nation for Judah to overhear. Rather than a collection of such oracles as found in Isaiah (13–23), Jeremiah (46–51), Ezekiel (25–32), Amos (1–2), and Zephaniah (2:4–15), Obadiah has an extended oracle against one nation. The nation was Edom, the small country south and east of the Dead Sea, that traced its history back to Esau, Jacob's brother (Gen. 25:30). Hostility and fighting dominated the relationship of the two nations (Judg. 11:17; Isa. 11:14; Mal. 1:4).

Obadiah introduces his prophecy as a **vision**. Many scholars see a prophetic vision as "a revelation of the divine word, usually at night during a deep sleep and sometimes associated with emotional agitation" though at times the prophet is awake (Num. 24:4,16). However received, "The emphasis in the revelatory vision was on the revelation of the divine word, which endowed the prophet with special knowledge of divine things, which he had to proclaim (Isa. 1:1; 2:1; 13:1; Amos 1:1; Mic. 1:1; Hab. 1:1)" (Jackie A. Naudé, *NIDOTTE* II, 58).

The problem for Israel lay in the experience of prophets with false visions (Isa. 30:10; Ezek. 21:29). Israel complained to God when no vision from God was available (1 Sam. 3:1). Thus "the prophetic vision primarily involved a revelation of God and his word, and only then a visual impact: God let it be known what he wanted or what he was going to do and showed it to someone whom he had chosen for this purpose" (Naudé, 59).

Obadiah's vision may have been rooted in a picture God showed him, but primarily it contained a message that God wanted his people to hear. Interestingly, Obadiah shares the message of verses 1–5 with Jeremiah 49:9,14–16. This shows that God could use a message already written and delivered in another context to reveal his will to a different audience. Obadiah may have repeated a message the audience knew Jeremiah had preached, or both prophets may have taken over material used in Israel's worship to cast it into forms God chose for the particular audience addressed.

Obadiah communicated the message in the prophets' normal mode of communication, using the messenger speech of "thus says the Lord" (author's translation). This formula occurs 136 times in the Old Testament, while "thus says Yahweh" occurs 293 times. The formula identifies the prophet as a chosen messenger of God sent from God's high court to the court of his people to announce God's decrees. Obadiah emphasizes his role as messenger by announcing: **We have heard a message from the LORD: An envoy was sent to the nations**. Thus the prophecy opens on a note of suspense, waiting for God's message—a message spoken to Israel but about Edom and sent as a warning to all the nations.

2. For Edom, the message was not good. For the other nations it could be a call to celebration unless they took the message to Edom as a symbolic reminder of what God would say to them too. Edom was big only in that it had tall, rough mountains. Otherwise, it was a nation that controlled a small territory and exercised minimal influence in international affairs. Its only hope for fame lay in its location on the trade route between Mesopotamia and the Red Sea or between Egypt to the west and Assyria and Babylon to the east. The exotic goods from Arabia and Africa traveled through Edom to get to customers in the north, east, and west. With no hopes for economic importance, Edom would be **small**. Not only that, Edom would be **utterly despised**.

3. **Pride** was Edom's problem. The Hebrew word *zadon* points to "presumptuousness, over-confidence" (*HALOT*). (See Deut. 17:12; Jer. 49:16.) Edom thought of themselves as dwelling safe and secure in their craggy, rocky **heights**. Their mountain stronghold in the city of Petra seemed impregnable. What enemy army would bother taking the time and energy required to climb the mountains with military equipment to break down the city's famous walls? So Edom claimed triumphantly: **Who can bring me down to the ground?**

4. God had the answer. They could become like an **eagle**, spreading their wings and soaring high into the mountains—even higher among the **stars** of heaven—to build their **nest**. But God declared, **From there I will bring you down**.

B Friends Will Be Your Foes (5–7)

SUPPORTING IDEA: *Friends turn against a proud, uncaring people.*

5. Rhetorical questions open this brief prophetic announcement of judgment coming on Edom. You would not expect **thieves** or even violent, devastating **robbers** to take everything you had. They would come in, take what they were looking for, and disappear. What awaits Edom is much worse. They will lose everything they have. Obadiah could react to such news only with a cry of lamentation. **Oh** (Heb. *'ek*) is used to introduce a cry of wailing and mourning for the dead or for disastrous news (2 Sam. 1:19).

Even harvesters who came to your vineyard would not take every single grape, even if they were harvesting your vineyard without your knowledge. Those harvesting the vineyard were supposed to leave some for the poor and needy (Deut. 24:21). Now Edom would have the role of picking what was left for the poor. So much for Edom's dreams of economic power!

6. The word **how** repeats the lamentation formula as Obadiah continues mourning over the tragic fate awaiting Edom. **Esau** is another name for Edom, calling the nation by its founding ancestor. The thieves and robbers illustration is completed here. These thieves and robbers do not have a limited appetite. They want everything and will conduct a search-and-find operation until they collect everything Edom owned. The great riches and possessions Edom thought were safely tucked away in their mountain hideaways will be discovered and carted away.

7. **Allies** is literally "all the men of your covenant." Edom had signed peace treaties and mutual protection agreements with surrounding nations or with a powerful, conquering overlord. The actions described in Obadiah 11–14 may indicate that Edom had willingly become a vassal of Babylon and signed an agreement with them before Babylon conquered Jerusalem in 586 B.C. Trust in treaties would prove as worthwhile for Edom as trust in geographical isolation.

But what would these allies do? The phrase **force you to the border** is not clear in Hebrew. The verb is an intensive form of "to send." The widespread meaning of the verb has given rise to many interpretations in the text: sending Edom's ambassadors back home without further agreements, sending Edomite battle refugees back home, driving Edom away from their homeland into exile. The most obvious explanation is that Edom's military powers have been remaining in self-confidence in their mountain strongholds. But that will not be enough. Invading enemy armies will force Edom to fight to defend its borders.

Friends are literally "men of your peace"—people who live together without fighting. It probably indicates parties who have signed a peace agreement with one another. What friends and allies Edom had! They were cheats and deceivers (2 Kgs. 18:29; Jer. 4:10). They ignored treaty obligations and commitments and would **overpower** Edom.

Those who eat your bread are those in friendly treaty relations who have been invited to political banquets and celebrations and who have eaten ceremonial meals sealing the covenant or treaty. They would **set a trap** for Edom. **But you will not detect it** reads literally "no understanding in it." Edom had a marvelous reputation for wisdom and understanding. But the reputation would not serve her in this situation. No one could explain what was happening to Edom. This was a vision that came from God—a prophetic oracle revealing what lies beyond human explanation.

Boasting over Your Brother (8–14)

SUPPORTING IDEA: *Turning on your brother in his time of dire need arouses God's wrath.*

8. God's conclusion for Edom is self-evident. The Lord asks a poignant question. The question centers **in that day**. Israel and her neighbors looked forward to a day when God would intervene and bring final victory for his people. That day would be one of celebration and joy. God repeatedly had to douse such hopes. The day would not be pleasant for people who opposed the Lord. This included Edom. On that day God would **destroy** what Edom was most proud of—her **wise** counselors. Their economic, military, and political advice would prove useless. Destruction from the Lord would come. Wise men hidden in the **mountains** could not stop him.

9. **Teman**, meaning "south," is another name for Edom derived from an early ancestor (Gen. 36:11). (See comments on Amos 1:12.) Teman may originally have been a tribal name given to the territory around the capital of Bozrah and gradually expanded to refer to all of Edom. Edom's soldiers forced to leave their mountain refuges would be **terrified**. The country's inhabitants would be led to **slaughter**.

10–11. God lists the specific charges against Edom. The list goes all the way back to the feud between **Jacob** and Esau (Gen. 27:1–45). From then on **violence** characterized the relationships between their descendants. Finally, Edom would get the **shame** they deserved for the way they had treated Israel. They would lose all national identity because God would see that they were **destroyed forever**.

The main charge against Edom revolved around the events surrounding the destruction of Jerusalem by Babylon in 586 B.C. Edom stood on the other side from Judah at that time, **aloof while strangers carried off his wealth**. As Babylon burned the city and carried away temple treasures (2 Kgs. 25), Edom made no effort to respond as a treaty partner or ally of Jerusalem. Instead they **were like one of them**. They acted like **foreigners** who had no relationship to Israel. They helped destroy their kinsmen in hopes of financial gain.

12–14. Obadiah turns to negative imperative verbs to warn Edom of the consequences of their attitudes and actions. He relieves the bitter experiences of Jerusalem's fall. He says literally, "Do not look on the day of your brother, the day of his misfortune. Do not rejoice over the sons of Judah in the day of their destruction, and do not make your mouth great in the day of trouble." Edom should have turned their heads away in horror from Jerusalem and its destruction. Instead Edom rushed in to find whatever of value they could carry away. Edom should have joined Jerusalem in mourning and lamentation, but Edom joined Babylon in celebration and rejoicing. Edom should have sat appalled and terrified at the sight of Jerusalem in ruins. Instead, they boasted of their part in the fray.

Obadiah continued: "Do not enter in the gate of my people in the day of their disaster. Do not look, even you, on his evil in the day of his disaster. Do not send away his wealth in the day of his disaster." The prophet echoed like a beating drum—the day, the day, the day, of his disaster, his disaster, his disaster. Edom deserved allies who would turn against them because they had turned against Judah in her most helpless moment.

Edom took three steps against Judah: (1) They entered the gate; (2) they examined the evil done to Jerusalem; and (3) they found and sent away anything of value for their personal use. They forgot one thing. God declared that these were his people. Babylon defeated Jerusalem. Babylon did not defeat Yahweh, the God of Jerusalem. He remained to fight another day. Edom, beware!

God had one last set of No! No! for Edom. "Do not stand over the crossroads to cut off his refugees. Do not deliver over his survivors in the day of trouble." Edom went one step further down the road to God's wrath. Edom was not content with getting valuables and running home. Edom stood at the highway intersections and captured the few surviving escapees from Judah. Edom participated as a full ally of Babylon, not as a friend, relative, and ally of Jerusalem.

𝔻 Drinking Your Deeds or Deliverance from Doom (15–21)

SUPPORTING IDEA: *God will eventually establish his kingdom and bring down the deeds of the wicked on their heads.*

15. Again the prophet turns to that glorious **day of the LORD** when people expect victory, celebration, and joy. This Day of the Lord is not just a local event with some community or country having reason to celebrate. Obadiah has expanded the Day of the Lord into international dimensions. **All nations** will participate whether they want to or not. Eye for an eye, tooth for a tooth will prevail. **As you have done, it will be done to you.** Retribution will return on Edom's head. Be ready. The Lord's marching orders are about to sound. The Edomites will face the Day of the Lord in all its horror.

16. Obadiah took up another metaphor from Jeremiah and his prophetic predecessors, that of God's cup of wrath poured out for his enemies to drink (Ps. 60:3). In 586 B.C. Jerusalem had drunk the cup on the temple mount, God's holy mountain (Isa. 11:9). Now Jerusalem's enemies, Edom included, would take their turn. God's punishing wrath would be so severe that the nations would leave no trace of their existence. They would **drink continually** until God's wrath had made them vanish.

The greatness of Edom, Moab, Ammon, Assyria, Babylon, and such is a matter of ancient records recovered from the sand. The world continues on as if these nations never existed. But Jerusalem has given us Jesus Christ, whose imprint on world history can never be erased and who is the only way to eternal salvation.

17. The prophet had another side of the picture for Jerusalem. World history would center on Mount Zion, God's earthly dwelling (Lam. 5:18). This would again be a **holy** place where God's people would live in holiness, obeying his word. Jacob, not Esau, would **possess** the **inheritance.**

18. The prophet changes imagery to a fire, an image often associated with God's anger. **House of Joseph** and **house of Jacob** are two ways of speaking of the Northern Kingdom applied to the entirety of God's people after the fall of the Northern Kingdom in 722 B.C. God's people will become his instrument to destroy Edom completely so that **there will be no survivors.**

19. Tersely and succinctly the prophet assumed the role of a new Joshua meting out the land to God's people. The text reads literally: "The Negev will inherit (or possess) Mount Esau, and the Shephelah the Philistines. They will inherit the field of Ephraim and the field of Samaria, and Benjamin, the Gilead." Instead of distributing it to tribes, he divides the land among the geographical entities that make up God's people. **The Negev** is the dry region south of Beersheba and Arad, northeast of the Sinai peninsula, and west of the Arabah below the Dead Sea. The Judean people living there will **occupy the mountains of Esau**, taking over Edom's land.

The Shephelah is the "strip of foothills along the western flank of Judah. The term means 'Lowlands' and must have been given by inhabitants living in the higher elevations" (Brisco, *Holman Bible Atlas,* 18). The Shephelah lay between the coastal plains and the western highlands just west of Jerusalem. Four valleys—Aijalon, Sorek, Elah, and Way to Hebron—cut across the Shephelah and led to major cities. Wars were fought in the cities protecting the valleys—Lachish, Azekah, Socoh, and Timnah.

Obadiah seems to indicate that such wars will become a thing of the past when God lets Judah's people of the Shephelah **possess the land of the Philistines** to the east. The residents of the Shephelah or some anonymous "they" of Judah will occupy **Ephraim**, which can also be called **Samaria**, a major division of the western mountains between Galilee and Judah. Samaria was also the city that served as capital of the Northern Kingdom before its destruction and the Assyrian name for its political province in the old Northern Kingdom.

Thus Judah would take over the territory of David's fiercest enemies, the Philistines, and of the old Northern Kingdom (Israel). **Benjamin** was the smallest of the tribes, lying between the northern and southern kingdoms, usually overshadowed by Judah, but actually containing the Judean capital of Jerusalem as well as Gibeon, Gibeah, Bethel, and Jericho. They would inherit or **possess Gilead**, the mountainous region west of the Jordan River between the Dead Sea and the Yarmuk River. In effect, God through Obadiah promised the original promised land to Judah again.

20. The Hebrew text of this verse offers many problems: the present text literally reads: "And the exiles—this army(?)—of the sons of Israel who [are?] Canaanites unto Zarephath and exiles of Jerusalem who in Sepharad will posses the cities of the Negev." The meaning and interpretation of almost every word can be debated. **This company** or army is a possible reading of a difficult Hebrew text. Stuart reads "the exiles of these possessions" (Douglas Stuart, WBC 31, 412). The reference is apparently to Israelites exiled from Samaria in 722 B.C., thus underlining the unity of Israel north and south and Israel living in Palestine and Israel in exile. The term *company* or *army* or *possession* further identifies these exiles as having military or financial power.

The Septuagint, the earliest Greek translation of the Old Testament, read this word as "the first," apparently clarifying these exiles as the first ones from northern Israel, not the last ones from Jerusalem. "Who are Canaanites" may identify the northern exiles as having so intermingled with the native inhabitants of the land that they no longer can be given a separate identity but can still be used by God. Others would change the Hebrew text and interpret these as Phoenicians or merchants (original meanings of the term *Canaanites*) whose land Israel was going to occupy in a new conquest.

The verb "will possess" appears only once in the Hebrew text at the end of the sentence but probably is expected to be supplied before "unto Zarephath." Zarephath was a city-state located near the tip of a promontory along the Lebanese Mediterranean Sea coast about fourteen miles north of Tyre and eight miles south of Sidon. "Since Zarephath was located on the coastal road in Phoenicia, it encountered many passing armies and therefore is occasionally mentioned in ancient records, but it never became an important city" (Ray L. Roth, *ABD*, VI, 1041). (See 1 Kgs. 17:8–24; Luke 4:26.) Archaeologists have shown Zarephath to be a pottery-manufacturing center. Obadiah pointed to this Phoenician coastal city as the new northern boundary of Israel.

Not only northern exiles but also those exiled from Jerusalem in 586 B.C. would join in the new conquest. These are identified as living in Sepharad. "The biblical text gives no indication of the location of Sepharad, but at least three possible locations have been suggested: a city in Spain, possibly Sefarad; a city located in Media; and the city Sardis, located in Lydia of Asia Minor" (John D. Wineland, *ABD*, V, 1089). The capital city of Lydia appears to be the most likely candidate according to current evidence, but many scholars still look north and east of Babylon. Whichever location is correct, Obadiah offered a call to far-off exiles to return to the Jewish homeland and occupy the southern cities (see Jer. 13:19; 32:44; 33:13; 2 Chr. 28:18).

Obadiah extends his view to include the citizens of the Northern Kingdom and the Southern Kingdom taken into exile and scattered among foreign nations.

21. Obadiah had one last word, directed at Edom, of course, but with a strong teaching for his own Jewish people. The word **deliverers** appears only in Obadiah. It refers to people like Joshua and the judges from the original conquest period who led God's people to dramatic victories. These will now reside on Mount Zion—the religious name for Jerusalem as the home of God's temple (2 Kgs. 19:31; Mic. 4:7). They would **govern** Edom who lived in **the mountains of Esau.** "Govern" translates Hebrew *shepot*, the term used for the judges in the Book of Judges. The Book of Judges concluded by blaming Israel's wretched condition on their lack of a king (Judg. 21:25).

The long history Obadiah looked back on showed that kingship had not solved Israel's problems. The problem was that they had never learned the lesson contained in Gideon's refusal to become king over Israel: "I will not rule over you, nor will my son rule over you. The LORD will rule over you" (Judg. 8:23). Obadiah said once more that Jerusalem's leaders would control Edom and other foreign territories, approximating the original promised land.

But Obadiah had one final shocking lesson for Israel—**the kingdom will be the LORD's.** Israel's new day of rulership would be vastly different from their previous efforts because now the Lord would be king over Israel and over all that Israel possessed. Only then could Obadiah promise, "On Mount Zion will be deliverance; it will be holy, and the house of Jacob will possess its inheritance" (Obad. 17).

MAIN IDEA REVIEW: *Edom exhibited pride, overconfidence, refusal to help in time of need, attacking when the other person was down, and helping the enemy qualify a person and a nation for God's judgment, while God's plan is for his people to be part of his kingdom.*

III. CONCLUSION

Forgiveness Seems Unjust, Unfair, Irrational

Simon Wiesenthal faced an agonizing decision and describes his dilemma in a book entitled *The Sunflower*. This young Polish soldier watched helplessly as German soldiers killed his grandmother on the stairway of her home and then forced his mother into a freight car filled with elderly Jewish women. Eventually, Wiesenthal counted eighty-nine relatives whom the Nazis had slaughtered.

Then one day on prison detail in a Nazi hospital, Wiesenthal received a summons. A nurse signaled him to accompany her up a stairway and down a hallway to where a lone Nazi soldier lay swathed in bandages.

In that musty hospital room, the soldier compelled Wisenthal to listen to his story. "I must tell you of this horrible deed—tell you because you are a Jew," the soldier began. Long separated from the lifestyle and faith of his Catholic upbringing by Hitler's Youth Corps, he found his military attachment in battle in the Ukraine village of Dnyepropetrovsk. Boobytraps killed thirty members of his unit. In revenge this soldier and his squad herded three hundred Jews into a three-story house, doused it with gasoline, and fired grenades into it. Drawn guns ensured that no one escaped.

The wounded soldier finally got to his point.

I am left here with my guilt. In the last hours of my life you are with me. I do not know who you are. I know only that you are a Jew and that is enough. In the long nights while I have been waiting for death, time and time again I have longed to talk about it to a Jew and beg forgiveness from him. I know what I am asking is almost too much for you, but without your answer I cannot die in peace.

Simon Wiesenthal stared out the window at the sunlit courtyard, looked at the bandaged soldier lying in the bed, and without a word left the room. But this decision haunted him the remainder of his life.

Philip Yancey concludes: "*The Sunflower* takes forgiveness out of the theoretical and thrusts it in the midst of living history. . . . I was struck by the terrible, crystalline logic of unforgiveness. In a world of unspeakable atrocity, forgiveness seems unjust, unfair, irrational" (*What's So Amazing About Grace?*, 111–12).

Israel faced Wiesenthal's question on two fronts. Could an exiled, homeless nation ever hope beyond hope to receive forgiveness from God? How would a forgiven people react to those whom God had used to punish them? Obadiah shows us one brief response to those issues. God would forgive Israel. One sign of that forgiveness would be the punishment of Edom, the relative who turned traitor when Babylon came to destroy Jerusalem and exile the nation. Another sign would be that God would restore Jerusalem and all Israel to power. The question remained: How would Israel treat Edom? Obadiah's book called Israel to learn lessons from Edom.

PRINCIPLES

- Pride goes before a fall and brings God's wrath.
- Turning traitor against your own people is always wrong.
- Attacking people who are down and out is wrong.
- Helping the enemy is wrong.
- God punishes people in the way they have punished others.
- God has a plan of deliverance and renewal for his people.

APPLICATIONS

- Check your pride at the door as you enter the house tonight and never pick it up again.
- Change your self-confidence to God-confidence.
- Find a way to show love to someone you perceive as your enemy.

- Give God freedom to rule your life and that of your family today and forever.

- Trust God to set up his kingdom and create a new way of life for his world.

IV. LIFE APPLICATION

Conflict and Resolution

The pastor preached against some things he thought the deacon was doing wrong in his business. The deacon voted against the pastor's plans for the church. A donnybrook threatened. With whom would the church side? Who would win the fights to come? Then the seasoned deacon came to the young pastor for a private talk. He described a way to go, admitting where he had been wrong and letting the pastor confess his own faults. This deacon put down his pride and restored a young preacher's sense of self-esteem and dignity. His love for the church and his pastor opened the door to fruitful ministry because he slammed the door on hatred and distrust.

Obadiah preached to two parties who had become violent enemies. He showed where Edom had let pride, self-confidence, and greed lead to hatred and betrayal of their treaty partner and relatives. His message can sound like a get-even speech of hatred, jealousy, and revenge. But it is not Obadiah's message. It is God's. God did not call on Israel to take revenge. He did not call Israel to arms. God promised to win the victory himself.

Meanwhile, Judah needed to learn the lessons Edom had not learned. So do we. What creates enemies in your personal, business, and church relationships? What attitudes do you have that maintain enmity rather than restoring friendship? How has a sense of self-confidence melded with greed to lead you down the wrong path to betray friends and run away from God?

V. PRAYER

Forgive us, Lord. Obadiah has described who we are—proud, self-reliant, greedy traitors who break agreements for momentary gain. Forgive our attitudes. Change the way we treat business acquaintances, fellow believers in church, extended family, and especially our own families. Your kingdom come, your will be done in our lives here on earth as it is in heaven. Amen.

VI. DEEPER DISCOVERIES

A. The Kingdom of God in the Old Testament (21)

Christ's central message could be reduced to a brief statement: "The kingdom of God is near. Repent and believe the good news!" (Mark 1:15) This message promised the fulfillment of God's plans in the Old Testament, where the kingdom of God is also an important theme. The Hebrew term *malkuth* appears ninety-one times in the Old Testament but only infrequently in reference to God's kingdom (Pss. 103:19; 145:11–13; 1 Chr. 17:14; 28:5). The Hebrew *melukah* appears twenty-four times with only a few referring to God's kingdom (Ps. 22:29). Most importantly the Old Testament refers to the kingdom of God with the brief acclamations, *Yhwh malak*, "Yahweh reigns as king" (Exod. 15:18; Ps. 96:10) and *Yhwh melek*, "Yahweh is king" (Deut. 33:5; Zeph. 3:15).

On coming out of Egypt, Israel proclaimed God's royal power over all nations (Num. 23:21). Gideon tried to teach Israel that no human could rule them because the Lord was their king (Judg. 8:22–23). In worship Israel used the cry "Yahweh reigns" or "Yahweh is king" to celebrate God's eternal kingship over Israel, foreign nations, the earth, and all other gods (Ps. 96:4).

Still, Israel had a human ruler, a king. In fact, it may be claimed that "the idea of the kingdom of God in the Old Testament was tied to David's kingdom" (Ralph L. Smith, *Old Testament Theology*, 408). The king was God's agent, carrying out God's will for his people. The king was so identified as the agent of God that he could be addressed as the son of God (Ps. 2:6–7) or even as *'elohim*, God (Ps. 45:6).

> The earthly king in Israel failed to bring in the kingdom of God and to achieve the goals of righteousness and justice for all (Ps. 72:1–2,4), but kingship was not a total failure. . . . The anointing of kings opened the door for the idea of a Messiah, an ideal anointed one who would come and perform the functions of an ideal king (Smith, *Old Testament Theology*, 410).

> According to the God-king ideology of Israel and its idealistic representation, the king has his place at God's right hand, he proclaims and executes God's sovereignty, and he mediates God's salvation to the world (Ps. 110). This representation of the Davidic king transcended a particular historical situation and was applicable to various messianic hopes (Isa. 9:5–6). Because of the narrow association of the Messiah with the dominion of God, the New Testament believers saw in Jesus the realization of the Messiah, and he was

therefore the Christ (John 4:25). Jesus is the Messiah, the son of David (Luke 19:38) (Philip J. Nel, *NIDOTTE*, II, 960).

Israel's neighbors proclaimed their pagan god as king of the heavens, king of earth, and king of the gods. Similarly, Israel could proclaim: "The LORD sits enthroned over the flood; the LORD is enthroned as King forever" (Ps. 29:10); and, "The LORD reigns, he is robed in majesty; the LORD is robed in majesty and is armed with strength. The world is firmly established; it cannot be moved. Your throne was established long ago; you are from all eternity" (Ps. 93:1–2).

Thus we can conclude with Ralph Smith: "Many scattered threads in the Old Testament point to a new, coming kingdom of God. Ideas such as a son of David, son of God, son of man, and suffering servant appear at different times and circumstances. They are never put together or related in any systematic form in the Old Testament. The New Testament brings all these ideas together and says that Jesus Christ is the fulfillment of all of them" (Smith, *Old Testament Theology*, 426).

VII. TEACHING OUTLINE

A. INTRODUCTION
1. Lead Story: Dancing with the Devil
2. Context: Shortly after Jerusalem fell to Babylon and the population of Judah was exiled, the prophet Obadiah appeared in Judah to condemn Edom, Judah's treaty partner and brother turned traitor and enemy. In so doing the prophet also caught Judah's ear.
3. Transition: Obadiah's message is brief but biting. Pride, self-confidence, betrayal, and picking on the fallen summon God's justice and punishment as quickly as anything. Judah may be exiled, but Judah will still overcome. Their victory, however, involved going back to the days before Saul and David and letting God be king, celebrating the kingship of God, not the kingship of Judah.

B. COMMENTARY
1. Punishing Pride (1–4)
2. Friends Will Be Your Foes (5–7)
3. Boasting over Your Brother (8–14)
4. Drinking Your Deeds or Deliverance from Doom (15–21)

C. CONCLUSION: FORGIVENESS SEEMS UNJUST, UNFAIR, IRRATIONAL

VIII. ISSUES FOR DISCUSSION

1. How does pride deceive you?
2. What areas of life most tempt church members to show pride?
3. How do you react when friends betray you?
4. Have you ever stood aloof and not helped people, as Edom did?
5. What difference does confessing God as king of the universe make in your everyday life?

Introduction to

Jonah

Get ready for a new experience. Jonah is different from all the other prophetic books in the Bible. Jonah is different from all the other books of the Bible—period! Jonah does not report on the preaching of a prophet like other prophetic books. Jonah does not make the prophet a hero like most of the Bible. Jonah does not give us straightforward theological or ethical teachings so we can memorize a verse and know something God wants us to do today.

Jonah tells a story—a story filled with irony, satire, character reversal, and humor. Jonah wants you to laugh. Jonah wants you to be surprised. Jonah constantly throws the unexpected at you and waits a second for you to react. Jonah provides a negative example of how not to be a messenger for God. Jonah wants you to turn the negative satire around into a positive message.

Jonah takes up the story of a well-known prophet—well-known at least in his time in Israel but known to us only through a verse in 2 Kings 14:25. Jonah gave King Jeroboam II of Israel (783–753 B.C.) the divine authority to extend the Northern Kingdom's territory almost to the extent of the Davidic kingdom. This made Jeroboam "the greatest of all the kings of northern Israel" (Walter C. Kaiser Jr., *A History of Israel*, p. 351). And for his time this made Jonah the greatest of all the prophets of the Northern Kingdom, certainly greater than Amos or Hosea in the minds of the people of Israel.

The author of Jonah knew another side to the prophet's story. In this side the heroes looked entirely different: pagan sailors, enemy citizens, the most vicious ruler known in his day, even cattle and a worm. Of course, the central hero was God. On the other side of the ledger stood Jonah. He was the laughable villain, the supreme example of how not to be God's messenger.

Who wrote this book? Seeing its portrait of the prophet, we immediately eliminate Jonah as the author. This is not first-person narrative but an inspired anonymous writer's satirical lesson based on the prophet's experience. To eliminate Jonah as the author throws wide open the question of when the book was written. The writer evidently was a pious reader of Israel's sacred literature, since many of his words and episodes remind us of other scriptural materials:

Jonah 1:2	Genesis 10:12; 18:20–21
Jonah 1:9	Genesis 1:9–10; Psalm 95:5
Jonah 1:10	Genesis 3:13
Jonah 2:2–9	Psalms 42:8; 103:4; 120:1; 142:4
Jonah 3:9–10	Jeremiah 18:7–8,11; 26:3–6
Jonah 3:9	Joel 2:14
Jonah 3:10	Exodus 32:14
Jonah 4:2	Exodus 32:12; 34:6; Joel 2:13
Jonah 4:2–3	1 Kings 19:4
Jonah 4:4,9	Genesis 4:5

Some commentators would use this along with what they consider late Aramaic linguistic traits to date the book quite late in Israel's literary history. Wilhelm Rudolph places it between the sixth and third centuries—between 600 and 200 B.C. (KAT, XIII2, p. 330). Leslie Allen speaks of "a later author who had no intention of teaching a history lesson but employed contemporary tradition as basic material for a didactic parable" and so dates the book between 550 and 350 B.C. (NICOT, p. 186).

Hans Walter Wolff uses the vocabulary, a free use and combining of historical names such as picturing Nineveh in size as the center of the Assyrian kingdom but describing it like the large city-state of the Persian period, and the changing of geographic realties to make Joppa the nearest port to Galilee to point to a postexilic dating. Literary dependence on what for Wolff are late parts of Jeremiah and on Joel means that Jonah cannot have been written before 350 B.C. Wolff would go further and see motifs taken from Greek literature so that the date of writing sinks to a time after 330 B.C. and most likely after 300 (BKAT XIV3, 54–56).

James Limburg lists the linguistic and related Scriptures evidence, concludes that "none of these linguistic, literary, or thematic considerations is decisive for settling the matter of the date of the composition of Jonah" and then decides that "taken together they point to a time after Jeremiah and after the composition of Deuteronomy–2 Kings, a time in the late exilic or the postexilic period" (OTL, 30–31).

Such evidence is not so convincing for Douglas Stuart, who suggests, "The actual composition of the book is not datable except within the broadest boundaries (about 750–250 B.C.)." Aramaisms may be vocabulary common to old Northwest Semitic languages. Dependence on "late parts" of Jeremiah may be better attributed to the consistent voice of "divine revelation" throughout Scripture rather than one writer having to borrow a concept from another.

One cannot prove if Jonah borrowed from Joel, Joel from Jonah, or both used a common source. Nineveh may not have been the capital of Assyria in terms we use today, but it was probably one among several royal residences, and "king of Nineveh" was a common way to refer to a king ruling a larger territory as shown by 1 Kings 21:1 referring to Ahab, the king of Israel, as king of Samaria. Thus Stuart concludes, "There is ample evidence to support the historicity of the book, and surprisingly little to undermine it" (WBC 31, 432–33, 440–42).

Similarly, C. Hassell Bullock argues:

> The book is a refined account of a prophetic career written for its theological value. Yet the author has not abused history in order to communicate that theology. The objections raised against the historicity of the book, though sometimes substantive in nature, are not sufficient to disqualify it as historical.

As for dating, Bullock says, "The book could have been composed any time between the middle of the eighth century and the canonization of the Twelve Prophets by the end of the fifth century," but then he concludes that a mid-eighth-century date is possible but that its northern air and pride in the prophet point to a time at least before or shortly after the fall of Samaria in 722 B.C. (*An Introduction to the Old Testament Prophetic Books*, pp. 48–52).

We must join Stuart in a critical questioning of the hypercritical approach to Jonah that seeks evidence for lack of historical reality and for reasons to provide a late date for the authorship of the book. While no evidence points to an exact date, it would appear that readers would identify much more with the issues the book raises if they were still prone to hate Nineveh and if they had some relationship, however faint, to the glory days of Israel. Nothing really points away from a date of writing at least by 700 B.C. when a remnant of northern Israelites still lived in the land of promise and Judah was suffering from mighty Assyrian attacks. The book would be even more strongly received by a Northern Kingdom watching Assyria take away its own territory between 735 and 722 B.C.

The dating of the book cannot be that much of a concern for us since the writer, unlike the writer of most prophetic books, did not give a clue as to when the writing took place. What is important for understanding the book is an appreciation for its literary mastery.

The writer of Jonah knew how to tell a story, keep readers interested, and force them to face the points that Jonah's example raised for their own lives. He did this by staging his narrative in seven brief scenes: (1) the prophet's dilemma (1:1–3), (2) the shipboard chaos (1:4–16), (3) the fishy delivery and thanksgiving (1:17–2:10), (4) the prophet's second chance (3:1–3a), (5) the prophet's preaching mission (3:3b–10), (6) the prophet's angry prayer (4:1–3), and (7) the divine dialogue (4:4–11). The scenes play against one another with two commissioning scenes (1 and 4), two conversion of pagans scenes (2 and 5), and two prayer scenes (3 and 6). This leaves only the climatic dialogue unpaired as the climatic point of the narrative.

Fourteen questions carry the message of the story, forcing the reader to answer the questions along with the person in the narrative (1:6,8,10,11; 2:4; 3:9; 4:2,4,9,11; some verses carrying more than one question). Skillfully, all the questions prepare the reader for the final and climatic question of Jonah 4:11—the question that goes unanswered so the readers must supply the answers for themselves.

Satirical irony keeps the reader laughing at the poor, pathetic excuse for a prophet until the realization dawns that the questions mean that the reader may be as pathetic as the prophet. Called to go east, the prophet goes west. Called as God's messenger, the prophet sleeps while pagan sailors pray. Seeking his own death, the prophet somehow leads pagan sailors to pray and sacrifice to the one true God. Caught in a fish's belly, the prophet sings a prayer of thanksgiving. Forced to proclaim God's message to Nineveh, the prophet speaks five words and sees the world's greatest spiritual revival break out.

Seeing his congregation repent, the prophet leaves to test God's faithfulness to his word of judgment. Delivered from scorching heat, the prophet falls in love with a vine while maintaining his hatred for a repentant people. Questioned by God about the value of his anger, the prophet prays a prayer protesting God's loving grace. Seeing a worm destroy his source of shade, the prophet protests angrily rather than asking why. Confronted with the ironic contrast between his love for a vine and God's love for a people, the prophet falls silent.

The Book of Jonah makes one major point.

> To experience the grace of God and not be willing to tell others of His compassion is a tragedy all must avoid. Messengers of God can neither limit the grace of God nor control its distribution, but they can prevent God's grace from having an effect on their own lives (Gary V. Smith, *The Prophets as Preachers*, p. 97).

This lesson you dare not miss: God expects your compassion to encompass everyone, especially your enemies.

Such compassion is more than a feeling of good will and an absence of anger. Such compassion calls for commitment. Such compassion seeks God's call to share his salvation with all sinners—the pagan, the enemy, the untouchable, the hated, the feared, the socially superior, the socially inferior. Should God not be concerned about the great cities of the world that teem with pagan people who are pagan because we have not let them hear the gospel message? If God is concerned for them, why aren't we?

Jonah 1:1–17

A Fish for One Who Flees

I. INTRODUCTION
A Funny Story That Makes You Cry

II. COMMENTARY
A verse-by-verse explanation of these verses.

III. CONCLUSION
I'm Going with You

An overview of the principles and applications from these verses.

IV. LIFE APPLICATION
Keeping Posted

Melding these verses to life.

V. PRAYER
Tying these verses to life with God.

VI. DEEPER DISCOVERIES
Historical, geographical, and grammatical enrichment of the commentary.

VII. TEACHING OUTLINE
Suggested step-by-step group study of these verses.

VIII. ISSUES FOR DISCUSSION
Zeroing these verses in on daily life.

"*I*t's always too soon to quit."

David Tyler Scoates

Jonah 1:1–17

IN A NUTSHELL

Jonah, a national hero because his previous prophecies had led to military victories, dislikes God's latest mission—to preach to the enemies in Nineveh. Fleeing God, he boards a ship going west rather than east, then goes down in the ship to sleep through a storm while the pagan sailors pray for deliverance. Awakened by the angry captain of the ship, he sees the sailors' lot fall on him as the culprit who is causing the storm. He answers their questions as briefly as possible and tells them to throw him into the sea to bring the storm to a halt. Finally, the rugged sailors do as Jonah asks, while they pray to God for forgiveness. God sends a special fish to swallow his off-track prophet.

A Fish for One Who Flees

I. INTRODUCTION

A Funny Story That Makes You Cry

"*Preach* Jonah, Daddy. Preach Jonah!" My boys' excited voices still ring in my ears. When "Professor Dad" got invited to preach, the boys wanted to hear Jonah again. They liked to laugh at a prophet who heard God say go east but purchased a ticket to the farthest western resort, at a prophet sleeping while pagan sailors prayed, at a thanksgiving prayer from a big fish's belly, at a five-word sermon bringing the greatest spiritual awakening in human history, and at a pouting prophet bawling God out for sending a revival.

Jonah is a funny story. It is supposed to be. But it is also a sad commentary on us as a people of God. While God tries to carry on a love relationship with the world, we selfishly seek to limit his love to us and the people we like because they are like us. We should laugh as we read Jonah and see the many ironic twists of the narrative. We should also cry as we let Jonah show us our prejudices and the limits we place on God.

II. COMMENTARY

A Fish for One Who Flees

> **MAIN IDEA:** *Faith is measured by acts of piety and trust, not by past history, family connections, or national ancestry.*

A Protesting Prophet (1:1–3)

> **SUPPORTING IDEA:** *The believer cannot escape God's call to mission.*

1:1. Jonah is a book of mission. It contrasts God's eternal mission of redeeming a lost world to humanity's ongoing mission of self-preservation and self-serving. Jonah exemplifies the intricate relationship between these two missions. Jonah became a national hero when he accomplished the first mission God gave him. Second Kings 14:25 shows how Jonah encouraged King Jeroboam to extend his territories, and the king successfully carried out the message of God that Jonah delivered.

The Book of Jonah presumes that we know the story from 2 Kings because Jonah is written in direct contrast to that story. Here Jonah again hears the **word of the LORD**—the message God has for this prophet. The Old Testament uses the expression *dabar Yahweh* about 438 times, 161 of these occurring in the prophetic books. This is the Lord's major way of revealing his will to his people.

Aside from the verse in 2 Kings and the Book of Jonah, we know nothing else about this prophet (see the Introduction to Jonah).

1:2. This message of God was different. It expanded Jonah's horizons. He must do more than report to the king. In this word of the Lord, God called Jonah to a truly God-sized task: preach God's message in the capital city of the most cruel enemy on earth. **Nineveh**, the capital city of the Assyrian empire, featured the great temple of Ishtar. Nineveh's ruins are located within modern Mosul, the second largest city of Iraq on the east bank of the Tigris River.

Genesis 10:11–12 credits Nineveh's founding to the ancient hunter Nimrod, and modern studies show its occupation in prehistoric times. The city's circumference reached almost eight miles. From about 1363 B.C. Nineveh flourished as a strong city-state until Sennacherib made it the capital of all of Assyria about 700 B.C. It fell to the Medes and Babylonians in 612 B.C. Archaeologists have uncovered many finds from Nineveh, including King Asshurbanipal's library.

Nineveh was not only great in political power and cultural sophistication; Nineveh had great **wickedness**. It was this wickedness that came to God's attention. This should bring comfort to Judah. God cannot just stand before wickedness and sin. God in his holiness must do something about such horrible conditions. And God was doing something. He was calling Jonah to **preach against** the city.

1:3. Jonah was not so sure about that calling. This mission went beyond his understanding of his mission with God. Jonah's response may have been something like, "Lord, you know I love you, but faith has limits. I will go anywhere you send me—just not to Nineveh. Lord, it's dangerous. Lord, we have many people here at home who need ministry. Lord, Nineveh does not deserve to hear your word. Lord, go ahead and destroy them. You do not have to send me to do that. It's vacation time for me. Call again when I come back and you have a better mission for me."

Yes, you read the text right: "Jonah rose to flee to Tarshish from the face of the Lord" (author's translation). God's prophet heard God's word and ran. Emotions took over, and he thought he could find a refuge where God was not present. Called to go east to preach, he sailed west. Tarshish represented the farthest point west from Palestine, though its exact location remains a mystery. Obviously, it was a seaport connected with ships (1 Kgs. 9:26–27). It was also a source of precious metals (Jer. 10:9). Scholars have pointed to Tartessus in southwest Spain, to a town in Sardinia, to an identification with Carthage in north Africa. Wherever Tarshish was, it was west, and Nineveh was east. Jonah chose to go west.

So **he went down**, first to **Joppa** and then into the **ship**, something he would continue to do (Jon. 1:5; 2:6). A journey from God's presence is a journey downward. The first station on the downward journey was Joppa (modern Jaffa south of Tel Aviv), the city that marked the northwest boundary of the tribe of Dan (Josh. 19:46). During their heyday the Egyptians used Joppa as a military fortress. Being the only navigable seaport between Egypt and Acco (later called Ptolemais), Joppa was important for Israel and was used to transport materials for the building of Solomon's temple (Ezra 3:7).

The text repeats Jonah's ultimate destination—from the face of God. A national hero for delivering God's victorious word to Jeroboam became a fleeing prophet, fearful of the consequences of God's message for the pagan city of Nineveh.

B Praying Pagans (1:4–6)

SUPPORTING IDEA: *Faith shows itself in surprising ways among people who do not meet the qualifications we set up.*

1:4. Jonah did not expect a new captain to take control of the ship, but the Hebrew word order places the Lord, the God of Israel, squarely in center stage. Much like a baseball pitcher, God picked up a "great wind and hurled it to the sea" (literal Hebrew). The result was "a great storm on the sea." The **ship threatened to break up** ("be shattered to pieces," author's translation). God and the ship conspired against Jonah's attempts to flee from God.

1:5. What do you do when God threatens you? The ship gave up and started to shatter in pieces. Each of the old "salts" (the Hebrew term for sailors) **cried out to his own god** for help and "hurled" away their wage-earning cargo **to lighten the ship**.

But Jonah. The prophet had **gone below** to the "inaccessible, innermost part" of the ship (*HALOT*). He thought he was fleeing from God and fleeing from everyone aboard the ship. After the emotional and physical exertion in refusing God's call and running from God's presence, he was tired. There was only one thing on Jonah's mind—**sleep**.

1:6. It didn't even take God to find Jonah. The ship's **captain** (literally, "the great one of the ropes") would do. He knew his ship and its passenger list. He found the missing passenger and snarled, "What's up with you, sound sleeper? Get up and pray to your God. Just perhaps, the God will call us back to mind so that we do not perish!" (author's translation). The captain woke the prophet up for a prayer meeting. The captain wanted every base covered, every god implored, so that finally the God (Hebrew text could be translated "gods," but this is not likely) would pay attention and do something.

ⓒ Seeking a Solution for Safety (1:7–12)

SUPPORTING IDEA: *God knows the guilty party and shows the innocent the way to safety.*

1:7. The **sailors** worked from the other end of the puzzle. They declared, "Let's punish the guilty and appease God." So they **cast lots**, an ancient way of finding the will of the gods or of God (see "Deeper Discoveries"). The pious sailors—not the priest or the prophet—cast lots. And God gave his revelation to the sailors, not the prophet. And, **the lot fell on Jonah.** He was the guilty one. Now everyone knew his secret. He was the one **responsible** for this calamity.

1:8. The prophet remained silent, not defending himself. The sailors pressed him: **Who is responsible . . . ? What do you do . . . ? Where do you come from?** They were full of questions.

1:9. Finally, the prophet spoke but only to give name, rank, and serial number. He was a **Hebrew.** This Hebrew term "does not occur very often and usually in the presence of (or from the lips of) foreigners (except Gen. 14:13; Exod. 2:12) to indicate the distinctive racial features of Israel and its ancestors" (*HALOT*). "Hebrew" was the way foreigners identified Israelites. Jonah may have seen himself as a bit of an outsider to Israel since he was fleeing from God.

Jonah gave one more description of himself to the sailors. In doing so he placed the divine name first in the sentence—a Hebrew method of centering attention on this name rather than on himself as subject of the sentence. Literally he proclaimed: "I myself am fearing Yahweh, the God of the heavens who made the sea and the dry land." Quite an appropriate answer for sea-weary sailors who lived most of their lives under the heavens and categorized life as on the sea or on the dry land. But it was not the normal Israelite confession of God because it ignored the people of Israel and God's miraculous acts in Egypt that created the nation.

Jonah's confession was similar to the confession of any citizen of the Ancient Near East when asked to describe the high god of their religion rather than the more personal, lower gods to whom they would turn every day. Thus Jonah spoke the sailors' language as he identified himself and his God to them.

1:10. What was the sailors' reaction? Literally "the men (not sailors) feared a great fear." The narrative moves away from the men's professional identity and places them on level ground with Jonah as a man. The NIV has it right: **This terrified them.** Their terror was heightened by Jonah's admission somewhere along the way that "from the face of the Lord (placed first in the sentence for focus and emphasis) he was fleeing." No wonder they had experienced such trouble! Of course, they wanted more details: "What is this you have done?" (author's translation). No doubt he had done something, but what would cause a man to run away from God?

1:11. Since the sailors were men of action, they did more than question why. They sought a solution to the problem: **What should we do to you to make the sea calm down for us?** Surely Jonah would know how to appease this God whom he had angered.

1:12. The prophet accepted the blame and knew the solution: **Pick me up and throw me into the sea.** For the sailors, Jonah's solution must have been logical. The sea god was attacking them. They would feed the sea god to cool his anger.

D Punishment and Piety (1:13–17)

SUPPORTING IDEA: *Faithful believers seek to save even the guilty and show their faith in pious worship.*

1:13. The sailors on the ship had too much human kindness to try Jonah's solution immediately. Surely something less drastic would work. They dug deeper into the sea with their oars to try to get to dry land. **But they could not.** "The sea continued storming over them" (author's translation).

1:14. The men had one more hope to save Jonah and themselves. They summoned God. They turned to Jonah's God, not to the pagan god of the sea. In desperation they accepted the fact of Jonah's guilt and knew it must be dealt with. So they offered a prayer that might sound very self-centered in another context, but God had shown that nothing they did could save Jonah.

So they prayed, "Please, God, do not let us perish on behalf of the soul of this man. Don't set innocent blood on us, for you have done just what you wanted to do." Guilt for innocent blood meant killing someone who did not deserve to die (Jer. 26:15). The sailors sought God's will with lots. They prayed to their gods. They tried to get Jonah to pray. They even prayed directly to Jonah's God. They feared what God would do if they killed Jonah. They confessed God's power to create the storm when and how he wanted to.

Here is complete role reversal—pagan sailors acting like the most pious Israelite, with the Israelite prophet fleeing from God like the most pagan foreigner.

1:15. "They lifted Jonah and hurled him to the sea. The sea stood up from its angry raging." Finally, after everything else had failed, the sailors sacrificed Jonah to the storm and the sea. Immediately, God stopped the sea, and it raged no longer.

1:16. Again, "the men feared the LORD even more" (HCSB). Their earlier terror gradually gave way to respect and worship, but the aspect of terror never completely left the scene. The storm terrified them. Jonah's confession terrified them. Their experience in prayer and action with God brought them to worship, so they offered **a sacrifice to the LORD and made vows to him.**

Worshipful fear did not remain a feeling or an emotion. It led to action, self-giving, and sharing.

1:17. "God arranged for **a great fish** (no species mentioned) to swallow Jonah." God will arrange for several things to happen before the narrative is complete. God was in pursuit of the fleeing prophet. The depths of the sea could not stop the hunt. So Jonah remained in the belly of the fish **three days and three nights**. How this could happen, the story does not say. Scientific details and explanations are not the narrator's concern. The fact is that God used a fish to preserve Jonah's life, and God made it possible for a man to live inside a fish three days. The Bible boldly confesses God's power to do what he wants to do. The Bible invites us to have the same boldness in confessing God's power.

> **MAIN IDEA REVIEW:** *Faith is measured by acts of piety and trust, not by past history, family connections, or national ancestry.*

III. CONCLUSION

I'm Going with You

In her book *Chicken Soup for the Woman's Soul,* Lois Krueger tells the story of Justin Carl, her four-and-one-half-year-old son. Lois and her husband were experiencing one of those hectic, go-in-a-hundred-directions days. Every direction they went they seemed to find Justin Carl in the middle getting into mischief. Over and over they told him, "Don't do that!" Finally, husband George sent Justin Carl to the corner. Not at all happy, he piped up, "I'm going to run away from home."

Lois stopped to remember a moment from her own childhood when she had spoken those words. The distant feelings of being unloved and lonely overcame her. She knew her son was crying, "Please notice me. I'm important, too."

"Okay, Jussie, you can run away from home," she whispered tenderly and started picking out clothes.

"Mama," he said, "what are you doin'?"

"We'll also need my coat and nightgown," Lois continued, packing the items in a bag and placing it by the front door. "Okay, Jussie, are you sure you want to run away from home?"

"Yeah, but where are you goin'?"

"Well, if you're going to run away from home, then Mama's going with you because I would never want you to be alone. I love you too much, Justin Carl" (pp. 172–73).

Just as Lois watched her son decide to run away from home, so God watched his wayward prophet flee. God loved Jonah even more than Lois loved Justin Carl, so God went with Jonah, seeking to show Jonah just how big his love was. Jonah's small love covered himself and his own people. God's big love covered all the world, even Nineveh and the pagan sailors on the ship. Jonah could not rest on past laurels, banking on what he had accomplished for God. Jonah had to follow God wherever he led.

PRINCIPLES

- The sovereign God sends you where he will in accordance with his purpose.
- The sovereign God uses unexpected people and things to achieve his purpose.
- The sovereign God delivers you even when you rebel.
- What you did for God yesterday needs to be validated by what you are doing today.
- Even those people whom you consider the worst of sinners can respond to God's power and come to worship him.

APPLICATIONS

- Never mark someone off as too far gone to be able to find God.
- Renew your commitment to God today.
- Volunteer with a mission group to witness to others about God's love.
- Listen for God's word of commission intended for you.
- Do not think your relationship with God is right because you have accomplished something with him in the past.

IV. LIFE APPLICATION

Keeping Posted

Charles Stanley in *The Wonderful Spirit-Filled Life* tells of his photographing experience on the small island of Inagua in the Bahamas. He was near the small commercial port where salt ships dock to load their cargo. Three fifty-foot-high posts were lined up several yards apart on one side of the loading area. Since the posts were on land rather than in the water, Stanley had a hard time figuring out why they were there.

Finally, he asked a local person about the posts. He learned that the water in the channel is too shallow for the large salt boats to enter. The boats must make their way to the dock through one long, narrow channel. As a ship's captain enters the harbor, he aligns the three posts so that from his perspective they are in a straight line, letting him see only one post. Then he knows he is in the deep channel and can safely maneuver to the dock (p. 165).

God had to teach Jonah a lesson—one also connected with the sea. Jonah had to learn the danger of trying to maneuver his life to suit his feelings and needs rather than aligning himself with God and his will. So we must learn that we cannot pick the mission to accomplish for God. We have to align our own lives with God, listen for his message to us, and steer ourselves only where he leads. God does not call us to determine what we want to do and then to ask him to bless our choices. Mission for God is not a smorgasbord of choices. It is a command to join God where he is at work.

V. PRAYER

God, you are everywhere. No matter how high we go, how deep we dive, or how far we run, we can never flee from your presence. Thank you for loving us so much that you are always near us. Teach us to love your presence so much that we will obey your word. Amen.

VI. DEEPER DISCOVERIES

Lots (1:7)

The Old Testament refers several times to lots as a means of discovering God's decision in a specific case. Lots were used to determine how to divide the promised land (Josh. 14:2), who was to lead the attack in battle (Judg. 20:9), who was the chosen king (1 Sam. 10:18–19), what families were to live in Jerusalem (Neh. 11:1), and how to allot the Levitical cities (Josh. 21:8).

Lots could apparently give yes/no, either/or decisions. The exact nature and method of using lots is lost in the mist of history. Apparently small stones or similar items were used, somewhat like dice. The result of a decision by lot was then specified as one's lot, especially in cases of the division of property (Josh. 15:1).

VII. TEACHING OUTLINE

A. INTRODUCTION

1. Lead Story: A Funny Story That Makes You Cry
2. Context: Israel was satisfied with itself, enjoyed control over its greatest extent of territory since Solomon, reveled in hating its enemies, and took God for granted as one who was required to bless them. Israel celebrated the great achievements of King Jeroboam. His

accomplishments came about because the faithful prophet Jonah had delivered God's message of blessing. So the people looked for further words from God sending them on further expeditions of conquest and victory. Instead, Jonah received a personal message from God—a message that called on him for decision.

3. Transition: This chapter introduces us to an unexpected but important element of God's character and nature. He has a mission for his people beyond their own borders, their prejudices, their self-satisfied attitudes.

B. COMMENTARY

1. Protesting Prophet (1:1–3)
2. Praying Pagans (1:4–6)
3. Seeking a Solution for Safety (1:7–12)
4. Punishment and Piety (1:13–17)

C. CONCLUSION: I'M GOING WITH YOU

VIII. ISSUES FOR DISCUSSION

1. How deeply is our church involved in God's mission outside our comfort zone?
2. What has made or would make me try to flee from God's presence?
3. What people today are most nearly in the position the sailors occupied in Jonah's day?
4. Does God still speak to people today and give them assignments they are expected to carry out?
5. How do you know when God is calling you to participate in a specific part of his mission?

Jonah 2:1–10

Praying from the Pit

I. INTRODUCTION
Dramatic Answers

II. COMMENTARY
A verse-by-verse explanation of these verses.

III. CONCLUSION
Emergency Thanksgiving

An overview of the principles and applications from these verses.

IV. LIFE APPLICATION
Off-Side Penalties

Melding these verses to life.

V. PRAYER
Tying these verses to life with God.

VI. DEEPER DISCOVERIES
Historical, geographical, and grammatical enrichment of the commentary.

VII. TEACHING OUTLINE
Suggested step-by-step group study of these verses.

VIII. ISSUES FOR DISCUSSION
Zeroing these verses in on daily life

Quote

"*F*or far too many of us, there are only two attitudes toward prayer—those who 'pray their way in' and those who 'pray their way out.' Most of us, unfortunately, take our prayer lives most seriously when we are trying to 'pray our way out.'"

L e o n a r d   S w e e t

Jonah 2:1–10

I N   A   N U T S H E L L

*F*rom a fish's belly, Jonah celebrates his deliverance with a song of thanksgiving. He confesses that God had answered his prayers uttered in the midst of hopeless distress, describes the situation he faced, and praises God for bringing him back to life when he remembered to pray. Jonah contrasts his situation of deliverance with idol worshippers who forfeit God's grace and concludes with a promise to worship and sacrifice to his God. And so the fish deposits Jonah on dry land.

Praying from the Pit

I. INTRODUCTION

Dramatic Answers

As a college senior, James Dobson received a call from home. His parents sounded anxious and upset. His forty-six-year-old dad had an "angry-looking sore" on his right hand that had refused to heal. That day a dermatologist diagnosed the sore as carcinoma, squamous cell—a type of skin cancer curable in the early stages but at that time dangerous if not treated early. The microscope showed Mr. Dobson had a "very mature" cell. The doctor did not know if it had spread to other parts of his body.

Six weeks of radiation treatment were recommended. Healing should then begin and take about another five weeks. At that point without healing, amputation might be the only option. For an artist, this virtually meant taking away the meaning of life and livelihood. Radiation began. So did intense prayer. Four weeks after radiation stopped, "no sign of healing had occurred."

The doctor began talking of the next step. Tension and concern dominated the family's life. Finally, five days into the fifth week, Mr. Dobson went to church leaders and asked for a special time of prayer that God would heal the cancer. Two days later the sore healed over, never to return (*When God Doesn't Make Sense,* pp. 96–97).

This account makes us realize that Jonah's story is only one example of answered prayers. Such stories of divine power in disastrous situations fuel the church's witness. But Jonah shows us another side to prayer. He not only prayed to get out of the fish and the sea; he also promised to pray and worship once he returned to dry land. His thanksgiving prayer from an unusual place can guide us in our prayer pilgrimage with God.

II. COMMENTARY

Praying from the Pit

> **MAIN IDEA:** *However desperate a person's situation, God listens to prayer and can bring deliverance.*

A Salvation from Sheol (2:1–2)

> **SUPPORTING IDEA:** *God listens to prayer from any location and out of any kind of distress.*

2:1. As usual, the narrator of Jonah's story surprises us. Jonah prays. What the sailors could not make the sleepy prophet do in chapter 1, the fish accomplishes in chapter 2. The Hebrew term for **prayed** (*yithpallel*) often refers to intercessory prayer for someone else (Num. 11:2; 1 Sam. 7:5). It is also a word for conversation and petition to God (2 Kgs. 19:20; Jer. 29:12). In Jonah's case it became a totally unexpected time of prayer, a prayer of thanksgiving looking back on God's act of salvation. Jonah described what happened when the fish snatched him from the water. He interpreted that as an act of divine deliverance.

The prayer is directed to **the LORD his God**. Suddenly Jonah was fleeing no more from God's presence. He was seeking God's presence in prayer and claiming God once more as his Lord. The fish converted the rebellious prophet into a prophet of prayer and thanksgiving. Oceans of ink have been spent trying to explain how Jonah could live **inside the fish**, literally "in the womb or entrails of the fish." The Bible expends no effort on such details. It simply assumes God can accomplish such miracles since the fish was sent by him (Jon. 1:17).

2:2. The opening words of the prayer present an interesting perspective. It is a report on what Jonah did in the past and how God responded. Jonah spoke of his **distress**. But God **answered**. At the moment the where and how of God's answer is not important. Jonah simply focused on his renewed relationship with God. This is the first part of deliverance. Prophet and Almighty God communicate with each other again.

Then Jonah explains a bit further: "From the belly of Sheol I cried for help." Sheol speaks of the deepest depths, the antithesis of the highest heavens (Prov. 9:18). Like *tehom* ("the depths") it is a dwelling place, one approached through gates and covered everywhere with dust (Isa. 38:10). The dead there have an existence of some kind, though their description as "shades" (*rephaim*) (Isa. 14:9) makes clear that theirs is a weak and unrewarding style of life (Isa. 14:10). There is no hope of deliverance from Sheol or the grave unless God himself intervenes—a possibility hinted at here and there in the Old Testament record (Ps. 56:13). Full assurance of victory over Sheol must await the revelation of the New Testament witness (1 Cor. 15:50–58) (Eugene H. Merrill, *NIDOTTE,* IV, 6–7).

The prayers of the Psalms often seek deliverance from or avoidance of Sheol (Pss. 49:15; 141:7) or see Sheol as the ultimate destiny of their enemies (Ps. 55:15). Thus Jonah joined a solid tradition in crying to God for deliverance from the land of the dead. Where was Jonah when he issued this cry? Our immediate reaction is to locate him in the belly of the fish, but the following verses locate him in the sea before the fish got him. The fish apparently represents a safe haven for Jonah, a God-given vessel of safety escorting him out of Sheol. From inside the fish Jonah can look back at his distressful times in the sea before the rescue occurred. He describes Sheol as "a hyperbole for his brink-of-death experience (as in Pss. 18:5; 30:3)" (Barker, *Breaking Old Testament Codes,* 229).

Ⓑ Prayer Overpowers the Pit (2:3–6)

> **SUPPORTING IDEA:** *Desperate situations, even those God has instigated, provide opportunity for prayer and for witnessing God's deliverance.*

2:3. Jonah describes his trouble in very personal terms. It was not an accident. It was a you-and-me confrontation. Jonah remembered the horror of the situation, a horror caused not only by his fear of the sea but even more by his knowledge that God **hurled** (or cast him out) **into the deep**. If God had put him there, then only God could deliver him, and Jonah knew he had become a rebel whom God might not want to deliver. Why would God deliver him when the threat came from **all your waves and breakers**? As Jonah pictured his plight, he was as good as dead. Any deliverance had to come from God.

2:4. In such a desperate situation, Jonah expressed one of history's greatest confessions of faith as he prayed, **I have been banished from your sight; yet I will look again toward your holy temple**. In the midst of the sea, this sounded like an insane pipe dream. Even repeating the prayer inside the fish made the prophet look foolish. What hope for escape did he have, yet he had faith he would once more enjoy worshipping in the temple in Jerusalem—or perhaps if he were tied to Jeroboam in the Northern Kingdom, the temple would be in Bethel.

2:5. Engulfing represents language of the Psalms (Pss. 18:4; 116:3) as does so much of Jonah's prayer. Jonah remembered the deep sea **waters** "up to the throat" (author's translation). He was **surrounded** by the **deep** (Heb. *tehom*). In poetic language this meant he looked death square in the face. The deep referred to the "primeval ocean, the primeval flood, one of the prominent elements in creation (Gen. 1:2; Ps. 104:6)" (*HALOT*). It can refer to the watery depths that surrounded the earth at the beginning of the creation week (Gen. 1:2) or subterranean waters that burst forth in the flood (Gen 7:11). Often *tehom* "acquires the meaning of the flood or depths that threaten existence (Exod. 15:5)" (C. Westermann, *TLOT,* III, 1412–13).

No matter how fearsome the deeps are for frightened humans, God is always in control of the flooding waters (Ps. 135:6). He uses these waters to bring blessing and victory to his people (Deut. 8:7). "*Tehom* is a component of the world that God created and in which he acts" (Westermann). It is a component God can destroy if he chooses (Amos 7:4). Caught in the midst of the depths, Jonah saw them only as the chaotic waters that were part of the formless void until God organized it into the heavens and earth. These chaotic waters were destined to be God's instruments in carrying out God's death sentence on Jonah.

2:6. Jonah sank as low as he could go, **to the roots** (or base or foundation stones) **of the mountains**. His journey downward that started in chapter 1 is finished. He reached the bars of the **earth**—the gates to Sheol or the underworld itself. He was in the **pit**, another term for the residence of the dead (Ezek. 28:8). Humanly speaking, escape was impossible. Jonah was there **forever**. Even entry into the residence of the dead was not eternal because God maintains control of **life** even in the realm of the dead. For Jonah this proved more than a theological statement of faith. He confessed to his own experience: **you brought my life up.**

C Failure to Pray Forfeits Grace (2:7–8)

> **SUPPORTING IDEA:** *No matter how near death a person may be, he can pray and find God listening, but failure to pray forfeits any hope of receiving God's grace.*

2:7. Feeling more and more feeble, Jonah remembered the one source of help that had never failed: **I remembered you,** LORD. Memory of God and what he had done in the past gave rise to new hope—new attempts to communicate with the Lord, to make connection and gain new blessing. He pictured God in his **holy temple,** the house of prayer, and sent his prayers there. The prayer was not to the temple, however, as if the place had some magical quality. His prayer was to God. Jonah's I/you conversation brought results.

2:8. Jonah had seen the plight of the sailors as each prayed to his own god without success. Jonah had entered the world of fleeing the Lord and looking for help elsewhere. He had a strong testimony from all this experience: **those who cling to worthless idols** "forsake their grace" (author's translation; cp. Ps. 31:6). This phrase can be taken in several ways.

Frank Page states the problem simply: "The primary difficulty in the verse is with the word *chasdam.* It is made up of a pronominal suffix meaning 'of them' and the word *chesed*, which can have several meanings, such as 'loyalty, obligation, faithfulness, kindness, grace, mercy'" (NAC 19b, 253). The problem is determining which meaning best fits in this case and whether the pronoun represents the object or the subject of the *chesed*. Page opts for the pronoun being the object of grace so that they receive God's grace, for "the overall thought here seems to emphasize that salvation comes from the Lord."

Leslie C. Allen claims:

> In light of the use of *chesed* in the intended parallel in 4:2, the suffix is not subjective, "their loyalty," "their devotion," but objective: the divine *chesed* previously shown and still available to them. His *grace*, the loyal love that rushes to the aid of his own at their first cry, in the psalm's present context, not only glances back to Jonah's deliverance but hints at that of the sailors who abandoned their own gods and relied upon Yahweh (NICOT 219–219 with note 28).

On the other hand, Joyce Baldwin puts it like this:

> The word *chesed* depicts the characteristic attribute of God as he is revealed in his covenant relationship with Israel. Jonah is convicted of his folly in forsaking such a God, and his advice is directed to his fellow Israelites who are guilty of the same thing (Hos. 4:12; Amos 5:26) and who have gone astray morally as a result. Jonah can say with conviction that those who forsake their covenant Lord for any other object of devotion need to appreciate what fools they are (*The Minor Prophets: An Exegetical and Expository Commentary,* vol. 2, pp. 571–72).

Douglas Stuart says:

> Worshiping them also shows a lack of faith in Yahweh. For any Israelite to trust in idol worship was a violation of the covenant. Covenant loyalty (*chesed*) was a mutual obligation both of God, the initiator of the covenant (Exod. 20:6, etc.), and of the Israelites to whom the covenant was given. Accordingly, one who broke the covenant's first commandment by having other gods had 'abandoned' his or her loyalty to Yahweh (WBC 31, 478).

The present context is a praise to God expressed first in the negative statement about worthless nothings and then in the positive vow to praise and worship and sacrifice. Part of that praise is to express the availability of God's grace, his love, his covenant faithfulness to his people, and to warn them of the danger of abandoning that grace when they abandon God. The Lord personifies grace, and he gives objective blessings because of his grace. Both are tied up in the meaning of "their grace."

D Salvation Summons Sacrifice (2:9–10)

SUPPORTING IDEA: *Having experienced God's salvation, people will bring offerings and worship the God of their salvation.*

2:9. Still in the belly of the fish, looking back at his desperation in the sea, Jonah looks forward to the temple experience. He believes he will once more see the temple. Once there he will carry out his obligations to God. He will sing a song of thanksgiving at a special thanksgiving ceremony. He will make the thanksgiving sacrifice and share it with family, friends, and priests. He will recount all that God has done to deliver him and will testify about God's goodness to him. This is Jonah's promise to God, and this is exactly what he will do when he sees the temple again.

Having reviewed all this, Jonah can only shout from the fish's stomach: **Salvation comes from the LORD.** This again is not a theological statement of belief. This is a personal confession. God had saved him. Standing at death's door, he cried for God's help and found God present at death's door. God had truly saved the prophet, and he wanted everyone to know about it. Most likely, he would repeat this song of thanksgiving at the thanksgiving service in the temple and elaborate on it for his friends.

2:10. We leave Jonah in the fish for a moment to listen to the rest of the story. God spoke to the fish, as clearly as he had spoken to Jonah. The fish served as God's messenger in a way comparable to the prophet serving as God's messenger. The fish did not reply. He simply got the biggest stomachache imaginable and **vomited Jonah onto dry land.**

MAIN IDEA REVIEW: *However desperate a person's situation, God listens to prayer and can bring deliverance.*

III. CONCLUSION

Emergency Thanksgiving

We took my son skiing in Austria for his eighteenth birthday. He had grown up in Switzerland and loved to ski the Alps. On day one of skiing, the ski patrol knocked on our door: "Your son has been flight-lifted down the mountain. He ran into a rock and has hurt his shoulder. We are checking to see what else may be injured."

"Danke" is all the German that would come from my mouth as we ran to find where Kevin was. Even as I ran, I prayed, "Thank you, Lord, that Kevin is still alive and that trained people were there to help him." Yes, I said a prayer of thanksgiving even before I knew the extent and consequences of Kevin's injuries. Quite often in life, we find ourselves in situations where we say "thank you" to God in the midst of crisis.

Jonah is certainly example number one. In the midst of the sea, he thanked God for deliverance. In the belly of the fish, he repeated that prayer, and certainly at the public thanksgiving service in the temple later, he repeated the prayer. We cannot say thank you to God too many times.

PRINCIPLES

- You may pray to God in any location, in any circumstances, for any reason.
- Even though you have rebelled against God and are fleeing from his presence, you can still pray in desperation and seek his deliverance.
- God answers prayers even when you are at death's door.
- Even as we suffer under God's discipline and punishment, we can pray to him and know that he hears.
- Praying to God means forsaking other gods and other objects of devotion and sources of hope.
- When God answers prayer, we should respond in thanksgiving and worship and give an offering to him.
- Deliverance always has its ultimate source in God.

APPLICATIONS

- List every reason you have to be grateful to God, and give him thanks for each item on the list.
- No matter how dark life may seem, do not give up; pray to God for help.
- Write out a story or song about how God has answered your prayer recently, then share it with your Bible study group.
- Search for the objects of devotion that have become false gods in your life, then get rid of them.
- Commit yourself to be loyal in participating in the worship services of your church.
- Remind yourself of promises you have made to God in the past, and fulfill any that you have not yet kept.

IV. LIFE APPLICATION

Off-Side Penalties

In his book *Iron Shoes,* Roy Angell relates a story told by Carey Barker, once captain of the Washington and Lee football team. Walking down a Richmond, Virginia, street late one evening just before dark, Barker saw a little boy sitting on the edge of the sidewalk, elbows on his knees, face in his hands, and a partially deflated football tucked under one arm. The boy looked so pathetic that Barker went over and sat on the curb beside him.

"What's the matter?" he asked. "Why are you sitting here like you have lost your best friend?"

Twisting around, the boy looked up into Barker's eyes. "Mister, you ever play football?"

"Sure did. I was fullback for two years."

"Then, Mister, you know what it means when a player is off side. The whole team, not just the player, gets penalized. Everybody in the grandstand that's rootin' for them gets penalized. Everybody that's pullin' for them on the radio gets penalized."

"You are so right, son," Barker replied, waiting anxiously to hear what the boy had done to be off side.

"Well, Mister, my daddy is off side. He came home drunk tonight. Mother had the nicest dinner ready. She was singing and smiling and happy as she put it on the table.

"Mister, he turned the table over and slapped Mother across the face. I sneaked out the back door and came back over here. Thought I'd kick a football around a while, but it ain't any fun to kick a football around by yourself. All the other boys have gone home" (pp. 68–69).

What do you do when every negative feeling in the world fills your soul, and you can do nothing about it? Jonah, who knew a bit about most of those feelings, shows us the only resource we have when despair invades life. He prayed to God, thanking him in advance for what he was going to do. He showed his trust in God when all human objects of trust had failed him.

V. PRAYER

God, sometimes we think every day is a "Jonah day" as we flounder in the sea of helplessness. Thank you that you are always there with us, ready to hear our prayer and deliver us from our despair. We trust in you and discard everything that we are tempted to put in your place. Amen.

VI. DEEPER DISCOVERIES

Salvation (2:9)

Old Testament salvation usually refers to a concrete, objective act of deliverance from danger and despair. It can be expressed by several Hebrew words, many of them related to the verb *yasha'*. "In general, the root *yasha'* implies bringing help to people in the midst of their trouble rather than in rescuing them from it. It is almost exclusively a theological term with Yahweh as its subject and his people as its object" (Robert L. Hubbard Jr., *NIDOTTE*, II, 556). This word is used especially to describes God's victory for Israel in the exodus (Exod. 14:13).

But the term is most at home in worship and prayer. Nearly half the psalms use some form of the root, and about 40 percent of its total occurrences appear in the Book of Psalms. "Theologically, Israelite worship and instruction supremely associated Yahweh with salvation" (Hubbard, 559).

When Old Testament believers raise laments or complaints to God, they often cry out *hoshi'ah,* "Save!" (Pss. 12:1; 71:2). Often God answers with the promise to save (Jer. 15:20). God is thus known as "my salvation" or "my help" (Mic. 7:7).

People like Jonah who see their prayers answered look back at the experience and testify that God has given them salvation (Isa. 25:9). They know that God alone can bring deliverance because human help is in vain (Hos. 14:3). But God expects the person being delivered to trust him and to repent of his sins (Isa. 30:15).

Jonah joined a long line of his ancestors in seeking God in his temple and lamenting, asking for salvation. He also joined a long line of people who had experienced God's deliverance and could proclaim, "Salvation comes from the Lord."

VII. TEACHING OUTLINE

A. INTRODUCTION

1. Lead Story: Dramatic Answers
2. Context: Having been thrown off the ship by reluctant sailors, Jonah found himself drowning in the sea, standing at the door to the place of the dead. The fleeing prophet became the fervent prophet, asking God to save him.
3. Transition: Chapter 2 repeats Jonah's prayer of desperation but looks back on it from the vantage point of salvation. That vantage point just happens to be the belly of a fish that God sent to help Jonah. In the fish, Jonah offers thanksgiving for his salvation and proclaims that only the Lord saves; all other gods are powerless.

B. COMMENTARY

1. Salvation from Sheol (2:1–2)
2. Prayer Overpowers the Pit (2:3–6)

3. Failure to Pray Forfeits Grace (2:7–8)
4. Salvation Summons Sacrifice (2:9–10)

C. CONCLUSION: EMERGENCY THANKSGIVING

VIII. ISSUES FOR DISCUSSION

1. When is thanksgiving prayer appropriate?
2. Should a promise to do something for God always accompany a prayer of thanksgiving?
3. What does it mean to you to confess that salvation is from the Lord?
4. Describe the difference between the realm of the dead described in Jonah and the realm of the dead described in the New Testament.
5. How did Jesus use the story of Jonah? (See Matt. 12:39–41; 16:4; Luke 11:29–32.)

Jonah 3:1–4:11

Pouting Against Pity

I. **INTRODUCTION**
Saying Good-bye

II. **COMMENTARY**
A verse-by-verse explanation of these verses.

III. **CONCLUSION**
Self-Centered or God-Centered?

An overview of the principles and applications from these verses.

IV. **LIFE APPLICATION**
A Vessel for God's Use

Melding these verses to life.

V. **PRAYER**
Tying these verses to life with God.

VI. **DEEPER DISCOVERIES**
Historical, geographical, and grammatical enrichment of the commentary.

VII. **TEACHING OUTLINE**
Suggested step-by-step group study of these verses.

VIII. **ISSUES FOR DISCUSSION**
Zeroing these verses in on daily life.

"*G*od is always sympathetic, but his sympathy is not always accepted. . . . God's most glorious extension of sympathy to a dying world was Christ, his Son. God sent Christ as the delegate of his sympathy to the misery of men. Ultimately his message of sympathy was rejected by the very ones to whom it was first extended, and Christ hung on a cross in complete humiliation."

B e t h   M o o r e

Jonah 3:1–4:11

IN A NUTSHELL

*G*od had a reason for sending the fish. Jonah had to go to Nineveh. This time when God called, Job went. But not with his whole heart. Once there Jonah started into the city, preached five Hebrew words, and then went back to see what would happen. The unexpected happened. Revival broke out. The king called everyone, even the animals, into fasting and mourning. He called on everyone to repent and give up his evil, violent ways. God had sympathy for such people, changed his course of action, and did not destroy the city.

This infuriated Jonah. Knowing God's character, he had expected something like this might happen. When the prophet got hot waiting for God to act, God provided a vine for shade. On the next day God sent a worm to destroy the vine. Jonah exploded, asking to die. God contrasted Jonah's attitude with his own. Jonah worried about vines, shade, and comfort. God worried about a huge, ignorant city that needed his salvation.

Pouting Against Pity

I. INTRODUCTION

Saying Good-bye

*S*aying good-bye is hard. Sometimes we hate to say good-bye to the silliest things. Going to college, I said good-bye to baseball cards. Going to seminary, I said good-bye to Texas. Going to the foreign mission field, I said good-bye to a church I loved and to a large part of my carefully collected library. Returning from the mission field, I waved good-bye to a lifelong mission dream along with a fluffy white dog. Coming to work at LifeWay, I said good-bye to a teaching career. Then a few years back, I had to say good-bye to my beloved spouse of thirty years.

God had good-byes for Jonah to say, but he had a hard time getting Jonah to say good-bye. Good-bye, fish; hello, mission assignment. Good-bye, Israel; hello, Nineveh! Good-bye to being famous and popular; hello to being strange and a foreigner. Good-bye, vine; hello, sunshine and heat. Good-bye, anger; hello, joy. Good-bye, prejudice; hello, mission devotion. Good-bye, hatred; hello, love.

Refusing to say good-bye, Jonah let anger and prejudice consume his life and lead him to the brink of death. What the sea depths and Sheol could not accomplish, refusing to say good-bye almost did.

II. COMMENTARY

Pouting Against Pity

> **MAIN IDEA:** *God loves the world so much that he seeks to save the world by leading every person in it to repentance from sin and commitment to a life of obedience.*

Mission Repetition (3:1–3)

> **SUPPORTING IDEA:** *God expects his people to carry out the mission assignments he gives to each of us.*

3:1–2. "One more try, Jonah. Nineveh is the destination I chose, not Tarshish. Are you going?"

"Nineveh? Capital of Assyria. Most cruel nation on earth. Our biggest enemy. That strange language. So far away. I won't know anyone. What will they do to me? You say you are going to judge and destroy them? Why tell them, then? Just do it! They deserve it. Go ahead and destroy the city. I'll tell people at home and let them see how great you are. I'll make sure you get the credit!"

"I am at work in Nineveh just now. I want you there."

"On my way, Lord. You delivered me from the sea. I'll deliver your message just as you say."

3:3. "Well, I'm finally here, Lord. I've traveled five hundred miles riding in a camel caravan just to get here. See, here I am in Nineveh, just like you said. What a big city."

"Yes, Jonah, it is a big city. Note what I have written about it. It is a 'great city to God.' It is not just big. It is a city that figures greatly in my plans. It is important to me, no matter how big it is."

The text says that Jonah crossed Nineveh with "a walking of three days." What does that mean? Scholars debate it extensively. Allen studied ancient sources to determine that a day's walk would be about seventeen miles, making the diameter of the city about fifty miles, much larger than ancient evidence seems to credit to Nineveh. Some sources do indicate the circumference of the city walls was about fifty miles, but an inscription from King Sennacherib at that time indicates he extended the city walls so they were seven and one-half miles in circumference. For Allen, then, the narrator is working with much later traditional material and using it to enhance the prophet's task (NICOT, 221).

Other scholars approach the problem by asking what "walking" means. Does "walking" refer to a stretch of road (HALOT), a visit (Wiseman, *Tyndale Bulletin* 30, 1979, 38), or a journey (DCH). Stuart follows Wiseman in seeing the three days referring to the time required to complete all the official protocol for a visit to city officials. Stuart thus assumes

> that his first and third days involved meetings and explanations, perhaps even formal hearings. . . . The popular notion that Jonah, virtually unnoticed, wandered into Nineveh casually and then, at various stages of his trip, suddenly began shouting his message, would be far from a realistic portrayal of the events. . . . Rather the narrator's point is that Nineveh was a "three-day visit city," a major diplomatic center of the ancient world, a city where a formal protocol was observed by official visitors (WBC 31, 487–88).

Allen then notes another explanation:

> In a major city a prophet would have to travel to various sections, speaking to different crowds, over a period of time. . . . Nineveh's population and importance made it necessary for Jonah to preach there for at least three days to be sure that God's message had been really heard by the bulk of the populace.

B Mission Results (3:4–10)

SUPPORTING IDEA: *God is free in his love for the world and can turn back from his decision to destroy a people when they repent and obey him.*

3:4. "Lord, I was not prepared for this. I'll walk around a while. Then I'll preach." So Jonah walked the city for a day, a note perhaps supporting Allen's last suggestion of the interpretation of three days' walk. Finally, he preached: "Yet forty days, Nineveh overthrown." If the narrator in his terse style intends for us to hear this as the totality of the prophet's sermon, it says much about Jonah's attitude. He went as far as possible before preaching, then preached only five words. His heart did not appear to be in stirring up a revival in Nineveh, just in passing God's minimum requirements.

3:5. The Ninevites believed God. Of all the unexpected twists in the Jonah story, this has to be the one we are least prepared for. "Believed" translates a verb from the Hebrew root *'aman*. The basic meaning is to be firm, trustworthy, or safe (*HALOT*). Thus it means to regard the one believed in as trustworthy, to have trust in that person or thing. It is often used for trust in God as the one able to do Godlike achievements (Gen. 15:6; Ps. 78:22). Nineveh was known as a religious city with temples to many gods, but in this instance the people of Nineveh turned their backs on all their national gods and personal gods and turned to the God of Israel who created the heavens and the earth. They recognized God's power and believed he would carry out the threats he had made through Jonah.

The citizens of Nineveh demonstrated their faith in concrete ways. They called a fast, eating no food. They dressed in sackcloth, the traditional clothing for mourning. These actions were taken by the entire population—from the biggest and most important to the smallest and least important.

3:6. The royal information agency did its job, securing the latest talk of the town and relaying it immediately to the king. The king joined "the greatest" in putting on mourning garments. The king of Nineveh would also be the king of the entire Assyrian Empire—one of the most powerful men on earth. Was not this the greatest spiritual revival in history?

Stuart goes to great lengths to show that possible loss of territories, a complete solar eclipse, and a major earthquake may have occurred during the reign of King Ashshur-dan III who ruled from 773 to 756 B.C., making the monarch ready to hear the prophetic word. But then he is forced to conclude: "There is, of course, absolutely no way to identify with confidence the king mentioned in Jonah 3:6" (WBC 31, 490–93). Still Stuart wants to hypothesize:

> A king such as Ashshur-dan III, during whose reign an agonizing confluence of omens and disasters (eclipse, earthquake (?), famine,

rioting) had occurred, whose capital (or at least common residence) may have been Nineveh, though this cannot be proved, and who was beset by international problems including continuing military failures against Urartu, was certainly the sort of king (among others) who might well have been predisposed to receive Jonah's message sincerely as a chance for respite from his troubles.

The Bible, however, gives the king no reason to listen to Jonah except the power of God's message on the people and on him.

3:7–8. The king **issued a proclamation**, literally "caused a cry for help to go out." The king thus called on all citizens to join him in a national cry for help. The king's nobles or royal advisory council (literally, "his great ones") joined in issuing the decree. The decree affected every living thing in the land. Humans and animals joined in refusing to eat or drink as they cried to God. The somewhat humorous sight of cows and sheep slipping on sackcloth to mourn emphasizes the severity of the crisis and the determination of the royal house to avert national tragedy.

The king's edict included the passive wearing of sackcloth and not eating. It also called for positive action. Everyone was to **call urgently on God**. Interestingly the generic *'elohim,* "god" or "God" or "gods" is used and not Yahweh, the personal name of God. Praying desperately for health was not enough. Each of the people must also "turn from his evil way" (author's translation)—the Hebrew way of calling for repentance. This evil way is specified as "the violence that is in their hands" (author's translation). The biblical prophets often accused Israel of violence against its poor and less fortunate population—the powerless people in society. Jonah may refer to such internal violence and social injustice here. He may also refer to Assyria's war practices by which they treated conquered nations and captive prisoners with cruelty.

3:9. In his decree the Assyrian king explained his purpose in asking for such drastic actions. "Who is the one knowing? The God may repent and become remorseful and turn away from his burning anger so that we do not perish" (author's translation). In spite of his royal status as the representative of the Assyrian gods on earth, the king made no promises. He expressed a hope that the people's actions would bring a divine reaction. Note Jonah's related reaction in 4:2.

The king credited God with the power to change things. If the Lord did not change his ways, then Assyria had no hope. Note the expression is now "The God" pointing to one, high, all-powerful God in control of his fate. Had the Assyrian king, like the pagan sailors, come to recognize the exclusive claim to deity made by Israel's God?

3:10. What do you expect to happen? People repented. So did God. He became remorseful. He changed his plans when the people changed their ways. No judgment for Nineveh. No destruction.

Here is a perfect picture of the biblical teaching that God is free to change. God announces his sentence on a guilty people and declares the punishment they must endure because of their guilt. But God's word is not the proverbial law of the Medes and the Persians that we find in Daniel. God's word is a message on mission. When the word accomplishes its mission so that the people respond to it in the way God desires, then he does not consider himself bound to carry out his word. God retains the freedom to repent, to become remorseful. As they "turned away from their evil ways" so "the God became remorseful concerning the evil that he had promised (literally spoken) to do to them."

Here the Hebrew term *ra'ah* ("evil") views actions from a human viewpoint as that which destroys or pains people. The important words here are the last two in Hebrew—"he did not do." Prayer, repentance, a change of attitudes and actions influence God. He reacts as a person in a personal relationship and changes his plans in accordance with the way people have changed their conduct.

Missionary's Misery (4:1–4)

> **SUPPORTING IDEA:** *Prejudice and hatred lead people away from God's loving plan to a demand for revenge and destruction.*

4:1. The people's not doing evil causing God not to do evil "was extraordinarily evil to Jonah, making him angry" (author's translation).

4:2–3. So what did Jonah do in his anger? He prayed, of course. The same word is used here as in Jonah 2:1. That is what all the psalms of lament and complaint teach us to do with our anger. But Jonah prayed in a special way. He bawled the Lord out for being God. He even quoted Scripture about the things in God's nature that he did not like (Exod. 34:6). "Jonah failed to recognize his privilege of being an instrument of God in a miraculous situation. Failing to recognize God's sovereign plan, he missed the joy of the situation. Much like Elijah (1 Kgs. 19:3–18), Jonah sank into a selfish state of mind" (Page, NAC, 276).

Can't you hear Jonah even now: "I knew it, God. I told you this would happen. You went back on your word just as I said you would. That is why I did not want to come to Nineveh. Then you would have zapped the city. But, no, you let the people repent. You did not bring judgment on them. I am a fool. What I preached did not happen. What will people back home think? I know you are the God of love, but love has its limits. Some people you are not supposed to love. Just kill me if you're going to be that way!"

As Stuart phrases it: "He was actually expecting God to suppress his own natural inclination to show mercy wherever possible. It was not simply the case that Jonah could not bring himself to appreciate Nineveh. Rather, to a shocking extent, he could not stand God!" (p. 503). Saving Nineveh was evil. Killing Jonah was good. What a reversal of values and attitudes!

4:4. God responded to Jonah's suicidal plea: "Is the anger you have causing something good to happen?" (author's translation). There was no way Jonah could answer yes to that question. Certainly he should have seen the answer. But he did not.

Ⓓ Choice of Concerns (4:5–11)

> **SUPPORTING IDEA:** *Prejudice and hatred lead to a concern for self while love and pity lead to a commitment to help and save.*

4:5. Without answering, the petulant prophet stomped angrily off, clear out of the city, presumably a day's journey. He set up shop east of the city, building himself a little booth and sitting in its shade "until he should see what would occur in the city."

4:6. As he had earlier prepared a fish, so now God prepared a **vine**, probably a castor oil plant. This provided shade for Jonah's head and shaded him "from his evil" (translated **discomfort** in NIV). Back to the spirit of chapter 2! "Jonah rejoiced with great joy because of the vine." This sounds like the worshipping congregation singing psalms of joy for God's deliverance. Jonah was easily satisfied. A fish and a vine furnished places and opportunities for him to worship just like he was in the temple.

4:7. Again God went into the preparing business. This time he prepared a wonderful **worm**. This was apparently the "so-called fruit-grub (*cochylis ambiguella Hüb.*), which attacks the grape" (*HALOT*). This special fruit grub, prepared and sent by God, "attacked the vine, and the vine withered away and dried up" (author's translation).

4:8. Another divine preparation! This time an **east wind**, "a scorching one." Here is the biblical affirmation that God controls every element of his creation and can use any element in it for his own purposes. If it takes a scorching wind to discipline his prophet and teach him a lesson, then God can prepare a scorching wind. The sultry wind joined by the searing sun did Jonah in. He fainted and "asked his soul to die."

4:9. God speaks for the first time since verse 4 with the exact same question asked there: "Is the anger you have causing something good to happen?" (author's translation) This time the question focuses on a specific cause of anger—anger **about the vine**. Incredibly Jonah answered a rhetorical question the wrong way. "The anger I have is causing something good even unto death." The prophet was so mad at God and his uncomfortable circumstances that he was ready to die rather than give up his anger. His anger blinded him to the absurdity of his feelings and his statements.

4:10. God tried to calm his prophet with a bit of simple reasoning. Let's compare your situation with my situation. You watched a vine get eaten away and got all worked up with concern and pity over the vine. Now this vine was something that just came to you. "You did not labor over it, and you did not make it grow. It appeared one night, and it was destroyed in one night" (Literally, "which was the son of a night and perished the son of a night"). Think about the real value of this vine. "Does my prophet love a one-day-wonder-gourd vine more than my eternal mission?"

4:11. "That's your situation, Jonah. Now look at mine. If you love the vine that much, can't I love Nineveh at least that much? Look at all the poor, innocent, ignorant people! Love them with me. Or love your prejudice. Which will it be?"

> **MAIN IDEA REVIEW:** *God loves the world so much that he seeks to save the world by leading every person in it to repentance from sin and commitment to a life of obedience.*

III. CONCLUSION

Self-Centered or God-Centered?

In her book *The Glorious Dawn of God's Story,* Anne Graham Lotz introduces us to Wang, a young man from one of the world's most repressive countries. When Wang was four, his brother taught him the Lord's Prayer. In spite of all her efforts, his mother could not lead him to faith in Christ. So Wang went off to join the national army with his mother's last words echoing her promise to pray for him daily.

Army life was unrewarding until Wang joined the wrestling team, became national champion, and received the athlete's share of the food. One night an intense longing for God filled his soul, so he prayed the Lord's Prayer. He began doing that before every match. He also asked God, if he were real, to "keep my mother safe until I can see her again." He did return home to his mother and went to church with her. He answered the pastor's invitation and gave his life to Christ.

Wang then became a successful mechanical engineer and eventually a wealthy man. But one day God called him to preach, so he gave up his lucrative job to pastor a church in a country that was hostile to religion. Years went by, and one day Wang got the government's permission to come to America.

Anne Graham Lotz was one of many Christians who admired Wang. She was moved by his story and did everything possible to help him adjust to his life in America. They provided everything he needed. Then one day Wang asked the Lotz family if they would lend him a television. As Anne writes, "My husband and I exchanged glances, then gladly gave our own TV to him for his use as long as he wanted it. As he took it, he looked at us and said, 'Don't you have anything larger?'"

"It seemed to either be a turning point in Wang's attitude or perhaps just an opening of our eyes to what was happening in his life," Lotz wrote.

> Wang began to wheedle sympathy from friends as he asked for a newer model car than the one he had been given, the latest set of *Encyclopedia Britannica*, designer clothing, and other items he wanted. We watched in sorrow as a truly great man yielded to the temptations of freedom, worshiped at the altar of materialism, and became consumed with greed and resentment of those who had what he wanted but couldn't get (p. 195).

Wang followed some of the same road Jonah did—the road from being a nobody to being a great somebody, the road from humble obedience and joy to greedy, prejudiced anger and frustration. What places a person on such a road? The Book of Jonah teaches us that this happens when we lose God's love for others and become consumed by our own desires and prejudices. We become self-centered instead of God-centered.

PRINCIPLES

- God's world is bigger than ours.
- God's love is bigger than his wrath.
- God wants to cure our prejudice and greed.
- God wants to use us in his mission if we will love people as he loves them.
- God accepts repentance and obedience from even the worst of sinners.

APPLICATIONS

- Check your hate list today and see how many people you need to remove.
- Check God's love list today and see how many people you need to learn to love as he does.
- Seek God's mission for your life and dedicate yourself to fulfilling it, no matter the cost.
- Repent of your sins and promise God you will obey him in everything he asks.
- Let God replace your anger and frustration with his love for people.

IV. LIFE APPLICATION

A Vessel for God's Use

In his own inimitable way, Mark Lowry tells about his next-door neighbor during his childhood. She was named Helen Hanft and had a son named Fritz. Mark writes:

> I used to beat the tar out of him. We'd start out wrestling, and he would end up runnin' home crying.
>
> I'll never forget Helen. She was short and had the hairiest toes I've ever seen on a woman. She was the only person I knew who could grow her own furry slippers. She wouldn't go barefoot because she was afraid of split ends.
>
> Helen didn't like me. I have no idea why. But when Mama was about thirteen months pregnant with my little sister, Helen walked up to Mama outside our house, pointed at Mother's stomach, and said, "I hope that child isn't like Mark."
>
> Mama swung around like only a pregnant woman can do and said, "Listen, here, Helen. One day God is going to use Mark."
>
> When I was a hyperactive kid coming home with notes from my teachers hanging on my lapels, Mama would read those notes, tuck me into bed, and she'd say, "Mark, one day God's going to use you" (*Out of Control*, pp. 20–21).

Jonah lived his life with the same message beating through his heart every day: "God's going to use you." Jonah experienced how God could use him in a marvelous way that prospered his nation and his people. Then one day Jonah discovered God wanted to use him in a way that had danger, fear, intrigue, and change written all over it. God wanted Jonah to witness to people he did not like, people he actually hated. Jonah was not sure he wanted to be used in the way God wanted to use him.

We face the same decision every day. We know God wants to use us. He saves us so we can serve him. Are we willing to serve him only in ways that are safe and popular? Or are we willing to go where he wants us to go and do what he wants us to do with the people he chooses to work with? Do we create the job description? Or does God?

I have wrestled with this decision all the time I have been writing this book because God has called a group of us to go to India and witness among the gypsy tribes there. I volunteered to go, but something keeps holding me back. Am I willing to enter territory where nuclear arms are being rattled back and forth? Am I willing to go to a country I know nothing about but its poverty and disease? Am I willing to talk to people who revere cows and worship hundreds of gods?

Ultimately I am answering *yes,* but still I must let God remove that last feeling of reluctance, fear, and doubt. Will you ask God to remove all your fear, anger, frustration, doubts, reluctance, prejudice—whatever it is that would prevent you from joining God in his work and letting him use you as he wants to do? God loves the whole world and everyone in it. Jonah loved only himself and people like him and his vine. Whom do you love?

V. PRAYER

Loving heavenly Lord, you have so much love. You spread it around the world. You call us to receive that love from you and to share it with people we do not know, people we do not like, people against whom we hold great prejudice. Cleanse our hearts of anger, reluctance, prejudice—whatever it is that keeps us from letting you use us in the way you have chosen. Here we are! Send us wherever you are at work and want us to join in. Amen.

VI. DEEPER DISCOVERIES

A. God's World Mission

Jonah in many ways represents the pinnacle of the Old Testament's missionary message. Missions, from a biblical perspective, has its ultimate source in God. He created the entire world and desires for the world to experience a love relationship with him. He is the God of all the earth (Isa. 54:5). From the very beginning of the Bible, God is never presented as a tribal god or one who is confined to certain geographical territory. He is the God of all the earth who acts so that all the peoples on earth may know him.

Mission became necessary when man sinned (Gen. 3) and especially when man's pride and sin led God to scatter the human race over the entire earth (Gen. 6–11). Human sin separated every person on earth from God and showed that only he could provide a solution to the sin problem. Sin also separated nations as a whole from the Lord and led to their judgment.

Mission began with God's call to Abraham—a call seeking blessing for all the nations of the world (Gen. 12). God's desire to bless all the people of the world is woven into the fabric of the Old Testament (Isa. 42:6–10). His blessings begin as Abraham and his descendants, Joseph, and then Moses encountered foreigners and entered foreign countries. The Lord's blessing is seen in that he controls even the territories and histories of other nations (Deut. 32:8). The successes of the nations are explained as God's way of raising up instruments to judge and discipline his own disobedient people.

Jonah is the clearest example in the Bible that missions is not a natural human idea or action. It is God's plan to redeem sinners. He commissioned Israel to be a kingdom of priests, a holy nation, representing him before all the other nations of the world (Exod. 19:5–6). Having known the nature, the care, and the love of God, Israel was to be a missionary nation to others. God's missionary strategy is quite different from what humans might devise. He does not use his omnipotent power to force the nations to recognize and serve him. Instead, he uses personal means. He called Israel to be a special, treasured people. They were to mediate between God and all other nations, seeking to bring all people to obey God, keep his covenant, and be his people.

Jonah also shows us how God's people, Israel, ignored God's missionary message and mandate. They grew comfortable in their own worship habits and proud of their nation's power and influence. They chose to conquer—not convert—the nations. But from the beginning, missionary work called for God's people to be a self-sacrificing, obedient people. Abraham was willing to sacrifice his own son, the agent through whom God had promised to work out his missionary purpose of blessing the nations. Abraham's obedience allowed God to bless him and to use his descendants to bless all the nations of the earth (Gen. 22:16–18).

God worked out his missions plan for the world by calling individual people in Israel such as Jonah, Moses (Exod. 3), and Isaiah (Isa. 6). God calls some people to special ministry in world missions. The individual whom God calls becomes "a prophet to the nations" (Jer. 1:5). Like Jonah, people frequently rebel against God's call and offer excuses, but God does not accept excuses from people whom he calls. He promises to be present with them in their mission (Jer. 1:7–8).

Jonah did not like having to work in a foreign country, but he was not the first to have to do so. Moses had to go back to Egypt where he was on the most-wanted criminal list. There God promised that he was already at work in the foreign country. He had "raised up" the foreign ruler because he had one purpose for him—"that I might show you my power and that my name might be proclaimed in all the earth" (Exod. 9:16). Knowing that God wants his name known in all the earth provides authority for missions.

Jesus took up the Old Testament call to missions and applied it to himself. He found that call summarized in Isaiah 61 (see Luke 4:16–20). In this chapter we see a summary of the Old Testament missionary message. Missions is a divine activity of the sovereign God. The Spirit of God calls people to the missions task. The Spirit of God anoints people for that task. Missions by nature involves preaching good news to society's poor. Missions goes beyond proclamation to deeds of love. Missionary preaching and action brings freedom from fear, sin, vice, superstition, and oppressive conditions.

B. God Repents or Relents (3:9–10; 4:2)

Two Hebrew terms (*shuv*, "turn"; *nicham*, "become remorseful") express God's freedom to respond to human prayer and human change. *Shuv* is the standard Hebrew word for repentance, expressing a turning around from one course of action to another, from one lifestyle to another. The biblical message calls sinners to turn to God for the first time or to return to him from their evil ways (Ezek. 14:6). This is what theologians call "repentance." It involves going back to God, the original starting point, for a new beginning.

Repentance by people is possible for one reason—repentance by God. He promises to turn to the person seeking forgiveness and reconciliation (see Mal. 3:7). His response to someone's plea for restoration is to turn away his anger (Hos. 14:4). Such turning and change of direction by God comes only because the Lord is a God of feeling and emotions. He has compassion on his people (Jer. 31:20).

God's repenting is based on his relationship with his people. He calls them to turn back to him so he can turn back to them (Zech. 1:3). He responded to Moses' prayer for him to turn away from his anger (Exod. 32:12) and to Rehoboam's humility (2 Chr. 12:12). He heard Israel's prayer for him to return after disciplining them (Ps. 80:14). Israel prayed for God to return because they trusted his covenant faithfulness and love (Ps. 6:4). Hezekiah renewed the covenant and pledged obedience to God, asking him to turn his anger away from Israel (2 Chr. 29:10).

The prophets called on Israel to return to God. Then God would "heal them of their turning away . . . love them freely for my anger has turned away from them" (Hos. 14:4, author's translation). Jeremiah called Israel to right worship and right ritual to prevent God's fury from flaring up, but then he announced judgment and called for mourning rituals because God's anger was not turned away (Jer. 4:1–8). God's conclusion for Jeremiah's historical moment was clear: "Because I have spoken; I have planned. I will not show remorse; I will not turn back from it (his plan to destroy) (Jer. 4:28, author's translation).

Still the prophets looked to the day when Israel could once again sing a victory hymn to the God whose anger had turned back because of his compassion (Isa. 12:1). They promised that after God had pulled Israel up by the roots he would return and show compassion to them (Jer. 12:15). What gives such prophetic assurance that "I will not turn back to destroy Ephraim" (Hos. 11:9 HCSB)? The answer is simple—"because I am God and not man" (Hos. 11:9).

God thus repents by turning from his anger against Israel because of his overwhelming love for them. He does this because he is divine not human. He does it because he made promises he intends to fulfill and plans he will bring to historical reality. He does it because he is faithful to his covenant and plans to see it fulfilled as outlined in Exodus 19.

Nicham, the second term used to express God's repentance, basically means to regret, to be sorry (Exod. 13:17), to console oneself (2 Sam. 13:39), to become remorseful (Jer. 8:6). It can even mean to avenge oneself (Esth. 9:16). Most often this verb involves feeling pain, and God is usually the subject. Many times the object of God's regret or repentance is a concrete disaster (expressed by Heb. *ra'ah,* literally *evil*) that he had announced or planned (2 Sam. 24:16). Such repentance is connected to God's faithful covenant love (Heb. *chesed;* Ps. 106:45).

On rare occasions divine repentance involves refusal to do something good (Jer. 18:10). Thus God's repentance "is never sorrowful resignation but always has concrete consequences" (*TLOT*). When the object of the Lord's repentance is a person (Ps. 90:13), the verb is often translated "to have mercy on," but "the translation 'to be sorry, feel sympathy for' is more correct" (*TLOT*). At times the verb appears to mean "cannot tolerate something any longer" (Gen. 6:6–7).

In all this, Scripture continues to claim that God is consistent and will not repent (Num. 23:19). Yet the hope continues to be maintained that the Lord will repent in remorse and pity (Jon. 3:9), and the repeated confession of faith that God is One who "relents from sending calamity" (see Joel 2:13). As H. J. Stoebe concludes:

> Despite frequent claims, there is no inherent contradiction between a more anthropomorphic statement of God's regret and a more spiritual understanding. This coexistence is based in the polarity of the experience of God. Yahweh is, on the one hand, the "jealous God" so he neither needs to regret a decision nor is he bound by it (Gen 6:6f.; 1 Sam 15:11,35); and he is, on the other hand, "gracious and merciful" so plans for disaster need not be his last word (*TLOT*).

As Mike Butterworth explains:

> The explanation seems to be that God does not capriciously change his intentions or ways of acting. It is the change in Saul's behavior that leads to this expression of regret. The reference is notable as being one of the rare occasions when God is said to repent or change his mind about something intended as good (cp. Gen. 6:6) (*NIDOTTE*).

That God repents is a part of God's nature as a loving, covenant-making God. It is a part of his freedom as one able to respond to the needs and cries of his people rather than being a robot programmed always to respond the same way. God's repentance is, however, always a reaction dictated by God's plans and God's decisions and always beyond human control. It is a free action of God in relation to his people and his purposes. It is never an automatic response brought about by some human reaction or response.

VII. TEACHING OUTLINE

A. INTRODUCTION
1. Lead Story: Saying Good-bye
2. Context: The final two chapters of Jonah provide the story's climax. Forced to go to Nineveh, Jonah faced the decision of what to do after he got there. Nineveh faced the decision of how to respond to what Jonah said. God faced two decisions: how to respond to Nineveh and how to respond to Jonah.
3. Transition: The story of decisions by Jonah, Nineveh, and God carries forward the ironic, satirical style of the first two chapters. We listen to hear the sneers and gasps between the lines. We laugh at the ineptitude and disobedience of the prophet, but then we have to turn the laughter into questioning. Is the author talking about Jonah and Israel, or is the author talking about me and my church? How closely does my attitude resemble that of Jonah?

B. COMMENTARY
1. Mission Repetition (3:1–3)
2. Mission Results (3:4–10)
3. Missionary's Misery (4:1–4)
4. Choice of Concerns (4:5–11)

C. CONCLUSION: SELF-CENTERED OR GOD-CENTERED?

VIII. ISSUES FOR DISCUSSION

1. What location or what people in your community is most like Jonah's Nineveh? What is your church doing to reach these people?
2. Are there some things you know about God that you would like to change?
3. Do you have some limits on where you will go for God?
4. In what way do the comforts of life that you enjoy prevent you from being what God wants you to be and from doing what God wants you to do?
5. What brings love and compassion into your life more than the lost people of the world?

Introduction to

Micah

PROPHECY PROFILE

- Uses courtroom language to convict Judah and Israel of their sins and sentence them to exile and destruction
- Uses prophetic oracle of salvation shared with Isaiah 2
- Lists God's requirements of doing justice, loving covenant faithfulness, and walking with wisdom and care
- Accuses people of insincere religion and unjust economic and political system
- Uses language of lament to show dire nature of situation
- Defends God as having done every good thing possible for the nation
- Attacks false prophets
- Gives hope for Israel's remnant
- Looks to new baby in Bethlehem for hope
- Referred to in Matthew 2:5–6; 10:35–36; Luke 12:53; John 7:42

AUTHOR PROFILE: MICAH THE PROPHET

- Southerner from Moresheth-Gath southwest of Jerusalem
- Spoke to Northern Kingdom and Southern Kingdom
- Name means, "Who is like Yah?" (or Yahweh)
- Claimed divine power and justice for his preaching but not for his opponents—the false prophets
- Felt called to lay out the sin of God's people
- His prophecy later helped save Jeremiah (Jer. 26:17–18)
- Used wide variety of literary forms to gain attention and make impression on his audience

READER PROFILE: KINGDOMS UNDER THREAT

- Prophesied under Jotham (750–731 B.C.), Ahaz (735–715 B.C.), and Hezekiah (729–686 B.C.)
- Probably ministered about 735–700 B.C.

- Israel and Syria formed alliance but could not stop onslaught from Assyria, leading finally from economic prosperity and pride to utter disaster with fall of Northern Kingdom in 722/721 B.C.
- People continued unjust economic practices against the poor even as disaster loomed
- Judah became vassal state of Assyria, rebelled, and paid the consequences, being saved at the last moment by divine miracle from the besieging Assyrian army
- Religious, economic, and political leaders conspired to keep the poor down and rob them of their possessions, particularly their part of the tribe's inherited land
- Religion became empty ritual combined with pagan practices expecting God's blessings without covenant obedience

Micah 1:1–2:13

Israel's Incurable Illness

I. INTRODUCTION
A Prophetic English Teacher

II. COMMENTARY
A verse-by-verse explanation of these verses.

III. CONCLUSION
God's Faithfulness

An overview of the principles and applications from these verses.

IV. LIFE APPLICATION
My Life Is My Business

Melding these verses to life.

V. PRAYER
Tying these verses to life with God.

VI. DEEPER DISCOVERIES
Historical, geographical, and grammatical enrichment of the commentary.

VII. TEACHING OUTLINE
Suggested step-by-step group study of these verses.

VIII. ISSUES FOR DISCUSSION
Zeroing these verses in on daily life.

Quote

"*H*is [Micah's] whole message might almost be summed up in this one sentence: Those who live selfish and luxurious lives, even though they offer costly sacrifices, are vampires in the sight of God, sucking the life-blood of the poor. His words fairly quiver with feeling."

G . L . R o b i n s o n

Micah 1:1–2:13

I N A N U T S H E L L

*G*od calls his people to court to hear the indictment against them. Their sins center in the capital cities of Samaria and Jerusalem, where false political and religious leaders have wounded the people of God through misuse of the sacrificial system and false prophecies, and through economic policies that strip the poor of their possessions. Thus an enemy will conquer God's people. But God will eventually lead them back home.

Israel's Incurable Illness

I. INTRODUCTION

A Prophetic English Teacher

"*You* never know, Jerry, what you'll end up doing." So Nancy Miller, an English professor at Hope College, changed the life of Gerald L. Sittser. His childhood dreams of becoming a medical doctor had carried all the way into college until an English professor encouraged a freshman to complete a writing course. Suddenly, his career path changed from medicine to ministry and eventually to college teaching. As Sittser writes:

> I ended up doing something far different from what I had assumed was God's will for my life. . . . My writing teacher proved to be a prophet. As it turns out, both course and teacher helped to prepare me for a vocation I never imagined at the time I would be doing (*The Will of God as a Way of Life*, pp. 13–14).

Micah could have echoed those sentiments. An unsophisticated young man from the Judean countryside, he never imagined he would rub shoulders with kings, prophets, and priests. He certainly did not expect that he would be God's servant to influence the history of his country. But God sent him to preach, and he obeyed.

In the same vein, Israel and Judah never expected to hear the words Micah proclaimed. They did not think of themselves as sick or guilty. Micah said sin was their incurable disease. Israel and Judah ended up straying far from where they thought God would lead them.

We need to listen carefully to God's message and to the words of godly people like Micah and Professor Miller. God may change drastically everything we assumed about his will and lead us on a different path. God may also use people to warn us when we have taken the wrong path. Listen up! God is speaking!

II. COMMENTARY

Israel's Incurable Illness

> **MAIN IDEA:** *God does not let his people continue sinning without warning them of the consequences of their sins, giving them the opportunity to change their lifestyle, punishing them for their sins, and fulfilling his promises to his people.*

A The Historical Setting (1:1)

> **SUPPORTING IDEA:** *God uses individuals he calls out in important historical moments to guide his people, to call them back to him, and to warn them of his punishment for their sin.*

1:1. The Bible anchors each of the prophets firmly in history. Their messages had specific meaning for God's people in specific historical situations. Micah entered the scene at a tumultuous and decisive moment in the history of God's people. The opening superscription describes his work with Samaria, the northern capital, and Jerusalem, the southern capital; but it makes no mention of northern kings.

King Uzziah of Judah (792–740 B.C.) had died. His son Jotham (750–731 B.C.) assumed sole reign of the Southern Kingdom after serving as coregent with his leprous father. Jotham joined his father in receiving praise from the author of 2 Kings (15:34; cp. 2 Chr. 27:2,6). He rebuilt one of the temple gates (15:35), among other building projects (2 Chr. 27:3–4), and conquered the Ammonites (2 Chr. 27:5). But the people of Judah did not follow Jotham's religious leadership (2 Chr. 27:2).

Ahaz (735–715 B.C.) succeeded Jotham as king of Judah. He faced a tough situation, as recorded in Isaiah 7. Rezin of Syria and Pekah of Israel tried to force Ahaz into joining their coalition to fight Assyria. Instead, Ahaz paid tribute to Assyria so Assyria would defeat the coalition (2 Chr. 28). Ahaz followed Israel's lead in one way. He took up their worship practices (2 Kgs. 16:2–4), even copying a Syrian altar (2 Kgs. 16:10–16). God did not let such sins go unpunished (2 Chr. 28). Ahaz lived to see the last days of the Northern Kingdom.

Hezekiah was one of the great, pious kings of Judah. He reformed the religion of Judah and cleaned out the temple (2 Kgs. 18–20). But he also had to face Sennacherib of Assyria, who destroyed most of the Judean countryside, took the cities east and south of Jerusalem, and besieged the holy city until God sent a plague against the Assyrian army (for an outline of the historical period, see "Deeper Discoveries").

B God's Terrible Testimony (1:2–7)

SUPPORTING IDEA: *God knows the sins of his people, and he announces his verdict against them.*

1:2. The Book of Micah begins with a legal summons, a form often found in the Old Testament (Judg. 5:3; Jer. 10:1; Mic. 3:1). Though one could limit the expressions **peoples** and **earth** to a more localized understanding of citizens of the land, the setting at the beginning of the book appears to indicate a universal expression here. Micah's message is not limited to one nation. It affects the entire universe. Again, **against you** could be read as "among you," but the context apparently calls for an accusation against the peoples for their sins leading to tragic results.

Verse 2 serves as an introduction not just to the following passage but to the entire book. It emphasizes the significance of the prophet's message and alerts the audience that they are both the jury hearing the case and the defendants accused of crime. In this understanding, the Lord of the universe is on the witness stand to describe the guilt of the universe. The courtroom scene is his **holy temple**—a reference to God's earthly locale in Jerusalem as well as his universal temple in heaven.

1:3. We expect to hear the Lord's witness. Instead, the court official who called us to hear the Lord's testimony changes his tune. He uses traditional language of theophany (Deut. 33:2; Ps. 68:8–9; Amos 1:2) to announce God's coming. God does not remain in his **dwelling place** in heaven to testify against his people. He comes down to walk the earth where they live. He hits only the **high places**. The immediate reference is to the mountains. God is so otherworldly that his footsteps take him from one mountain to the next. But high places also represent the illegal worship places that Israel loved. These are places for God to stomp on as he makes his way through the earth.

1:4. God's coming brings astonishing results. Figurative, poetic language shows earth's transitory nature and God's unmatched, unimaginable power. Earth's most majestic features, its mighty **mountains**, melt at God's presence.

1:5. Why does God enter the courtroom to witness? Why does he walk to earth to come to his peoples? Because of their **sins**. These belong to **Jacob** and the **house of Israel**. These were terms for the Northern Kingdom, yet Micah was a southerner. Most of his proclamations affected Judah, not Israel. This may represent an early phase in the prophet's ministry before the destruction of Samaria, Israel's capital, in 722 B.C. The final phrase of this verse shows that Micah did not leave Judah out. Sin had infested both the north and the south. In both nations sin centered in their capital cities. Both nations faced judgment because of these sins.

1:6–7. Guilty Judah and Israel must pay for their crime. Samaria faced total destruction of its magnificent buildings and the powerless **idols** on whom the people depended for protection. **Temple gifts** is the same Hebrew word translated **wages of prostitutes** (Ezek. 16:31,34,41) at the end of the verse. Israel's worship featured cultic fertility rites involving prostitution (see discussion in Hosea 1–2). The judge has come, heard the case against the people, and announced the indictment and the sentence.

C Mourn for Zion's Misery (1:8–16)

SUPPORTING IDEA: *The appropriate response to God's sentence is to mourn for God's guilty people.*

1:8. The prophet responded emotionally to God's announcement of Israel's sentence. Prophets were loyal citizens who identified with the nation's fate. Before calling the nation to mourning, the prophet entered into traditional mourning practices himself. **Weep** represents a Hebrew term, *saphad*, for singing a lament or mourning (Gen. 23:2; Zech. 7:5). **Wail** signifies howling or screaming in lamentation (Jer 47:2; Joel 1:5,11,13). Going **barefoot** was a sign of mourning (2 Sam. 15:30), although the Hebrew term appears only here in the Old Testament. Going naked apparently refers to stripping off the main garments until a person is left in a loincloth, the Israelite male's underwear (Job 22:6). Such sadness so encompassed the prophet that he lost his prophetic gift for words and moaned like an animal.

1:9. The realization hit the prophet that no longer would the nation just hear prophetic judgment; they would actually experience it. Israel, the Northern Kingdom, would experience disaster. Samaria was as good as dead. But this had consequences for Micah's homeland. Jerusalem stood under indictment just as Samaria did. Could Jerusalem's final curtain call be far behind? Feeling pain for his people, the prophet expressed his inner feelings while symbolizing for the people their only proper response.

1:10–12. In beautiful Hebrew poetry and word play, Micah begins to lament for his people. He echoes David's lament over Saul (2 Sam. 1:20). As Saul's kingdom fell, so would David's. But Judah must not share the news with their Philistine neighbors in Gath. There was no reason to cause the enemy more joy or to encourage the Philistine cities to join the Assyrian conquerors. This would be even more ironic if, as seems probable, Gath had been reduced to almost nothing at this time.

Then Micah addressed Judean cities within a ten-mile radius of his hometown of Moresheth Gath in a series of word plays. These cities were on the traditional path of military invaders and were certainly attacked by Sennacherib in 701 B.C. But just because Sennacherib attacked them does not mean that the prophecy had to happen in Sennacherib's day. Certainly he was not the first conqueror to follow this natural invasion route. The setting is apparently before the last blow was struck to Samaria. Micah could describe the desperate situations of southwestern Judah and its capital city because he had already heard God's pronouncement of his sentence.

1:13. Lachish was an important military and economic center thirty miles southwest of Jerusalem. Anyone who wanted to attack Jerusalem from the south had to go through Lachish (2 Kgs. 18:17). The army protecting Lachish receives one final order—hitch the horses to the chariot. This time they must retreat, fleeing for their lives rather than attacking or defending the city.

The second part of the verse tantalizes interpreters. How could Lachish be the beginning of sin? Certainly Jerusalem was the center of sin (Mic. 1:5). Was Lachish a center of false worship? Or was the military outpost just a reflection of Judah's reliance on their own military power rather than on God? Or did Lachish have a historical moment we cannot pinpoint in which they initiated some sinful practice? The comparison to the sins of Israel would seem to say that Lachish was importing foreign gods into Judah. Perhaps they maintained ancient worship practices or imported some false gods from nearby Philistia. Whatever the exact meaning, the sin proved disastrous to Judah.

1:14. Micah takes up wedding imagery to describe the sorrow his own town must face (Mic. 1:1). Judah and its political/military leaders are losing the town just as a father has to watch a daughter leave the family home for her husband's dwelling. And the irony is that the person losing also has to pay a dowry to the one receiving the daughter (1 Kgs. 9:16). Israel has to pay Assyria tribute and lose control of a valuable agricultural center as well.

Aczib means "deception," and this city will live up to its name. Could this indicate that the city would capitulate to the conquerors without a fight? Certainly Israel's rulers would be deceived in their reliance on the military strength they had planted in Aczib. But why the kings of Israel? Certainly this cannot refer to the Northern Kingdom! The prophet assumes the destruction of the north so that the Southern Kingdom stands alone as representative of the ancient covenant people, Israel.

1:15. The word plays continue as God speaks in first person. Another of Judah's defense outposts faces destruction by a **conqueror**. The problem is not the conqueror's power. The problem is God's power in bringing the conqueror. No one can oppose God's conqueror. Coming to **Adullam** retraces David's flight from Saul (2 Sam. 23:13). Is this a continued threat to Judah's cities as God, Israel's glory, comes to destroy? Or has the Assyrian conqueror taken over the glory of Israel? Or is Judah's king the glory who has had to retreat like David and hide in the caves of Adullam? Or is it simply the nobles of Judah's court or military who hide out?

Perhaps the answer is all of the above, as Smith concludes: "Rather than identifying one specific person, it is probably better to suggest that **glory of**

Israel points to all that is glorious in the nation. It will all be debased and forced to run for cover in a cave" (NIV Application, 454).

1:16. If you face such a disastrous future, how do you respond? Micah had only one solution for Judah—follow his example. You have seen me **in mourning**, he declared. You join me. Shaving the head was apparently a part of pagan rites (Lev. 21:5) but also a part of mourning rituals (Ezek. 27:31). Judah must mourn its own children—children whom they cannot bury—because they are among the living dead. The Assyrians have taken them into exile.

Micah issues no call to repent. He offers no hope for the future. He simply paints a picture of inevitable destruction and punishment. He calls for lamentation and no other response. This must occur before anything else he pictures can happen. Any hope in Micah is hope after disaster.

Woe to Bedtime Plotters (2:1–5)

SUPPORTING IDEA: *Economic sins guarantee eternal loss.*

2:1. Micah follows his own lament and his call to Israel to lament with a woe oracle that imitates the mourning at a funeral. The "deceased" are Israelite economic leaders. The workday is not sufficient for their evil. They take their diabolic plans home and stew over them as they lie down to sleep. Such plans are both deceptive and violent. The evildoers are up at dawn to bring such plans to reality. This denies the expectations of their victims because morning symbolized a new day of hope and justice, partially because the king meted out justice in the morning (2 Sam. 15:2; Zeph. 3:5).

What's the payoff? The pride in accomplishing what they planned—pride in their own power. **Power** here reads literally, "For there is to El their hands." El can refer to a Canaanite god, to the one all-powerful God, or to extraordinary, godlike power. These power brokers of Israel play God as they exercise power over their helpless victims.

2:2. They break the basic covenant expectations God has set out for Israel (Exod. 20:17). In spite of their overwhelming power and authority, they want more. Everything they see, they claim for themselves. In so doing they **defraud** or exploit their poor victims. The verb here applies to brutal actions that take advantage of the weaker party in a legal contract (Lev. 19:13; Amos 4:1). It can even involve blackmail (Ezek. 18:18).

These Israelite leaders call in debts and force poor people to give them their houses, leaving families homeless or even further in debt as renters from the powerful. This breaks the nature of Israelite religious and economic policy. The houses represented the poor people's occupation of the land God had given Israel for an inheritance. The exploitation involved taking houses and land from poor, powerless fellow Israelites—land that God had assigned the family forever (Num. 27:1–11). The best example of such action is Ahab's seizing of Naboth's vineyard in 1 Kings 21.

2:3. God's heart-shattering **therefore** sounds forth. Joined with the messenger formula of "thus says the Lord," this announces God's sentence on sinful Israel. The economic planners face a divine planner. These power brokers will face a situation in which they are powerless. **You cannot save yourselves** is literally, "an evil which you cannot remove from there your necks." These people are up to their necks in trouble, or they are yoked together in trouble and cannot get rid of the yokes. They have created evil. God will bring the evil back on their necks.

2:4. The sinners will get what they deserve. People will take up a *mashal*, a Hebrew term for proverbs or traditional sayings. The people will lament (NIV, **taunt**) with a song of lament. Fields and lands taken through exploitation will change hands again. Now even **my people's possession** is divided up, God declares. This is the portion of inheritance God gave his people and may refer either to the entire nation or to the particular part entrusted to the exploiter's family. They will lose what they stole as well as what originally belonged to them.

2:5. Still the chastened power brokers had hope. Periodically, new family conditions made it necessary to divide a tribe's land again among the clans of the tribe as Joshua did in Joshua 13–21. When this time came, could these people use their intelligence and influence to get their land back? Oh, no! Micah declared. When that time comes, you will not be there, nor will any agent be there to represent you. You will have disappeared in exile.

The People's Perfect Prophet of Prosperity (2:6–11)

SUPPORTING IDEA: *People cannot shut up God's prophet and choose their own who will promise prosperity.*

2:6. Micah got into an argument, at least in literary fashion, with other prophetic figures in Israel. The Bible speaks often of false prophets. We stand in wonder how anyone could follow false prophets and ignore or persecute true ones like Micah. But Israel had neither a term for false prophets in their dictionary nor criteria for determining a true prophet since a true prophet was known only when his word was fulfilled (Deut. 18:21–22). Micah had company in being called to silence (Isa. 30:10).

The exact meaning of verse 6 is difficult to determine. The last phrase is translated differently by various translators of the Bible. The NIV translation puts the entire verse in the mouth of the false prophets. The Hebrew text apparently puts only the first line in their mouths. Thus Smith translates: "'Do not give sputtering prophecy,' they sputter. They are not sputtering prophecies concerning these things; shame will not be removed." Similarly,

Waltke translates: "'Stop prophesying,' they prophesy. They do not prophesy about such things so their shame will not depart" (MP, 642). Allen puts only the second line in the prophet's mouth: "'Stop your preaching,' they preach. They should stop preaching in this vein: 'Humiliation won't overwhelm us'" (NICOT, 292).

The syntax and speakers are not easily clarified, but the purpose of the verse is clear. Micah and his supporters face a group of prophets, perhaps employed by the temple, who deny the doom and gloom of Micah. They continue to promise prosperity while Micah demands a new way of life or destruction.

2:7. The argument continues. Micah mocks the prosperity prophets, apparently quoting their question to him: Does the **Spirit of the LORD** become impatient? Or are these things his work? These prophets apparently think it ridiculous to say God's patience can run out so that he acts in judgment. Micah has a strong answer for them. God's words **do good** for those who do what is right. Now the opponents must place themselves in a category. Are they doing what is right or not?

2:8. This verse has received all sorts of emendations and changes. It reads quite literally, "And yesterday my people to (or perhaps as) an enemy was rising up. From the front of a robe, splendor you strip off; from those passing by, security, that is those returning from war."

Apparently the prophet accused the money-grabbing landowners of sending the poor peasants to war, then becoming their enemy when they returned from battle. Any war booty they had won was taken by the rich, and the security they should have in returning to their homes was taken away by these land grabbers. While away in battle, the poor would not have been able to raise crops or make money, so now the rich took away the security of their homes (see Mic. 2:2).

2:9. Not only the returning warriors but also their wives faced the ravages of the greedy. They were driven from the comfort of their own **homes**. The self-satisfied rich take God's **blessing** (literally, his splendor) from the women's **children**. This must refer to the inheritance God gave his people so they could enjoy their plot of land forever and so they would be a people representing God's splendor to the world. Now all God's plans must be annulled because rich people will not let poor people inhabit their God-given land and fulfill their God-given mission.

2:10. The prophet issues marching orders. If these self-indulgent, greedy, immoral land grabbers were going to act this way, then they must experience the same type of misery they were dishing out. They must leave their land. It was no longer the promised God-given **resting place** (1 Kgs. 8:56). God's people are called to be holy people. They cannot live in a **defiled**, unclean land. Israel has become such a land because these unjust people have made it so.

2:11. Micah rounds off the argument with a reference back to the original argument with the prophets. They bear the major guilt because they had not warned these ruthless Israelites. What's more, the prophets apparently profited from such injustice. They were among those ordered to march away from the land into exile. These people did not want a prophet filled with God's spirit. They wanted a prophet who provided spirits for their thirst, so they could drink their cares away. Lies and deception were the tools of the rich as they exercised their scams on the poor. They should get a prophet just like them. They have refused God's word. Now they will have a prophet who will lead them into a stupor where they are unable to understand God's word. They just use the prophet to order more **beer.**

⬛ The Lord Leads the Remnant (2:12–13)

SUPPORTING IDEA: *God preserves a remnant for himself and leads them like a shepherd leads his flock.*

2:12. Surprise! God again does the unexpected, bringing the section to an end with a promise to save a **remnant** of his people. He does not promise to lift the verdict of judgment against the guilty, heartless rich. He realizes that a poor remnant exists—those who have been loyal to him through the hard times. They have suffered from unjust treatment by the rich. They have suffered with the nation through the exile, having to stay in the land and scratch out a living under foreign rulers.

The Old Testament constantly refers to God as Shepherd (Ps. 23:1; Ezek. 34:12; Rev. 7:17). God will protect the people and provide them with a place to live like a shepherd provides a safe pen for his sheep. The last line continues the comparison of sheep and people: "They will make an uproar from men." As sheep crowd together noisily in a sheep pen, so the remnant will fill God's pen, bumping together with bleats of joy.

2:13. The image reverses from penning up the people in safety to breaking out through a city **gate** after having been penned up in it, apparently under siege. This fits the imagery of 701 B.C. when God lifted the Assyrian siege and freed the people whom Sennacherib had not killed. Israel would again celebrate under God as king and deliverer. God was faithful to judge the wicked and march them into exile. He was faithful to protect the pious remnant and defeat their enemies.

MAIN IDEA REVIEW: *God does not let his people continue sinning without warning them of the consequences of their sins, giving them the opportunity to change their lifestyle, punishing them for their sins, and fulfilling his promises to his people.*

III. CONCLUSION

God's Faithfulness

God is consistently faithful. Israel may suffer an incurable sin disease. God will march forth bringing wailing and mourning in face of divine destruction and disaster. He pronounces the funeral dirge over such a sinful people, who are given to self-centered grabbing of material possessions. When people ignore him and his stated covenant expectations, God does not ignore them. He will turn their songs of joyful partying into whines of grief.

Religious leaders are not exempt from sin disease and will not escape the divine judgment. They cannot silence God's true prophets with their false theology of prosperity. People who give no heed to God's plan for his people will find that they must heed God's marching orders into exile. But God is faithful not only to judge. He is faithful to his beleaguered remnant and promises salvation, hope, and a new day for them.

PRINCIPLES

- God warns his people when they disobey.
- God is aware of the sin of his people.
- Sin inevitably brings judgment.
- God's basic moral standards remain absolutely true.
- God protects the poor and punishes those who abuse them.
- God sometimes uses disaster to bring about his purposes.
- God expects ministers to preach the truth, not what satisfies the audience.
- God the king will eventually bring salvation to faithful people.

APPLICATIONS

- Confess your sins to God before it is too late.
- Measure yourself by how you treat the poor, not by how much property you own.
- Never think you are immune from God's judgment.
- Walk in God's commandments.
- Teach God's absolute trust to yourself and others.
- Trust God to fulfill his promises of salvation in his timing.

IV. LIFE APPLICATION

My Life Is My Business

In her book *Battling the Prince of Darkness*, Evelyn Christenson shocks us by relating a conversation overheard in a seminary coffee shop. A young protégé of her husband's was finishing a doctoral program. He reported on the main conversation at the seminary coffee breaks. "They are discussing whether it is enough to preach the truth, or do they have to live it, too. One of the future pastors stated decisively, 'I'll preach the truth—but my personal life is my own business'" (p. 66).

Hosea found laypeople and prophets with the same attitude. Worship on the day God set aside was OK, but the Ten Commandments were out of style. Daily life was directed by greed and desire, not by personal piety and indebtedness to God's grace. The same attitudes prevail today. God called Israel to mourn their demise. Is he doing any less for us? Will we hear his warnings before it is too late?

V. PRAYER

Lord, forgive us, forgive us, forgive us! Remove our pride. Take away our greed. Center our eyes on you, not on us. Teach us to be a part of the faithful remnant, not of the immoral majority. Amen.

VI. DEEPER DISCOVERIES

The Historical Setting (1:1)

Our dating and historical description are based on the following outline of the history of Israel. Different scholars assign different dates for various kings and events since many kings first reigned with their fathers as corulers before taking full control after the father's death.

The Assyrian Period

A. Tiglath-pileser III (745–727 B.C.)

1. Collects tribute from Menahem (742 B.C.) of Israel and Rezin of Damascus (738 B.C.).

2. Israel and Damascus join in revolt and try to force Judah to participate by besieging Jerusalem in Syro-Ephraimitic War (734 B.C.).

3. Ahaz (735–715 B.C.) of Judah summons Tiglath-pileser to help, bringing destruction of Damascus and reduction of Israel to small city-state around Samaria (732 B.C.) with new king Hoshea (731–723 B.C.) (2 Kgs. 16:5–17:1).

B. Shalmaneser V (727–722 B.C.)

1. Besieges Samaria (724–722 B.C.).
2. Samaria is then captured either by him or by Sargon II.

C. Sargon II (722–705 B.C.)

1. Subdues rebellions in Babylon, Hamath, Gaza, and Samaria, while collecting tribute from Judah (720 B.C.). Egypt defeated for first time.
2. Hezekiah (715–687 B.C.) becomes king of Judah, bringing religious and political reforms (2 Kgs. 18).
3. Ashdod revolt is put down (712 B.C.).
4. Babylonian revolt fails (710 B.C.).

D. Sennacherib (705–681 B.C.)

1. Subdues rebels in Assyria and Babylon.
2. Defeats Phoenicians, Philistines, and Egyptians (701 B.C.).
3. Destroys most Judean cities and besieges Jerusalem (701 B.C.) but has to retreat to Nineveh (2 Kgs. 18:13–19:37; Isa. 36–37).

VII. TEACHING OUTLINE

A. INTRODUCTION

1. Lead Story: A Prophetic English Teacher
2. Context: A proud nation found itself losing its power, possessions, and finally its population because they had lost their desire to hear the prophetic word.
3. Transition: Micah entered the scene with God's word of judgment on his people's sin. Joy must dissolve into grief. Would God's people hear God's message of judgment as faithfully as they heard his word of prosperity?

B. COMMENTARY

1. The Historical Setting (1:1)
2. God's Terrible Testimony (1:2–7)
3. Mourn for Zion's Misery (1:8–16)
4. Woe to Bedtime Plotters (2:1–5)

5. The People's Perfect Prophet of Prosperity (2:6–11)
6. The Lord Leads the Remnant (2:12–13)

C. CONCLUSION: GOD'S FAITHFULNESS

VIII. ISSUES FOR DISCUSSION

1. What is the purpose of the language of theophany? Is it always the same?
2. What can you do to symbolize your grief for your sins before God?
3. Which of the Ten Commandments do you habitually ignore or break?
4. How does your attitude toward possessions measure up to God's expectations?
5. What do you understand the Bible to teach about the remnant? Who are they? How can you recognize them? Must they always suffer? What promises do they represent?

Micah 3:1–5:15

Breaking the Lord's Silence

"*I* would rather lose in a cause that will some day win,

than win in a cause that will some day lose."

W o o d r o w   W i l s o n

Micah 3:1–5:15

IN A NUTSHELL

*G*od calls the unjust rulers of his people to attention to announce his silence. He will respond neither to their prayers nor to their prophets. He speaks only through the Spirit-filled Micah, announcing judgment on the nation's sins. But that is not God's final words. In the last days God will rule with his remnant from his temple in Jerusalem and establish peace among the nations. The instrument of this renewal will be a baby from Bethlehem who will shepherd God's people.

Breaking the
Lord's Silence

I. INTRODUCTION

We Heard from Him

*T*he gleam in her eyes, brightened by tears in the corners, remains bright in my memory. She broke her usual silence during prayer time in our Bible study. "We heard from him this week. For the first time in fifteen years, we heard from our son. Pray for him and for us."

Can you imagine the anguish of fifteen years of silence? The son's silence had driven the parents into silence. I did not even know they had a son. Now cautious joy filled the room. Could this be the beginning of a marvelous reconciliation and renewal?

Micah had to create just the opposite mood for Israel. He announced God's silence to his people. He would not respond to their prayers or give words to their prophets. Judgment was God's only message for the hour. But then that changed. Micah could announce a new word from God—a promise to break the divine silence.

How do you respond to God's silence? What expectations do you have that he will break that silence? Have you met the baby of Bethlehem who broke God's silence once and for all and assured us that God will be there for us?

II. COMMENTARY

Breaking the Lord's Silence

> **MAIN IDEA:** God is not bound to speak to his people. He can retreat in silence from a sinful people until he decides to relieve the time of judgment and speak peace to his people once more.

Sin Sends Silence (3:1–12)

> **SUPPORTING IDEA:** God's silence comes when he must judge an unresponsive, sinful people.

3:1–4. The setting for these verses is that the Northern Kingdom had apparently disappeared from history. Judah, the Southern Kingdom, had taken over the ancient titles the north had assumed since the time of Jeroboam I.

Micah used not only ancient national titles to address the people. He also reached back into history for official titles. **Leaders** (*ro'she*) is literally heads.

> Such an "office" appears to be rooted originally in tribal structures, within which it denotes someone who exercises military and juridical authority. Most important, however, is its integrative function: the chief is responsible for the well-being and common life of the community. . . . With the disappearance of tribal structures, somehow the title together with its functions—the juridical more than the military—gradually penetrated other social organizations.

Early on in the monarchy the king was seen as the nation's head (1 Sam. 15:17). (See W. A. M. Beuken, *TDOT,* XIII, 248–59.)

Rulers (*qetsine*) appears only twelve times in the Old Testament (Josh. 10:24; Judg. 11:6,11; Prov. 6:7; Isa. 1:10; 3:6–7; 22:3; Dan. 11:18; Mic. 3:1,9). Early in Israel's history the *qatsin* was a military leader. Isaiah almost mocked the current leadership by refusing to use modern titles of king and judge. Micah may have done the same thing. He wanted the leaders to take up the role their venerable ancestors exercised in a way that established the nation in the land and protected its most vulnerable members. Instead, they were following a self-centered, nation-destroying job description. Micah may have used *ro'sh* to designate judicial and administrative leadership and *qatsin* to point to military leadership. At least he was calling current leaders to remember history and function as God's leaders rather than usurping more recent titles from their neighbors and functioning as neighboring kings did.

Micah spelled out God's expectations for leaders of his people—establishing justice. But his ironic question turned into a courtroom accusation. He asked if they even knew what justice was all about and described how they functioned. They hated **good** and loved **evil**, just the opposite of God's way. They were cannibalizing the nation they should protect, particularly its poorest, most helpless members.

So it was time for God to announce his sentence against these heartless, crooked leaders. The sentence is placed in the indefinite future with the ominous **then.** On this occasion judgment comes in unexpected form—divine silence rather than divine action. The holy God will hide his face in the presence of the leaders' evil. Without God's presence, they cannot prosper. Thus they finally call to God in desperation for help, but no help will be forthcoming. Prayers receive no answer when God declares his silence.

3:5–7. The authoritative messenger formula, "Thus says the Lord" or **This is what the LORD says,** empowers Micah's judgment on those responsible for hearing God's message and conveying it to the leaders. Divine silence encompassed even the prophets who were thronging the royal court to support the king. Their word should reveal to the nation God's path. Instead they **lead my**

people astray. Why would prophets quit proclaiming God's message? They were preaching for a paycheck. The king wanted to hear **peace** rather than judgment.

Micah had a sentence to fit the crime. He introduced it with the prophetic **therefore** that added foreboding to the following words. Every method they used to determine the divine will would vanish (see "Deeper Discoveries"). They would have to **cover their faces** in shame because there was **no answer from God.**

3:8–12. One prophet remains unsilenced, ready to speak God's word. How could Micah make such an audacious claim for himself? Because he experienced God's Spirit. His audience could receive this claim in various ways. Did this just send the prophet into raving ecstasy (Num. 11:17,25)? Or was Micah empowered by God to proclaim his word (Neh. 9:20,30)? The people might even think deception was involved (Ezek. 14:9).

Micah saw the presence of the Spirit of the Lord as a positive proof of his prophetic validity. His audience did not necessarily agree. Micah saw his words as filled with **power . . . justice and might.** The audience may have perceived him as an ecstatic egomaniac gone mad. Still the prophet maintained his mission. He had to tell Israel of their sins (Mic. 1:5) and seek to establish God's justice among his people (Mic. 2:2).

Micah addressed the same Israelite leaders here (v. 9) as in verse 1. Israel's leaders who were supposed to establish justice hated it instead. They were distorting **all that is right.** They had turned God's job description for them upside down. They preyed on the poor rather than praying for them. They justified injustice and called wrong right.

Apparently Micah picked up the politicians' pride in their greatest achievement as the prime example of their sin before God. King Hezekiah had resurrected the city of Jerusalem, making it once again resemble Zion, the city of God magnificent enough for God to reside there. Second Chronicles 32 shows the building of new walls and the marvelous architectural feat of the Siloam tunnel.

Micah asked, "At what price?" Thousands of hours of sweat labor for poverty-stricken laborers wanting to get back to their small plot of land and farm it before one of Jerusalem's big land owners called in a debt and confiscated the home place (Mic. 2:2). This was not a labor of the heart for these people. It was murder because only at the price of hundreds killed in accidents could such huge stones be cut and put into place. Thus Israel's proud leaders deserved the death sentence (Num. 35:33; 1 Kgs. 2:32).

The heads of Micah 3:1,9 were guilty. So were the religious leaders—priests and prophets. All agreed on one thing. Their major goal was money in their pockets. Bribery, lies, and wicked behavior were tolerated when they produced money for them. At the same time these corrupt leaders used theology to protest the prophet's judgment oracle. Their prosperity, their building achievements in the city of the Lord showed that God was among them. Thus his presence protected them. They thought **disaster** (literally, evil) would not come upon them. They were God's people.

"Not so!" bellowed the prophet with his threatening **therefore**. Zion, the city they claimed God protected, the city they labored so carefully on at the expense of so many lives—this Zion would become a wheat field, plowed up for sowing. Jerusalem would become **a heap of rubble**. Even the temple was not exempt. Bushes would cover the temple grounds because no building would remain.

A century later Micah's prophecy would serve in Jeremiah's defense when the religious leaders wanted to pronounce the death penalty on him (Jer. 26:7–19). Neither in Micah's day nor in Jeremiah's could the prophecy bring the people back to God and save the city of Jerusalem from damage and eventual destruction (2 Kgs. 25:9).

𝔹 The Temple Teaches Torah Again (4:1–8)

> **SUPPORTING IDEA:** *God's silence is not eternal. His eternal plan for his people includes renewing the power of his temple city and drawing the nations to worship him there.*

4:1–2. The first part of this vision also appears in Isaiah 2:2–4. Isaiah's conclusion transforms the announcement of salvation into a call to worship by introducing Isaiah 2:5. Micah's form, however, is a public commitment to God or a confession of faith as seen in Micah 4:5. Apparently, both Isaiah and his younger contemporary Micah used the same announcement of salvation from the Jerusalem **temple** to speak to God's people. This would mean that God used the temple ritual as a source for his inspired word. Micah had just described the destruction of Jerusalem. The holy city functioned unexpectedly as the center of world salvation in this section. The **last days** are still within world history, with separate nations acting.

Israel used the same language as her Near Eastern neighbors in talking about the national temple as the highest mountain on earth where the deity fights battles for his people (cp. Pss. 46; 48). Micah applied this language to the temple in Jerusalem even though Jerusalem was not the highest of the mountains Israel could see. Jerusalem would be high and lifted up because God was at work there, causing his purpose for the world to be realized. The emphasis is not on the height of Jerusalem. The emphasis is on the unheard of—foreign nations coming to Jerusalem to worship. God's hope always encompasses the world, not just one small nation (Gen. 12:1–4).

The prophet took up the popular theology of the people's hymnody and shifted the emphasis, pointing everything to the future. Only in the last days would Zion occupy such an exalted position. God would no longer battle the nations. Jerusalem could no longer glory in the hope that nations would march to her with large gifts and tribute for her victorious king.

The prophetic hope is that God's word will become the world's weapon. Military academies and weapons will vanish. People will learn to live life according to God's ways. They will obey his teachings. Nations will come to Jerusalem not because a victorious king forces them to but because they are attracted to Jerusalem by the God who lives there and the teaching he dispenses.

4:3. No longer will nations have to fight to settle their differences. In Jerusalem God will be the great mediator who settles all human disputes without battle. Military weapons will become obsolete. The world's only war will be on poverty and hunger. Micah puts even stronger emphasis than Isaiah does on the miracle of foreign nations coming to Jerusalem because he enhances Isaiah's "many peoples" to **strong nations far and wide**.

4:4–5. God's last days change relationships on the international scene. They also change relationships at the personal level. No longer do capricious, greedy leaders bribe, steal, and murder their way across the countryside accumulating property. Now each clan and each family has secured his own **vine and fig tree**. Vines and figs were Israel's most profitable crops. Fear vanishes on the international and the individual level. Doubt should also vanish. Behind the announcement of salvation stands the word of **the LORD Almighty**, or more literally, Yahweh of Hosts—the leader of the heavenly armies with power to put down any earthly rebellion.

For once Israel hears God's message, believes, and responds with a confession of faith and commitment. They will not longer follow the gods of the nations. They will no longer enter into the intrigue of international politics. Other nations may do as they please, but Israel would **walk in the name of the LORD our God for ever and ever**. This commitment separates God's people from the gods of all other peoples. But this comes only in the last days. First, God's punishments must be endured. Exile comes before life under the vine and fig.

4:6–8. But what happens to the exiles in a foreign land? Can they share Micah's hopes? Can they expect to find their fig tree in the land of promise? Or must they endure exile forever? God excludes none of his people from his promise. He will take the initiative. He will find the lame and the exiles, those unable to help themselves and those unable to return to the land. These are people who are suffering for their sins. They are the ones God has **brought to grief**. But grief is not God's last word.

God has transforming power. He uses it for his people. His remnant theology works. He punishes a people, only to gather from them a faithful remnant to receive his blessings. Returning home, they will not have to involve themselves in local politics to find a leader strong enough to protect them from the nations. God will be king as he always intended to be (see Judg. 8:23; 1 Sam. 8:6–9). This time nothing will interfere. Human fears and human jealousies will not get in the way. God will be king of Israel **from that day and forever.**

In Micah 4:8 God addresses the city of Jerusalem directly with images of her strength and glory. The **watchtower of the flock** could also be translated "the tower of Eder" as in Genesis 35:21. Here it pictures Jerusalem as a military fortress able to protect the straying flock that God has gathered as his remnant. The **stronghold** is the Hebrew *'ophel,* a geographical part of Jerusalem that joined the ancient Jebusite city (2 Sam. 5:6–10) with the temple area and Solomon's palace. The name was gradually expanded until it took in the entire temple area. What Jerusalem originally ruled, they would rule again, with God as the monarch making the laws and decisions.

Micah ends verse 8 with the phrase, **kingship will come to the Daughter of Jerusalem.** Did he refer to divine kingship as elsewhere in this context? Did he prepare for the messianic theology to come later? Or did he refer to a restoration of Davidic rule—this time in obedience to God?

Ⓒ Preparing to Participate in God's Plans (4:9–5:4)

> **SUPPORTING IDEA:** *Enduring God's silence in exile prepares his people to participate in his plans for renewal and restoration.*

4:9. The prophet sees a hopeless, suffering, lamenting people and throws rhetorical questions at them quickly. Now, in these circumstances, they need to explain why they are suffering. How could an enemy king possibly be able to surround their city and starve them out? They have been so quick to trust their king to help. Where is he when they need him? Do they call on an earthly king instead of the heavenly king? Famous for wisdom and counsel since the time of Solomon, Israel now has no counselor. How can this be? Have they not turned to God for counsel?

4:10. Micah had no immediate word of comfort. They might escape a besieged city for a while but only to dwell in the open countryside without a home. Still, exile was Judah's destiny. Immediate hope was not on the horizon. Here the prophet looked down the halls of history, past the period of Sennacherib and Assyria, to the greater threat of Babylon. Judah's problem was not solved with the escape in 701 B.C. Judah would be disciplined for its sins, but discipline would be postponed until 586 B.C. when the Babylonians leveled Jerusalem and the temple. This 701 B.C. reprieve was not salvation; it was disaster delayed.

The bigger picture includes a final frame of future hope. This is painted in two words: **rescued** and **redeem.** Rescue (Heb. *nitstsal*) refers to deliverance from a difficult situation as when Jacob wrestled with the divine stranger

(Gen. 32:30). To redeem is to buy back something that was once legally yours (Ruth 3:13). The term can be applied to the avenger of blood (Num. 35:12,19–27; 1 Kgs. 16:11), but most often it refers to God buying back his lost people (Exod. 6:6; Job 19:25; Lam. 3:58). Lost and hopeless in Babylon, Israel would see God reclaim his people just as he had saved them in the exodus from Egypt.

4:11. The same word **now** that introduced Micah 4:9 begins this section and Micah 5:1. The prophet repeatedly calls the people to look at the present circumstances caused by their neglect of God. The victorious nations are ready to defile Jerusalem by entering it and destroying it. They will subject the holy temple to shame and public display.

4:12. Micah uses a strong Hebrew construction to draw a contrast between the plans that international powers make and the plans that God makes. The Lord's plan is his wise counsel or advice (Ps. 33:11; Jer. 32:19). As the nations make plans to destroy Jerusalem, God plans to reap his harvest among the nations.

4:13. Finally the prophet calls his people to action. They are to join the Lord in his harvest field. He will equip them to defeat the international enemies. Just as in the days of Joshua's conquest, they will put the enemy to the sacred ban. They will **devote** to God the wealth and possessions the enemy has gained through illegal means. This is holy war. It will prove that God is **the Lord of all the earth**—a title connected with Joshua's holy war conquests (Josh. 3:11,13).

5:1. This verse is Micah 4:14 in the Hebrew text. The prophet makes a word play whose exact meaning is not clear. The most common meaning of the Hebrew verb is to slash one's body in pagan mourning rituals (Deut. 14:1). The term here more likely means to band together like an army (Jer. 5:7). Jerusalem is then addressed as a **city** (literally, daughter) of *gedur*—a noun that may mean wall or troops (Ps. 18:29) or furrow (Ps. 65:10) or perhaps incision. Modern translators render the verse differently.

The second part of the verse shows the basic meaning. Israel is in danger. The enemy threatens their ruler. Israel must react. Again the language takes Israel back to their beginnings. The word for **ruler** is *shophet*, the term used for Israel's first deliverers or judges in the Book of Judges. Being struck on the cheek is a sign of humiliation (Ps. 3:7) and defeat. Israel must either collect its troops for one last battle or, more probably, gather in its walls in grief, waiting for the end.

5:2. Using the same strong Hebrew construction to show contrast as in 4:12, Micah portrays a ray of hope from an unexpected source. The small village of Bethlehem Ephrathah takes center stage. Five miles southwest of Jerusalem, it was just off the major highway leading south to the Negeb. Bethlehem's most famous native was David (1 Sam. 16:1–13). Micah picks up the Davidic connection to note that Israel must go back to Bethlehem to get a new David since the present line of Davidic rulers is passing from historical importance. This resembles Isaiah's call for a ruler from the "stump of Jesse" (Isa. 11:1), thus **from of old, from ancient times**—at least clear back to the beginning of the Israelite monarchy if not all the way to eternity.

Hope for the present is lost, but God's plans go far beyond the present. He has hopes for a new ruler for Israel. This ruler will come for the Lord. He will fulfill God's plans and be obedient to God, unlike the current Israelite rulers. This new ruler appeared in the person of Jesus of Nazareth, providentially born in his family's ancestral hometown (Luke 2:1–7). The Hebrew term for rule (*moshel*) picks up the promise of Deuteronomy 15:6 that Israel would rule the nations, and it alludes to the ironic claim of Gideon that neither he nor his sons would rule Israel because God would rule them (Judg. 8:22–23).

5:3. The prophet resorted to mysterious language to complete his threat/promise motif. He begins with the prophetic "therefore" that often introduces the sentence God is imposing on a guilty people. The punishment is pictured as God giving up or abandoning Israel—another image of exile and loss of Jerusalem. Such exile is only temporary. A woman in labor will give birth.

This has received many interpretations: (1) the mother of the messianic ruler; (2) more precisely, Mary, the mother of Jesus; (3) Bethlehem, the town of the promised ruler, since towns are often pictured as women; (4) Israel or Jerusalem as the seedbed of the Messiah; (5) a royal princess or queen in the period of the exile. The language is closely related to Isaiah 7 and the promise of a newborn son. As with that promise, so this one has progressive fulfillments. It could even refer to the birth of Cyrus and the Persian release of Judah from Babylonian exile or to the Persians as the mother of that release.

The rest of his brothers shows Micah's concern for all God's people. The identity of the rest depends on the perspective of the newborn child. The rest may be those in Jerusalem awaiting the return of the exiles, the Southern Kingdom awaiting the restoration of the ten lost tribes of the north or, most likely, the people in exile in Babylon returning to join those already in Jerusalem awaiting the birth of the child of Bethlehem.

Whatever the exact historical meanings in Micah's day, here the contemporary importance can hardly be downplayed. God prepared centuries in advance for his people to understand Jesus as the Messiah fulfilling the promises to Israel. God is the Lord of restoration and reunion. He does not punish his people to dissolve them but to prepare them for renewal and reunion. God's plan focuses on all his people from all the nations of the earth because he remains Lord of all the earth.

5:4. Micah completes this complex promise of salvation with a job description for Messiah. Messiah will be the good shepherd feeding his flock. He will assume David's original role (2 Sam. 5:2) and even that of the tribal leaders before David (2 Sam. 7:7). The shepherd image continued to refer to God's dealing with his mistreated people (Isa. 40:11; Ezek. 34:13–23). With divine **strength** and **majesty** the promised shepherd will protect his people. All the world will hear of the new ruler's greatness.

𝔻 The Refreshing Remnant (5:5–9)

SUPPORTING IDEA: *God uses his remnant to bring peace and security to his people after they have suffered for their sins.*

5:5. The NIV unnecessarily places the first line of this verse with verse 4 as the conclusion to the preceding sermon. Instead the Hebrew form here parallels the opening of verses 7 and 10. The entire section from Micah 5:5 through 5:15 describes God's way of **peace.** Its introduction reads literally, "And this will be *shalom,* peace, wholeness, completeness, security." This is most usually interpreted as "This One—the Messiah." The Hebrew text could have written, "He is [their, our] peace," but that does not appear here. Verses 5–6 describe peace. Verses 7–8 describe the remnant. Verses 10–15 describe that day.

One stark word follows *shalom*—Assyria. Does that mean Assyria is the source of peace? At least Micah caught the audience's attention. What they heard did not sound like peace. Assyria enters *our* land and treads on *our* fortified palaces where our king lives. This sounds like a picture of disaster. But the prophet turned it around: **we will raise against him.** Some interpreters cannot see this as a realistic hope on Micah's part, so they see him placing these words as ironic false hopes in the mouth of his audience. Nothing in the context forces us to such a strained interpretation. Micah does seem to avoid the term *king* at all costs. **Shepherds** picks up the image from the previous section, while *nesikey,* **leaders,** utilizes a term elsewhere reserved for foreigners (Ezek. 32:30). While Israel cannot recognize them, leaders stand waiting for God's call.

5:6. **Rule** is again the word for "to shepherd." Ironically, these shepherds use swords on their unruly flock. **Nimrod** was a primeval hero in Babylon who extended his territory into Assyria (Gen. 10:9–12). Micah again picks up ancient tradition to find a parallel term for Assyria. That Babylon is meant here is possible but not likely. **Drawn sword** represents a small change of the Hebrew text based on the difficulty shown by the early translations and on the reading of the Vulgate and the early rabbis.

The NASB maintains the Hebrew: "The land of Nimrod at its entrances." Hebrew parallelism does not always have to be exact, so the NASB reading may be preferred here. Again as in 4:10 Micah describes salvation as God's rescue from the enemy, changing from a plural to a singular subject here. Using the same verbs as in verse 5, Micah promised that because Assyria entered the land and trod the border, God would rescue his people. Note the emphasis here on divine activity. The leaders were to be used of God. As with the promised messianic ruler of verse 2, they must come for God and not for themselves.

5:7. Micah stepped back a moment to remind the people that these promises were not immediate. They represented hope for the **remnant**, not for the entire nation. Punishment would trim the people to a bare remnant before God's salvation. The invading Assyrians would get their due in God's timing. The remaining exiles who survived the Assyrian and Babylonian captivities would appear to be refreshing **dew** watering the land and sudden showers watering the grass. One must remember, however, that dew and showers come at God's command and not in response to human wishes. Records show that many Israelites blended into the prosperity of the Babylonian exile. They gave no reason to believe they would cause their rulers problems.

5:8–9. Micah knew differently. Like rain or showers, God's remnant waited only for God's timing. Then they transformed their appearance. Assyria and/or Babylon in all their power could not withstand the onslaught of God's remnant. They will stand victorious while his enemies will taste defeat and destruction. The *your* of verse 9 is singular and may refer either to God or to the remnant addressed as a collective group. Thus verse 9 may be seen as a concluding song of praise or as a final promise of victory.

E God's Day of Destruction (5:10–15)

> **SUPPORTING IDEA:** *God will destroy everything and everyone who prevents people from obeying him.*

5:10. The meaning of this entire oracle is open to various interpretations. The *I* is God's first person direct address. But who is *you?* The most obvious answer is Israel although the previous section dealt with Assyria. The entire section appears to be an oracle condemning Israel. Then we read in the final verse of wrath on the nations. Is this a reference to the two nations of Judah and Israel who are expected to obey God? Or is it a reference, as the Hebrew term *goyim* normally is, to the pagan nations? In what way are pagan nations supposed to listen to or obey the Lord? Does the final verse turn the entire section into a backhanded oracle of salvation for Israel just because the nations suffer? The tone of the passage is dark, not light. Any salvation it pictures is dim at best. God's final statements in this larger passage leave one sensing the divine power to punish rather than the promise to provide salvation.

The opening salvo of destruction attacks Israel's military might. With Assyria looming outside the walls of Jerusalem, God threatens to dismantle all the Israelite fighting forces.

5:11–14. Next in line are Israel's towns and villages with their military fortifications. Having stripped Israel of all physical hope for victory, God attacks their spiritual powers. The first is **witchcraft**. This represented a way to determine the will of a deity worshipped by pagan religions but forbidden to Israel (Exod. 7:11; 22:18). Magic (sorcery or witchcraft) was common in the Ancient Near East and was inseparable from the practice of pagan religions.

Casting **spells** represents the work of the soothsayer who could interpret signs (Lev. 19:26; Jer. 27:9). Exactly how this representative of pagan religion and politics worked we do not know, but their allure for Israel was strong. The **Asherah** was a Canaanite goddess of fertility. Trees or special wooden poles were an integral part of such worship. The symbolic poles or trees were also called Asherah (Deut. 7:5; Isa. 17:8). God's answer for those who worshipped in such pagan ways was simple. He would root them out of their hometowns and their favorite worship sites and then destroy the towns.

5:15. Micah ends this section on a mysterious note. It does not sound like a happy note, since it is full of **anger and wrath**, and **vengeance**. The end is near for nations that have not listened. This sounds like a concluding statement to the entire section, 3:1–5:15. God's enemies will suffer the consequences for not obeying him. But who is included? Certainly Assyria and Babylon! Perhaps some of Israel's jealous, greedy neighbors. And probably most of Israel and Judah except for that remnant of promise. As other prophets show with oracles against foreign nations (e.g., Isa. 13–23; Amos 1–2), Judah and Israel can find themselves included in God's oracles against foreigners. Those who will listen find that God breaks his silence in actions of destruction.

> **MAIN IDEA REVIEW:** *God is not bound to speak to his people. He can retreat in silence from a sinful people until he decides to relieve the time of judgment and speak peace to his people once more.*

III. CONCLUSION

When God Says Nothing

Silence can mark our relationship with God. We long to hear his voice and understand his ways and his plans, but we stare into the darkness hearing nothing. At such times we must put our house in order, making sure no worldly practices have separated us from God so that his anger muffles his voice. We know in the long run that God is there for his people, but the short run may require patience until God reveals himself in his timing according to his plans.

PRINCIPLES

- All people know basic principles of right and wrong, good and evil.
- Human sin brings God to shut down his revelation pipeline and communicate to his people through his silence.
- God's ministers may cause God's people to sin.
- At times God's only message is to call attention to the sin of his people.
- God's eternal plan looks to a day of salvation when all nations will worship him.
- God's salvation comes to the remnant of his people through the Messiah to be born in Bethlehem.

APPLICATIONS

- Confess your sins to God right now.
- Pay homage to Jesus Christ.
- Do not fret over God's silence.
- Trust God to win the victory in his time.
- Let God shepherd you rather than letting worldly leaders guide your paths.
- Represent the forces of peace, not war, in this world.
- Pray that God will reveal his plan of salvation for the remnant of this generation.

IV. LIFE APPLICATION

Groaning into the Silence

A time of God's profound silence remains fresh in my memory after eight years, in spite of the fact that God has granted a new start, a new family, and a new job. I spent four months watching Mary die. Then I spent nine months screaming into the darkness, asking God why and receiving no answers. God's silence remains real in today's world. Our modern communication technology will never reach to heaven and amplify God's voice. He speaks only as he chooses, and his speech may bring darkness and destruction rather than light.

We must be sure we belong to the promised remnant, not to the immoral majority. As such, we must learn to trust God and his eternal plans even in the dark silence. We know he has once and for all shined his light into our darkness through the birth of his Son Jesus. As Jesus groaned at God's seeming silence in the garden of Gethsemane (Mark 14:32–42) and at being forsaken on the cross (Mark 15:34), so we may groan in times of misery. But even such groaning into the silence represents faith that some day God's answer will come.

V. PRAYER

Lord, break your silence! Hear our prayer. Show us your way through this dark hour. Even as we wait for you to speak, guide our steps into paths of good and right, not wrong and evil. Keep us as part of your faithful remnant. We trust you, O Silent One. Amen.

VI. DEEPER DISCOVERIES

Prophetic Revelation (3:6–7)

God silenced the prophets. They could no longer serve as his messengers, conveying his word. Silence came not from shutting the prophets' mouths. It came from shutting their pipelines to revelation. Micah lists several key terms in prophetic revelation.

Visions (*chazon*) is often used in titles of prophetic books to show the basic mode of prophetic revelation (Obad. 1). People sought visions from a prophet (Ezek. 7:26). The report or contents of such a vision could be written down (2 Chr. 32:32) or kept secret for future revelation (Dan. 9:24). The vision came from God to communicate his message and his will (Ps. 89:19). But prophets could not require such visions. They came at God's initiative and could be rare or nonexistent (1 Sam. 3:1). Normally distinct from dreams, at times visions were much like dreams (Dan. 7:1). Prophets could pretend to receive visions and lie to the people (Jer. 14:14).

Many of Israel's neighbors practiced various forms of divination (*qosem*). These included consulting the dead (1 Sam. 28:8) and manipulating arrows or examining animal livers (Ezek. 21:21–23). These were often seen as false, sinful means of revelation (2 Kgs. 17:17; Zech. 10:2), forbidden to Israel (Deut. 18:10–14). But divination could be seen as a way to find God's oracle or God's revelation to his people (Isa. 3:2). Micah did not clearly condemn divination as a false means of revelation. He did declare that God would take away any power the diviners had to determine his or any god's will. He said that some prophets practiced divination ("tell fortunes," Mic. 3:11 NIV) for payment.

Since Israel had no specific term for false prophets, *nebi'im* covered both true and false prophets. Micah referred to the false variety who sought visions and omens in the night and then told the people what the people wanted to hear and were willing to pay for (Mic. 3:6). But the prophets' day in the sun was over. Night and darkness would surround them, so they could not reveal any visions they might have.

A **seer** (*chozeh*) received the vision (*chozon*). Many of Israel's prophets bore the title (1 Chr. 21:9). Amaziah the priest considered Amos a seer (Amos. 7:12). God warned his people through prophets and seers (2 Kgs. 17:13), but he could also silence prophets and seers (Isa. 29:10) who told the people what they wanted to hear (Isa. 30:10).

VII. TEACHING OUTLINE

A. INTRODUCTION

1. Lead Story: We Heard from Him
2. Context: Chapters 3–5 lead God's people from his words and works of punishment and destruction to a strange mixture of hope in light of divine silence. God's people have to learn they cannot manipulate God with pious prayers, ritualistic worship, or powers from the pagan world. He speaks and acts when, where, and how he wills.
3. Transition: How do we respond when God is silent? We can increase our religious activity. We can give up and go the way of the world in disgust. We can depend on our own resources and wisdom. Or we can listen patiently for God's message, ready to obey what we know and respond to what we hear when his silence ends.

B. COMMENTARY

1. Sin Sends Silence (3:1–12)
2. The Temple Teaches Torah Again (4:1–8)
3. Preparing to Participate in God's Plans (4:9–5:4)
4. The Refreshing Remnant (5:5–9)
5. God's Day of Destruction (5:10–15)

C. CONCLUSION: WHEN GOD SAYS NOTHING

VIII. ISSUES FOR DISCUSSION

1. What does it mean to say that God is silent?
2. Can human action or inaction cause divine silence?
3. How should we respond to divine silence?
4. Can we say that God is silent today in light of the coming of Jesus Christ?
5. In the silence, how can we be sure we are part of God's victorious remnant?

Micah 6:1–7:20

The Righteous Requirements

I. **INTRODUCTION**
What's Expected?

II. **COMMENTARY**
A verse-by-verse explanation of these verses.

III. **CONCLUSION**
Nothing to Offer God

An overview of the principles and applications from these verses.

IV. **LIFE APPLICATION**
Standing Before the Judge

Melding these verses to life.

V. **PRAYER**
Tying these verses to life with God.

VI. **DEEPER DISCOVERIES**
Historical, geographical, and grammatical enrichment of the commentary.

VII. **TEACHING OUTLINE**
Suggested step-by-step group study of these verses.

VIII. **ISSUES FOR DISCUSSION**
Zeroing these verses in on daily life.

Quote

"*I*mportant principles may and must be inflexible."

A b r a h a m   L i n c o l n

Micah 6:1–7:20

IN A NUTSHELL

*G*od takes Israel to court to show that history is on his side; that justice, mercy, and humility are his expectations; that economic abuse is cause for his judgment; that God is the only source of hope for a deceitful generation; and that God will ultimately show his incomparable character by saving his people.

The Righteous Requirements

I

I. INTRODUCTION

What's Expected?

I will never forget my first (and only) college math class. The instructor came directly out of a Ph.D. program at Los Alamos National Laboratory. He had apparently never taught before. Some thirty students entered class the first day with trepidation and fear written all over our faces. "What's he like?" "What have you heard?" "What should we expect?" Questions flew across the room. The first day we learned what he expected, and were we shocked! No one had ever put together a syllabus like that. We wanted a college math credit, not a full-time job in higher math research.

In a similar vein the people of Israel kept shaking their heads. Is there no way we can please God? What does the prophet expect from us, anyway? God made his covenant to be our Lord back in Egypt. What more is necessary?

As he closed his book, Micah thundered forth God's expectations to his people—expectations most of the people were not ready to handle. God's expectations of his people remain the same. Are you ready to listen to them and fulfill them?

II. COMMENTARY

The Righteous Requirements

> **MAIN IDEA:** *God's salvation does not come automatically, because he brings expectations to his people. A people who refuse to meet those expectations may have to suffer punishment and discipline before experiencing God's mercy, forgiveness, and compassion.*

God's Case for Righteousness (6:1–8)

> **SUPPORTING IDEA:** *The God who saved his people expects righteousness, not ritual.*

6:1–2. God calls Israel to the courtroom to **plead** their **case**. The only mediators who can hear the case between God and his people are elements of

---

the natural world. So Israel must testify before the mountains and hills. God initiates the action, charging his people with serious crimes.

6:3–5. God maintains an intimate relationship with Israel, addressing them as **my people.** He wants them to justify their actions by showing how their God did them wrong. Has he expected too much? God shows he has the right to make demands on his people. Consider what he had done for them. He rescued them from **the land of slavery** and set them free (Exod. 20:2). He provided leadership for them in the person of Moses, along with his brother Aaron and sister Miriam. God had done all his people needed, what they could not do for themselves (see "Deeper Discoveries").

God not only delivered Israel from Egypt. He led them into the promised land, Shittim to Gilgal being the final leg of the journey (Num. 25:1). All this should represent one thing for Israel—God is righteous. **Righteous acts** is the plural of the term *righteousness.*

6:6–7. Here is the heart of Micah's book. A witness representing Israel takes the stand. Rather than giving testimony, the witness begins asking questions like an attorney. He uses the language of a pilgrim traveling to God's worship center. The pilgrim expects to have something in his hands as a gift for the master of the worship center as he comes to bow down in homage and worship. The pilgrim knows the requirements. He should follow traditional sacrificial practices. Such offerings stretched all the way back to Noah (Gen. 8:20), Abraham (Gen. 22:2), and Moses in Egypt (Exod. 10:25). **Burnt offerings** were one of God's first demands on his people (Lev. 1:3–17).

The witness decides this was not sufficient to acknowledge all that God had done and all that he expected. So he takes flight in hyperbole. Will **thousands of rams** please God? What if they are accompanied by **ten thousand rivers,** or perhaps trenches, filled with the **oil** that a person uses with other offerings?

If that is not enough, should the worshipper go further and offer a special kind of sin offering—his oldest son? The witness appears to be ready to do anything God requires, even take up the pagan practice of child sacrifice (1 Kgs. 11:5). Drastic conditions led Israelites to this drastic solution (2 Chr. 28:3). Israelite law condemned any thought of child sacrifice to the Lord (Deut. 18:10). God's righteous acts proved his loyalty to Israel and showed no court of law could possibly condemn him. But Israel's witness could show that Israel was willing to give God anything he demanded. How could the court condemn Israel?

6:8. The Israelite witness receives a direct answer, with the prophet mediating the divine message. God has already revealed what is **good.** What is good is what the Lord requires. What is good is what God's covenant stipulations require—the stipulations mediated through Moses on Sinai. Leviticus 19:18, echoed in the New Testament (Matt. 19:19; Rom. 13:9), summarizes the stipulations as "love your neighbor as yourself." Amos summed it up with, "Seek good, not evil, that you may live. Then the LORD God Almighty will be with you, just as you say he is. Hate evil, love good; maintain justice in the courts. Perhaps the LORD God Almighty will have mercy on the remnant of Joseph" (Amos 5:14–15). He added: "But let justice roll on like a river, righteousness like a never-failing stream!" (Amos 5:24).

Isaiah's version of this requirement reads:

> Wash and make yourselves clean. Take your evil deeds out of my sight! Stop doing wrong, learn to do right! Seek justice, encourage the oppressed. Defend the cause of the fatherless, plead the case of the widow. "Come now, let us reason together," says the LORD. "Though your sins are like scarlet, they shall be as white as snow; though they are red as crimson, they shall be like wool. If you are willing and obedient, you will eat the best from the land; but if you resist and rebel, you will be devoured by the sword (Isa. 1:16–20).

Over and over in many versions, God showed Israel his expectations of a covenant people. But again and again, Israel refused to listen.

Micah's version of God's requirements is simple and to the point. The people he faced hated good and loved evil (Mic. 3:2). Their "hands are skilled [literally good] in doing evil" (Mic. 7:3). They must learn a new lifestyle. They must **act justly**. The Hebrew text says to do *mishpat*. Israel's leaders should have been experts in this (Mic. 3:1), but only the prophet was (Mic. 3:8). The leaders "despise justice" (Mic. 3:9). Their emotional commitment should be centered on **mercy** (Heb. *chesed*)—on covenant faithfulness and commitment to care for the other person. Instead, Israel wanted mercy only for themselves. God delighted to show mercy to his people, but they refused to reflect that mercy in their dealings with other people (Mic. 7:18,20).

The Hebrew term for **humbly** occurs only here in the Old Testament, so its meaning is not clear. Recent discussion centers on being careful and cautious. Smith summarizes it nicely: "Micah is warning against carelessly or presumptuously doing things your own way instead of being attentive to do God's will. Such a walk with God is humble in that it puts a person's will in a secondary position and gives prudent attention to doing his will" (NIV Application, 554).

This is the root of religion, the core of the covenant, the point of piety, and the essence of Christian commitment. God does not expect regulated religious activities. God wants personal relationships with other people and with him—relationships that place the other at the center of our concern. Actions are not controlled by legal writings but by genuine commitments.

B Desolation for the Deceitful (6:9–16)

SUPPORTING IDEA: *People and nations who do not meet God's requirements face his judgment.*

6:9. Translation problems face us in this verse. The Hebrew text reads: "The voice of Yahweh to the city calls while prudent success he sees your name; listen you all, O tribe (or rod) and who appointed it." Every translation changes the text in one way or another. Perhaps the prophet pictures God warning his people, the city of Jerusalem as representative of the entire nation. The person who shows regard for the divine name is prudent and successful, the Hebrew term carrying both connotations. This implies that many people are misusing the divine name and that they will face serious consequences.

God's call is simple: Pay attention to the **rod** in my hand, the rod representing an instrument of punishment and military defeat (Isa. 9:4; 10:5,15,24). Pay attention also to the one who appoints it—the Lord, who gives the punishing rod to whomever he desires. Whatever the exact meaning of the verse, it portrays God coming to judge his people.

6:10. Again the text of this verse challenges the translator. The Hebrew text apparently reads: "Still is there (or is a man of) a wicked house [with] treasures of wickedness, while a lean ephah (or measure of grain) is cursed?" Most translations change the Hebrew text somewhat. God addresses his people directly. He sees them as a wicked family hoarding treasures they have obtained through wicked and unjust means. One of these is using unjust weights in buying and selling grain—a practice on which God has placed a curse. God's people know better, but they do not do better. They have a sin habit they cannot kick, a greed practice they cannot break.

6:11–12. Continuing in the same vein, God asks the guilty people to assume God's role as judge. The accused stands with a bag full of weights that do not weigh what they are supposed to weigh. The accused also has a scale set up to indicate the wrong weight. Thus when the accused sells something, the amount is always more than it should be. When the accused buys something, the purchase weighs less than it should. This has produced a wealthy class and a poor class. The wealthy have used deceit and lies to gain their wealth. These practices have resulted in violent actions against the poor. The wealthy were stealing their money, homesteads, and inherited land—a path to slow death.

6:13–15. The English translation **therefore** represents a different Hebrew construction from the deadly *therefore* that introduces most prophetic announcements of guilt. The Hebrew text may best be interpreted as, "And even I myself have begun to strike you (with the rod of verse 9?; or have made sick, striking you), causing desolation because of your sins." God in his loving faithfulness cannot wait any longer. He has to act on such a guilty people. He will isolate them from all source of life. They will stand appalled at their situation. They have food to eat, but it does not satisfy. The rest of verse 14 is difficult to translate because of obscure words. The proper reading may be: "While your dysentery is in your innards. You cause to flee but cannot bring to safety, but if you do rescue, I will give [it] over to the sword."

Verse 15 changes to an agricultural image. Neither the grain harvest nor the grape harvest will produce anything useful. Thus all is futile. Food makes these people sick. If they try to rescue themselves or someone else from the situation, they do not succeed. If they do seem to succeed, then God brings death. Whatever the exact meanings of the difficult terms of verse 14, the intention is clear. God is bringing futility to the land so that all activity, even the basic actions of eating and farming, fail. Death is God's final word for his people.

6:16. The people have not obeyed God and his way of justice. Which way have they followed? The way of the wicked Omride dynasty of kings that ruled in Israel! Judah has patterned itself after the pagan worship introduced into Israel rather than after the perfect worship introduced at Sinai by the Lord. **Omri** (885–874 B.C.) had great material success, but the Book of 1 Kings condemned him: "But Omri did evil in the eyes of the LORD and sinned more than all those before him" (1 Kgs. 16:25).

Omri's son Ahab was worse:

> Ahab son of Omri did evil in the sight of the LORD more than all who were before him. And as if it had been a light thing for him to walk in the sins of Jeroboam son of Nebat, he took as his wife Jezebel daughter of King Ethbaal of the Sidonians, and went and served Baal, and worshipped him. He erected an altar for Baal in the house of Baal, which he built in Samaria. Ahab also made a sacred pole. Ahab did more to provoke the anger of the LORD, the God of Israel, than had all the kings of Israel who were before him (1 Kgs. 16:30–33).

Walter Kaiser declares: The two most infamous names in the history of northern Israel are probably King Ahab and Queen Jezebel (*A History of Israel*, 326).

Thus God is ready to **therefore** Israel, pronouncing his sentence upon their injustice and the religious infidelity they learned from Omri and Ahab. God's people face horrific atrocities. Enemies will hiss at them in scorn and **derision**. Shameful taunting will be their burden. You can feel the divine heart hurting as God calls them **the scorn** of *my* people (NIV's **the nations** follows the Greek LXX, not the Hebrew text).

[C] Lament over the Land (7:1–7)

SUPPORTING IDEA: *A sinful people cause God's minister to mourn in anguish while waiting for God's salvation.*

7:1. Unable to persuade his people with normal prophetic preaching or with courtroom language, Micah turned to a funeral tone. He mimicked the funeral oration as he described his own pain and agony. The agony came not from his sin and punishment since he was filled with justice (Mic. 3:8). The agony came because the prophet shared God's faithful love and mercy for his people. He began with another unusual word meaning **misery** or woe and occurring elsewhere only in Job 10:15. Micah's ministry appears as barren as the agricultural land under God's curse.

7:2. Vivid description shows what has brought the prophet to lamentation. People with faithful loyalty to God, the **godly** (Heb. *chasid*) have vanished from the land. **Not one upright man remains.** Where are they? They lie in ambush, out for blood. Every person in Israel has a net waiting to capture his own family members.

7:3. God requires people to know what is good (Mic. 6:8). Israel is good at **doing evil** with **both hands** (cp. Mic. 3:1). Both the government official serving the king and the judge in charge of maintaining justice ask for payment for any favor they do. If you can pay, you get what you want. If you are poor, the government takes what you have. "The great one is speaking the desire of his soul, and they twist it together." The antecedent of "they" is not stated. It may be underling officials or the aforementioned judge and official. The great one or **the powerful** might be a hidden reference to the king, so that corruption goes all the way to the top. Only the king does not have to pay. Everyone else in the system is out for himself.

7:4. Looking at the list of government staff, Micah concludes even the **best of them** is as useful as a brier that sticks in a person's flesh. The upright should receive God's help (Mic. 2:7), but Israel's government distorts all that is upright (Mic. 3:9). Thus no upright person remains (Mic. 7:2). Those who claim to be upright help as much as a hedgerow of thorns pricking at one's side. Such a government mess can have only one result. **Watchmen** may refer to the prophets who have been God's messengers to the people and have announced judgment to them. The Day of the Lord they announced is at hand. They may expect a visitor, but an unwanted one. The visit will have one result—confusion (Isa. 22:5).

7:5–6. The confusion is already apparent, extending to one's closest relationships. So the prophet offers advice. Neighbors, friends, lovers, family members—do not trust anybody. A son makes a fool of his father. The daughter stands against her mother. Home becomes a battlefield. No wonder the prophet laments.

7:7. Finally, the prophet turned his eyes away from the situation at hand. Raising his eyes heavenward, he professed his faith in God. Unable to trust any person, he can trust God. **I watch** picks up the word used for watchmen in verse 4. Micah played the prophetic role even as people refused to listen. Whereas the day of the watchmen brought an unwanted visitation, Micah waits **in hope**. He, too, expects a visit from God, but this is not a visit to bring confusion. This visit brings salvation. How can the prophet be so sure of this when he has announced just the opposite for his people? His assurance comes through prayer. He has asked God for salvation and rests assured that **my God will hear me**.

𝔻 A Confident Case in God's Court (7:8–13)

SUPPORTING IDEA: *A prophetic announcement of judgment against God's people does not provide enemies the opportunity to boast and rejoice because God will use them for a while to punish his people but will eventually punish the enemies as well.*

7:8–10. Laments often lead to praise and confidence. So the prophet ended his lament with a statement of hope. Now he extends that to express confidence in God's salvation for his people. Micah lets fallen, destroyed Jerusalem warn their enemies. Don't **gloat** (literally, rejoice). You may have won the battle now, but look out. Jerusalem will rise again. How can a fallen city make such an audacious claim? God is the Lord who turns **darkness** into **light**. Finally, Jerusalem answers God's call to respond to his legal claims against them (Mic. 6:1–3). Jerusalem confesses, **I have sinned**. The people must acknowledge that God's rage is justified; their punishment is deserved.

Unexpectedly, Jerusalem changes its tune from confession of sin to confession of faith. God who argued the case against Jerusalem will now argue Jerusalem's case. He will become the defense attorney arguing for a reduction of the sentence. Then he will do justice. Jerusalem will leave the darkness and enter God's light. There they will discover God's *tsedeq,* his righteousness, his reestablishment of the world order out of the chaos and confusion he had created because of Jerusalem's sins. Here is the starting point for the New Testament concept of God justifying sinners and declaring them righteous (Rom. 1:16–17).

Enemy rejoicing will suddenly cease. The bitter taunt: **Where is the Lord your God** will no longer echo through Jerusalem's streets. The city will see the enemy trampled as Jerusalem had been defeated. Now **shame** will cover the enemy.

7:11–13. The defeat of enemies is only one side of the picture. Jerusalem will be restored, its boundaries extended beyond the present city. This future time will see the international power structure change. People from throughout the world will flood back to Jerusalem. Are these exiled Jews, or does the prophet refer to nations coming to pay tribute in Jerusalem and worship Jerusalem's God? Barker (NAC 20, 129) is probably correct in seeing parallel prophetic passages pointing to representatives of foreign nations coming to worship (Ps. 2:8–12; Isa. 60:11–12). In coming to Jerusalem, the foreigners escape disaster back home because **the earth will become desolate**.

How can the entire earth be decimated? Only through an act of God! Why would God act? To punish the wicked nations for **their deeds**. In God's court, his people find him faithful to his covenant promises. He punishes his people, then argues their case to declare them righteous while condemning the wickedness of the nations he used to punish them.

🄴 Sending Our Sins to the Sea (7:14–20)

SUPPORTING IDEA: *Because of his loving nature, God answers prayer with promises of salvation.*

7:14. The Book of Micah comes to a conclusion with a conversation between the prophet and God. The prophet prays that God will again be the Good Shepherd for his people (Ps. 23:1–6; Jer. 13:17).

Micah and his people need divine leadership. They live alone in isolation because the enemy has isolated them, barring them from commerce with the nations or their neighbors. They had to retreat to the forest, away from civilization's protection.

> A forest in biblical times referred not only to large trees, but also to shrubs, herbs, and smaller vegetation with animals roaming in it. In biblical times, the Levantine landscape must have been far more densely forested than at present. For this reason the forest is also used figuratively for danger (esp. wild animals in it threatening people). Ancient people feared that the forest would overgrow ordered civilization (L. Cornelius, *NIDOTTE*, 3623).

This feared forest lies in the midst of an orchard (rather than NIV **pasturelands**). The people not only have to bear loneliness and fear of the dark forest. They know that just beyond the lonely forest lies the lovely orchard that they cannot reach.

Micah prays for a reversal of fortunes. May the Good Shepherd take Israel, his flock, to the marvelous pasturelands of Bashan (Ezek. 27:6) and Gilead east of the Jordan River. To answer this prayer, God would have to restore this area to Israelite control. It had been lost long ago to Syria and Assyria.

7:15. God answers his prophet's prayer in marvelous fashion. Victory comparable only to the exodus miracles is in the offing for God's people. God will be the Shepherd King leading his people to victory over the enemy once again.

7:16–17. The powerful nations that threaten and control Israel will see the new exodus miracles and gasp. **Deprived of all their power** is literally "from all of their strength," a phrase that is unclear. It could mean because of all their strength, indicating shame that all the power of the people cannot match God's miracles or even in spite of all their strength. The prophet draws a contrast between what is expected from the nations and what they can deliver when they face God.

The nations will not be able to speak or hear. Thus the communication needed by an army is nonexistent. The images may also include the meaning of being dumbfounded and yet refusing to hear God's orders that could save them and of remaining silent in the presence of a superior.

The proud armies will be reduced to crawling on the ground, groveling before the superior power. Thus they are pictured as unclean and unacceptable before God (Lev. 22:5), akin to the accursed serpent of Genesis 3:14. They will be forced to hide, then to come out of their hiding places and surrender. They will fear both God and Israel (or if the singular you is taken literally, the prophet). Such fear is not the beginning of wisdom but the onset of doom.

7:18–20. The divine promise sends the prophet into ecstatic joy, praising his incomparable God. The Lord's uniqueness is seen in his pardoning and forgiving sin. But such pardon is not universal. It does not even affect all Israel. Pardon is restricted to Israel's **remnant**. The God who punishes in anger does not remain **angry forever**. **Mercy** or faithful covenant love wins out in the end. God's nature as love turns from anger to his true delight—showing mercy to his people. Anger turns to faithful love and to **compassion** (Heb. *racham*)—the deep love a mother has for her children and God has for his people.

The promise of victory over the Genesis serpent finds a new expression as God treads Israel's sins under his foot. Put another way, he will **hurl all our iniquities into the depths of the sea**. Here is forgiveness. Nothing can escape from God's foot or from the ocean depths. Forgiveness need not be questioned or repeated. God has dealt with our sins and declared us righteous, innocent in his sight. That is salvation from the enemy and from sin.

Micah's book ends where Israel's story began—with the promises to Abraham (Gen. 12). A thousand years separated Abraham and Micah, but God still remembered his promise and kept it. The present situation may look dim and dark, covered in divine judgment. But God listens when his people pray and comes to redeem them as he did in Egypt. Almost a thousand years after

Micah, God came in the person of his Son, Jesus Christ, to prove once and for all that he is faithful to his covenant promises.

> **MAIN IDEA REVIEW:** *God's salvation does not come automatically because he brings expectations to his people. A people who refuse to meet those expectations may have to suffer punishment and discipline before experiencing God's mercy, forgiveness, and compassion.*

III. CONCLUSION

Nothing to Offer God

Micah 6–7 presents some of the greatest teachings in the Bible on prophecy. The passage calls us before God's court of justice and demands that we state our case. We feebly offer our side of the story, only to find that God knows the entire picture. God has done everything we could have asked of him. We try to bribe our way through life and through the heavenly court. But nothing we bring to God can affect his decision. We are guilty. We must turn from guilty actions to God's requirements. Then we can experience divine mercy, forgiveness, and hope.

PRINCIPLES

- Everyone must face the divine Judge.
- God's requirements call us to act in justice, faithfulness, and wisdom with God and with other people.
- Following human powers reveals our weakness and leads to God's judgment.
- God's judgment removes all our resources and places us squarely before him and him alone.
- Our hope for salvation rests on God's mercy and compassion.

APPLICATIONS

- Confess your sins to God today.
- Determine what earthly powers control your life and surrender those powers to God.
- List areas of your life where you are most likely to be unjust, unfair, and unloving.
- Ask forgiveness from people whom you have treated unjustly; then ask forgiveness from God.
- Let God be your only hope for salvation.

IV. LIFE APPLICATION

Standing Before the Judge

No one likes to go to court. When you step up to the bench, you know nothing can change what is coming. All you can do is hope the judge is merciful and your sentence will not be too severe.

The Bible takes this picture one step further. You step up to the bench, look up to the judge, and find you are facing God. He is bringing the indictment against you. What can you do? Israel tried all sorts of excuses and alibis. They pointed to everything they were ready to do for God. He rejected their plan and called for a simpler one—love justice, act in faithfulness, and live life according to God's directions.

What is your plea when you face God the Judge? You can't say, "The devil made me do it" or "I will give you anything I own." You can't follow the world's way of bribery. You can't even point to personal suffering and self-sacrifice. So confess your sins now. Let God declare you innocent and righteous. Start meeting God's expectations. Then you can truly say, "I watch in hope for the LORD, I wait for God my Savior; my God will hear me" (Mic. 7:7)

V. PRAYER

Great Judge of the universe, we have played the world's games too long. We have tried to pretend we are one thing, when we are really something different. We relate to you as the world's businesses too often relate to one another, thinking the strong and rich will win out in the end. We confess our sin. Please forgive us. Hurl our sin into the depths of the sea and let us know for sure that you are God our Savior. Amen.

VI. DEEPER DISCOVERIES

A. The Exodus

Historically and theologically the exodus is the most important event in the Old Testament. More than a hundred times in all parts of the Old Testament except the Wisdom Literature, the Lord is proclaimed as the one who brought the people of Israel "out of the land of Egypt, out of the house of bondage" (Deut. 5:6 NKJV). Israel remembered the exodus as God's mighty redemptive act. She celebrated it in her creeds (Deut. 26:5–9). She sang of it in worship (Pss. 106; 135).

The prophets constantly reminded Israel that election and covenant were closely related to the exodus (Isa. 11:16; Hag. 2:5). The exodus in the Old

Testament was to Israel what the death and resurrection of Christ was to Christians in the New Testament. Just as Israel commemorated her deliverance from Egyptian bondage in the feast of Passover, Christians celebrate their redemption from sin in the observance of the Lord's Supper (Luke 22:1–20; 1 Cor. 11:23–26).

B. Balaam (6:6)

Balaam is the non-Israelite prophet whom Balak, king of Moab, promised a fee if he would curse the invading Israelites. Balaam was one of many prophets of eastern religions who worshipped all the gods of the land. Many of these false teachers had great power and influence. When they pronounced a blessing or a curse, it was considered true prophecy. When Moses led his people across the wilderness, God commanded him not to attack Edom or Moab (Deut. 2:4–9). He did not. When Edom attacked, "Israel turned away from them" (Num. 20:21). As the great nation journeyed north on the east side of the Jordan River, King Balak of Moab faced the invasion of Israel. Balak sought a strategy other than battle to stop Moses. He decided to use a prophet to curse Israel. Balaam was chosen.

Balak sent his messengers with fees to secure Balaam's services. Balaam asked God's permission to curse Israel. Permission was refused, but Balaam journeyed to confer further with Balak. On this journey, Balaam's donkey talked with him as he traveled a narrow trail (Num. 22:21–30; 2 Pet. 2:16). Here Balaam clearly understood that an angel's drawn sword enforced his obedience to speak only God's message to Balak. Later in four vivid messages Balaam insisted that God would bless Israel (Num. 23–24). God used Balaam to preach truth. He even spoke of a future star and scepter (Num. 24:17)—a prophecy ultimately fulfilled in the coming of Jesus as the Messiah.

Balak's actions brought God's anger on Moab (Deut. 23:3–6). In a battle against the Midianites, Balaam died (Num. 31:8; Josh. 13:22). Balaam could not curse Israel, but he taught the Moabites to bring the men of Israel into Baal worship with its immorality. For this God would punish Israel. What Balaam could not accomplish with a curse, he did through seductive means.

VII. TEACHING OUTLINE

A. INTRODUCTION

1. Lead Story: What's Expected?
2. Context: Micah sets up a context of a divine courtroom as he turns to complete his book. God calls all people into that courtroom to determine what they must do to please him.

3. Transition: God can testify to everything he has done for his people. His people can only reply, "What could I possibly do to please you? Nothing I give is enough." What reply does God expect from you?

B. COMMENTARY
1. God's Case for Righteousness (6:1–8)
2. Desolation for the Deceitful (6:9–16)
3. Lament over the Land (7:1–7)
4. A Confident Case in God's Court (7:8–13)
5. Sending Our Sins to the Sea (7:14–20)

C. CONCLUSION: NOTHING TO OFFER GOD

VIII. ISSUES FOR DISCUSSION

1. Do you truly believe you must face the divine Judge one day?
2. What church accomplishments can you list before God to show you deserve to be declared innocent?
3. What areas of justice and injustice most need the church's attention today?
4. What does it mean to hope in God?
5. What signs and proofs of God's faithfulness to his promises can you witness to?

Glossary

Achor, Valley of—Place name meaning "trouble," "affliction," or "taboo." The valley in which Achan and his household were stoned to death (Josh. 7:24–26). Later it was part of the border of Judah. It is the subject of prophetic promises in Isaiah 65:10 and Hosea 2:15.

adultery—An act of unfaithfulness in marriage that occurs when one of the marriage partners voluntarily engages in sexual intercourse with a person other than the marriage partner. Several Old Testament prophets, including Hosea, used adultery as a metaphor to describe unfaithfulness to God, especially unfaithfulness involving participation in Canaanite fertility rituals.

Baal—The chief god among a multitude of Canaanite gods and worshipped as the source of fertility.

Beeri—Otherwise unknown father of Hosea, the prophet.

bride price—A gift the bridegroom or his parents gave to the bride's family to seal the covenant of marriage.

covenant—A contract or agreement expressing God's gracious promises to his people and their consequent relationship to him (see Exod. 19–24; Josh. 24).

Day of the Lord—God's time of decisive intervention in history to save or to judge his people; the final day of judgment in the end time.

Ephraim—Name of the most prominent Israelite tribe in the north; a less frequently used name for all of Israel, the ten northern tribes after 931 B.C.

fertility cults—Pagan religious worship practices involving sexual intercourse to imitate the supposed world of the gods and ensure the fertility of the land to produce crops.

festival—A time of national worship and celebration at the central worship place. Israel celebrated three such annual gatherings—Booths in the fall; Passover in the spring; and Weeks in the summer.

Gomer—Hosea's unfaithful wife who was a prostitute

high place—A pagan worship center usually located atop a hill or mountain and featuring sacred poles, idols, and sacred trees.

Israel—Name given to Jacob and then borne by the ten northern tribes when the United Kingdom divided in 931 B.C. after Solomon's death.

Jehoshaphat, Valley of—Place-name meaning "valley where Yahweh judged." Place to which the Lord summons the nations for judgment (Joel 3:2).

Jehu—Founder of a strong dynasty in the Northern Kingdom through the violent murder of Ahab, Ahaziah, Jezebel, and Ahab's seventy sons; ruled Israel 841–814 B.C.

Jeroboam II—Strongest king of Israel (Northern Kingdom); ruled Israel about 793–753 B.C.

Jezreel—One of Hosea's sons, whose name symbolized the evil nature of the dynasty of Jehu that began with much bloodshed in the Valley of Jezreel. The name also symbolized that God will sow seeds of prosperity after the destruction (Hos. 1:4–5,10–2:1).

Jezreel—A city located at the eastern end of the fertile Valley of Jezreel; winter capital of the Northern Kingdom (Israel) and site of Jehu's horrific acts.

Judah—The name of one of twelve sons of Jacob; then the name of the largest tribe among the twelve tribes; finally, the name borne by the two southern tribes when the United Kingdom divided in 931 B.C.

justice—The central ethical idea in the Old Testament deriving from the nature of God and his expectations that Israel would develop a societal order that gives opportunity and fairness to all citizens (Amos 5:6–7,15; Mic. 6:8). It is the standard God sets by which he punishes and blesses his people (Amos 7:7–9).

Lo-Ammi—Symbolic personal name meaning "not my people." Son of Hosea the prophet whose name God gave to symbolize Israel's lost relationship with him because of their sin and broken covenant.

locust—A species of insect that periodically multiplies in astronomical numbers and devours all vegetation as it swarms across a region. The locust plague is used as a symbol for what God's judgment will be like (Joel 2:1,11,25; Rev. 9:3,7; cp. Exod. 10:3–20; Deut. 28:38).

Lord of Hosts—*Yahweh Sabbaoth*; ancient name for Israel's God, indicating he was the commander of all heavenly and earthly armies; NIV translates as Lord Almighty.

Lo-Ruhamah—Symbolic personal name meaning "without love." Name that God gave Hosea for his daughter to symbolize that Israel, by rebelling against God and serving foreign gods, had forfeited God's love (Hos. 1:6).

Negeb—Dry, infertile, rocky land south of Beersheba.

New Moon—A monthly celebration featured in Israel's worship but also used as a time to celebrate in pagan worship.

Sabbath—Seventh day from sundown Friday to sundown Saturday when Israel celebrated God's creation rest and their delivery from slavery in Egypt. Israel developed rigid rules defining rest from work on the Sabbath.

sackcloth—A garment of coarse material fashioned from goat or camel hair and worn as a sign of mourning or anguish.

Samaria—The only major city founded by Israel (Northern Kingdom); location of the royal residence of the kings of Israel after Omri.

Sennacherib—King of Assyria, 705–681 B.C. He conquered most of the cities south and east of Jerusalem and besieged Jerusalem in 701 B.C.

Septuagint—The Greek Old Testament; oldest translation of the Hebrew Bible into another language; shows some variation in preserving the text of the Old Testament.

sycamore-fig tree—A tree in the Jordan Valley whose fruit was inferior to that of the fig tree. The fruit had to be punctured to make it edible and was used as food by the poor. Amos identified himself as one who tended these trees (Amos 7:14).

theophany—An appearance of God to a person; often described in terms of storms and earthquakes.

Yahweh—The personal name of Israel's God, usually translated "LORD."

Zion—Name of original part of Jerusalem and then of entire city as God's home on earth.

Bibliography

Abbreviations

AB	Anchor Bible
ABD	*Anchor Bible Dictionary*
BBC	Broadman Bible Commentary
BKAT	Biblischer Kommentar—Altes Testament
CBC	Cambridge Bible Commentary
DCH	*The Dictionary of Classical Hebrew*
EEC	An Exegetical and Expository Commentary: The Minor Prophets. Ed. Thomas Edward McComiskey.
FOTL	The Forms of the Old Testament Literature
HALOT	*The Hebrew and Aramaic Lexicon of the Old Testament*
KAT	Kommentar zum Alten Testament
MP	*The Minor Prophets: An Exegetical and Expository Commentary.* Ed. Thomas Edward McComiskey.
NAC	New American Commentary
NICOT	The New International Commentary on the Old Testament
NIDOTTE	*New International Dictionary of Old Testament Theology and Exegesis*
NIV Application	The NIV Application Commentary
OTL	Old Testament Library
TDOT	*Theological Dictionary of the Old Testament*
TLOT	*Theological Lexicon of the Old Testament*
TWOT	*Theological Wordbook of the Old Testament*
WBC	Word Biblical Commentary
WEC	The Wycliffe Exegetical Commentary

Commentaries

Allen, Leslie C. *The Books of Joel, Obadiah, Jonah, and Micah.* NICOT. Eerdmans, 1976.

Andersen, Francis I., and David Noel Freedman. *Hosea.* AB 24A. Doubleday, 2000.

Andersen, Francis I., and David Noel Freedman. *Micah.* AB 24E. Doubleday, 1980.

Baldwin, Joyce. *Jonah.* MP. Baker, 1993.

Barker, Kenneth L. *Micah.* NAC 20. Broadman & Holman, 1999.

Boice, James Montgomery. *The Minor Prophets*. 2 vols. Zondervan, 1983, 1986.

Butler, Trent C. *Joshua*. WBC 7. Word, 1981.

Ferreiro, Alberto. *The Twelve Prophets*. Ancient Christian Commentary on Scripture. XIV. Ed. Thomas C. Oden. InterVarsity, 2003.

Finley, Thomas J. *Joel, Amos, Obadiah*. Moody, 1990.

Garrett, Duane. *Hosea, Joel*. NAC 19A. Broadman & Holman, 1997.

Honeycutt, Roy L., Jr. *Hosea*. BBC 7. Broadman Press, 1972.

Jeremias, Jörg. *The Book of Amos*. OTL. Westminster John Knox, 1995.

Limburg, James. *Jonah*. OTL. Westminster/John Knox Press, 1993.

Magonet, Jonathan. *Form and Meaning: Studies in Literary Techniques in the Book of Jonah*. The Almond Press, 1983.

Mays, James L. *Amos*. OTL. London: SCM Press, 1969.

Mays, James L. *Hosea*. OTL. London: SCM Press, 1969.

Mays, James L. *Micah*. OTL. London: SCM Press, 1976.

McKeating, Henry. *Amos, Hosea, Micah*. CBC. Cambridge, 1971.

Niehaus, Jeffrey. *Obadiah*. MP. Baker, 1993.

Page, Frank. *Jonah*. NAC 19B. Broadman & Holman, 1995.

Robinson, G. L. *The Twelve Minor Prophets*, 1926. Reprint. Baker, 1967.

Rudolph, Wilhelm. *Hosea*. KAT XIII 2. Gütersloher, 1966.

Rudolph, Wilhelm. *Joel, Amos, Obadja, Jona*. KAT XIII 2. Gütersloher, 1971.

Rudolph, Wilhelm. *Micha, Nahum, Habakuk, Zephanja*. KAT XIII 2. Gütersloher, 1975.

Smith, Billy K. *Amos, Obadiah*. NAC 19B. Broadman & Holman, 1995.

Smith, Gary. *Hosea, Amos, Micah*. NIV Application. Zondervan, 2001.

Smith, Gary V. *Amos*. Zondervan, 1989.

Smith, Ralph L. *Micah-Malachi*. WBC 32. Word, 1984.

Stuart, Douglas. *Hosea-Jonah*. WBC 31. Word, 1987.

Waltke, Bruce. *Micah*. MP. Baker, 1993.

Watts, John D. W. *The Books of Joel, Obadiah, Jonah, Nahum, Habakkuk and Zephaniah*. CBC. Cambridge, 1975.

Wolff, Hans Walter. *Hosea*. BK XIV 1 1965. Neukirchener, 1969.

Wolff, Hans Walter. *Joel, Amos*. BK XIV 2. Neukirchener, 1969.

Wolff, Hans Walter. *Micha*. BK XIV 4. Neukirchener, 1982.

Wolff, Hans Walter. *Obadja, Jona*. BK XIV 3. Neukirchener, 1977.

Zvi, Ehud Ben. *Micah*. FOTL XXIB. Eerdmans, 2000.

Reference Works

Botterweck, G. Johannes, Helmer Ringgren, and Heinz-Josef Fabry, eds. *TDOT*. Vols. I–XIII. Grand Rapids: Eerdmans, 1974–.

Brand, Chad, et. al. *Holman Illustrated Bible Dictionary.* Nashville: Broadman & Holman, 2003.

Brisco, Thomas. *Holman Bible Atlas.* Nashville: Broadman & Holman, 1998.

Bullock, C. Hassell. *An Introduction to the Old Testament Prophetic Books.* Chicago: Moody Press, 1986.

Clines, David J. A., ed. *DCH.* Sheffield, 1993–.

Freedman, David Noel. *ABD.* 6 vols. Doubleday, 1992.

Gerstenberger, Erhard S. *Psalms, Part I,* FOTL XIV. Eds. Rolf Knierim and Gene M. Tucker. Grand Rapids: Eerdmans, 1988.

Hallo, William H., and K. Lawson Younger Jr., eds. *The Context of Scripture.* 3 vols. Brill, 1997–2003.

Harris, R. Laird, Gleason L. Archer Jr., and Bruce K. Waltke, eds. *TWOT.* 2 vols. Chicago: Moody Press, 1980.

Jenni, Ernst, and Claus Westermann. *TLOT.* Trans. Mark E. Biddle. 3 vols. Hendrickson, 1997.

Kaiser, Walter. *A History of Israel.* Nashville: Broadman & Holman, 1998.

Koehler, Ludwig, Walter Baumgartner, and Johann Jakob Stamm. *HALOT.* Trans. M. E. J. Richardson. Brill, 1994.

Redditt, Paul L., and Aaron Schart. *Thematic Threads in the Book of the Twelve.* Beihefte zur Zeitschrift für die alttestamentlich Wissenschaft 325. Ed. Otto Kaiser. Walter de Gruyter, 2003.

Sandy, D. Brent, and Ronald L. Giese Jr., eds. *Cracking Old Testament Codes.* Nashville: Broadman & Holman, 1995.

Smith, Gary V. *The Prophets as Preachers: An Introduction to the Hebrew Prophets.* Nashville: Broadman & Holman, 1994.

Smith, Ralph L. *Old Testament Theology.* Nashville: Broadman & Holman, 1993.

VanGemeren, Willem A. *NIDOTTE.* 5 vols. Grand Rapids: Zondervan. 1997.

Von Rad, Gerhard. *Theology of the Old Testament.* 2 vols. Trans. D. M. G. Stalker. New York: Harper & Row, Publishers. 1965.

Vriezen, Th. C. *An Outline of Old Testament Theology.* 2nd ed. Oxford: Basil Blackwell, 1970.

Zimmerli, W. *Hermeneia: Ezekiel.* Augsberg Fortress, 1979.

Other Works Cited

Ahlström, G. W. *Joel and the Temple Cult of Jerusalem.* Brill, 1971.

Angell, C. Roy. *Iron Shoes.* Nashville: Broadman Press, 1953.

Angell, C. Roy. *Shields of Brass.* Nashville: Broadman Press, 1965.

Arthur, Kay. *Lord, Is It Warfare?* Portland: Multnomah, 1991.

Blackaby, Henry T., and Claude V. King. *Experiencing God.* Nashville: Broadman & Holman, 1994.

Brown, H. Jackson Jr., and Robyn Spizman. *A Hero in Every Heart.* Nashville: Thomas Nelson, 1996.

Browning, Robert. "Bishop Blougram's Apology."

Cartledge, Tony. *Intrigued, How I Love to Proclaim It: Adventures in Thinking Theologically.* Macon, Ga.: Smyth & Helwys, 2003.

Chekhov, Anton Pavlovich. *The Selected Letters of Anton Chekhov.*

Christenson, Evelyn. *Battling the Prince of Darkness.* Wheaton Ill.: Victor Books, 1990.

Crabb, Larry. *Inside Out.* Colorado Springs, NavPress, 1988.

Cymbala, Jim. *Fresh Faith.* Grand Rapids: Zondervan, 1999.

Dobson, James. *When God Doesn't Make Sense.* Wheaton, Ill.: Tyndale House, 1993.

Graham, Billy. *Hope for the Troubled Heart.* Dallas: Word, 1991.

Krueger, Lois. *Chicken Soup for the Woman's Soul.* Deerfield Beach, Fl.: Health Communications, 1996.

Lewis, C. S. *Mere Christianity.* The Barbour Christian Library. New York: Macmillan, 1943, 1945, 1952.

Long, Michael G. *Martin Luther King, Jr. on Creative Living.* St. Louis: Chalice Press, 2004.

Lotz, Anne Graham. *The Glorious Dawn of God's Story.* Dallas: Word, 1997.

Lowery, Mark. *Out of Control.* Dallas: Word, 1996.

Lucado, Max. *The Great House of God.* Dallas: Word, 1997.

Lucado, Max. *When Christ Comes.* Nashville: Word, 1999.

Moore, Beth. *A Heart like His.* Nashville: Broadman & Holman, 1999.

Patterson, Dorothy Kelley. *BeAttitudes for Women.* Nashville: Broadman & Holman, 2000.

Shanahan, John M. *The Most Brilliant Thoughts of All Time.* Cliff Street Books, HarperCollins, 1999.

Sittser, Gerald L. *The Will of God as a Way of Life.* Grand Rapids: Zondervan, 2000.

Stanley, Charles. *The Wonderful Spirit-Filled Life.* Nashville: Thomas Nelson, 1992.

Stewart, Tracey, with Ken Abraham. *Payne Stewart.* Nashville: Broadman & Holman, 2000.

Sweet, Leonard, with Denise Marie Siino. *A Cup of Coffee at the Soul Café.* Nashville: Broadman & Holman, 1998.

Yancey, Philip. *What's So Amazing About Grace?* Grand Rapids: Zondervan, 1997.

Zacharias, Ravi. *Cries of the Heart.* Nashville: Word, 1998.

Also Available...

THE HOLMAN NEW TESTAMENT COMMENTARY

Save preparation time when you teach or preach the New Testament. This easy -to-use 12-volume set, which can be purchased as a set or one volume at a time, gives you the freedom to prayerfully appropriate the Scriptures as you spend more time directly with the text. It's like having a team of researchers doing the work for you. Available at your local Christian bookstore or visit us online at www.broadmanholman.com.